Werner Gephart / Jürgen Brokoff / Andrea Schütte /
Jan Christoph Suntrup (Hrsg.)
Tribunale

GEFÖRDERT VOM

Schriftenreihe des
Käte Hamburger Kollegs
»Recht als Kultur«

Herausgegeben von Werner Gephart

Band 4

*Werner Gephart / Jürgen Brokoff /
Andrea Schütte / Jan Christoph Suntrup*
(Hrsg.)

Tribunale

Literarische Darstellung
und juridische Aufarbeitung
von Kriegsverbrechen im
globalen Kontext

VITTORIO KLOSTERMANN
Frankfurt am Main · 2014

recht als kultur
käte hamburger kolleg
law as culture
centre for advanced study

Bibliographische Information der Deutschen Nationalbibliothek

Die Deutsche Nationalbibliothek verzeichnet diese Publikation in der
Deutschen Nationalbibliographie; detaillierte bibliographische Daten
sind im Internet über *http://dnb.dnb.de* abrufbar.

1. Auflage 2014

© Vittorio Klostermann GmbH · Frankfurt am Main · 2014
Alle Rechte vorbehalten, insbesondere die des Nachdrucks und der
Übersetzung. Ohne Genehmigung des Verlages ist es nicht gestattet,
dieses Werk oder Teile in einem photomechanischen oder sonstigen
Reproduktionsverfahren oder unter Verwendung elektronischer Systeme
zu verarbeiten, zu vervielfältigen und zu verbreiten.
Gedruckt auf alterungsbeständigem Papier ⊚ ISO 9706
Satz: post scriptum, www.post-scriptum.biz
Umschlaggestaltung: Jörgen Rumberg, Bonn
Umschlagabbildung: Werner Gephart,
Hannah Arendt, den Eichmann-Prozess beschreibend, 2012
Druck und Bindung: Hubert & Co., Göttingen
Printed in Germany
ISSN 2193-2964
ISBN 978-3-465-04200-6

Vorwort der Herausgeber

Als rechtliche Institution ist das Tribunal untrennbar mit dem kulturellen Phänomen der Öffentlichkeit verbunden. Die Sache, die im Tribunal zur Verhandlung und das heißt immer auch: zur Darstellung kommt, ist von allgemeiner Relevanz. Sie tangiert das öffentliche Interesse einer Gemeinschaft, auf welchen politischen, rechtlichen und kulturellen Bedingungen diese Gemeinschaft im Einzelnen basieren mag. Das gilt für die antike römische Gerichts- und Rednerbühne ebenso wie für die Videoübertragung eines laufenden Gerichtsprozesses oder Tribunals im Internet, die zumindest der Idee nach auf die Herstellung einer weltweiten, globalen Öffentlichkeit abzielt.

Spätestens seit der Arbeit der Juristin und Medienwissenschaftlerin Cornelia Vismann (1961–2010) über *Medien der Rechtsprechung* (Frankfurt a. M. 2011) ist die Tätigkeit gerichts- und tribunalförmiger Jurisdiktion ins Zentrum auch der rechtskulturellen und kulturwissenschaftlichen Reflexion gerückt. In diesem Rahmen gilt es nicht nur die »unhintergehbar theatrale Dimension des Rechtsprechens« (Vismann) zu berücksichtigen, sondern zugleich auch die rechtliche Dimension von ›Verhandlungen‹ auf der Theaterbühne, mit anderen Worten: die rechtliche Dimension von kulturellen Artefakten, literarischen Texten überhaupt. Man kann in diesem Kontext mit guten Gründen auf die Überlegungen der Schaubühnenästhetik im 18. Jahrhundert (von Gottsched bis Schiller) oder auf die gleichermaßen theatralen wie forensischen Versuchsanordnungen Heinrich von Kleists zurückgehen. In besonderer Weise und mit besonderer Dringlichkeit aber stellt sich die Frage nach der rechtlichen, kulturellen und literarischen Relevanz von Tribunalen für die Zeit nach dem Zweiten Weltkrieg.

Seit der Einrichtung des *International Military Tribunal (IMT)* in Nürnberg unmittelbar nach Kriegsende sind Gerichtsprozesse und Tribunale immer wieder von Schriftstellern, Philosophen und Intellektuellen beobachtet worden. Das heutige kulturelle Wissen über diese Prozesse und Tribunale, das über juristische Aspekte im engeren Sinne hinausgeht, verdankt sich weitgehend den Schriften dieser Autoren. Hannah Arendts Bericht *Eichmann in Jerusalem* (1963) ist unter diesen Schriften sicher das bekannteste Werk.

Die Vielschichtigkeit der rechtlichen Einrichtung Tribunal hat Wissenschaftler aus verschiedenen Disziplinen zusammengeführt, um gemeinsam die rechtlichen, kulturellen und literarischen Aspekte dieser Einrichtung einer grundlegenden Analyse zu unterziehen. Juristen, Soziologen und Historiker sind an dieser Analyse ebenso beteiligt wie Literatur- und Kulturwissenschaftler. Darüber hinaus ist von Beginn an die Erweiterung (und Korrektur) des wissenschaftlichen

Blicks auf die zu untersuchende Problematik ein Ziel der gemeinsamen Arbeit gewesen. Aus diesem Grunde kommen im vorliegenden Band auch Rechtspraktiker, Schriftsteller und Filmschaffende zu Wort, die sich auf je eigene, nicht minder wichtige Weise mit Tribunalen beschäftigt haben.

Bonn, im Juli 2013

Jürgen Brokoff, Werner Gephart,
Andrea Schütte, Jan Christoph Suntrup

Inhalt

JAN CHRISTOPH SUNTRUP
Einleitung: Über die rechtliche, kulturelle und literarische Bedeutung
von Tribunalen 9

Erster Teil
Tribunale als Rechtskultur:
Historische, soziologische und juristische Perspektiven

ANNETTE WIEVIORKA
Observations sur des procès nazis :
de Nuremberg à Klaus Barbie 29

WERNER GEPHART
Memory, Tribunals and the Sacred 39

CHRISTOPH FLÜGGE
Die juristische Aufarbeitung von Kriegsverbrechen am *International
Criminal Tribunal for the former Yugoslavia (ICTY)* in Den Haag 57

Zweiter Teil
Lokale Ungerechtigkeit, Kultur und globales Recht:
Tribunale als Globalisierungsphänomen

ANDREAS TH. MÜLLER
International Criminal Tribunals as a Phenomenon of Globalization 71

CHANDRA LEKHA SRIRAM
Tribunals, Legacies, and Local Culture: Lessons from Some African
Experiences with International Criminal Justice 97

JOACHIM J. SAVELSBERG
Tribunals, Collective Memory, and Prospects of Human Rights 117

Interludium
Documenting war crimes

Interludium: Documenting war crimes
Podiumsdiskussion mit Rob Lemkin, Ali Samadi Ahadi, Werner Gephart
und Annette Wieviorka im Anschluss an die Vorführung des Dokumentarfilms »Enemies of the People«
Moderation: Alexander Glodzinski 137

Dritter Teil
Recht sprechen: Tribunale als theatralische Erscheinung

DŽEVAD KARAHASAN
Tribunal, Theater und das Drama des Rechts 151

JÜRGEN BROKOFF
Übergänge. Literarisch-juridische Interferenzen bei Peter Handke
und die Medialität von Rechtsprechung und Tribunal 157

SVJETLAN LACKO VIDULIĆ
Geteilter Erinnerungsort? Der Internationale Gerichtshof für das
ehemalige Jugoslawien als Topos regionaler Erinnerungskulturen 173

Vierter Teil
(Post-)Jugoslawien: Theater und Literatur der Gegenwart

ANDREA SCHÜTTE
Peter Handkes Literatur der Fürsprache 189

ANDREA SCHÜTTE
Imaginäres Interview mit der kroatischen Autorin Dubravka Ugrešić 215

MIRANDA JAKIŠA
Postdramatisches Bühnen-Tribunal: Gerichtstheater rund um das ICTY . . 223

Die Autorinnen und Autoren 243

Jan Christoph Suntrup

Einleitung
Über die rechtliche, kulturelle und literarische Bedeutung von Tribunalen

Tribunale gehören zu den ambivalenten Einrichtungen der Rechtsgeschichte, da ihr Name nicht mit der zivilisierenden Kraft der Rechtsstaatlichkeit, mit den fairen Verfahrensregeln, die eine »ordentliche« Gerichtsverhandlung idealerweise auszeichnen, verbunden wird, sondern mit deren Gegenteil. Das Revolutionstribunal, das Robespierre und seine Anhänger 1793 in Frankreich einrichteten, war ebenso ein Werkzeug des Terrors, der Willkür und des Machtmissbrauches wie die Tribunale, die Stalin in Moskau gegen Dissidenten und Rivalen inszenierte. Das von Intellektuellen eingesetzte Russell-Tribunal wiederum war kein rechtliches Organ, sondern verurteilte symbolisch die Kriegsverbrechen der amerikanischen Armee in Vietnam – ein Versuch, die Weltöffentlichkeit aufzuklären, der sich gleichwohl mit dem Vorwurf des Schauprozesses konfrontiert sah. Während das Tribunal seinen schlechten Ruf als Instrument des Unrechts niemals gänzlich loswurde, steht sein Name in jüngerer Zeit hingegen auch für internationale und hybride Institutionen, deren Aufgabe die Be- und Verurteilung fundamentalen Unrechts ist: Die strafrechtliche Verfolgung von Kriegsverbrechen und »Verbrechen gegen die Menschlichkeit«,[1] wie sie etwa im Tribunal gegen Adolf Eichmann und vor allem in den wegweisenden Tribunalen zu den Jugoslawienkriegen und dem Völkermord in Ruanda erfolgte.

Als Instrumente des internationalen Strafrechts haben diese speziellen Gerichtshöfe seit einigen Jahren nicht nur das Interesse der politologischen und rechtswissenschaftlichen Disziplinen geweckt, sondern auch kultur- und geisteswissenschaftliche Ansätze inspiriert, die den Blick auf die Verfahrenstechniken, auf die Rechtskultur von Tribunalen richten. Die deutsche zeithistorische Forschung hingegen hat schon länger die juristische »Bewältigung« der national-

---

[1] Die Angemessenheit dieser deutschen Übersetzung von »crimes against humanity« ist bekanntlich von Hannah Arendt in ihrem Bericht über den Eichmann-Prozess radikal in Frage gestellt worden: »Das den Nürnberger Prozessen zugrunde liegende Londoner Statut hat [...] die ›Verbrechen gegen die Menschheit‹ als ›unmenschliche Handlungen‹ definiert, woraus dann in der deutschen Übersetzung die bekannten ›Verbrechen gegen die Menschlichkeit‹ geworden sind – als hätten es die Nazis lediglich an ›Menschlichkeit‹ fehlen lassen, als sie Millionen in die Gaskammern schickten, wahrhaftig *das* Understatement des Jahrhunderts« (Arendt: Eichmann in Jerusalem, S. 398 f.).

sozialistischen Vergangenheit, wie sie in den Nürnberger Prozessen begann und in den Frankfurter Auschwitz-Prozessen weitergeführt wurde, zum Thema gehabt, den Focus aber verstärkt in letzter Zeit auf den gesellschaftlichen Einfluss und die erinnerungskulturellen Effekte dieser Verfahren gerichtet.[2]

Die historische Entwicklung internationaler Straftribunale

Mit den Tribunalen gegen deutsche und japanische Kriegsverbrecher, die nach Ende des Zweiten Weltkriegs in Nürnberg und in Tokio abgehalten wurden, wurde politisches und rechtliches Neuland betreten. Ideen für internationale strafgerichtliche Institutionen hatte es bereits zuvor gegeben: Gustav Monnier sprach sich im 19. Jahrhundert vergeblich für die Einrichtung eines internationalen Strafgerichtshofs aus, der Verletzungen der ersten Genfer Konvention aus dem Jahre 1864 verhandeln sollte, während der Prozess gegen den Landvogt Peter von Hagenbach, der 1474 in Breisach eröffnet wurde, bisweilen, in anachronistischer Weise, als erstes »internationales« Tribunal bezeichnet wird.[3] Auch nach dem Ersten Weltkrieg hatte es Überlegungen gegeben, Kriegsverbrecher auf juristischem Weg zur Rechenschaft zu ziehen. Im Artikel 227 des Versailler Vertrags wurde die Absicht erklärt, Kaiser Wilhelm II. »wegen schwerster Verletzung des internationalen Sittengesetzes und der Heiligkeit der Verträge« vor ein internationales Sondergericht zu stellen, ein Plan, der zum einen an der mangelnden Bereitschaft der Niederlande, den Kaiser auszuliefern, scheiterte, der zum anderen aber auch auf Skepsis im Lager der Siegermächte stieß, da ein solches Tribunal das Prinzip der nationalen Souveränität untergraben hätte.[4]

Somit stellte das Internationale Militär-Tribunal von Nürnberg einen historischen Präzedenzfall für die juristische Aufarbeitung von Kriegsverbrechen dar, die nicht nur den gewohnten Zustand der rechtlichen Straflosigkeit von Führungspersonen krimineller Regime, sondern auch ihre außergerichtliche Behandlung durch die Siegermächte beendete, wie Robert H. Jackson, der amerikanische Chefankläger in Nürnberg, in seiner Eröffnungsrede betonte: »That four great nations, flushed with victory and stung with injury stay the hand of vengeance and voluntarily submit their captive enemies to the judgment of the law is one of the most significant tributes that Power has ever paid to Reason. [...] If these men are the first war leaders of a defeated nation to be prosecuted in the name of

---

[2] Vgl. Wamhof: Gerichtskultur und NS-Vergangenheit.
[3] Vgl. Popovski: Legality and legitimacy, S. 391.
[4] Vgl. ebd., S. 393; vgl. auch den Beitrag von Andreas Th. Müller in diesem Band.

the law, they are also the first to be given a chance to plead for their lives in the name of the law«.[5]

Wenn sich die Prozesse von Nürnberg und Tokio als einflussreich für die Kodifikation des humanitären Völkerrechts erwiesen, das mit der Genozid-Konvention von 1948 und den Genfer Konventionen von 1949 auf eine neue Basis gestellt wurde, scheiterten alle Gedankenspiele, eine permanente internationale Strafgerichtsbarkeit einzurichten, die diese grundlegenden normativen Texte hätte implementieren und ihnen damit erst im vollen Sinn Gesetzeskraft verleihen können, an der Logik des Kalten Kriegs.[6] Erst nach dem Fall des Eisernen Vorhangs wurde dieser erneuten Phase der Straflosigkeit ein Ende bereitet.[7] Die internationale Staatengemeinschaft vermochte es zwar sowohl während der Jugoslawienkriege als auch angesichts der Massenmorde in Ruanda nicht, eine konsequente Interventionspolitik zu entwickeln, die den Massakern Einhalt gebot, das Ziel der Strafverfolgung der Verantwortlichen wurde aber nolens volens wieder aufgegriffen. Die vom UN-Sicherheitsrat beschlossene Installation zweier Ad-hoc-Tribunale, des *International Criminal Tribunal for the former Yugoslavia* (ICTY) 1993 und des *International Criminal Tribunal for Ruanda* (ICTR) 1994 zur Aufarbeitung der Kriegsverbrechen war die Folge, die richtungsweisenden Charakter für die Weiterentwicklung des internationalen Strafrechts hatte, bildete die Arbeit der Tribunale doch das Vorbild für die Einrichtung des permanenten Internationalen Strafgerichtshofs, der schließlich 2002 seine Arbeit aufnahm. Darüber hinaus zeigt die Bildung von diversen, oft als »hybrid« bezeichneten Sondertribunalen, die Elemente des jeweils nationalen und internationalen Rechts verbinden, von der zunehmenden Etablierung der Strafverfolgung verantwortlicher Eliten in Post-Konflikt-Gesellschaften, etwa zu beobachten in Sierra Leone, Kambodscha oder Ost-Timor.[8] Mit diesen Praktiken ist, folgt man Ruti Teitel, ein entscheidender Paradigmenwechsel in den Internationalen Beziehungen markiert. Das internationale Rechtsregime hat sich zunehmend von seinem Fokus auf die staatliche Sicherheit und Souveränität gelöst und eine neue Art der Normativität entwickelt, die die Sicherheit von Völkern und Personen in den Mittelpunkt rückt – mit deutlichen Spuren im Kriegsvölkerrecht, bei der Artikulation von Menschenrechten

---

5 Jackson: Opening statement.
6 Vgl. Popovski: Legality and legitimacy, S. 395.
7 Die NS-Verbrechen waren natürlich auch in der Zwischenzeit stets Gegenstand der juristischen Bewältigung auf nationaler Ebene gewesen, wie die Frankfurter Auschwitzprozesse, das Eichmann-Tribunal in Israel oder der französische Prozess gegen Klaus Barbie zeigen. Für die Verurteilung neuerer Kriegsverbrechen und Menschenrechtsverletzungen, die nicht vor den zuständigen nationalen Gerichten verhandelt wurden, gab es jedoch keine internationale Instanz, die dieses Defizit der Straflosigkeit beheben konnte.
8 Vgl. Nouwen: ›Hybrid courts‹, sowie Müller in diesem Band.

und eben auch im Internationalen Strafrecht, die alle zusammen konstitutive Elemente eines neuen »Humanity law« bilden.[9]

Legalität und Legitimität von Tribunalen

Diese neuen strafrechtlichen Institutionen sind nun nicht nur von großer politischer und juristischer Bedeutung, sondern werfen auch die kulturwissenschaftliche Frage nach der möglichen eigenen Funktionslogik der Tribunale auf. Denn schon das Alltagsverständnis von »Tribunal« suggeriert, dass es sich bei diesem Phänomen um eine eigene rechtskulturelle Form handelt, die sich von der des normalen Gerichts signifikant unterscheidet. Die jüngsten wissenschaftlichen Funktionsanalysen vergangener und aktueller Straftribunale verfolgen deshalb zumindest implizit das Ziel, dem generellen Unterschied von Gericht und Tribunal auf die Spur zu kommen.

Jeder Versuch, diese Differenz zu fixieren, wird schon durch divergierende kulturelle Vorverständnisse und Sprachgewohnheiten erschwert. Christoph Flügge weist in seinem Beitrag zu diesem Band darauf hin, dass im Englischen der Tribunal-Begriff unbeschwerter verwendet wird als im Deutschen und eben *per se* keine Sonderform der Gerichtsbarkeit bezeichnet. Nicht zufällig wird deswegen der ICTY in der deutschen Debatte zwar oftmals, in Anlehnung an den englischen Titel, als »Haager Tribunal« bezeichnet, offiziell führt er aber den Namen eines Strafgerichtshofs. In der Tat weisen die Haager Prozesse auch viele Elemente auf, die man idealtypisch einem ordentlichen Gericht zuschreiben würde, so wie das Vorgehen nach einer transparenten verfahrensrechtlichen Ordnung, die faire Anhörung der Angeklagten und die ergebnisoffene, faktenorientierte Urteilsfindung. Dass das Ziel des ICTY nicht die voreingenommene und hastige Aburteilung der Angeklagten ist, offenbart sich in den langwierigen Verfahren, an deren Ende durchaus die Möglichkeit spektakulärer Freisprüche stehen kann, wie der in der Revision erlangte Freispruch für den kroatischen General Ante Gotovina dokumentiert.[10] Gleichwohl begleitet viele der in den letzten 20 Jahren in Angriff genommenen internationalen oder hybriden Straftribunale, wie schon ihre Vorläufer, die Unterstellung, selektive Justiz im Stile eines Schauprozesses zu betreiben. Dieser Vorwurf trifft insbesondere das Jugoslawien- und das Ruanda-Tribunal, weil sie mit dem gleichen Problem konfrontiert waren wie die Ad-hoc-Tribunale in Nürnberg und Tokio: Weil eine Anklage allein auf Basis des beste-

---

9 Vgl. Teitel: Humanity's law.
10 Dieses Urteil verstärkte natürlich gerade in Serbien die Wahrnehmung des Haager Tribunals als politisches, antiserbisches Gericht (vgl. Martens: Nicht nur Nationalisten).

henden Rechts nicht möglich war, musste eine neue Rechtsgrundlage geschaffen werden, die die Strafverfolgung legalisierte, was aus rechtsstaatlicher Sicht zu großen Bedenken führt: »Der Grundsatz *nulla poena sine lege* wird in Tribunalen ausdrücklich ignoriert – was mit der außergewöhnlichen Dimension begründet wird, in der sie agieren. Die fehlende oder bloß lose Bindung an das gesetzte Recht eröffnet Tribunalen einen weiteren Aktionsradius als ihn Gerichte haben. Sie können all das verhandeln, was eine öffentliche Angelegenheit werden soll. [...] Das Tribunal, das jenseits der Gesetze einsetzt, ist demnach die Form, einem überwundenen Regime den Prozess zu machen«.[11]

Ungeachtet der realen Verfahrensgerechtigkeit war diese labile rechtliche Grundlage von jeher ein Einfallstor für fundamentale Kritik.[12] Die Einrichtung der Tribunale für das frühere Jugoslawien und für Ruanda wurde durch Beschlüsse des UN-Sicherheitsrates initiiert (Resolutionen 808, 827 und 855), was einen Präzedenzfall darstellte, da nie zuvor der Sicherheitsrat, der als nicht-repräsentatives, historische Machtstrukturen reflektierendes Organ selbst an einem großen Legitimitätsdefizit leidet, eine juristische Institution ins Leben gerufen hatte.[13] Die Gründung des Internationalen Strafgerichtshofs (ICC), dessen Status keinesfalls unumstritten ist, geht hingegen auf einen internationalen Vertrag (Rom-Statut) zurück, der von mittlerweile mehr als 120 Ländern ratifiziert wurde (bekanntlich nicht von Großmächten wie den USA, Russland und China), so dass der Gerichtshof auf einem ungleich festeren legalen Fundament steht, zumal er nicht retroaktiv tätig werden kann.[14] Diese Rechtsbasis schützt ihn jedoch nicht vor Anschuldigungen, seine Praxis der Strafverfolgung voreingenommen und lokal fixiert auszuüben, ein Vorwurf, der angesichts der Tatsache, dass der ICC trotz seines universalen Anspruchs bisher ausschließlich Fälle auf dem afrikanischen Kontinent verfolgt hat, immer wieder aufkommt.[15]

Tribunale als Schau-Prozesse – pädagogische und identitätspolitische Elemente aus kulturwissenschaftlicher Sicht

Wenn Tribunale als Schauprozesse bezeichnet werden, schwingt dieser Vorwurf der selektiven, meist außerrechtlichen Justiz der Ausnahme mit – ob bei den

---

11 Vismann: Medien der Rechtsprechung, S. 161.
12 So fragte Peter Handke, ob nicht die Einrichtung des ICTY ein »Gewaltstreich ›im Namen der Humanität‹«, ein »Gewaltstreich der ›Welt‹ gegen die Staaten« sei (Handke: Rund um das Große Tribunal, S. 18).
13 Vgl. Popovski: Legality and legitimacy, S. 397.
14 Ebd., S. 402 ff.
15 Vgl. Müller, in diesem Band.

Nürnberger Prozessen, die oft als »Siegerjustiz« wahrgenommen wurden,[16] ob im Eichmann-Tribunal, wo etwa Hannah Arendt die Rechte des Angeklagten beschnitten sah,[17] oder im Bezug auf den ICTY, der laut Martti Koskenniemi nur dann der Gefahr eines umfassenden Schauprozesses hätte entgehen können, wenn auch die Verstrickung der westlichen Politik in die Dynamik der Jugoslawienkriege verhandelt worden wäre,[18] was faktisch nur sehr begrenzt der Fall war. Doch die Frage nach dem Schau-Charakter von Tribunalen wird in den letzten Jahren noch weit grundlegender gestellt, um zu untersuchen, was in solchen Prozessen zu welchem Zweck zur Schau gestellt wird. Versteht man Recht nicht nur als Regelwerk, sondern als soziale Praxis, wird deutlich, dass bestimmte Rituale und Strategien des Zur-Schau-Stellens konstitutiv für das Recht, das immer eine ostentative und theatralische Seite hat, sind: »Die Performanz des Rechts ist das Rechten: die Aufführung einer Verhandlung«.[19] Selbst ein »moderner« Strafgerichtsprozess lässt sich unter diesen Vorzeichen noch als theatralisch geformte Darbietung verstehen, die in ihrer vorgegebenen Nüchternheit als »Nicht-Inszenierung inszeniert« wird.[20]

Trotz dieser essentiellen Theatralität jeden »Rechtens« heben sich Tribunale, zumindest idealtypisch, von anderen Rechtsformen dadurch ab, dass sie darauf abzielen, eine möglichst große Öffentlichkeit zu erreichen: »Zuschauer sind für ein Tribunal [...] konstitutiv. Sie sind das, was die Tragödienzuschauer in der Antike und was die Umstehenden für die mittelalterlichen Verfahren gewesen sind. Ihr Sehen entscheidet. Schaut niemand hin, versinkt ein Tribunal in der Bedeutungslosigkeit. Um eine Sache von Relevanz zu werden, muss ein Tribunal darum bemüht sein, dass alle schauen«.[21] Ein Gericht hingegen ist, ebenfalls idealtypisch, aus Gründen der Transparenz zwar zu einer gewissen öffentlichen Rechenschaftspflicht genötigt,[22] auf der anderen Seite aber immer darum bemüht, Öffentlichkeit zu limitieren, um einer Tribunalisierung der Verfahrensabläufe entgegenzuwirken – nicht ohne Grund verbietet das deutsche Gerichtsverfassungsgesetz die »öffentliche Vorführung« von Prozessen, wobei die Auslegung dieses Grundsatzes stark umstritten ist.[23]

---

16 Vgl. Koskenniemi: Between impunity, S. 5.
17 »Jetzt zeigte sich, daß Israel das einzige Land der Welt war, wo Entlastungszeugen nicht vernommen werden konnten und wo die Verteidigung gewisse Belastungszeugen, nämlich jene, die für vorhergegangene Prozesse eidesstattliche Erklärungen abgegeben hatten, nicht ins Kreuzverhör nehmen konnte« (Arendt: Eichmann in Jerusalem, S. 332).
18 »Having finally moved away from the Scylla of impunity [...] the West is now heading either towards a lesson in history and politics in which its own guilt will have to be assessed, or to the Charybdis of show trials« (Koskenniemi: Between impunity, S. 19).
19 Schwarte: Angemessenes Unrecht, S. 135.
20 Schild: Die Strafgerichtsverhandlung, S. 117
21 Vismann: Medien der Rechtsprechung, S. 151.
22 Ebd.
23 So lehnte das Oberlandesgericht München bei der Verhandlung der sogenannten NSU-Morde

Tribunale wenden sich an ein großes Publikum, weil sie didaktisch-pädagogische Ziele verfolgen, die sich aus der Natur der Verbrechen ergeben, die sie verhandeln. Konfrontiert mit den schlimmsten Menschenrechtsverletzungen werden Tribunalen vielfältige Gerechtigkeitserwartungen entgegengebracht, die die Anforderungen an ein normales Gericht bei Weitem übersteigen. So kann argumentiert werden, dass die Verurteilung der Täter auf symbolische Weise einen Beitrag zur Affirmation fundamentaler Werte einer wie auch immer gearteten »moralischen Gemeinschaft« leistet[24] – bisweilen wird in diesem Geist sogar die Idee von »liberal show trials« verteidigt, die gerade in Gesellschaften, die Schauplatz von grausamen Verbrechen geworden sind, der pädagogischen Vermittlung liberaler Normen dienen sollten.[25] Solche Vorschläge knüpfen an Strategien der normativen Transformation von Gesellschaften an, wie sie unter dem Stichwort der *transitional justice* seit einiger Zeit diskutiert werden.[26] Die gerechte »Bewältigung« der Vergangenheit wird dabei an gezielte erinnerungspolitische Maßnahmen geknüpft, die außergerichtlicher Art sein können, wie im Fall der südafrikanischen Wahrheits- und Versöhnungskommission, während in anderen Fällen Tribunalen selbst die Mission der Erinnerungsbildung und -bewahrung überantwortet wird. Die Einschätzung Cornelia Vismanns, das Haager Tribunal ziele auf »ein Gerichtsverfahren plus Geschichtslektion, Täterbestrafung plus Opferforum, Aburteilung konkreter Taten plus Thematisierung des Bösen« ab, zeugt von diesem ambitionierten Versuch, mit juristischen Mitteln das kollektive Gedächtnis zu prägen. Eine solche Nutzung des Rechts für außerrechtliche Zwecke hatte Martin Walser bereits im Frankfurter Auschwitz-Prozess am Werk gesehen, habe dieser doch eine Bedeutung erhalten, »die mit dem Rechtsgeschäft nichts mehr zu tun hat. Geschichtsforschung läuft mit, Enthüllung, moralische und politische Aufklärung einer Bevölkerung, die offenbar auf keinem anderen Wege zur Anerkennung des Geschehenen zu bringen war«.[27]

Schon die wegweisenden Nürnberger Prozesse hatten eine offensichtliche erzieherische Funktion, die sich nahtlos in die amerikanische Politik der *reeducation* der deutschen Bevölkerung einfügte. Robert Kempner, der Stellvertreter

im Frühjahr 2013, trotz der nur begrenzt zur Verfügung stehenden Presseplätze im Gerichtssaal, eine Video-Übertragung der Verhandlung in einen benachbarten Raum mit Bezug auf diesen Passus ab. Ob eine solche Übertragung als »öffentliche Vorführung« einzustufen wäre, bleibt jedoch noch juristisch zu klären (vgl. Tretbar: Videoübertragung; vgl. auch Gephart: Recht als Kultur, S. 277ff.).

24 Vgl. hierzu Koskenniemi: Between impunity, S. 9f.
25 So argumentiert Osiel: Mass atrocity, S. 65f.: »The orchestration of criminal trials for pedagogic purposes [...] is not inherently misguided or morally indefensible. The defensibility of the practice depends on the defensibility of the lessons being taught – that is, on the liberal nature of the stories being told«.
26 Vgl. hierzu grundlegend: Teitel: Transitional justice, sowie die nützliche Übersicht bei Graf/Kainz/Taibl: Transitional justice.
27 Walser: Unser Auschwitz, S. 189.

von Hauptankläger Robert H. Jackson in Nürnberg, sprach über das Tribunal als »the greatest history seminar ever held«.[28] Wie »Geschichte« in Tribunalen zur Sprache kommt, hängt dabei nicht zuletzt von der Art der Beweisführung ab. Die primäre Berufung des Nürnberger Verfahrens auf schriftliche Dokumente erwies sich in didaktischer Hinsicht als eher ambivalent: »This reliance on written documents, however well suited to bringing history into the courtroom, deprived the trial of a compelling human element: the voice of memory, the words of victims«.[29] Wenn im Gegensatz dazu Chefankläger Gideon Hausner im Eichmann-Prozess großen Wert auf die Aussage überlebender Opfer des Holocausts legte, geschah dies zum einen, um diesen Opfern durch das eigene Bezeugen ihres Leids Gerechtigkeit widerfahren zu lassen, zum anderen aber auch, um der israelischen und der Weltöffentlichkeit ein lebendes und anschauliches Zeugnis von den Nazi-Verbrechen zu liefern.[30] Nicht die nüchtern-faktische Dokumentierung von Wahrheit stand im Zentrum des Eichmann-Prozesses, sondern die durch persönliche Betroffenheit der Opfer authentisch-unmittelbar wirkende narrative Bezeugung des Unrechts, die zum Bezugspunkt kollektiver Identitätsbildung werden sollte.

Man kann hier einen Sonderfall des *legal storytelling* erkennen, der narrativen Dimension des Rechts, die seit einigen Jahrzehnten Gegenstand vor allem der US-amerikanischen Literaturwissenschaft ist. Die Historikerin Annette Wieviorka hat im Eichmann-Prozess die kulturgeschichtliche »Entstehung des Zeugen«[31] gesehen, die offensichtlich nicht die Figur des juristischen Zeugen hervorgebracht, sondern eine neue testimoniale Form eingeführt habe, die laut Michael Bachmann folgende Züge aufweist: »Zeugenschaft [erscheint], vor der inhaltlichen Dimension, primär als ein Erzählmodus, mit dem sich Geschichte immer neu – und glaubhaft – vermitteln lässt. Sie bricht das unfassbare Gesamtgeschehen auf in eine Reihe von greifbaren Ereignissen [...], denen die anwesenden Zeugen leibliche Präsenz verleihen«.[32] Dieser Zeuge ist also kein unbeteiligter, neutraler Gerichtszeuge, sondern ein »moralischer Zeuge«, der die Rolle des Opfers und des Zeugen in sich eint[33] und als »Erinnerungs-Mensch« zum Träger von Geschichte wird.[34] Das Hören seiner Stimme im Zuge der Beweisführung dient nicht nur der juristischen Wahrheitsfindung, sondern einer übergeordneten erinnerungspolitischen Mission: »Was im Gerichtssaal beginnt, setzt sich in einer sozialen Praxis und Politik der Anerkennung außerhalb des Gerichtssaals fort. Auf Urteil und Schuldspruch folgt die sekundäre Zeugenschaft der Gesellschaft in Form einer

---

28 Robert Kempner, zit. nach Douglas: The didactic trial, S. 514.
29 Douglas: The didactic trial, S. 515.
30 Ebd.
31 Wieviorka: Entstehung des Zeugen.
32 Bachmann: Der abwesende Zeuge, S. 109 f.
33 Vgl. Assmann: Der lange Schatten, S. 88.
34 Wieviorka: Entstehung des Zeugen, S. 152.

Erinnerungskultur, die von der Solidarität mit den Opfern getragen ist und historische Verantwortung übernimmt«.³⁵

Spätere Tribunale haben ihren eigenen Weg der Dokumentierung und persönlichen Vermittlung von Verbrechen und Leiden gesucht. Das ICTY hat während seiner langjährigen Prozessführung Millionen von schriftlichen Materialien angehäuft, aber auch den Raum für die Narrationen von Opfer-Zeugen geboten.³⁶ Der Rechtskultur des Tribunals kommt also eine Gedächtnisfunktion zu, die in der Geschichts- und Kulturwissenschaft die Frage aufgeworfen hat, »ob nicht das strafjuristische Vorgehen und hierbei insbesondere der öffentliche Prozess als Aufarbeitungsmodus, der Aspekte der Vergangenheit unter spezifischen Vorzeichen, nach bestimmten Regeln und Kriterien organisiert, ein eigenes erinnerungskulturelles Genre etabliert«.³⁷ Die Behandlung von Kriegsverbrechen und Menschenrechtsverletzungen erfolgt in unterschiedlichen institutionellen Arenen, die geschichtliche Faktizität nach ihrer eigenen Logik (re-)konstruieren. Der nach bestimmten Kriterien konstruierte juristische Fall deckt sich nicht zwangsläufig mit den Ergebnissen historischer Analysen, denen ganz andere Methoden zur Verfügung stehen. Die Repräsentation von Verbrechen und das Verständnis von Schuld unterliegt in Gerichtsverhandlungen, woran Lawrence Douglas erinnert hat, juristischen »Filtern«, die durchaus rechtskulturell variieren können: Erstens stellen die Beweisregeln einen spezifischen epistemologischen Focus dar, der bestimmt, was als justiziable »Wahrheit« vor Gericht anerkannt wird. Zweitens präsentiert die Formulierung der Anklagepunkte schon einen Rahmen für die Deutung der Geschichte, der bei vergangenen Prozessen, gerade bei komplexen Verbrechen wie Genoziden, nicht immer angemessen war. So konnte der Frankfurter Auschwitz-Prozess, um eine nachträgliche Anwendung des in den 1950er Jahren beschlossenen Gesetzes zur Kriminalisierung des Genozids zu vermeiden, die Beschuldigten nur für das Delikt des einfachen Mordes anklagen, mit gravierenden Konsequenzen für die Art der Beweisführung.³⁸ Drittens wirken Konzep-

---

35 Assmann: Der lange Schatten, S. 90.
36 Vgl. den Beitrag von Christoph Flügge in diesem Band. Die Arbeit des ICTY zeigt im Übrigen deutlich die Gefahren auf, die mit der Zeugenvernehmung verbunden sind, solange die Verteidigungsseite das Recht zum Kreuzverhör hat: »Witnesses contradict themselves and each other, memories change, or remain inscribed in the words that have been used to give shape to them, lose their immediacy and turn into a myth. A vigorous cross-examination leads even the most reliable witness to a state of confusion. In the end, memory may not have been served but undermined – not to say anything of the dignity of the victims who, like the young woman who survived the Racak massacre in January 1999, testified about it in the Hague in May 2002, and whose evidence was reduced to a series of panicky ›I don't know‹ statements by a bullying Milosevic« (Koskenniemi: Between impunity, S. 33).
37 Wamhof: Gerichtskultur und NS-Vergangenheit, S. 13. Vgl. auch die Beiträge von Werner Gephart und Svjetlan Lacko Vidulić in diesem Band.
38 Den Angeklagten musste nämlich in diesem Prozess für eine Verurteilung das Motiv der »Mordlust« nachgewiesen werden, was den generellen Zuständen in der Todesfabrik Auschwitz über-

tionen der Zurechnung als zusätzlicher Filter – der ICTY hat gerade wegen der schwierigen Behandlung kollektiver Verbrechen, denen mit den Mitteln des individuellen Strafrechts äußerst schwierig zu begegnen ist, die juristische Figur des »joint criminal enterprise« entwickelt, die ein elaborierteres Verständnis individueller Schuldzurechnung ermöglichen soll.[39] Denn die Überforderung traditioneller juristischer Kategorien mit neuartigen Verbrechen hatte schon Hannah Arendt in ihrem Bericht über den Eichmann-Prozess konstatiert: »[U]m die Frage von Schuld und Unschuld, um die Möglichkeit, Recht zu sprechen und Gerechtigkeit zu üben im Interesse des Verletzten wie im Interesse des Angeklagten, geht es in jedem Strafprozeß; auch im Eichmann-Prozeß konnte es um nichts anderes gehen. Nur daß hier das Gericht mit einem Verbrechen konfrontiert war, das es in den Gesetzbüchern vergeblich suchen wird, und mit einem Verbrecher, dessengleichen man jedenfalls vor Gericht vor den Nürnberger Prozessen nicht gekannt hat«.[40]

Wirkung von Tribunalen und Varianten der Vergangenheitsbewältigung

Wenn Tribunalen, explizit oder implizit, die Aufgabe zugewiesen wird, Geschichte festzuhalten und zu dokumentieren, bleibt also stets zu berücksichtigen, dass im Prozess letztlich die Produktion von justiziablem Wissen im Vordergrund steht, das Ergebnis einer spezifischen verfahrensrechtlichen Rationalität ist, die historische Erkenntnisse selektiv wahrnimmt, die aber auch in Konkurrenz zu anderen Versuchen der Vergangenheitsbewältigung und der Repräsentation von Verbrechen und Schuld tritt.[41] Welche dieser Unternehmungen schließlich eine

---

haupt nicht gerecht wurde: »Wenn man mit wehleidiger Lust (die sich auch als nationaler Protest äußern kann) in der Zeitung die brutalen Fakten zur Kenntnis nimmt, vergißt man leicht, daß all diese mittelalterlich bunten Quälereien eher gegen das System veranstaltet wurden. Unsere Nationalsozialisten waren ja erst am Anfang. Persönliche Grausamkeit hätte über kurz oder lang kaum mehr eine Rolle spielen dürfen. ›Fleißaufgaben‹ nannte der ehemalige ›Häftling‹ Dr. Wolken die grausamen Praktiken der SS-Chargen. Man vergißt angesichts der einprägsamen Folterer, daß das schlechtere Idealisten waren als die besseren Idealisten, die das System entworfen hatten. Es sollte wirklich, wie Ossietzky sah, die ›Zeit des desinfizierten Marterpfahls‹ werden« (Walser: Unser Auschwitz, S. 193; vgl. auch Douglas: The didactic trial, S. 517).

[39] Douglas: The didactic trial, S. 518. Vgl. auch Burkhardt: Individuelle Zurechnung sowie grundlegend Jakobs: System der strafrechtlichen Zurechnung; Fauconnet: Responsabilité; Gephart: Symbol und Sanktion.

[40] Arendt: Eichmann in Jerusalem, S. 67f.

[41] Dass die Perspektive des Strafrechts deswegen »verzerrend« sei, wie in vielen Studien argumentiert wird, ist zumindest eine missverständliche Formulierung, wenn man sich die konstruktivistische Rolle des Rechts, aber auch anderer Rationalitäten bewusst macht: »Denn [...] was der Fall ist, wird im Verfahren mit seinen juridischen Praktiken erst hergestellt, d.h. der Prozess hantiert nicht mit einer ideellen, vorgefundenen Wirklichkeit, die dann verzerrt werden könnte, sondern mit

dominante Rolle bei der Geschichtsschreibung und der Bildung eines kollektiven Gedächtnisses einnehmen kann, hängt von gesellschaftlichen Wirkfaktoren ab, die nicht *a priori* zu bestimmen sind. Während für den deutschen Kontext von einer auch öffentlich wirksamen »Juridifizierung der NS-Vergangenheit« gesprochen wird,[42] ist die Strahlkraft jüngerer Tribunale noch gar nicht definitiv einzuschätzen. Das Haager Tribunal etwa arbeitet durch die permanente, nur leicht zeitversetzte Übertragung seiner Prozesse im Internet unter Bedingungen der maximal möglichen Transparenz, ohne dass hierdurch schon auf eine bestimmte Rezeption geschlossen werden könnte. Allerdings wird oft lamentiert, die fehlende »organische« Beziehung des Tribunals zum Ort des Unrechts stehe seinen didaktischen Zielen entgegen, da der Versuch einer *transitional justice* als Fernjustiz zum Scheitern verurteilt sei.[43] So kann Den Haag, das nicht nur das ICTY, sondern auch den Internationalen Strafgerichtshof sowie zahlreiche andere Gerichte und Sondertribunale beheimatet, wahlweise als »legal capital of the world«[44] oder als »Nicht-Ort«[45] bezeichnet werden, der weit entfernt von den Verantwortlichen und Betroffenen der verhandelten Verbrechen situiert ist. Auf der anderen Seite ist es nicht von der Hand zu weisen, dass die Erfolgsaussichten von nationalen und hybriden Straftribunalen bisweilen durch Korruption, politische Einflussnahme und mangelndes Aufklärungsstreben kompromittiert werden.[46]

Diese Diskussion über die soziale Einbettung von Tribunalen lenkt den Blick darauf, dass die juristischen Narrationen einer weiteren diskursiven, medialen Vermittlung bedürfen, um prägenden Einfluss auf eine Erinnerungskultur zu entwickeln.[47] Hier sind Deutungskonflikte zwischen politischen Eliten, Wissenschaftlern, Künstlern und anderen sozialen Gruppen an der Tagesordnung, die zu je eigenen Darstellungsversionen von Verbrechen samt Schuldinterpretationen gelangen. Intellektuelle, die sich bei ihrer Kritik gesellschaftlichen Unrechts selbst nicht selten juristischer, zum Teil tribunalhafter Formen bedient haben,[48] sind dabei auch immer wieder als genaue Prozessbeobachter in Erscheinung getreten, was zur Etablierung eines eigenen literarischen Genres der Gerichtsberichterstat-

---

seiner justiziell hergestellten Wirklichkeit, die sich der Repräsentation ihrer Akte in der medialen Rückspiegelung in der Öffentlichkeit nicht immer entziehen kann« (Wamhof: Gerichtskultur und NS-Vergangenheit, S. 18).

[42] Vgl. ebd., S. 13.
[43] Vgl. Vismann: Medien der Rechtsprechung, S. 359 f.; ähnlich Koskenniemi: Between impunity, S. 11, und Douglas: The didactic trial, S. 519.
[44] Vgl. Müller in diesem Band.
[45] Vismann: Medien der Rechtsprechung, S. 359; Vismann behauptet, dass gerade die für das Tribunal zentrale Medientechnik der Internet-Übertragung die Justiz zu einem »ortlosen Unternehmen« mache (ebd.).
[46] So van Ooyen: Politische Bedingungen, S. 27, der sich vor allem auf die Situation in Kambodscha bezieht.
[47] Vgl. hierzu grundlegend Savelsberg/King: Law and collective memory.
[48] Vgl. Suntrup: Die Intellektuellen.

tung geführt hat, wenn man nur an Arendts Eichmann-Studie, Harry Mulischs »Strafsache 40/61« über das gleiche Verfahren,[49] Martin Walsers Kommentar des Frankfurter Auschwitz-Prozesses[50] und Peter Handkes »Umwegzeugenberichte« vom ICTY[51] denkt. Im Medium des Films wiederum kann eine Prozesskritik mit anderen ästhetischen Mitteln betrieben werden, wie Hans-Christian Schmids Spielfilm »Sturm« über das Haager Tribunal bezeugt, während ein Dokumentarfilm wie »Enemies of the people« über die Massenmorde in Kambodscha[52] einen Einblick in die Dynamik und Abgründe kollektiver Verbrechen verschafft, die in juristischen, aber auch anderen diskursiven Kategorien kaum adäquat zu adressieren sind. Die Aufarbeitung von fundamentalen Verbrechen endet somit nicht selten in einem Kampf der Deutungen und Erinnerungen, der durch unterschiedliche ästhetische Darstellungsmittel, institutionelle Logiken und strategisch auftretende »mnemonic entrepreneurs«[53] geprägt ist.

Über die Beiträge des Bandes

Die in diesem Buch versammelten Texte dokumentieren die Ergebnisse einer Tagung des Käte Hamburger Kollegs »Recht als Kultur« und des Instituts für Germanistik, Vergleichende Literatur- und Kulturwissenschaft der Universität Bonn vom Frühjahr 2012, die sich der literarischen und medialen Darstellung und der juristischen Aufarbeitung von Kriegsverbrechen und damit dem Proprium von Tribunalen widmete.

Annette Wieviorka stellt mit dem Blick auf ausgewählte Prozesse gegen Nazi-Verbrecher heraus, dass diese nicht nur als juristisches Instrument, sondern als Mittel der Geschichtsschreibung und kollektiven Identitätsbildung zu betrachten sind. In Anknüpfung an ein Konzept Pierre Noras könnten diese Tribunale somit als »lieux de mémoire«, als »Erinnerungsorte« tituliert werden. Während die Nürnberger Prozesse durch die Dokumentierung und Archivierung von Beweisstücken als Initiator einer didaktischen, auch an die Nachwelt gerichteten Aufarbeitung von Auschwitz gelten können, schätzt Wieviorka den Eichmann-Prozess als in mehrfacher Hinsicht bedeutsam ein. Nicht nur habe er den Versuch dargestellt, dem jüdischen Volk (auch der Diaspora) ein »universales Narrativ« zu geben, sondern auch eine neue Art der Öffentlichkeit eingeführt, wurden doch

---

49 Vgl. Mulisch: Strafsache 40/61.
50 Vgl. Walser: Unser Auschwitz.
51 Vgl. Handke: Rund um das Große Tribunal, sowie ders.: Tablas von Daimiel; vgl. zu Handke auch die Beiträge von Brokoff und Schütte in diesem Band.
52 Vgl. die Diskussion »Documenting war crimes« über diesen Film in diesem Band.
53 Savelsberg, in diesem Band.

zum ersten Mal Bilder dieses Tribunals gefilmt und – als »Event« – weltweit gesendet, um die Verankerung des Genozids im kollektiven Gedächtnis zu fördern. Auch den späteren Prozessen gegen Nazi-Verbrecher in Frankreich kann in erster Linie eine pädagogische und dokumentarische Funktion zugesprochen werden.

Werner Gephart knüpft direkt an die Überlegungen Wieviorkas an, indem er auf den Fehler hinweist, dass »Erinnerung« traditionellerweise nicht als Kategorie im Reich des Normativen beachtet wird. Dabei dienen Gerichtsprozesse wie das Eichmann-Tribunal im hohen Maße der symbolischen Repräsentation der kollektiven Ordnung, der Repräsentation von Recht und Unrecht. Gephart argumentiert, dass zur Verankerung im kollektiven Gedächtnis nicht nur das Zur-Sprache-Bringen von elementaren Wahrheiten und Überzeugungen beiträgt, sondern auch die quasi-religiöse Tabuisierung, wenn es um das Undarstellbare und Unaussprechliche geht. Daran anknüpfend wirft er die Frage auf, ob man in diesem Sinne von einer »Sakralisierung des Holocausts« reden kann, die eine Sphäre des Unberührbaren, des Tabus als Grundpfeiler einer Kultur errichtet. Zudem verdeutlicht der Beitrag, dass auch Gerichtsverhandlungen auf ihren Bezug zum religiösen Symbolismus hin untersucht werden können. Ihre rituelle Ordnung kann als Liturgie gelesen werden, deren Verletzung zwar nicht als Sakrileg, aber als gravierende kulturelle Irritation wahrgenommen wird – ein hochaktuelles Problem, wenn man sich etwa die lokale Implementierung globaler Rechtsnormen vor Augen führt, wo verschiedene rechtskulturelle Prozesslogiken aufeinandertreffen.

Christoph Flügge meldet aus seiner Sicht eines Richters am Internationalen Strafgerichtshof für das ehemalige Jugoslawien Zweifel an, ob die Charakterisierung seiner Arbeit und anderer Sondergerichte als »Tribunal«, eine Rechtsform, die schnell mit Schauprozessen assoziiert werde, tatsächlich angebracht ist, da das ausschließliche Ziel des ICTY die strafrechtliche Verfolgung von Kriegsverbrechern sei. Zugleich gesteht Flügge aber ein, dass die historische und auch didaktische Bedeutung der Prozesse kaum zu leugnen ist. Diese drückt sich in der systematischen Archivierung eines detailreichen Wissens über die Kriegsverbrechen genauso aus wie in den Episoden, in denen betroffene Opfer die historische Gelegenheit bekommen, vor Gericht ihre Geschichte zu erzählen.

Die folgenden Texte weisen den neuartigen Tribunalisierungsformen ihren Platz im Rahmen einer Globalisierung normativer Ordnungen zu. *Andreas Th. Müller* wirft einen Blick auf die Genese des Internationalen Strafgerichtshofs, dessen globaler Anspruch sich daran reibt, dass wichtige Staaten wie China, Russland und die USA sein Wirken ablehnen. Die symbolische Bekräftigung universalistischer Normen verdeutlicht Müller anhand einer Analyse der Präambel des Römischen Statuts des IStGh: Alle Kulturen werden hier als fragile universale Werte- und Leidensgemeinschaft repräsentiert, die die Straflosigkeit schlimmster Verbrechen nicht länger tolerieren dürfe. Gleichwohl führt dieser universale Anspruch zu Herausforderungen, wenn bei der Rechtsprechung des Gerichtshofs unterschiedliche rechtskulturelle Verfahrensregeln kollidieren oder die vermeintliche Fixierung auf Verbrechen in Afrika den Vorwurf provoziert, mit zweierlei Maß zu messen.

Chandra Lekha Sriram untersucht das spannungsreiche Verhältnis von Fällen der strafrechtlichen Tribunalisierung in Afrika im Bezug zur lokalen Kultur. Sie zeigt, dass Straftribunalen in Post-Konflikt-Gesellschaften zwar einerseits die Aufgabe der Verurteilung und Vergeltung zugesprochen wird, andererseits aber auch die weit größere Herausforderung, als Element einer »transitional justice« Versöhnung zu stiften und politische Identitäten zu transformieren, was leicht zu Ziel- und Rollenkonflikten führt. Gerade durch das Streben nach einer sozialen Transformation kommt der Sichtbarkeit von Tribunalen und ihren medialen Ausstrahlungen in die lokale Bevölkerung große Bedeutung zu. Zugleich birgt die symbolische Auflading der Strafprozesse aber auch die Gefahr der Manipulation für die falschen Zwecke. Die Bilanz Srirams, wie es den Tribunalen gelingt, sowohl das Ausmaß des zuvor erlittenen Unrechts in der Konfliktgesellschaft darzustellen als auch die Legitimität des Verfahrens seiner strafrechtlichen Aufarbeitung zu verdeutlichen, fällt schließlich, nicht zuletzt wegen der zu hohen Erwartungen an die Strafprozesse, gemischt aus.

Auch *Joachim Savelsberg* widmet sich den gesellschaftlichen Effekten von Tribunalen, die er als kulturellen Mechanismus, das kollektive Gedächtnis zu prägen, vorstellt. Savelsberg betont hierbei nicht nur die unterschiedlichen Logiken der Vergangenheitsbewältigung von Recht und Geschichtswissenschaft, sondern demonstriert, wie Strafverfahren auch zur selektiv verfälschten Überlieferung von Gräueltaten beitragen können. Am Beispiel des Massakers von amerikanischen Soldaten in My Lai während des Vietnamkriegs illustriert er, wie die juristischen Urteile in Teile der Geschichtsschreibung eingegangen sind, der dadurch die essentiellen Ausmaße des Massakers verborgen geblieben sind. Die historische Wahrheit lässt sich folglich nicht auf das reduzieren, was justiziabel ist.

Das Interludium »Documenting war crimes« diskutiert den Beitrag der Kunst zur Memorierung und Repräsentation abgründiger Verbrechen. Dokumentiert ist hier die Podiumsdiskussion, die sich auf der Bonner Tribunale-Tagung im Anschluss an die Vorführung des preisgekrönten Dokumentarfilms »Enemies of the people«, der den Massenmord der *Khmers rouges* in Kambodscha ins Visier nimmt, entsponnen hat. Dem Regisseur *Thet Sambath* ist es für diesen Film im Laufe vieler Jahre und Gespräche nicht nur gelungen, zum ersten Mal einen der Hauptarchitekten der Morde, Nuon Chea alias Brother Two, zu einem Geständnis vor der Kamera zu bewegen, sondern auch die traumatischen Erfahrungen von Menschen aus der kambodschanischen Bevölkerung für die Nachwelt festzuhalten. Co-Regisseur und Co-Produzent *Rob Lemkin* verdeutlicht in der hier abgedruckten Diskussion, dass ihr Werk auf eine dokumentarische, aber auch ästhetische Weise eine Erklärung des Unvorstellbaren versucht habe, die dem eingerichteten Sondertribunal in Kambodscha nicht offenstehe. Er hält aber auch fest, dass der Film als unersetzlicher Beitrag zur Aufklärung und Erinnerung in Kambodscha seine Wirkung momentan noch nicht entfalten kann, da er der kambodschanischen Öffentlichkeit aufgrund politischer Entscheidungen vorenthalten wird.

Die weiteren Untersuchungen konzentrieren sich auf die Jugoslawienkriege der 1990er Jahre und die Rolle des ICTY. *Dževad Karahasan* vergleicht in seinen Reflexionen literarische Darstellungsformen des Bösen, wobei er sich für eine Literatur ausspricht, die das Böse und Abnorme nicht zu verurteilen, sondern zu erkennen versucht, wie er es schon bei Aischylos und anderen Klassikern beobachtet. Die metaphysische Unterscheidung von absolut »gut« und »böse« verstelle den Blick für die kontingenten Umstände, die manchmal den Weg der Menschen bestimmten. Durch einen strikten Dualismus gehe das ethische Gefühl verloren, das davor schütze, ins falsche Lager zu geraten, ein Gefühl, das auch ein ästhetisches sei.

Jürgen Brokoff widmet sich aus kulturwissenschaftlicher Perspektive der konzeptuellen Differenz von Gericht und Tribunal und bezieht diese auf Peter Handkes literarisch-essayistische Prozessbeobachtungen des Internationalen Strafgerichtshofs für das ehemalige Jugoslawien. Er konzediert Handke, wichtige Einsichten in Eigenheiten des Tribunals gewonnen zu haben, so etwa seine didaktische Funktion, die aus rein juristischer Sicht ein außergerichtliches Element sei. Die bekannte politische Ablehnung des Tribunals durch Handke habe ihn jedoch dazu geführt, seine eigene Prozessbeobachtung und auch ein späteres Theaterstück selbst »tribunalförmig« zu verfassen, indem er Zeugen, Richter und andere Beobachter durch Insinuation als illegitim darstelle. So sitzt Handke letztlich über das Jugoslawientribunal literarisch selbst zu Gericht und begreift sich dabei als Für-Sprecher jener, die öffentlich nicht zu Wort kommen.

Andrea Schütte führt diesen Gedanken anhand einer Werkanalyse Handkes weiter. Sie verweist auf bedeutende Stränge in Handkes literarischen und auch politischen Schriften, in denen dieser Literatur grundsätzlich als »Fürsprache« in diesem Sinne konzipiert. Partei zu ergreifen heiße, für andere und im Namen anderer zu sprechen, wobei die unbedingte Fürsprache, wie Schütte zeigt, auf eine Freund-Feind-Logik zurückgreift. Letztlich verweist das zornige Engagement und das Streben nach Gerechtigkeit für andere auf den Sprecher selbst. So sehe sich Handke als Partisan und Widerständler, als Stellvertreter der serbischen Interessen, der sich auch stellvertretend gekränkt und erzürnt fühle und so als »selbstaffizierter Fürsprecher« auftrete.

Svjetlan Lacko Vidulić thematisiert die erinnerungspolitische Dimension von Tribunalen, indem er die Frage aufwirft, ob Den Haag, der Sitz des Strafgerichtshofs für den Jugoslawienkrieg, auf dem Weg ist, ein kroatischer Erinnerungsort zu werden. Dabei kommt er zu dem Ergebnis, dass »Haag« im kollektiven Gedächtnis untrennbar mit dem Narrativ des »Heimatkrieges«, also der nationalistischen Sichtweise auf den Verlauf der Jugoslawienkriege verbunden ist und somit, selbst nach dem Freispruch von General Gotovina, noch stark negativ konnotiert ist. Vidulićs Einschätzung der Wirkung des Tribunals deckt sich mit den Erfahrungen Srirams im afrikanischen Kontext: Das während der Strafprozesse archivierte Wissen über die Wahrheit des Krieges kommt nur langsam und selten, durch politische Manipulation, »ungefiltert« bei der Bevölkerung an, so dass die pädagogische Wirkung des Tribunals bisher gering ausfällt. Allerdings sind, so Vidulić, »Erinnerungslandschaften« stets dynamisch zu denken, Ergebnisse von Deutungs- und symbolischen Kämpfen, so dass nicht ausgeschlossen werden kann, dass die marginal vorhandenen kritischen und differenzierten Narrative der Vergangenheitsbewältigung später an Gewicht gewinnen.

Ein persönlicher Blick auf die zentrale Frage von Schuld und Verantwortung während der Jugoslawienkriege kommt in den Textpassagen *Dubravka Ugrešićs* zum Vorschein, die *Andrea Schütte* für ein imaginäres Interview mit der Autorin ausgewählt hat. Ugrešić reflektiert dabei über die Ursachen des Krieges, die Rolle der Intellektuellen, die Perspektive als Exilantin, aber auch die mediale Darstellung der Kriegsgräuel.

Die ästhetischen Möglichkeiten des Theaters, Kriegsverbrechen inszenatorisch zu verarbeiten, werden schließlich im Beitrag *Miranda Jakišas* erörtert. Wie Jakiša an bestimmten Inszenierungstechniken des Autors Oliver Frljić nachweist, verfügt das Theater über eigene Mittel, Unrecht sichtbar zu machen und damit, in Anlehnung an den französischen Philosophen Jacques Rancière, eine neue »Aufteilung des Sinnlichen« zu bewirken, die Grenzen verschiebt und eine neue ästhetische und moralisch-politische Ordnung schafft. So kann aus diesen Inszenierungen nicht nur ein Plädoyer für die Aufarbeitung der Vergangenheit herausgelesen werden, sondern auch ein neues kulturelles Performanzverständnis, in dem das Theater zum Theater-Gericht wird.

Diese Studien demonstrieren durch ihre unterschiedlichen Zugangsweisen, welch große Bedeutung der Tribunalforschung im Rahmen einer kulturwissenschaftlichen Analyse des Rechts und der Literatur zukommt. Es wird deutlich, dass Recht nicht nur ein System von Normen darstellt, sondern über eine symbolische Dimension verfügt und sich durch variierende Organisations- und Prozessformen auszeichnet,[54] die je eigene wirklichkeitsgenerierende Effekte zeitigen. Der globale Anspruch des Rechts, wie er in der Entwicklung des internationalen Strafrechts zur Geltung kommt, wirft zudem die Frage nach der möglichen Harmonisierung normativer Ordnungen auf, die immer wieder an lokalen Gegebenheiten

---

[54] Dieser differenzierten Analyse verschiedener Dimensionen des Rechts kommt im Forschungsprogramm des Käte Hamburger Kollegs »Recht als Kultur« ein zentraler Stellenwert zu (vgl. Gephart: Für eine geisteswissenschaftliche Erforschung von Recht).

scheitert. Nicht nur das Wesen des Rechts, sondern auch seine Grenzen kommen somit in der Arbeit von Tribunalen auf instruktive Weise zum Vorschein, wenn es auf mangelnde Akzeptanz stößt oder mit abgründigen Verbrechen konfrontiert wird, denen juristische Kategorien allein nicht gerecht werden.

Literatur

Arendt, Hannah: Eichmann in Jerusalem. Ein Bericht von der Banalität des Bösen, München / Zürich 2011.

Assmann, Aleida: Der lange Schatten der Vergangenheit. Erinnerungskultur und Geschichtspolitik, München 2006.

Bachmann, Michael: Der abwesende Zeuge. Autorisierungsstrategien in Darstellungen der Shoah, Tübingen 2010.

Burkhardt, Sven-U.: Individuelle Zurechnung kollektiven Verhaltens, in: Arno Pilgram et al. (Hg.): Einheitliches Recht für die Vielfalt der Kulturen? Strafrecht und Kriminologie in Zeiten transkultureller Gesellschaften und transnationalen Rechts, Wien 2012, S. 41–54.

Douglas, Lawrence: The didactic trial: Filtering history and memory into the courtroom, in: European review, 14, 4, 2006, S. 513–522.

Fauconnet, Paul: La responsabilité. Étude de sociologie, Paris 1928.

Gephart, Werner: Symbol und Sanktion. Die Theorie der kollektiven Zurechnung von Paul Fauconnet, Opladen 1997.

Gephart, Werner: Recht als Kultur. Zur kultursoziologischen Analyse des Rechts, Frankfurt a. M. 2006.

Gephart, Werner: Für eine geisteswissenschaftliche Erforschung von Recht im Globalisierungsprozess: das Projekt, in: Werner Gephart (Hg.): Rechtsanalyse als Kulturforschung, Frankfurt a. M. 2012, S. 19–53.

Graf, Wilfried / Valerie Kainz / Agnes Taibl: Transitional justice: zwischen globalen Normen und lokalen Kontexten, in: Arno Pilgram et al. (Hg.): Einheitliches Recht für die Vielfalt der Kulturen? Strafrecht und Kriminologie in Zeiten transkultureller Gesellschaften und transnationalen Rechts, Wien 2012, S. 97–124.

Handke, Peter: Rund um das Große Tribunal, Frankfurt a. M. 2003.

Handke, Peter: Die Tablas von Daimiel. Ein Umwegzeugenbericht zum Prozeß gegen Slobodan Milošević, Frankfurt a. M. 2006.

Jackson, Robert H.: Opening Statement before the International Military Tribunal, http://www.roberthjackson.org/the-man/speeches-articles/speeches/speeches-by-robert-h-jackson/opening-statement-before-the-international-military-tribunal/ (letzter Zugriff: 24.05.2013).

Jakobs, Günther: System der strafrechtlichen Zurechnung, Frankfurt a. M. 2012.
Koskenniemi, Martti: Between impunity and show trials, in: Max Planck Yearbook of United Nations law, 6/1, 2002, S. 1–35.
Martens, Michael: Nicht nur Nationalisten. In Serbien kritisieren auch Menschenrechtler den Freispruch für die kroatischen Generäle, in: Frankfurter Allgemeine Zeitung, 19.11.2012., S. 10.
Mulisch, Harry: Strafsache 40/61. Eine Reportage über den Eichmann-Prozeß, Berlin 1996.
Nouwen, Sarah M. H.: ›Hybrid Courts‹. The hybrid category of a new type of international crimes courts, in: Utrecht law review, 2/2, 2006, S. 190–214.
Osiel, Mark: Mass atrocity, collective memory and the law, New Brunswick, NY/London 1997.
Popovski, Vesselin: Legality and legitimacy of international criminal tribunals, in: Richard Falk et al. (Hg.): Legality and legitimacy in global affairs, Oxford 2012, S. 388–413.
Savelsberg, Joachim J./Ryan D. King: Law and collective memory, in: Annual review of law and social science, 3, 2007, S. 189–211.
Schild, Wolfgang: Die Strafgerichtsverhandlung als Theater des Rechts, in: Reiner Schulze (Hg.): Symbolische Kommunikation vor Gericht in der Frühen Neuzeit, Berlin 2006, S. 107–124.
Schwarte, Ludger: Angemessenes Unrecht – Gerechter Zufall: Modelle rechtlicher Performanz, in: Paragrana, 15/1, 2006, S. 135–147.
Suntrup, Jan Christoph: Die Intellektuellen und die juristischen Formen, in: Archiv für Rechts- und Sozialphilosophie, 4, 2012, S. 494–509.
Teitel, Ruti G.: Transitional justice, Oxford/New York 2002.
Teitel, Ruti G.: Humanity's law, Oxford/New York 2011.
Tretbar, Christian: Kommt die Videoübertragung im Gerichtssaal?, in: Der Tagesspiegel 3.5.2013, verfügbar unter: http://www.tagesspiegel.de/politik/nsu-prozess-kommt-die-videouebertragung-im-gerichtssaal/8158066.html (letzter Zugriff: 24.05.2013).
van Ooyen, Robert Chr.: Politische Bedingungen einer effektiven internationalen Strafgerichtsbarkeit, in: Internationale Politik und Gesellschaft, 3, 2007, S. 23–35.
Vismann, Cornelia: Medien der Rechtsprechung, Frankfurt a. M. 2011.
Walser, Martin: Unser Auschwitz, in: Kursbuch, 1, 1965, S. 189–200.
Wamhof, Georg: Gerichtskultur und NS-Vergangenheit. Performativität – Narrativität – Medialität, in: ders. (Hg.): Das Gericht als Tribunal oder: *Wie* der NS-Vergangenheit der Prozess gemacht wurde, Göttingen 2009, S. 9–37.
Wieviorka, Annette: Die Entstehung des Zeugen, in: Gary Smith (Hg.): Hannah Arendt Revisited: »Eichmann in Jerusalem« und die Folgen, Frankfurt a. M. 2000, S. 136–159.

Erster Teil

Tribunale als Rechtskultur: Historische, soziologische und juristische Perspektiven

Annette Wieviorka

Observations sur des procès nazis : de Nuremberg à Klaus Barbie

Certains procès ne sont pas seulement des épisodes juridiques, même s'ils le sont aussi. Ils sont de véritables « lieux de mémoire », comme Pierre Nora les a définis : des lieux matériels ou idéels, réinvestis au cours de l'histoire de significations différentes. C'est bien évidemment le cas du procès de Nuremberg et de celui d'Adolf Eichmann qui a débuté le 11 avril 1961 à Jérusalem, second grand procès lié au nazisme. Aucun autre procès ne peut être comparé aux procès de Nuremberg et à celui de Jérusalem quant à leurs postérités internationales, même si certains – je pense aux procès de Francfort pour l'Allemagne ou de Klaus Barbie pour la France – ont eu un impact important, mais confiné dans un cadre national.

Le procès de Nuremberg qui s'est tenu du 20 novembre 1945 au 1er octobre 1946, constitue un événement majeur de l'histoire du XXe siècle. Pour la première fois, les plus hauts responsables d'un Etat furent traduits devant une Cour de justice internationale. Dès lors, ce procès est entré dans l'Histoire comme un événement à part entière, suscitant immédiatement une abondante littérature. Les historiens s'attachèrent à en dégager les prémisses, à en décrire les acteurs, à en analyser le déroulement. Nous n'y reviendrons pas. Les juristes interrogèrent sa légitimité et ne cessèrent de débattre de ses prolongements. Nuremberg est un moment du droit international.

La postérité, juridique et mémorielle, n'a retenu de ce procès qu'un des quatre chefs d'accusation, le crime contre l'humanité, désormais inscrit dans le droit international. Or pour les Américains, les vrais maîtres d'œuvre du procès, la question de la criminalité nazie était seconde au regard de ce qui leur importait : le complot (*conspiracy*) et le crime contre la paix. Leurs *boys* avaient traversé à deux reprises l'Atlantique, en 1917 et 1944, pour venir au secours de leurs alliés. Ils souhaitaient que cette situation ne se reproduisît point en mettant la guerre hors la loi. Ainsi, l'article 6 du statut de tribunal adopté à Londres par les quatre puissances organisatrices du procès[1] qui énumère les chefs d'accusation fait du « crime contre

---

[1] Le 8 août 1945, les Etats-Unis, le Royaume Uni, l'URSS, le Gouvernement provisoire de la République française signaient deux documents appelés respectivement « Accords de Londres du 8 août 1945 » et « Statut du Tribunal militaire international », ce statut faisant partie intégrante de l'accord. Les gouvernements des Nations Unies pouvaient adhérer à l'Accord, ce que firent ceux de Grèce, Danemark, Yougoslavie, Pays Bas, Tchécoslovaquie, Pologne, Belgique, Ethiopie, Australie,

la paix » le premier chef d'accusation. Ils sont ainsi définis : « (…) la direction, la préparation, le déclenchement ou la poursuite d'une guerre d'agression ou d'une guerre de violation des traités, assurances ou accords internationaux, ou la participation à un plan concerté ou un complot pour l'accomplissement de l'un quelconque des actes qui précèdent ».

Le point de vue des Soviétiques et des Français est fort éloigné. Les représentants des deux pays sont hostiles au « complot contre la paix ». Les Français le seront avec constance. Au moment des délibérations, le juge Donnedieu de Vabres remet à ses collègues un mémorandum. Il met purement et simplement en cause le concept de *Conspiracy*, dans la charte du Tribunal comme dans l'acte d'accusation. Pour lui, ce concept est inconnu, en droit international comme en droit continental. Donnedieu de Vabres fait l'unanimité contre lui. Le juge soviétique, le major général I. T. Nikitchenko s'insurge : « Nous sommes des gens pratiques, pas un club de discussion. » Quant aux Américains, ils pensent que si le complot est écarté, il faut écarter en même temps les crimes contre la paix. Bref, c'est l'architecture du procès, et par conséquent le procès lui-même, qui est en cause. D'autant que les crimes de guerre comme les crimes contre l'humanité doivent, pour être jugés, être en lien avec le complot contre la paix. Ils n'existent donc pas en soi, mais dans le seul contexte de la Seconde Guerre mondiale, définie comme une guerre d'agression par l'Allemagne. Pour Telford Taylor, qui fait partie de l'accusation américaine et aura la responsabilité des procès successeurs qui se sont ensuite tenus à Nuremberg, Donnedieu de Vabres pose la mauvaise question au mauvais moment. Le professeur français, tout en s'inclinant, restera sa vie durant sur cette même position.[2]

Pour les Soviétiques comme pour les Français, le cœur du procès est le jugement sur les crimes qui ont été commis sur leurs territoires lors de l'occupation allemande. Dans la division des tâches entre délégations, les Américains et les Britanniques ont en charge l'accusation de crimes et complots contre la paix, les Français et les Soviétiques celles de crimes de guerre et crimes contre l'humanité commis respectivement à l'Est et à l'Ouest, quand, selon le statut du tribunal, ils ont été commis en lien avec le crime contre la paix.

Ces différences de perspective se reflètent dans le choix des témoins appelés à la barre par les différentes accusations. Pour un procès de cette envergure, ils ne sont guère nombreux : vingt-neuf en tout.[3] En effet, l'accusation américaine a opté pour un procès s'appuyant essentiellement sur des documents écrits, et ses témoins

---

Honduras, Norvège, Panama, Luxembourg, Haïti, Nouvelle Zélande, Inde, Uruguay et Paraguay. Tous ces documents figurent dans le premier des 42 volumes des minutes du procès et des documents qui y furent présentés publiés dans les quatre langues du procès (français, allemand, russe, anglais) en 1947. Ils sont aussi disponibles sur internet sur plusieurs sites, parmi eux : http://avalon.law.yale.edu/subject_menus/imt.asp

[2] Sur ces questions, nous renvoyons à Taylor : Procureur à Nuremberg ; pour la traduction française et Falco : Juge à Nuremberg.

[3] Tisseron : France et le procès de Nuremberg, pp. 194–200.

sont appelés pour documenter le fonctionnement du régime nazi. Certains d'entre eux, tels le SS-*Gruppenführer* Otto Ohlendorf, seront d'ailleurs jugés et condamnés à mort lors d'un des douze procès successeurs que les Américains mènent seuls à Nuremberg entre 1947 et 1949. Ohlendorf est condamné à mort le 18 avril 1948, pendu le 8 juin 1951.[4] Les accusations française et soviétique ne bénéficient pas de documents permettant d'éclairer la mécanique criminelle au plus haut niveau. Le récit des témoins pallie en partie ce manque. Dans ce domaine, note Antonin Tisseron, la France occupe une place particulière : c'est la nation qui appelle le plus de témoins – onze – à la barre du tribunal. Elle est aussi la seule à ne convoquer aucun dirigeant nazi, alors que les témoins des accusations américaine et britannique (sept pour les Américains, deux pour les Britanniques) étaient tous allemands (SS, officiers de l'*Abwehr*, officiers nazis, opposants au nazisme...), à l'exception du médecin tchèque interné à Dachau, le Dr Franz Blaha. Les témoins de l'accusation française sont dans leur majorité des résistants déportés dans les camps nazis, qui viennent expliquer ce qu'était la vie dans ces camps. Aucun témoin juif pourtant n'est appelé à témoigner d'Auschwitz. Le procureur adjoint Charles Dubost a choisi pour évoquer ce camp, Marie-Claude Vaillant-Couturier, une grande figure du monde communiste, résistante, déportée à Auschwitz dans un convoi de 230 femmes, pour la plupart communistes.[5]

Dans l'économie du procès, les Soviétiques sont les derniers à porter l'accusation. Le procureur soviétique Rudenko prend la parole le 8 février 1946. L'accusation soviétique, à la différence de l'accusation américaine, n'a pas dans ses prisons de hauts responsables nazis, sinon un général, Erich Buschenhagen, et un transfuge de choix : le maréchal Paulus, le vaincu de Stalingrad, un témoin surprise qui fait sensation et à qui est dévolu le rôle d'expliquer comment fut préparée la guerre d'agression contre l'Union Soviétique, ce qui présente aux yeux des Soviétiques l'insigne avantage de sauter par-dessus la période du pacte germano-soviétique. Paulus est le premier des neuf témoins de l'accusation soviétique, et son témoignage et les questions qui lui sont posées par les avocats des accusés et les juges occupent la journée du 11 et la matinée du 12 février.[6] Sept autres témoins sont appelés entre le 22 et le 27 février. Deux d'entre eux témoignent de la destruction des Juifs, Samuel Rajzman, qui du ghetto de Varsovie fut transporté à Treblinka où il passa une année,[7] et Abraham Sutzkever. Ce sont, pour l'ensemble du procès, les deux seuls Juifs à évoquer le sort des leurs.

---

[4] Earl : The Nuremberg SS-Einsatzgruppen Trial.

[5] Ce convoi était celui de l'écrivain Charlotte Delbo qui en a été l'historienne. Cf. Delbo : Le convoi du 24 janvier 1943.

[6] L'épisode Paulus occupe cinquante pages des transcriptions du procès, cf. : Tribunal militaire international : Procès des grands criminels de guerre, pp. 260–310.

[7] Il ne faut pas le confondre avec Chil Rajchman, lui aussi interné à Treblinka, auteur de « Je suis le dernier Juif : Treblinka (1942–1943) ».

En effet, l'écrivain soviétique Ehrenbourg – correspondant de guerre, il est alors immensément populaire – a placé le grand poète yiddish «premier» sur la liste des témoins.[8] Ehrenbourg n'a qu'une force de proposition. Une commission secrète, surnommée «Commission Vichynski», a été établie pour diriger de Moscou le procès de Nuremberg. C'est elle qui décide de tout. C'est donc elle qui détermine le contenu des témoignages, lesquels n'ont rien de spontané. Ils ont auparavant été rédigés. Cette rédaction, écrit Sutzkever dans l'entrée de son journal datée du 16 février, dure 5 heures. Les témoins sont aussi préparés à un éventuel contre-interrogatoire par des agents du NKVD.[9]

Le Journal de Sutzkever permet de saisir son état d'esprit. Il se réjouit de voir Berlin et Nuremberg en ruines. Il médite sur son intervention. Ainsi le 21 février, à 6 heures du soir: «Le nom de Nuremberg est entré dans l'histoire pour l'éternité: les lois de Nuremberg, le procès de Nuremberg. Symbole: là d'où est parti le mot d'ordre d'extermination du peuple juif vont être jugés les criminels. Et moi, peut-être le seul poète yiddish rescapé de toute l'Europe occupée, je viens au procès de Nuremberg non seulement pour déposer, mais comme témoin vivant de l'immortalité de mon peuple.» Le 22 février: «Si c'est techniquement possible, je parlerai en yiddish. La question technique est le seul obstacle éventuel. Ce sera la première déposition du procès en yiddish. Je prie Dieu qu'on trouve un traducteur.» Le 23 février: «Nous ne savons pas quand nous allons comparaître. Il est à craindre qu'une partie de nos témoignages ne pourront être entendus (...). Notre comparution se complique. J'apprends en dernière minute que quatre d'entre nous seront appelés (...). Qui seront les quatre? Vais-je en faire partie? Dieu seul le sait.» Le 25 février: «Les chances que je puisse témoigner sont de plus en plus faibles (...). Demain prend fin le réquisitoire soviétique. J'ai le sentiment qu'il y a des réticences concernant ma présence à la barre des témoins. Qu'y puis-je faire? En fait, l'idée m'est désagréable. Mais qu'y puis-je?»

«Eh! Tout à l'heure, le procureur Smirnov est venu me voir! Je dois témoigner demain matin. Mais en russe! Vais-je réussir l'examen? Vais-je remplir correctement ma mission à l'égard de l'histoire, à l'égard de mon peuple? Dieu seul le sait!»

Effectivement, Sutzkever témoigne le 27 février, en russe. Son témoignage dura 38 minutes en y incluant les questions que lui posa le procureur Smirnov, dont les cinq premières furent filmées.[10]

---

[8] Sutzkever: Mon témoignage au procès de Nuremberg.

[9] Jusqu'à la disparition de l'Union Soviétique suivie par l'ouverture (partielle) de ses archives, il n'existait pas d'études sur la façon dont l'Union Soviétique avait organisé sa participation au procès de Nuremberg. Une lacune qui est désormais en grande partie comblée. Ces renseignements sont tirés de l'article de Hirsch: The Soviets at Nuremberg.

[10] Ces images sont notamment consultables au centre d'enseignement multimédia du Mémorial de la Shoah. Merci à Laurence Voix pour son aide avisée.

Le témoignage de Sutzkever – il suffit de l'écouter pour le constater –, est un témoignage largement appris par cœur, probablement à partir du protocole rédigé à Moscou. Il est énoncé avec une certaine lenteur (Sutzkever, de son propre aveu, maîtrise mal le russe). Mais la lenteur et les silences dont il est émaillé sont le lot de bien des interventions au procès de Nuremberg et sont dus au système de traduction simultanée, l'immense majorité, sinon la totalité, des traducteurs soviétiques étant de plus incompétents.[11] Le président Geoffrey Lawrence avait d'ailleurs demandé à Iakov Grigorev, paysan du district de Pskov qui avait témoigné la veille du jour où Sutzkever témoigna : « Veuillez répondre lentement et après avoir attendu un instant car la question doit être traduite et c'est ensuite votre réponse qui doit être traduite. »[12]

Reste la question de la langue du témoignage. Il n'eut guère été difficile pour l'accusation soviétique, si elle en avait eu le désir, de trouver dans ces années un interprète russe-yiddish, les locuteurs courants dans ces deux langues étant encore très nombreux. Il aurait alors été possible techniquement d'organiser cette traduction comme cela fut fait pour la « citoyenne polonaise » Severina Shmaglewskaya, qui parla d'Auschwitz. Elle succéda à la barre à Sutzkever, côte à côte avec une interprète qui traduisait du polonais en russe avant que les traducteurs ne fassent à leur tour la traduction vers les autres langues du procès, le français, l'anglais et l'allemand[13]. Il s'agit donc bien d'une volonté politique de gommer le yiddish. La demande de Salomon Mikhoels que le *Livre noir* fût traduit dans « la langue nationale » était, elle aussi, restée sans réponse.[14] Le peuple yiddish et ses écrivains qui avaient survécu en Union Soviétique entraient dans une longue agonie : assassinat de Mihkoels, en janvier 1948, arrestation des dirigeants du Comité juif antifasciste, procès à huis clos, exécution de treize d'entre eux dans la nuit du 12 août 1952.

Le témoignage de Sutzkever à Nuremberg reçut peu d'attention. Il vint après l'évocation de Katyn qui donna lieu à une violente controverse et peu avant le fameux discours de Churchill à Fulton (5 mars 1946). La défense des « grands criminels nazis » se fit accusatrice à l'égard de l'Union Soviétique, dévoilant le cadavre dans le placard qu'étaient les protocoles secrets du pacte germano-soviétique. La « Grande Alliance » du temps de la guerre faisait place à la guerre froide, même si elle se survécut le temps de finir le procès. D'autre part, l'heure n'était pas venue de mettre au cœur de la criminalité nazie le génocide des juifs, ni d'ériger le témoin en porteur de morale ou d'histoire. Quand Sutzkever témoigne, la salle est inattentive, bruyante, et Geoffrey Lawrence doit intervenir pour faire cesser les multiples bavardages.[15]

---

[11] Hirsch : The Soviets at Nuremberg, p. 723.
[12] Tribunal militaire international : Procès des grands criminels de guerre, p. 260.
[13] Cf. les séquences filmées du procès.
[14] Altman : Préface, p. 29.
[15] La traduction du « Journal de Nuremberg » d'Abraham Sutzkever par Gilles Rozier et sa pu-

Ainsi, même si la destruction des Juifs d'Europe est bien présente lors du procès de Nuremberg, elle est comme diluée dans l'ensemble d'une criminalité nazie multiforme. Le terme de génocide, que vient d'inventer le juriste Raphael Lemkin, ne s'installe pas alors. Il le fera lors de la discussion à l'ONU et la ratification par un certain nombre de pays de la convention pour la prévention et la répression du crime de génocide (1948).

Le procès de Nuremberg est un élément de la construction du monde issu de la Seconde Guerre mondiale, avec la création de l'ONU, de l'UNESCO, du FMI… Il est un exemple, sinon le seul exemple, totalement réussi même s'il fut justement critiqué, de ce que l'on appelle désormais « la justice transitionnelle ». Peut-être parce que pour la seule fois dans l'histoire se retrouvent trois conditions qui permettent l'exercice de la justice : une guerre tout à fait terminée par la capitulation sans conditions de l'Allemagne ; des accusés aux mains des accusateurs ; des archives qui permettent d'administrer la preuve.

Le procès d'Adolf Eichmann pourrait être lu comme un complément à celui de Nuremberg. Ben Gourion, le Premier ministre israélien, avait voulu qu'il fût « un Nuremberg du peuple juif ». Il se tient quinze années après la fin de la Seconde Guerre mondiale : ce n'est donc pas une justice transitionnelle, mais un jalon dans l'interminable jugement des criminels nazis. Le nazisme a en effet été le seul régime dont les protagonistes ont été jugés, quel que soit le temps séparant leurs actes de leurs procès. Des procédures en Allemagne précédèrent ou suivirent ce procès, de ceux de Francfort au procès d'Ivan Demanjuk tenu à Munich en 2011 ; la France fut le théâtre de trois procès : celui du Nazi Klaus Barbie (1987) ; celui du milicien Paul Touvier (1994) ; celui du fonctionnaire de l'Etat français, Maurice Papon (1998).

La question de la guerre et de qui l'a déclenchée s'estompe très vite au profit de la seule qualification, la plus problématique à Nuremberg, celle de crime contre l'humanité. Le crime contre l'humanité est défini dans l'article 6 des statuts du Tribunal. A y regarder de près, les mêmes actes relèvent du crime de guerre et du crime contre l'humanité. Le seul ajout concerne « les persécutions pour des motifs politiques, raciaux ou religieux ». Ces persécutions devant avoir été commises « à la suite de tout crime entrant dans la compétence du tribunal ou en liaison avec ce crime », les pays qui persécutent leurs minorités en dehors de la Seconde Guerre mondiale étaient donc à l'abri des poursuites.

Pour juger Adolf Eichmann, Israël se mit dans le sillage du procès de Nuremberg et de la Convention sur la prévention et la répression du crime de génocide. L'acte d'accusation comporte quinze chefs d'accusation. Les quatre premiers relèvent d'un

---

blication dans la revue Europe mit au jour cette participation au procès (1995). Je l'ai évoquée dans L'Ere du témoin (1998). Depuis, elle fait partie du savoir commun sur le procès.

crime en apparence nouveau, le crime contre le peuple juif. Il est défini par la loi israélienne de 1950 sur la répression des « crimes nazis et de leurs collaborateurs ». Cette loi, quand elle fut adoptée, ne visait pas les anciens nazis. Nul ne pensait qu'ils prendraient le risque de se rendre en Israël. Elle visait les juifs accusés de collaboration : Kapos dans les camps de concentration, membres des conseils juifs ou des polices juives des ghettos. Ils furent l'objet d'une quarantaine de procès. Une deuxième série d'accusations relève des « crimes contre l'humanité » (5, 6, 7, 9 à 15). Un seul chef d'accusation l'est pour « crimes de guerre ».

Les « grands » (major) criminels jugés à Nuremberg l'ont été surtout par rapport à leur position à la tête de l'Etat et non par rapport à l'ampleur de leurs crimes. Ils avaient commis leurs crimes dans plusieurs pays. Ainsi, le commandant d'Auschwitz, Rudolf Höss, qui témoigna en faveur de son supérieur hiérarchique Ernst Kaltenbrunner dans l'objectif de montrer que ce dernier ne s'était jamais rendu à Auschwitz, ne fut pas jugé à Nuremberg, mais à Varsovie et pendu à Auschwitz.

Le procès d'Adolf Eichmann fait entrer la Shoah dans l'histoire et la constitue en évènement spécifique dans la Seconde Guerre mondiale. Le génocide des Juifs est ainsi distingué des autres aspects de la criminalité nazie.[16] La distance temporelle des faits explique que pour la première fois, un historien en la personne de Salo Baron, premier titulaire de la chaire d'histoire des Juifs à l'Université Columbia est cité à la barre des témoins. Sa présence atteste le passage du temps, la nécessité de rappeler un contexte – celui de la vie juive qui a précédé la Shoah – qui s'éloigne des mémoires. Si le procès de Nuremberg visait à établir un certain nombre de faits historiques, à produire un récit de ce qu'avait été la Seconde Guerre mondiale, le procès Eichmann vise la transmission, notamment à la jeunesse israélienne. Abba Eban, alors ministre de l'Education et de la Culture, l'énonce clairement. La procès doit contribuer à réduire certains fossés qui menacent la cohésion nationale : fossé qui oppose « la nouvelle classe moyenne des villes à la vieille élite rurale née du mouvement kibboutz » ; entre « la population qui avait été élevée en Europe – et leurs enfants sabras – et les immigrants orientaux » ; entre les générations : « les jeunes nés au soleil, sous le vaste ciel, étaient attirés par une conception plus simple de l'existence, moins tourmentée, mais aussi plus superficielle intellectuellement que celle des premiers pionniers. » Dernier fossé enfin, celui entre « les sabras très réalistes, et les Juifs de la diaspora, plus sentimentaux, plus compliqués, plus introvertis, mais aussi plus créateurs ». Pourtant, précise encore Abba Eban, « certains souvenirs communs rappelaient souvent aux Israéliens que l'histoire avait traité l'ensemble du peuple juif d'une manière

---

[16] Sur ce procès, nous nous permettons de renvoyer à notre ouvrage Eichmann. De la traque au procès.

telle qu'en fin de compte leur destin était indivisible. L'un des grands moments de vérité de l'unification fut la capture et le procès d'Adolf Eichmann ».[17]

Ce procès marque ce que j'ai appelé « l'avènement du témoin ».[18] C'est en toute lucidité que le procureur Gidéon Hausner décide de faire reposer le procès sur deux piliers : les documents et les témoins. « Ce n'est que par la déposition des témoins, écrit-il, que les événements pourraient être évoqués au tribunal, rendus présents aux esprits, parmi le peuple d'Israël et parmi les autres peuples, d'une manière telle que les hommes ne pourraient pas reculer devant la vérité ». Cette vérité qui ne peut être touchée du doigt qu'en appelant à la barre les survivants « en aussi grand nombre que le cadre du procès pouvait l'admettre et de demander à chacun un menu fragment de ce qu'il avait vu et de ce qu'il avait vécu (...) Mises bout à bout, les dépositions successives de gens dissemblables ayant vécu des expériences différentes ; donnaient une image suffisamment éloquente pour être enregistrée. Ainsi espérais-je, écrit Hausner, donner au fantôme du passé une dimension de plus, celle du réel ».[19]

Les conséquences de cette option sont multiples. Elle permet d'intégrer les survivants à la société israélienne ; elle fait, selon l'expression de Hannah Yablonka, entrer leur histoire dans le code génétique israélien[20]. Elle marque aussi le mouvement qui intronise le témoin comme porteur d'histoire et de mémoire.

Pour la première fois, ce procès est filmé en intégralité pour la télévision. Le 8 novembre 1960, un accord est conclu entre l'Etat d'Israël et un petit producteur de télévision américain, Capital Cities Corporation Company. Le 10 mars, les juges autorisent le filmage à condition qu'il soit invisible et inaudible. Il ne s'agit pas de constituer des archives, mais de filmer la totalité du procès et de proposer les vidéos aux télévisions du monde entier. Le tournage est confié à un réalisateur communiste américain, pionnier dans son pays du film documentaire, Leo Hurwitz. Avec ma collègue Sylvie Lindeperg, nous avons étudié en détail comment le procès fut filmé. La présence d'un grand nombre de journalistes, la possibilité, en léger différé, de montrer les images, en RFA et aux Etats-Unis principalement, fait de ce procès un des tout premiers « global media event »[21].

En 1964, le parlement français adoptait une loi rendant le crime contre l'humanité imprescriptible. Si Hitler ou Mengele réapparaissaient, il serait ainsi possible de les juger. Il faut attendre les années soixante-dix pour qu'émerge en France, très largement à l'initiative de Serge Klarsfeld, l'idée de juger les responsables de la déportation des Juifs de France. Le 23 octobre 1979 s'ouvre à Cologne le procès de Kurt Lischka, de Herbert Hagen et d'Ernst Heinrichsohn, tous trois condamnés

---

17 Eban : Mon pays, p. 181.
18 Cf. Wieviorka : L'Ere du témoin.
19 Hausner : Justice à Jérusalem, p. 384.
20 Yablonka : The State of Israel vs. Adolf Eichmann.
21 Lindeperg / Wieviorka : Les deux scènes du procès Eichmann.

à des peines de prison[22]. Pourtant, c'est le procès de Klaus Barbie (1987), responsable de la Gestapo de Lyon, extradé de Bolivie qui est l'objet de toutes les attentions. Il s'agit là d'une première en France : jamais, en effet, un procès n'avait pris pour centre le génocide des Juifs. Bourreau de la Résistance, Barbie avait été jugé pour ces faits par contumace en 1952 et 1954, et condamné à mort. Ces faits sont désormais prescrits. Il ne peut donc être inculpé que de crimes contre l'humanité, sous condition que ces crimes n'aient pas été jugés. C'est le cas de la déportation des enfants d'Izieu et de celle des personnes raflées dans les locaux de l'Union générale des israélites de France sur Sainte-Catherine à Lyon. Ce procès est suivi de celui du milicien Paul Touvier (1994) et de Maurice Papon (1998). Ces trois procès présentent des points communs. De très nombreux témoins sont appelés à la barre, et témoignent de la Shoah et pas nécessairement des actions des accusés. Ils sont très fortement médiatisés. Ils sont filmés dans leur intégralité, les films devant servir à l'histoire. Surtout, il s'agit moins de punir que de prendre prétexte de ces procès pour donner une leçon d'histoire aux jeunes générations.

Inexorablement, les temps du nazisme s'éloignent et ses contemporains disparaissent. Cet épisode appartient désormais principalement à l'histoire, même s'il demeure vivant par les multiples travaux des historiens, évocations littéraires, films... La question pourtant de la façon dont ont été jugés les responsables de ce régime criminel reste une grande question d'actualité. Comment juger les criminels d'Etat ? Qui sont-ils ? De simples rouages obéissants aux ordres ? Quel type de tribunal ? National ? International ? Mixte ? La justice doit-elle être aveugle aux problèmes politiques que peut poser un procès ? Examiner comment la justice fut rendue peut aider à répondre à ces questions qui relèvent autant du droit que de l'éthique.

Bibliographie

Altman, Ilya : Préface. In : Ilya Ehrenbourg et Vassili Grossman (éd.) : Livre Noir sur l'extermination scélérate des Juifs par les envahisseurs fascistes allemands dans les régions provisoirement occupées de l'URSS et dans les camps d'extermination en Pologne pendant la guerre de 1941–1945. Textes et témoignages réunis par Ilya Ehrenbourg et Vassili Grossman, Arlea 1999, p.22.
Delbo, Charlotte : Le convoi du 24 janvier 1943, 1965.

---

[22] Sur les accusés de Cologne et leur procès, voir notamment Georges Wellers: Le cas Kurt Lischka, Wellers: Le procès de Beate Klarsfeld, et Klarsfeld: Le verdict.

Earl, Hilary : The Nuremberg SS-Einsatzgruppen Trial, 1945–1958: Atrocity, Law and History, Cambridge 2010.

Eban, Abba : Mon pays. L'épopée de l'Israël moderne, Paris 1975.

Falco, Robert : Juge à Nuremberg. Souvenirs inédits du procès des criminels nazis, Nancy 2012.

Hausner, Gidéon : Justice à Jérusalem. Eichmann devant ses juges, préface de René Cassin, introduction par Barbara Tuchman, Paris 1966.

Hirsch, Francine : The Soviets at Nuremberg. International law, propaganda, and the making of the postwar order, in : American historical review, juin 2008, pp. 701–730.

Klarsfeld, Serge : Le verdict du procès de Cologne, in : Serge Klarsfeld (éd.) : Mémoire du génocide : un recueil de 80 articles du « Monde Juif », revue du Centre de Documentation Juive Contemporaine, Paris 1987, pp. 474–485.

Lindeperg, Sylvie / Wieviorka, Annette : Les deux scènes du procès Eichmann, in : Annales ESC, Vol. 63, juin 2008, pp. 1249–1274.

Rajchman, Chil : Je suis le dernier Juif : Treblinka (1942–1943), traduit du yiddish par Gilles Rozier, préface d'Annette Wieviorka, Paris 2009.

Sutzkever, Abraham (Avrom): Mon témoignage au procès de Nuremberg, in : Europe, août-septembre 1995, p. 140–153 (traduit du yiddish par Gilles Rozier).

Taylor, Telford : Procureur à Nuremberg, Paris 1998.

Tisseron, Voir Antonin : La France et le procès de Nuremberg, thèse sous la direction d'Annette Wieviorka, Université Paris 1-Panthéon-Sorbonne, 2013.

Tribunal militaire international : Procès des grands criminels de guerre devant le Tribunal militaire international, T. 8, Nuremberg 1947.

Wellers, Georges : Le cas Kurt Lischka devant les spectateurs de la télévision de la République fédérale allemande, in : Serge Klarsfeld (éd.) : Mémoire du génocide : un recueil de 80 articles du « Monde Juif », revue du Centre de Documentation Juive Contemporaine, Paris 1987, pp. 451–454.

Wellers, Georges : Le procès de Beate Klarsfeld, in : Serge Klarsfeld (éd.) : Mémoire du génocide : un recueil de 80 articles du « Monde Juif », revue du Centre de Documentation Juive Contemporaine, Paris 1987, pp. 455–473.

Wieviorka, Annette : L'Ere du témoin, Paris 1998.

Wieviorka, Annette : Eichmann. De la traque au procès, Bruxelles 2011.

Yablonka, Hannah : The State of Israel vs. Adolf Eichmann, New York 2004.

Werner Gephart
Memory, Tribunals and the Sacred

Introduction

Any introduction to the sociology of law, any book about legal theory will tell you about the stabilisation of normative expectations by way of legal structures, analyses of the ›force du droit‹[1] will underline the symbolic and ritual dimension of law, whereas all theories connecting law and coercion point out the importance of Weber's ›Erzwingungsstab‹.[2] Integration, conflict resolution, rationalization of the world, even absorption of collective feelings are assigned to the law, at least in Durkheim's theory of law and punishment,[3] but *commemoration* is not the tool and the aim of the ›realm of normativity‹, to use a term made famous by Michel Foucault.[4]

The same holds true for the analysis of religion: management of contingency, expressing collective identity,[5] integration and creation of sociality, giving a meaning to the world and taking a standpoint (›Stellungnahme in der Welt‹): This is the catalogue of functional attributes of religion we are accustomed to. It is thanks to Mme Hervieu-Léger that a supplementary function has been brought into the discussion, namely the memorial one.[6] For the religious sphere it means to raise the question of ›where we come from‹ and to offer some solutions on how to deal with the complexity of the world and how to cope with the most horrible threat posed by modern thought: contingency.

For the legal sphere it means that law represents more than just a relatively autonomous space of constructing and applying normative orders in the social world, but also that law entails its own history, so much that its ›authority‹, as Louis Assier-Andrieu formulates in his beautiful book *L'autorité du passé*,[7] derives from the past. In this vein I have tried to show in my own studies how court buildings may be read as legal cultures petrified in stone,[8] where procedural orders,

---

[1] Bourdieu: La force du droit.
[2] Cf. Gephart: Einleitung, p. 39, 41.
[3] For a comprehensive perspective of Durkheim's theory of law, including his perspective on religion, see Gephart: Gesellschaftstheorie und Recht, pp. 321–418.
[4] Cf. Gephart: The realm of normativity in Durkheim and Foucault.
[5] Cf. Gephart/Waldenfels (eds.): Religion und Identität.
[6] Cf. Hervieu-Léger: Le pèlerin et le converti, pp. 23 et seqq.
[7] Cf. Assier-Andrieu: L'autorité du passé.
[8] Cf. the chapter on ›Orte der Gerechtigkeit. Gerichtsarchitektur zwischen Sakral- und Profanbau‹ in: Gephart: Recht als Kultur, pp. 237–253.

symbolic references, techniques of impressing and gestures of the ›force du droit‹ are engraved in marble or other precious materials we know from buildings of the late nineteenth century in Europe. To understand law is to understand it as a medium of collective memory,[9] an indicator of legal history, but also as a privileged space for the construction of a memory that embraces the collective history of a people – a space where ›truth‹ is found by way of respective truth rituals entailing different meanings for the historian, the political scientist, the sociologist or the jurist.[10]

Therefore I propose a more general reading of the interconnectedness of memory, law and the sacred (1.), leading to some fundamental questions of where to situate the logic of tribunals in contemporary societies on the move to globalization (2.).

1. Understanding Collective Memory and the Law

1.1. The Durkheimian Concept of Collective Memory

Collective memory is, unfortunately, not an explicit concept or a well-defined topic directly dealt with by Durkheim. But it seems to be very close to what he defined as the *conscience collective* in *The Division of Labour*, meaning: ›L'ensemble des croyances et des sentiments communs à la moyenne des membres d'une même société [qui] forme un système déterminé qui a sa vie propre‹!¹¹ On the other hand, in *The Elementary Forms*,[12] Durkheim deals with rituals and directly refers to *rites commémoratifs*.

We can find the inner link between history, memory and the construction of sociality in primordial communities in the belief in their common origin. The myth of origin is therefore one of the most powerful means of establishing a community's unity. At a very basic level, we find a close connection between mechanisms of collective memory on the one hand, and, on the other, institutions guaranteeing the collective identity in social life. Memory as one aspect of the diffuse *conscience collective* may be analysed with regard to the elementary forms of social life, which we recognise as central characteristics of the *conscience collective*.

On the *symbolic level*, it is important to know how commemorative symbols work. Heroes, holy events and material signs might evoke the past and stand for

---

[9] See also the recent work by Joachim Savelsberg, who came on a parallel path to similar conclusions. Cf. Savelsberg/King: Law and collective memory; see also his contribution in this volume.
[10] Cf. the introduction by Jan Christoph Suntrup, in this volume.
[11] Durkheim: De la division du travail social, p. 46.
[12] Cf. Durkheim: Elementary forms, book III, chapter IV.

the group's bond with its history. Destruction of these symbols is tantamount to destruction of the group itself. Eradicating history means cutting off social life from its sources. On the other hand, what we can observe in a revival of nationalism is exactly the struggle for those symbols which represent the past of a community and a claim for a specific collective identity.

In a *normative dimension,* it is interesting to observe – and thereby to understand memory as a *fait social* – that those beliefs and convictions of a community that constitute its memory are more or less obligatory and normatively imprinted. It is not up to the individual to construct his or her collective past, for the specific identity of a community is necessarily constituted within a complex normative system. This is, of course, very clear for religiously grounded communities for whom the myth of origin is a central component of religious *representations.* But other elements of a people's history, such as the Shoah or other atrocities and the memory of them, can also become constitutive of collective identities. It is for this reason, that the German penal code regards denial of the Holocaust as a criminal act directed against a community.

The *organisational aspect* helps us to understand why collective memory does not, so to say, simply work by itself, but is shaped by values and interests that are transformed into different forms of social organisation. Socialising agencies, such as schools, religious communities, and ›ethnically-grounded‹ communities, organize – more or less systematically – the transmission of their past from one generation to the next by structures of collective memory. The French tradition addresses institutions specialising in the preservation of the past as the multitude of ›lieux de mémoire‹, as Pierre Nora entitled them.[13] Such studies attend, e. g., to memorial stones of the First World War, the national flag, education and the army, the Collège de France, the Académie Française, and so on. These loci of memory stand between reality and imagination, where the collective memory is concentrated through the agency of commemorative organisations celebrating specific *commemorative rituals.*

In his reading of Spencer and Gillen, Durkheim makes the very important remark that nearly every ritual contains elements of collective commemoration. The central passage needs to be cited at length:

›The form this enactment takes can only serve to resurrect the clan's mythic past. But the mythology of a group is the whole set of its common beliefs. The traditions whose memory this mythology perpetuates are expressed in the way the society imagines man and the world; it is a morality and a cosmology, even as it is a history. The rite, then, does and can only serve to support the vitality of these beliefs, to prevent them from fading from memory – that is, in short, to revive the most essential elements of the collective consciousness. By this means, the group periodically reanimates the feeling it has of itself and its unity;

---

[13] Cf. Nora (ed.): Les lieux de mémoire.

at the same time, the nature of the individuals as social beings is reaffirmed. The glorious memories that are revived before their eyes, and with which they feel allied, give them a feeling of strength and confidence. One is more certain of one's faith when one sees its relation to the distant past and the great things it has inspired.‹[14]

The passage contains important elements for our analysis of the memorial function of tribunals, specifically the *welding of history, identity and memory* as a central part of the ›conscience collective‹, which is periodically enlivened by rituals representing and creating the identity of the group. The effects of collective effervescence are added to these elements, so the glorified past directly leads us to new ideals and projects for the future: ›A day will come when our societies will once again experience times of creative effervescence and new ideas will surge up, new formulas will arise that will serve to guide humanity for a time‹.[15] Are tribunals not endowed with such a magic power to lead from a condemnation of the past to the creation of something new, a new society, new type of mankind? Is the impression wrong that this was also an intended function of the Eichmann trial, as Annette Wieviorka evokes in her analysis?[16]

Commemorative symbols, norms, a commemorative social organisation and rituals as specialised or non-specialised social organisations form the basis of collective memory. Its relation to the *Sacred* is obvious. For whether we start from the normative definition of religion in the second volume of l'Année sociologique,[17] or whether we take the differentiation between the *Sacred* and the *Profane* as the theoretical starting point,[18] the collective memory is not subject to discussion. Its reality is not to be contested; it is, so to say, invulnerable. Though the selection of certain material signs as sacred objects is mainly arbitrary, according to Durkheim's anti-essentialist theory of religion, there is no doubt that its collectively imagined past stands at the centre of what a community holds to be sacred. Religion is the symbolisation of society and its forces, which, in turn, depend on the vitalising power of memory.

Seen in the light of this theoretical analysis, remembrance of the Shoa reveals the following features.

---

[14] Durkheim: Elementary forms, pp. 279 et seq.
[15] Durkheim: Elementary forms, p. 323.
[16] Cf. Wieviorka, in this volume.
[17] Durkheim: De la définition.
[18] Owing to the universalistic extension of Durkheim's notion of religion as defined by the pure differentiation of sacred and profane, the sacred can no longer be regarded as a substantialised concrete section of reality (cf. Durkheim: Elementary forms).

1.2. »Digression: Remembrance of the Shoa«

Arno Mayer has commented that he cannot ›reason with dogmatists who seek to reify and sacralize the Holocaust for being absolutely unprecedented and totally mysterious‹.[19] This view parallels former remarks of Siegfried Kohlhammer, citing Howard Jacobson, that there is a ›perverse sacralisation‹ of the Holocaust.[20] In his fascinating study on ›Holocaust tourism‹, Jack Kugelmass spoke about the birth of a cosmogenic time, or even a ›Holocaust-Religion‹,[21] to cite the critical formula by Adi Ophir ›Sanctifying the Holocaust‹.[22]

In accordance with Durkheim's thought, I would insist that there is, for good sociological reasons, a kind of a religious dimension in recalling the Shoa. This view, however, entails some ambiguity. It is e. g. not absolutely clear to which commemorative community the rituals of remembering the Holocaust in Germany should refer. It is paradoxical and deeply tragic. It is true that – as it seems well established – the power of Auschwitz was needed and helped to create the state of Israel.[23] It remains uncertain, however, which sort of identity-building emerged in Germany, especially of the German non-Jewish community, the sons and daughters of ›the willing executioners‹, as well as of those who resisted the régime.

Using the multidimensional model developed above, we may distinguish: On the *symbolic level*, there is a whole host of problems regarding adequate representation, if representation of those atrocities is possible at all. The discussion concerning the Central Holocaust Memorial in Berlin was revealing. Neither the act of creating a monument in itself, nor creating a monument to compensate for horror and crime seemed to be reasonable. The attempts at ›anti-monumentalism‹ look more convincing as they do not pretend to represent either events or structures, but only memory itself. I think of those reflexive and in this sense post-modern memorials, where the disappearance of collective memory is displayed. The *memorial mise-en-scène* in Hamburg-Harburg, realised by Esther and Jochen Gerz, is a most impressive example.[24] A twelve-meter column was covered with a lead sheath, on which passers-by were invited to scratch their names. During the period of this ›memorial action‹, the monument was continuously eroded until it literally dwindled into meaningful insignificance.

In the city of Bonn, the public burning of books ordered by the Nazis in 1933 throughout Germany inspired two artists in the year 2013 to a commemorative

---

19 Mayer: Memory and history, p. 446.
20 Kohlhammer: Anathema, p. 505.
21 Kugelmass: Weshalb wir nach Polen reisen, p. 156.
22 Cf. Ophir: On sanctifying the Holocaust.
23 See, e. g. Friedländer/Seligman: Das Gedenken an die Schoa in Israel.
24 Cf. Schmidt-Wulffen: Ein Mahnmal versinkt.

sign that is embedded in a commemorative ritual. The memorial by Andreas Knitz und Horst Hoheisel, rendered to the public 80 years after this annihilation of culture, consists of books of bronze showing titles and authors of many books burned back then. These ›book marks‹, integrated into the Bonn market place, condense near the stairs of the town hall, where the books were burned in 1933. In addition, a collection of books by authors, whose works fell prey to the incineration, is retained in a weatherproof chest, which is annually opened at the anniversary of the burning in order to read the works out and donate them afterwards to the public, whereupon other books are collected in the chest.

In the *normative dimension*, any denial of the Holocaust as a conscious and nearly successful attempt to exterminate the Jews is subject to prosecution in Germany.

Concerning the *organisational dimension*, it is, as Arno Mayer notes, obvious that in today's context of declining media attention, collective memory cannot be formed and preserve itself ›without organisation and orchestration‹.[25]

What sort of collective identity could materialize from that unimaginable catastrophe, the Holocaust, given that the people responsible for it were not expelled, but ›integrated‹ into a society that was rebuilding itself? This is to my understanding the theoretical issue at the root of the famous historians' debate in Germany.[26] Habermas was very critical of those who thought that an ›understanding‹ of the executioners' motive implied a moral sympathy with the criminals. Therefore, a project of ›identification‹ was regarded as highly dangerous. But perhaps identification could be imagined otherwise than generally thought. A more delicate and ambiguous project than to identify with the victims, as far as we were allowed to do that at all, the goal would be to ›identify‹ in a virtual way with that part of the perpetrators as a subtle reference to the potential for such behaviour in all of us, hoping that we can exactly define where this identification would necessarily fail. Not self-accusation for a collective guilt that cannot exist as such,[27] as the self-declared ›disinfectors of the past‹ claim to fear, but a highly sophisticated and moralised ›identification‹ and: rejection of the perpetrators' acts might provide the foundation for a ›remembrance-community‹. ›Sacralisation‹ of memory should not be avoided as such, it would rather have to gain its prominent place in the utopian project of founding a ›civil religion‹ in Germany that strives for a responsibility for memory as an element of building commonness in German society.

---

25 Mayer: Memory and history, p. 450.
26 Cf. the collection of the respective essays and my comment in: Soziologische Revue 12, 1989, pp. 314–318; see as well Gephart: Gesellschaftstheorie und Recht, pp. 215–236.
27 It would be most interesting to read the theory of Paul Fauconnet: La responsabilité, in this context. The question of ›guilt‹ is fundamentally dealt with by Jean-Louis Fabiani: On social guilt, in: Werner Gephart / Jan Christoph Suntrup (eds.): Rechtsanalyse als Kulturforschung II (forthcoming).

Durkheim could not have thought the unthinkable. He could not have foreseen that one day his theory of solidarity-producing commemorative rituals would have to be applied to a society with the most negative and unique content to its collective memory. Nor was such a thought possible for Maurice Halbwachs, the famous analyst of collective memory who was murdered on 16 March 1945 in Buchenwald, when he had just written his book on memory.[28]

How may we now, after those preliminary but nonetheless fundamental reflections about the place of memory in modern global society relate collective memory to the law and its procedural form that underlies the legal culture of tribunals?

1.3. Collective Memory and the Law

There are many places in which collective memories, the ›lieux de mémoire‹, as Pierre Nora famously named them, are produced, if not fabricated. Museums, schools, the army are symbols of a society as a commemorative symbol (flags, emblems, bibles). Law can be such a place of national pride: for the French, the *Code Napoléon* is certainly such a symbol. The Dôme des Invalides ist a ritual place of Napoleonism in which the legal-prophetic act of codification is emblematically celebrated. In Germany, the *Bürgerliches Gesetzbuch* hardly holds comparable identity-lending power. That ›legal culture‹ inscribes itself in procedural codes and leads to witnesses of procedural history in stone can be particularly well observed in the vicinity of Bonn, for instance at the court buildings at Reichensperger Platz in Cologne.

To the extent that court buildings themselves become *lieux de mémoire*, the ideal type of the ›court‹ is in a privileged position vis-à-vis gyms (during the Stammheim Trial) or other mobile venues of tribunalization which are harder to preserve.

In ›*traditional* legal cultures‹,[29] the reference to the past is a decisive component of the belief in law, in the absence of which the legitimacy of the ultimately forcible *enforcement* of the law can hardly be maintained. In ›*legal-rational* legal cultures‹, which are based on procedural validity cultures, the faith in the contingently possible creation of the New in law is a central component of the faith in law. ›*Charismatic* legal cultures‹, naturally, are in principle hostile to law, and the dictator hates no profession more than the legal one. Revolutionary law does not reference the past, unless it is a fictional *tausendjähriges Reich*, and only looks to the future. Fascist systems also cultivate a culture of remembrance which relies

---

[28] Cf. Halbwachs: La mémoire collective.
[29] The distinction of a legal-rational, a traditional and a charismatic type of legal culture is obviously inspired by Weber's famous theory of domination and authority.

on key moments of ›the movement‹: the march to Rome, the celebrations around the Schlageter monument, etc.

According to the ideal-type of the legal-rational legal culture, a charismatic aberration of law is transformed into a legal-rational form and – according to this ideal-typical development scheme – is then also able to assume functions of historical establishment of truth, thus entering into collective memory. Naturally, such a process remains entangled in the dilemma of ›transitional justice‹, that is to require revolutionary change in order to achieve the institutionalization of a new ›legal-rational legal culture‹. Such revolutionary change entails – much as in the Nuremberg Trials – the creation of new law which is retrospectively applied to the culprits. Past injustice is thus brought into focus, injustice which was committed through the communication medium of ›law‹ and thus also involves judicial (or perhaps rather *injudicial*) personnel: naval judges, judges at the People's Court (*Volksgerichtshof*), those applying the *Volksschädlingsverordnung*, etc. The fact that these culprits, when tried under the law of the Federal Republic of Germany, are under the protection of the principle of *nulla poena sine lege* and furthermore the possibility of invoking the ›perversion of justice‹ article in the German criminal code (§ 339 STGB) in their defence has hindered the prosecution and adjudication in the system of criminal law attribution.[30] These self-imposed barriers inherent to a system based on the rule of law are cast aside during times of the revolutionary charisma of tribunals in order to finally – and this is perhaps their crux – abolish themselves.

To what extent the trials in the Federal Republic of Germany, from the Nuremberg Trials to the Frankfurt Auschwitz Trial, have left traces in collective memory requires detailed analysis. For whether law can serve as an effective ›lieu de mémoire‹ empirically hinges upon a plethora of circumstances: orchestration by the media, acceptance in a society wishing to ward of victor's justice, increased or also decreased attention, its relationship to memorials and commemorative rituals, as already alluded to above. This charismatic moment is carried out through the medium of the tribunal which, in a legal-rational legal culture, increasingly takes on the form of a ›court‹.

The distinctive feature of law in a place of remembrance, however, resides in the fact that criminal regimes are characterized precisely by their perversion of the relationship between justice and injustice: without the systematic deprivation of rights, successively incorporated into legal institutions belonging to the legal system, i. e. the deprivation of the status as citizens, the Holocaust would not have been possible. In law, therefore, the criminal regime is programmed as being ›just‹, thereby necessitating a reprogramming from an ›illegal‹ to a ›legal culture‹ during the systemic change. However, such an act cannot be carried out by the pressing of a button, but rather involves a complicated process of legal-cultural change.

---

[30] Cf. the introduction by Jan Christoph Suntrup, in this volume.

Charismatic transformations and the shock of the rule of injustice are thus capable of being commemorated. Likewise commemorable, however, is the contribution of revelatory justice contributing to collective memory in such a way that the incriminating deeds are defined as reproachable in a lasting and unequivocal manner, but are simultaneously removed from discussion, thereby rendering them taboo and therefore ›sacralized‹ in the Durkheimian sense, as developed above.

2. Tribunals: The Penal Proceedings as a Ritual of Eternal Truth

Even if there have been certain attempts to establish a sharp difference between the legal proceeding and the ritual – as in the instructive work of Marie Theres Fögen[31] – because according to Luhmann the ritual is characterised by the absorption of contingencies[32] and could not be reflexively turned as in the code of procedure, this theoretical demarcation does not seem to hold: On the one hand, there certainly are reflexive rituals, as the Passah ritual demonstrates, where e. g. the hermeneutics of the ritual can be treated ritually but at the same time reflexively in the character of the understanding, non prudential son etc.[33] On the other hand, the hint of the Luhmannian theory formation to the function of the exclusion of contingent possibilities in the ritual is absolutely helpful, as we will see.

A brief glance at legal proceedings reveals how close they are to the religious dimension of social life.[34]

2.1. Symbolic Dimensions of Legal Life

The theories for the justification of penalty are closely connected to basic patterns of interpreting the world.[35] The image of the gods always comprises the wrathful, punishing god, either as functional god inside the pantheon[36] or in his capacity as the ›one‹ god. The modern punishment theories seem to slip into this gap as

---

[31] Cf. Fögen: Ritual und Rechtsfindung.

[32] Cf. Luhmann: Legitimation durch Verfahren.

[33] When I was awarded the ›Ordre national du mérite‹, I could find out that a speech on the ritual differences in Germany and France is not opposed to the effect of consecration! Cf. Gephart: Sur le rôle de l'honneur dans les sociétés modernes.

[34] For this parallel see an early version in Gephart: Strafe und Verbrechen.

[35] In the dualistic conception of the transcendent creator god, punishment has a different character than in the mundane asceticism of self-discipline.

[36] For the sociological background of the pantheon formation please also refer to the ›systematische Religionssoziologie‹ of Max Weber in Weber: Wirtschaft und Gesellschaft, p. 250.

soon as the religious legitimisation of punishment is no longer defensible in the secular state.[37]

Professional actors have superseded the old gods and their profane interpreters who pay special attention to cultivating their distinction from the ›laymen‹:[38] Their language is a ›secret‹ one, their knowledge remains incomprehensible to the layman, and this distinction is symbolised by way of sophisticated arrangements: from the judge's robe — a garment the shape of which[39] maintains the proximity to the priest's clothing — up to the spatial symbolisation of the ›secret‹. For the audience of the criminal proceedings, including the ›sinner‹, the bench steps out of a holy zone into a profane ›public‹, just as the ›holy of holies‹, the ›sacristy‹, and other holy rooms[40] remain secretive to the ›layman‹ and are covered by the mystery[41] of the unknown.

Law is therefore not conceived in terms of the theatre metaphor, very much put forward by Cornelia Vismann[42] in a long tradition to speak about penal justice as the ›theatre of threat‹ (Theater des Schreckens),[43] but in the light of a competing metaphorical model: that of the liturgy of religious events, regulated by holy norms, exercised at holy places during holy times by a priest-like personnel who tries to reconcile the profane and the sacred.

2.2. Ritual Dimensions

The procedure[44] itself is surrounded by the aura of the holy and ceremonial. The ritual arrangement accurately determines the permissible steps of the actors,

---

[37] Of course, the strange confounding of penal and state theories, e.g., in Hobbes, Pufendorf, Kant and Rousseau is deeply rooted in the disenchantment of the religious legitimisation of the state on the one hand, and the religious justification of punishment on the other.

[38] The entire sociology of professions does not only metaphorically live on the priest-layman dyad.

[39] As an alternative, intercultural differences can be derived, e.g., from the ›effet de manche‹ of the pleading lawyer in France.

[40] This spatial aspect of the social organisation of the penal proceedings would require an intensive interpretation, which — besides the architectural relationship with religious rooms — should consider the ›choreographic‹ equivalents, the meaning of the ›holy books‹, the sequencing of the opening, main, and closing rituals.

[41] For the function of the secret please also refer to the respective digression in Simmel: Soziologie, pp. 383 et seqq.

[42] Cf. Vismann: Medien der Rechtsprechung, pp. 19 et seqq.

[43] How much performing cultures are differentiated and interwoven in the same time is the central topic of the Käte Hamburger Centre for Advanced Study ›Interweaving performance cultures‹ at Berlin. For a systematically and historically most useful analysis of theatre see Biet/Triau: Qu'est-ce que le théâtre? In this volume see especially the contribution by Miranda Jakisa.

[44] The study of Niklas Luhmann ›Legitimation durch Verfahren‹ unintelligibly does without the suggesting reference to religious sociology. The attempt to initiate a normative legitimation through procedures must fail, of course. What remains is the long-supporting idea of *self-binding* through the

which are fixed inside the holy books⁴⁵ – absolutely incomprehensible for laymen. The social event of the process therewith imposes on the actors – other than in the ceremonial practice – a much stronger uncertainty of behaviour, which deprives the defendant step by step of all social appearances, profession, origin, and life, to be offered as just a ritual sacrifice to the fascinated crowd as nude ›offender‹.⁴⁶ The rituals of accusation, defence, swearing in and the judgment produce an atmosphere of emotive tension, of pity,⁴⁷ and the existential fear of all the potential ›sacrifices‹ who would become both the offender and the object of offence. The reconstruction of the offence provides the ›public‹ with a pictorial description of the event, which enables this public to vividly participate in the nightmare. The participants do not necessarily agree on the object of the cult: ›order‹, ›justice‹ and ›guilt‹ are the pitiless emblems of Justitia, who – with her allegoric blindness⁴⁸ – causes the laymen to develop heretic doubts.

2.3. The Legal Community as a Cult Community

Between the judge-priests and the vague public, the ›parish‹⁴⁹ mediates as community of all those who still believe in justice, but who – as heretics – are also at the mercy of the implacable sword of the law. Their community is built on the spiritual basis of the ›belief in commonness‹,⁵⁰ in belonging to the same legal order and: *ritual community*, even if the distribution of the ›legal goods‹ sure enough distinguishes between the more and the less privileged. The *belief* in the legal

---

enlacement in roles. In how far both the religious sociology of Luhmann (see also Luhmann: Funktion der Religion, and Luhmann: Soziale Systeme, p. 60) entail necessary changes is a question that would have to be further discussed (for more information on the ›Theoriewende‹ see also Gephart: Gesellschaftstheorie und Recht, pp. 97 et seqq.).

⁴⁵ In contrast to this, the type of the ›loose leaf compilation‹ which materially expresses the changeability of the law must be assessed as ›profanisation‹.

⁴⁶ The Fakultätenbild ›Jurisprudenz‹ (1907) by Gustav Klimt seems like a symbolic interpretation of this concept. Cf. my interpretation in Gephart: Recht als Kultur, pp. 271–274.

⁴⁷ Some perpetrators tried to profit from this situational effect, as the Eichmann trial sadly showed.

⁴⁸ For more information on the pictorial display of justice please also refer to Pleister/Schild (eds.): Recht und Gerechtigkeit im Spiegel der europäischen Kunst. A new light will be thrown on the blindfoldedness of Justice by the study of José González García: La Mirada de la Justicia/Ikonographie der Gerechtigkeit (forthcoming in the Schriftenreihe ›Recht als Kultur‹).

⁴⁹ In his systematic religious sociology, Max Weber has worked out the autonomy of the configuration of priests, laymen, and parish as compared to the simply religious ideas. See also §5 of the religious sociology, in Weber: Wirtschaft und Gesellschaft, pp. 275–279, where Weber virtually gets in touch with Emile Durkheim, whose social basis of religion internally lacks a theoretical differentiation which is structured by Weber in accordance with ideal typical forms.

⁵⁰ Just as for Weber the issue of legitimacy was transformed to the legitimacy *belief*, the question of the reality level of religious, ethnic, and cultural community melts into the community *belief*. See also Weber: Wirtschaft und Gesellschaft, p. 235.

order supersedes the vanished belief in the extraterrestrial justice. Thus, the ceremonial gains its own reason for legitimacy, and the lost idea of the community that leapfrogs religious classes and races⁵¹ returns inside of the feelings of the ›legal community‹, the members of which shall feel committed to each other as *legal comrades*.⁵² At last, the celebration of law releases mysterious powers where priests, parish and community reconcile with each other within the sacrifice. The judge's verdict⁵³ eases the tension of the fight between god and the devil, between good and evil. The word produces, according to speech act theory, the illucutionary binding effect of decisions and releases the individual power of the *force du droit*, if this can be expected in accordance with the rules of the cult. Just as the believer does not only ›know‹ more, but is actually more ›able‹, a mood of ›effervescence‹ has diffused within the procedure, where judges, priests, the public, and the defendant are carried by the pathos of the holy and are raised above themselves. Or he is simply mystically transformed, as Hannah Arendt put it.⁵⁴ The ›deontic power‹ of the sentence, as John R. Searle⁵⁵ calls it, is therefore backed by the institutional setting, and the religious forces unleash the ritual dynamics in the realm of normativity.

2.4. Sacred and Profane Times of Legal Life

These times of ›effervescence‹ are periodically interrupted; the spectator is discharged to everyday life just as the believer is, the judge gets rid of his gown and returns to the profane world, where he takes his place in the queue of the laymen just because of his social inconspicuousness.⁵⁶ However we should not exagger-

---

⁵¹ The problem of the universal community is described as conversion of the fraternal ethics into the flattening ethics of the ›others‹ in Nelson: Der Ursprung der Moderne. Weber had reserved the term of fraternity ethics for this phenomenon, while in Mead the universalistic jump already appears with the character of the ›generalised other‹ (cf. Mead: Mind, Self and Society).

⁵² In his ›Struktur der Moderne‹ Richard Münch mainly refers to the ›common‹ component of law.

⁵³ The judge's verdict is paradigm of the speech act, the binding impact or illocutionary binding effects of which Jürgen Habermas tries to derive from the immanent rationality of speech (see also Habermas: Theorie des kommunikativen Handelns II, p. 112), while we can find a religious sociological root of the binding word in Durkheim; see also the interesting review by Durkheim: Richard Lasch. See also Gephart: Gesellschaftstheorie und Recht, pp. 409 et seqq.

⁵⁴ During an interview with Joachim Fest, she explains the logic of the trial: ›Und das ist das eigentlich Großartige am Gerichtsverfahren, nicht? Es findet da eine wirkliche Verwandlung statt. Denn wenn der jetzt sagt: »Ich war doch nur ein Bürokrat«, dann kann der Richter sagen: »Du hör mal, deswegen stehst Du nicht hier. Du stehst deswegen hier, weil Du ein Mensch bist und weil Du bestimmte Sachen gemacht hast« und diese Verwandlung hat etwas Großartiges‹ (Arendt: ›Eichmann war von empörender Dummheit‹, p. 164).

⁵⁵ Cf. Searle: Making the social world, p. 8 et seq.

⁵⁶ If we believe what the reports on famous judges tell us; of course, besides the local gods there

ate this breakfast sociology of the law. The ›banalisation of the Sacred‹ keeps on going against the demand for the sacral to become permanent. The unity of the cult, however, is created in legends and myths, the – for modern societies – constitutive part of which cultivates the myth of equality and justice, which is even supplemented by the idea of a fraternity, that is evoked in many images[57] and tales. Thus, the values of the sacral legal community are upvalued to become holy things, the violation of which requires strictly described purification rites,[58] to maintain the irrevocable borders between the holy and the unholy. Besides, as Annette Wieviorka reminds us in her contribution, the witness role of Abraham Sutzkerer was felt as a ›sacred‹ obligation.[59]

2.5. Places of Justice

Just as the holy spaces[60] of law should be considered places of justice,[61] the sites of purification themselves are permeated by the character of the holy: magic places of betterment which are designed to lead the victim back from the state of evil to the world of the good through pure presence and ascetic rites. These ›rites de passage‹ require the utmost ritual arrangements and – last but not least – also a spatial discrimination which suppresses the evil and lets the good grow in peace.

---

are local judges, who are stylised to types by the local press; and this does not only apply to the British legal system.

[57] The educational handling of law in TV series and shows on ›my‹ right in everyday life could be interpreted from this point of view of sociology of religion. The simulacrum of justice mediated by Court TV shows has also the function to simulate the understandability of the law for the laymen (see Gephart: Recht als Kultur, pp. 277–281).

[58] The visiting committees are a particularly interesting case for the purification from political iniquities. The processing of political immorality is without any doubt impressed by the respective political culture or un-culture. Thus, political scandals in Great Britain (e.g. Profumo), the USA (Watergate), and in the Federal Republic of Germany (Flick) developed and ›processed‹ in absolute different ways. The culturally impressed purification techniques have in common that they are fulfilled as a ritual. From the sociological point of view, we must not forget the positive function of the scandal and the ritual processing. It is an interesting dogmatic question whether the juristic insecurities in the application of the code of criminal procedure can be restricted to the visiting committees through a functional consideration of the individual processes. For more information on Watergate please also refer to the attempt, inspired by the sociology of religion, by Jeffrey C. Alexander: Culture and political crisis.

[59] Cf. Wieviorka, in this volume.

[60] The legal protection of inviolable precincts belongs to the modern sacralisation of the space. See also Simmel: Soziologie, pp. 687–790.

[61] For more information on legal court architecture under religious sociological aspects please see also Gephart: Versteinerte Rechtskultur; as continuation Klemmer/Wassermann/Wessel: Deutsche Gerichtsgebäude. Von der Dorflinde über den Justizpalast zum Haus des Rechts; and a more detailed version in Gephart: Recht als Kultur, pp. 191–281.

2.6. Some Specific Traits of Tribunals

Along these lines and much inspired by Cornelia Vismann's marvellous study,[62] an ideal-typical distinction of tribunal and court may be drawn in the following way by using the analytical distinctions developed above:

	Tribunal	Court
Symbolic	Agonic	Theatralic Table, velum
Normative	– Loose connection to pre-established norms – Invention, definition and application uno actu – Coded signs as evidence	– Nulla poena sine lege – Differentiation of the creation of norms and its application – Inquisition and ›épreuve‹
Organizational	– Tribunal community as spectators' community – Close to ›people's justice‹ – No local fixation – Judge and attorney function undifferentiated	– Neutrality, collective bindingness, truth-relatedness – Dedifferentiated courtroom – Differentiation of judge and attorney
Ritualistic	– Ritualistic correctness	– Procedural legitimation
Functions	Melting of – truth – memory – pedagogical instruction – identity building – historical investigation	– Procedurally generated truth – Imputation of personal guilt

The main difference therefore lies in the degree of functional, spatial and normative differentiation that makes the tribunal, in its ideal-type, a direct voice of the undifferentiated ›conscience collective‹,[63] as represented by the present

---

[62] Cf. Vismann: Medien der Rechtsprechung, pp. 146–183.

[63] Peter Handke's condemnation of the ›Great Tribunal‹ entails, albeit its historically and politically mislead judgements, profound insights into the de-differentiation of the legal culture represented by Court TV Shows and the ›Great Tribunal‹, as Handke denounces the ICTY. Cf. Handke: Rund um das Große Tribunal, p. 17; for a critical assessment of Handke's reading see Jürgen Brokoff in this volume.

›foule‹,⁶⁴ whereas the court type differentiates among its personnel, its normative orders, its spatial organization and local fixation in permanent courtrooms. Spoken in an evolutionary way, one could say that the great tribunals dealing with accusations of crimes against humanity, from the Nuremberg Trials to the court in Den Haag, try to change tribunal peoples' justice to court justice, from formal substantive ritual by way of ordeals, prophecies etc. to the formally rationalized type of modern law in Weber's sense.⁶⁵

›Realism‹ about Humanity's Law, as Ruti Teitel⁶⁶ rightly names the evolutionary path in normative globalization, therefore does not mean disenchanting the validity of the values protected by the Nuremberg charter and its successors as ›crimes against humanity‹. Rather, a realist view has to take into consideration how the emerging global legal culture of ›Humanity's Law‹ relates to local conditions of implementation and national cultures of constructing truth by way of legal institutions. According to situational factors in the process of change from a culture of injustice to a real ›legal culture‹ approach, they may more closely correspond to either the ideal type of a ›tribunal‹ or that of a ›court‹. But their creative power to install a new normative order, a new legal and moral conscience, together with other institutions does not permit, in my understanding, the denouncement in advance of any kind of tribunal about a society's criminal past as a ›show trial‹. Nevertheless, without showing, without use of the media, without a public discourse of the threatened collective feelings, the *conscience collective*, the formation of a civil society seems unfeasible. Such a civil society would be no longer or not newly rediscovered as religiously founded, but rather be based on the paradoxical pillars of a *religion civique* that declares certain values simply untouchable, in the formal sense of a ›taboo‹.

The circle of ›Memory, Tribunals and the Sacred‹, then, is not a vicious one, but a balanced set of dynamic forces in society even when evil enters the scene. But as we know from Goethe's Faust, who did not take a lawyer as in the States,⁶⁷ the circle sign may irritate the devil.

---

64 For an interesting study of the crowd with reference to classical authors see Rubio: La foule.
65 For an interpretation of Weber's argument of juristic rationalisation see my introduction (Gephart: Einleitung) to the volume on law as part of the historical and critical edition of ›Economy and Society‹ (MWG I/22-3).
66 See Teitel: Humanity's law.
67 This was to be learnt by Yoram Shachar's talk ›When Faust takes a lawyer‹, July 12, 2011 at the Käte Hamburger Centre for Advanced Study ›Recht als Kultur‹.

List of references

Alexander, Jeffrey C.: Culture and political crisis: Watergate and Durkheimian sociology, in: Jeffrey Alexander (ed.): Durkheimian sociology: Cultural studies, Cambridge 1988, pp. 187–224.

Arendt, Hannah: ›Eichmann war von empörender Dummheit‹. Aus einer Rundfunksendung vom 9. November 1964 (Gespräch mit Joachim Fest), in: Martin Wiebel (ed.): Hannah Arendt. Ihr Denken veränderte die Welt, Munich 2012, pp. 150–176.

Assier-Andrieu, Louis: L'autorité du passé. Essai anthropologique sur la common law, Paris 2012.

Biet, Christian / Christoph Triau: Qu'est-ce que le théâtre?, Paris 2006.

Bourdieu, Pierre: La force du droit. Eléments pour une sociologie du champ juridique, in: Actes de la recherche en sciences sociales 64, 1986, pp. 3–19.

Durkheim, Emile: De la définition des phénomènes religieux, in: L'Année sociologique 2, 1897/98, pp. 1–28.

Durkheim, Emile: Richard Lasch: Der Eid. Seine Entstehung und Beziehung zu Glaube und Brauch der Naturvölker, Stuttgart 1908, in: L'Année sociologique, 11, 1910, pp. 460–465.

Durkheim, Emile: De la division du travail social, Paris 1973.

Durkheim, Emile: The elementary forms of religious life, Oxford / New York 2001.

Fauconnet, Paul: La responsabilité. Etude de sociologie, Paris 1928.

Fögen, Marie Theres: Ritual und Rechtsfindung, in: Corian Caduff / Johanna Pfaff-Czarnecka (eds.): Rituale heute. Theorien – Kontroversen – Entwürfe, Berlin 1999, pp. 149–164.

Friedländer, Saul / Adam Seligman: Das Gedenken an die Schoa in Israel. Symbole, Rituale und ideologische Polarisierung, in: James E. Young (ed.): Mahnmale des Holocaust. Motive, Rituale und Stätten des Gedenkens, Munich 1994, pp. 125–135.

Gephart, Werner: Strafe und Verbrechen. Die Theorie Emile Durkheims, Opladen 1990.

Gephart, Werner: Versteinerte Rechtskultur. Zur kultursoziologischen Analyse von Gerichtsbauten, in: Heinz Mohnhaupt / Dieter Simon (eds.): Vorträge zur Justizforschung. Geschichte und Theorie, Vol. 1, Frankfurt a. M. 1992, pp. 401–431.

Gephart, Werner: Gesellschaftstheorie und Recht. Das Recht im soziologischen Diskurs der Moderne, Frankfurt a. M. 1993.

Gephart, Werner: The realm of normativity in Durkheim and Foucault, in: Mark S. Cladis (ed.): Durkheim and Foucault: perspectives on education and punishment, Oxford 1999, pp. 59–70.

Gephart, Werner: Sur le rôle de l'honneur dans les sociétés modernes, in: Voyages sociologiques. France – Allemagne, Paris 2005, pp. 184–190.

Gephart, Werner: Recht als Kultur. Zur kultursoziologischen Analyse des Rechts, Frankfurt a. M. 2006.

Gephart, Werner: Einleitung, in: Werner Gephart/Siegfried Hermes (eds.): Max Weber-Gesamtausgabe I/22,3: Wirtschaft und Gesellschaft. Die Wirtschaft und die gesellschaftlichen Ordnungen und Mächte. Nachlaß. Teilband 3: Recht, Tübingen 2011, S. 1–133.

Gephart, Werner/Hans Waldenfels (eds.): Religion und Identität. Im Horizont des Pluralismus, Frankfurt a. M. 1999.

Habermas, Jürgen: Theorie des kommunikativen Handelns. Vol. 2: Zur Kritik der funktionalistischen Vernunft, Frankfurt a. M. 1981.

Halbwachs, Maurice: La mémoire collective, Paris 1950.

Handke, Peter: Rund um das Große Tribunal, Frankfurt a. M. 2003.

Hervieu-Léger, Danièle: Le pèlerin et le converti. La religion en mouvement, Paris 1999.

Klemmer, Klemens/Rudolf Wassermann/Thomas Michael Wessel: Deutsche Gerichtsgebäude. Von der Dorflinde über den Justizpalast zum Haus des Rechts, Munich 1993.

Kohlhammer, Siegfried: Anathema. Der Holocaust und das Bilderverbot, in: Merkur, 48, 1994, pp. 501–509.

Kugelmass, Jack: Weshalb wir nach Polen reisen. Holocaust-Tourismus als säkulares Ritual, in: James E. Young (ed.): Mahnmale des Holocaust. Motive, Rituale und Stätten des Gedenkens, Munich 1994, pp. 153–161.

Luhmann, Niklas: Funktion der Religion, Frankfurt a. M. 1977.

Luhmann, Niklas: Legitimation durch Verfahren, Frankfurt a. M. 1983.

Luhmann, Niklas: Soziale Systeme, Frankfurt a. M. 1984.

Mayer, Arno J.: Memory and history. On poverty and remembering and forgetting the judeocide, in: Rolf Steininger (ed.): Der Umgang mit dem Holocaust. Europa, USA, Israel, Vienna 1994, pp. 444–457.

Mead, George Herbert: Mind, self and society, Chicago 1934.

Münch, Richard: Struktur der Moderne, Frankfurt a. M. 1984.

Nelson, Benjamin: Der Ursprung der Moderne, Frankfurt a. M. 1986.

Nora, Pierre (ed.): Les lieux de mémoire, 3 vol., Paris 1984–1992.

Ophir, Adi: On sanctifying the Holocaust. An anti-theological treatise, in: Tikkun, 2, 1987, pp. 61–67.

Pleister, Wolfgang/Wolfgang Schild (eds.): Recht und Gerechtigkeit im Spiegel der europäischen Kunst, Cologne 1988.

Rubio, Vincent: La foule, Paris 2008.

Savelsberg, Joachim J./Ryan D. King: Law and collective memory, in: Annual review of law and social science, 3, 2007, pp. 189–211.

Schmidt-Wulffen, Stephan: Ein Mahnmal versinkt. Ein Gespräch mit Esther und Jochen Gerz, in: James E. Young (ed.): Mahnmale des Holocaust. Motive, Rituale und Stätten des Gedenkens, Munich 1994, pp. 43–49.

Searle, John R.: Making the social world, Oxford 2011.

Simmel, Georg: Soziologie. Untersuchungen über die Formen der Vergesellschaftung, Frankfurt a. M. 1992.

Teitel, Ruti G.: Humanity's law, Oxford/New York 2011.

Vismann, Cornelia: Medien der Rechtsprechung, Frankfurt a. M. 2011.

Weber, Max: Wirtschaft und Gesellschaft, Tübingen 1972.

Christoph Flügge

Die juristische Aufarbeitung von Kriegsverbrechen am *International Criminal Tribunal for the former Yugoslavia (ICTY)* in Den Haag

In diesem Beitrag möchte ich meine Tätigkeit als Richter des *Internationalen Strafgerichtshofs für das ehemalige Jugoslawien* (ICTY) darstellen und einen Einblick in unsere dortige Arbeitspraxis ermöglichen.[1] Dabei kommt mir – anders als anderen Autoren – eine schwierige Rolle insofern zu, als ich faktische Verantwortung trage für die Aufarbeitung der Verbrechen, die sich in Jugoslawien zugetragen haben. Um nicht das Risiko einzugehen, zu viel zu offenbaren und deshalb für befangen erklärt zu werden, kann ich mich über einzelne Verfahren nicht direkt äußern.

In meinem Beitrag will ich die Arbeit des ICTY nicht bewerten, nicht verteidigen und nicht kritisieren. Dies steht mir als Beteiligtem nicht zu. Seit 2008 bin ich Richter dort. Wenn ich im Folgenden einen kleinen Eindruck von unserer Arbeit zu vermitteln versuche, gibt mir das Gelegenheit, einige Missverständ-

---

[1] Die Diskussion über Tribunale, die auf der Bonner »Tribunale«-Tagung im April 2012 stattgefunden hat, war sehr lehrreich für mich, weil sie eine seltene disziplinübergreifende Auseinandersetzung mit dem Thema Tribunale darstellte. Besonders dankbar bin ich für den Beitrag von Dževad Karahasan (vgl. in diesem Band), stellt er doch ein Plädoyer für Humanismus dar, wie ich es selten gehört habe, und zugleich ein flammendes Plädoyer gegen die Todesstrafe. Man sollte sich im Klaren darüber sein, dass die Todesstrafendebatte überall immer wieder auftaucht, und selten habe ich so klar wie bei Karahasan formuliert gesehen, dass man bestimmte Situationen nicht einfach nach dem Schema »Gut«-»Böse« oder »Schwarz«-»Weiß« beurteilen sollte. Die Todesstrafe lässt aber keinen Spielraum, sie bedeutet »lebendig« oder »tot«, und genau deshalb ist sie im Rahmen der Strafgerichtsbarkeit zu vermeiden.
    Ich empfinde es als ausgesprochen befruchtend und interessant, mit Nicht-Juristen darüber zu diskutieren, wie unser juristischer Alltag in Den Haag aussieht. Cornelia Vismann, auf deren einschlägige Arbeiten in diesem Band immer wieder hingewiesen wird, war in den 80er Jahren im Amtsgericht Berlin-Tiergarten, wo ich Strafrichter war, meine Referendarin. Sie war eine sehr interessierte, mich sehr anregende Persönlichkeit. 2010 hat sie sich wieder bei mir gemeldet, weil sie nach Den Haag kommen wollte, um sich mit unseren Medien zu beschäftigen. Leider hat aber ihre Krankheit eine Reise unmöglich gemacht, so dass das, was sie in ihrem Buch über den Haager Strafgerichtshof schreibt (vgl. Vismann: Medien der Rechtsprechung), Erkenntnisse aus zweiter Hand geblieben sind. Diese sind jedoch sehr verdienstvoll, sehr interessant zu lesen. Ich stimme nicht mit allem überein, aber ich bin dankbar, dass ein Mensch wie Cornelia Vismann sich so intensiv mit dieser Seite der Justiz und ihrer Vermittlung an Außenstehende beschäftigt hat.

nisse klarzustellen. Diese fangen schon mit dem Begriff »Tribunal« an. Für mich war früher der Begriff ganz eindeutig besetzt: Ein Tribunal ist der Ort für einen Schauprozess, für ein Verfahren, dessen Ergebnisse vorher feststehen. Im Englischen scheint sich der Sprachgebrauch nicht mit unserem deutschen Verständnis von »Tribunal« zu decken, so dass ich jedenfalls im Kontext des Tribunals in Den Haag den englischen Tribunal-Begriff als gleichbedeutend mit dem deutschen »Gericht« ansehe. Nicht umsonst ist die deutsche Bezeichnung in der offiziellen Übersetzung nicht etwa »das Jugoslawientribunal«, sondern »Internationaler Strafgerichtshof für das ehemalige Jugoslawien«. Eine der bedeutendsten Nachfolgeorganisation, der »International Criminal Court« (ICC), heißt im Deutschen »Internationaler Strafgerichtshof«.

Mit dieser semantischen Frage »Gericht« oder »Tribunal« möchte ich mich hier nicht weiter auseinandersetzen. Aus meinen folgenden Schilderungen wird aber hoffentlich deutlich, dass es sich beim ICTY nicht um ein Schauprozesstribunal handelt, sondern wirklich um ein Gericht.

Zu diesem Zweck möchte ich mit einem Zitat beginnen, das die deutsche Geschichte im besonderen Maß betrifft. Der Hauptankläger im Nürnberger Prozess gegen die Hauptkriegsverbrecher, Robert H. Jackson, betonte am 21. November 1945 in Nürnberg: »Die Vernunft der Menschheit verlangt, daß das Gesetz sich nicht genug sein läßt, geringfügige Verbrechen zu bestrafen, die sich kleine Leute zuschulden kommen lassen. Das Gesetz muss auch die Männer erreichen [und ich füge hinzu: es sind tatsächlich fast ausschließlich Männer, C.F.], die eine große Macht an sich reißen und sich ihrer mit Vorsatz und im gemeinsamen Ratschlag bedienen, um ein Unheil hervorzurufen, das kein Heim in der Welt unberührt läßt«.[2]

Damit ist der wichtigste Punkt angesprochen, um den es geht. Von 1945/46, dem Nürnberger Kriegsverbrechertribunal, bis 1993 sind Staatenlenker, Präsidenten, Heerführer für ihre Untaten straflos gewesen. Nirgendwo gab es eine konsequente internationale Aufmerksamkeit oder Verfolgung, im Gegenteil: Man hat ihnen meistens Asyl gewährt, etwa Jean-Bédel Bokassa, dem selbst ernannten Kaiser des Zentralafrikanischen Kaiserreichs, der Zuflucht in Frankreich gefunden hat. Darum gab es seit langem, insbesondere von Menschenrechtsorganisationen wie *Amnesty International*, die Forderung, der Straflosigkeit für diese Hauptverantwortlichen ein Ende zu bereiten. Mit der Gründung des ICTY, wie sie in den Resolutionen des Weltsicherheitsrats vom 22. Februar 1993 und vom 25. Mai 1993 vorgesehen war, ist ein entscheidender Schritt in diese Richtung getan worden. Und da immer wieder die Legitimität des Haager Strafgerichtshofs in Frage gestellt wird, möchte ich darauf hinweisen, dass die UN-Charta es ausdrücklich gestattet, auch mit juristischen Mitteln, nicht nur mit Friedensmissionen, Blauhel-

---

2 Jackson: Grundlegende Rede, S. 7.

men, nicht nur mit bewaffneten oder unbewaffneten Missionen tätig zu werden, sondern eben auch mit juristischen Mitteln einzugreifen bei solchen Konflikten.

Aus der Resolution von Februar 1993 geht hervor, welch große Erwartungen mit der Einrichtung des Tribunals verbunden wurden: »Expressing once again its grave alarm at continuing reports of widespread violations of international humanitarian law occurring within the territory of the former Yugoslavia, including reports of mass killings and the continuance of the practice of ›ethnic cleansing‹«. Deswegen bestand das Bedürfnis, effektive strafrechtliche Maßnahmen zu ergreifen, »effective measures to bring to justice the persons who are responsible for them«. Dies wurde mit der Hoffnung verbunden, dass die Errichtung eines internationalen Tribunals »would enable this aim to be achieved and would contribute to the restoration and maintenance of peace«.³

In der Resolution vom 25. Mai 1993 heißt es, nachdem alle möglichen Maßnahmen in Erwägung gezogen wurden, im entscheidenden Schlüsselsatz: »The Security Council [...], acting under chapter VII of the Charter of the United Nations [...] decides hereby to establish an international tribunal for the sole purpose of prosecuting persons responsible for serious violations of international humanitarian law committed in the territory of the former Yugoslavia«.⁴ »The sole purpose« ist hier zu betonen, denn ein Strafgericht sollte eigentlich ausschließlich dafür da sein, individuelle strafrechtliche Verantwortlichkeit und Schuld zu prüfen und gegebenenfalls festzustellen und abzuurteilen. Keine andere Aufgabe kommt ihm zu. Darum sind die vielfachen kritischen Hinweise auf das Tribunal von interessierter Seite, dass in Den Haag Staaten auf der Anklagebank sitzen, völlig fehl am Platze. Es sind vielmehr individuelle Handlungen, die verhandelt werden, mutmaßliche Taten von Staatspräsidenten wie Milošević, Milutinović und Karadžić, auch von Ministern, Ministerpräsidenten – hier gäbe es zu viele Namen aufzuzählen – oder von Heerführern, Generälen wie Ratko Mladić und Ante Gotovina. All diese standen oder stehen in Den Haag persönlich vor Gericht.

Die kroatische Regierung zum Beispiel hat dieses Prozedere jedoch völlig falsch verstanden. Als Gotovina im April 2011 in erster Instanz verurteilt wurde, hat die kroatische Regierung mit dem Hinweis protestiert: »Wir gehen in die Berufung!« Nun ist es undenkbar, dass ein Staat in einem individuellen Strafverfahren in Berufung geht. Aber die Regierung hat es damit nicht genug sein lassen, sondern sie hat tatsächlich einen formalen Antrag gestellt und beantragt, an dem Berufungsverfahren beteiligt zu werden. Dieser Antrag ist mit einem sehr knappen und kurzen Entscheid der Berufungskammer zurückgewiesen worden mit

---

[3] Alle Zitate: Security Council: Resolution 808, http://www.un.org/ga/search/view_doc.asp?symbol=S/RES/808(1993), (letzter Aufruf: 06.05.2013).

[4] Security Council: Resolution 827, http://www.un.org/ga/search/view_doc.asp?symbol=S/RES/827(1993), (letzter Aufruf: 06.05.2013).

der Erklärung, dass es für ihn keine rechtliche Grundlage gebe, und mit einigen Hinweisen darauf, was das Wesen eines Strafprozesses ausmacht. Weder Staaten noch sonstige kollektive Entitäten wie Firmen oder Gesellschaften können vor ein Strafgericht gestellt werden, sondern im Strafprozess nur Individuen.

Dass Personen der Befehlsebene gerichtet werden, stellt eine Neuheit dar. Sicherlich sind unter den Angeklagten auch solche, die nicht zu der obersten Befehlsebene gehörten, etwa der serbische Lokalpolitiker Duško Tadić, der der allererste Angeklagte war. Tadić saß schon in München in Haft, als das Tribunal in seinen Anfängen darum bemüht war, überhaupt Zugriff auf die Angeklagten zu bekommen. Er wurde nach Den Haag überstellt und sein Verfahren hat Rechtsgeschichte gemacht, weil das erste Urteil und die Berufungs-Entscheidung viele Grundsätze des internationalen Strafrechts entwickelt haben. Man muss dabei bedenken, dass es bis zur Gründung des Tribunals 1993 kein kodifiziertes Völkerstrafrecht gab, sondern lediglich Völkergewohnheitsrecht. Ein solcher Zustand bringt große Probleme der Legitimität mit sich. Mit der Gründung unseres Tribunals im Mai 1993 gab es nun ein Statut mit materiellen Strafbestimmungen. Die Artikel zwei bis fünf machen deutlich, worum es geht: die Verletzung der Genfer Konventionen, Kriegsverbrechen, Völkermord und Verbrechen gegen die Menschlichkeit.[5] Damit existierte nunmehr eine materiellrechtlich akzeptable und verlässliche strafrechtliche Grundlage.

Im Allgemeinen wird, insbesondere in Deutschland, wo die Berichterstattung sehr zurückhaltend ist, immer nur Bericht erstattet, wenn es um drei Namen geht, nämlich um Milošević, Karadžić und Mladić. Kaum jemand weiß, dass immerhin 161 Personen angeklagt worden sind, einige Verfahren laufen noch heute. Häufig herrscht dabei die Meinung vor, dass die Verurteilungsrate des Gerichts bei annähernd 100 Prozent läge. Aber es handelt sich eben nicht um Siegerjustiz oder Tribunaljustiz. Ungefähr jedes fünfte Urteil ist ein Freispruch. Auch ein Freispruch bedeutet aber nicht, dass der jeweilige Angeklagte unschuldig ist, sondern nur, dass seine Schuld nicht »beyond reasonable doubt«, also ohne vernünftigen Zweifel, festgestellt werden konnte. Dieser Vorgang ist Zeichen von Rechtsstaatlichkeit, so schmerzlich er auch im Einzelfall sein kann.

In dem schon erwähnten Fall Gotovina, der ja selbst in der Berufung 2012 freigesprochen wurde, finde ich sehr eindrucksvoll, dass beinahe nie über die verschiedenen Urteile über die ursprünglich drei Angeklagten berichtet wurde. Die Zeitungen haben nur über Gotovina und seinen Prozess geschrieben, in dem er in erster Instanz zu 24 Jahren Haft verurteilt worden war. Dass in erster Instanz einer der beiden anderen Angeklagten ebenfalls verurteilt und einer freigesprochen worden war, weil man seine Schuld nicht sicher nachweisen konnte, wurde

---

[5] Vgl. Statut des Internationalen Strafgerichtshofs für das ehemalige Jugoslawien, http://www.icls.de/dokumente/icty_statut_dt.pdf (letzter Aufruf: 06.05.2013).

unterschlagen. Nach dem in zweiter Instanz erfolgten Freispruch der beiden in der ersten Instanz Verurteilen hat sich die öffentliche Reaktion in der Region allerdings in das Gegenteil verkehrt. Während kroatische Politiker das Tribunal nun lobten, kündigten viele serbische Politiker ihre Bereitschaft zur Kooperation mit dem ICTY auf.

Am ICTY sind etliche Verfahren eingestellt worden oder die Anklagen sind zurückgezogen worden. Manche Verfahren sind an die regionalen *War Crimes Chambers* in Sarajevo, Belgrad und Zagreb verwiesen worden. Dort sind, für meine Begriffe, überraschend viele Urteile herausgekommen. Denn die Tatsache, dass beispielsweise in Belgrad ein serbischer Richter serbische mutmaßliche Kriegsverbrecher wirklich verurteilt, habe ich zuvor nicht für möglich gehalten. Die meisten Verfahren am ICTY sind mittlerweile zumindest in erster Instanz abgeschlossen, wobei noch einige große Verfahren, etwa zu Mladić, Karadžić und Hadžić, andauern. Auch wenn oft der Vorwurf aufkommt, dass die internationale Gemeinschaft mittlerweile vor allem darauf bedacht sei, Geld zu sparen, so dass kein Ende der Prozesse in Sicht sei, kann erfreulicherweise festgestellt werden, dass alle Verfahren tatsächlich abgeschlossen werden. Lediglich neue Anklagen werden nicht mehr erhoben, und zwar schon seit vielen Jahren nicht mehr, weil die mutmaßlichen »großen Fische« alle bereits vor Gericht gestellt worden sind. Aber die Staatsanwaltschaft hat natürlich viel mehr Material gesammelt und kooperiert intensiv mit den Staatsanwaltschaften in Sarajevo, Zagreb und Belgrad. Hier gibt es Verbindungsstaatsanwälte, die regelmäßig die Informationen austauschen. Die Materialien, die die Staatsanwaltschaft zusammengetragen hat, werden auch im Hinblick auf andere Tatverdächtige ausgewertet und übergeben. Es war von möglichen 10.000 Beschuldigten die Rede, auch wenn es natürlich nie möglich sein wird, diese Fälle so gründlich und aufwändig wie in Den Haag aufzuarbeiten. Ein solches Vorhaben würde alle Strukturen überfordern und wahrscheinlich so viele Jahrzehnte dauern, dass der zuvor gewünschte Effekt dann vielleicht nicht mehr erreicht werden könnte.

Ich möchte daran erinnern, wie sich die Situation 1993, als das Tribunal gegründet worden ist, darstellte. In der UN-Resolution 808 und in der öffentlichen Begleitung herrschte die Vorstellung vor, dass mit der Einrichtung eines Tribunals die gegenwärtigen Kriegsverbrechen gestoppt und weitere verhindert werden könnten und vielleicht auch Frieden wiederhergestellt werden könnte, wie es in der oben zitierten Resolution hieß. 1993 dauerte die Belagerung Sarajevos schon ein Jahr an, übrigens eine Belagerung, die erst 1996 endete und somit zur längsten des 20. Jahrhunderts geworden ist. Sie hat sogar länger gedauert als die deutsche Belagerung Leningrads. Der Krieg in Jugoslawien, auch das muss bedacht werden, hat deutlich länger gedauert als der Zweite Weltkrieg.

An dieser Stelle möchte ich das Augenmerk auf die Haltung der Deutschen gegenüber dem Kriegsgeschehen in Jugoslawien richten und die Frage stellen, ob ich, ob wir alle diese schlimmen Ereignisse aus unserer deutschen Perspektive überhaupt angemessen wahrgenommen und unsere Folgerungen daraus gezogen haben. In einigen Beiträgen dieses Bandes ist die Wut über die Geschehnisse thematisiert worden. Ich habe aber meine Zweifel, ob dieses Gefühl der Wut auch in der deutschen Reaktion anzutreffen war. Für viele, auch für mich persönlich, gilt, dass die Ereignisse auf dem Balkan so unverständlich waren, dass es nicht einmal für angemessene Empörung reichte. Waren wir zu sehr mit der gerade erst errungenen deutschen Einheit und den Demokratiebewegungen in Mittel- und Osteuropa beschäftigt, um noch Interesse für diesen europäischen Krieg aufbringen zu können? Jedenfalls ist es noch heute bemerkenswert, dass zwei andere europäische Staaten zerfielen, ohne dass es zu nennenswertem Blutvergießen kam, nämlich die Sowjetunion und die Tschechoslowakei.

Nachdem 1993 das ICTY eingerichtet worden war, dauerte die Belagerung Sarajevos weiter an. Zwei Jahre später wurden die Massaker von Srebrenica und Žepa verübt, und 1999, weitere vier Jahre später, fand der Krieg im Kosovo statt, der Tausende von Toten forderte und 800.000 Menschen aus dem Land trieb. Also lässt sich die Schlussfolgerung ziehen, dass die Einrichtung eines Tribunals allein weder Kriege beendet noch zukünftige Kriegsverbrechen verhindert. Es gab damals die Hoffnung, dass ein solches Tribunal zur Versöhnung beitragen kann – »reconciliation« taucht in politischen und gesellschaftlichen Debatten als Ziel immer wieder auf. Doch wie kann unter solch extremen Umständen, wie sie im Krieg herrschen, eigentlich Versöhnung stattfinden? Die ethnische Säuberung war in weitesten Teilen erfolgreich, sie hat stattgefunden und alles verändert. Die Nachbarn, die sich wieder hätten versöhnen können, sind entweder tot oder leben nicht mehr am gleichen Ort, so dass eine Versöhnung kaum möglich ist.

In Deutschland, ich ziehe zur Erinnerung immer wieder diesen Vergleich heran, war die Lage nach dem Krieg ähnlich. Auch hier konnte es keine wirkliche Versöhnung geben, da die Deutschen in der Hitler-Zeit die Juden umgebracht hatten. Versöhnung kann es nur unter Überlebenden geben, und Vergebung kann nur dann geschehen, wenn der Vergebende auf der Opferseite steht. Deswegen ist meine Hoffnung, dass im Bereich des früheren Jugoslawien ein lang anhaltender Prozess der Versöhnung stattfindet, sehr gering. Die Hoffnung ruht, wie in Deutschland, eher auf den nächsten Generationen, die vielleicht irgendwann darüber nachdenken, was wirklich passiert ist, welchen Beitrag ihre Eltern oder Großeltern auf dieser oder jener Seite geleistet haben und welche Schuld sie auf sich geladen haben.

In diesem Zusammenhang ist die Arbeit des Tribunals jedoch ausgesprochen wichtig, weil es dort Tatsachenfeststellungen gibt und dokumentierendes Material archiviert wird. Ein typisches Verfahren, an dem ich beteiligt war, hat drei Jahre gedauert. In dieser Zeit haben wir 130 Zeugen gehört, was 18.000 Seiten Protokoll ausmacht. 3.000 Dokumente haben wir entgegengenommen und als Beweismittel zugelassen. Das ist die Basis einer Beurteilung der Vorwürfe gegen einen Angeklagten. Insgesamt sind im elektronischen Archiv des Tribunals etwa 9 Millionen Dokumente enthalten. Mittlerweile ersticken wir beinahe im Material, aber die Staatsanwaltschaft muss schließlich ihren Fall präsentieren, damit wir auf dieser Grundlage und auf Basis der Dokumente, die die Verteidigung vorlegt, die juristischen Schlussfolgerungen ziehen können.

Der Arbeitsalltag ist nur in dem Maße politisch, wie jedes Gericht politisch ist. Justiz ist immer politisch, Recht ist politisch, aber der juristische Arbeitsalltag darf nicht von politischen Einflüssen abhängig sein, wie ich betonen möchte. Immer wieder wird gesagt, das Tribunal sei ein Instrument der internationalen Gemeinschaft gegen Serbien oder gegen Kroatien, gegen eine Volksgruppe oder Nation, doch dieses Urteil bildet unseren Arbeitsalltag nicht richtig ab. Mein Arbeitsalltag ist vielmehr mit dem eines Richters an einer großen Strafkammer eines Landgerichts in Deutschland vergleichbar. Die jeweils drei Richter einer Strafkammer des ICTY sind dabei auf die Mitarbeiter angewiesen, die uns mit aller Kraft assistieren, weil die Aufgabe durch die Richter allein gar nicht zu bewältigen ist. Wir haben unsere Regularien und unseren beruflichen juristischen Alltag, und das schützt uns vor manchen schockierenden und emotional tief belastenden Dingen.

Wir sind im Übrigen kein europäisches Gericht. Nicht Europa ist repräsentiert in unserem Tribunal, sondern es ist ein von den Vereinten Nationen eingesetztes Gericht. Dort sind derzeit insgesamt 18 Richter aus vielen Teilen der Welt präsent, z. B. aus China, aus den Vereinigten Staaten von Amerika, aus Rußland, aber auch aus Malta, Belgien, Pakistan, Trinidad und Tobago, aus Deutschland und Südafrika. Dies soll deutlich machen, dass es sich bei diesen Nationen eben nicht um »Siegermächte« handelt.

Wir haben ein geregeltes Gerichtsverfahren, das für Kontinentaleuropäer erst einmal sehr fremd ist, weil es sich an die angloamerikanische Verfahrenspraxis anlehnt, was ich sehr bedauere, und nicht so sehr kontinental-europäisch geprägt ist. Aber auch diese Praxis funktioniert, und letztlich ist es beim Umfang dieser Verfahren entscheidend, dass überhaupt eine Methode gefunden wird, um auf eine formalisierte Weise die umfangreichen Aufgaben zu bewältigen. So haben wir Verfahrensregeln, die den Umgang mit den am Prozess Beteiligten festlegen: Wir schütteln weder mit den Angeklagten die Hände noch mit Verteidigern oder Staatsanwälten, aber wir gehen höflich miteinander um, denn eine gute, ruhige Atmosphäre in einem Gerichtssaal ist in jedem Strafprozess die Voraussetzung, um der Wahrheit wenigstens ein bisschen auf die Spur zu kommen. Herrscht keine ruhige Atmosphäre mit höflichen Umgangsformen vor, sondern ein aufgebrachter und aufgeregter Verhandlungston, ist es kaum möglich, der Wahrheit näherzukommen. Wenn wir als Richter eintreten, erheben sich alle. Alle verneigen sich vor dem Gericht, und wir verneigen uns vor allen anderen, was ein bemerkenswertes, mir aus Deutschland so nicht bekanntes Ritual ist, das die Geste ausdrückt: »Lasst es uns gemeinsam versuchen«. Die meisten Angeklagten werden in diese Praxis miteingeschlossen, auch sie stehen auf, auch wenn es welche unter ihnen gibt, die ihre Probleme damit haben und diese auch zeigen.

Wir hören dem Unmittelbarkeitsprinzip folgend Zeugen an, das, jedenfalls weitgehend, auch bei uns herrscht, mit den nötigen Einschränkungen, um das Verfahren nicht zu sehr in die Länge zu ziehen. Auch manche Zeugenaussagen, die früher getätigt worden sind, werden schriftlich als Beweismittel zugelassen. In jedem Verfahren werden 100, 200 oder noch mehr Zeugen gehört. Unsere Aufgabe besteht darin, zwei verschiedene Sachverhalte festzustellen. Zum einen muss ermittelt werden, welche Dinge in diesem Dorf oder in jener Stadt passiert sind, und zum anderen muss die Verbindung dieser schrecklichen Massaker zum individuellen Angeklagten, der in einem spezifischen Verfahren vor Gericht steht, hergestellt werden. Hier gilt es herauszufinden, welcher Art die Befehlskette war und an welchen Taten der Angeklagte beteiligt war. Um diese Informationen zu erlangen, sind Zeugen vonnöten, die über Interna reden, was die Verhandlungssituation manchmal sehr kompliziert. Diese Personen sagen nun über ihre ehemaligen Vorgesetzten und deren Beteiligung an bestimmten Verbrechen aus, was für die Betroffenen oft nicht einfach ist. Deswegen sind in solchen Fällen manchmal auch intensive Schutzmaßnahmen erforderlich.

Schließlich sagen vor allem Opfer aus, unter anderem die Überlebenden eines Massakers. Ich möchte zwei Beispiele nennen: Im ersten Fall sagt eine Frau aus, die zu einer Familie gehört, die ihr Gebäude für die OSZE-Beobachtermission in einem Dorf im Kosovo vermietet hatte. Unmittelbar vor Ausbruch des Kosovo-Krieges ist die OSZE mit ihren Beobachtern abgezogen, worauf die gesamte Familie, 42 Menschen, an einem Tag ermordet wurde – manche direkt noch auf der Straße, während die anderen in eine Pizzeria getrieben wurden, wo sie mit Handgranaten beworfen, mit Maschinenpistolen beschossen und mit Brandsätzen angezündet worden sind. Ein Polizeilastwagen hat die Leichen daraufhin abgeholt und weggeschafft. Zwei Frauen in diesem Leichenberg auf dem Lastwagen lebten noch und es gelang ihnen, sich vom Lastwagen fallen zu lassen. Wenn eine solche Frau dann vor einem sitzt und darüber berichtet, ist das ein Moment, in dem man realisiert, warum man als Richter in Den Haag ist.

Das zweite Beispiel ist das einer jungen Frau: Diese Kosovo-Albanerin, die als Kunststudentin in England lebt und fließend englisch spricht, war 24, als sie als Zeugin auftrat. Als 14-jährige, zehn Jahre zuvor, wurde sie mit ihrer ganzen Familie von einer paramilitärischen Einheit, den sogenannten *Scorpions*, aufgereiht und anschließend unter Beschuss genommen. Als das Mädchen wieder aus ihrer Ohnmacht erwachte, war die Großmutter verstümmelt, die Mutter und alle Geschwister waren tot, während nur ein Vetter überlebt hatte. Wenn man als Richter einer solchen Zeugin gegenübersitzt, die unter Tränen, aber mit ruhiger Stimme berichtet, was ihr widerfahren ist, und dann am Schluss sagt: »Und vielen Dank, dass Sie mir zugehört haben; dass ich meine Geschichte erzählen konnte. Und wenn Sie mich brauchen, komme ich wieder« – dann stockt einem der Atem, auch im Gericht.

An dieser Stelle möchte ich noch einmal auf die deutsche Geschichte zurückkommen. Nach 1945 haben die Deutschen den Opfern nicht zugehört, weil kaum jemand mit der Wahrheit behelligt werden wollte. Erst der Auschwitzprozess zu Beginn der 60er Jahre – und er ist gegen Widerstand der Justizbehörden vom damaligen Generalstaatsanwalt Fritz Bauer in Hessen durchgesetzt worden – hat letztlich dazu geführt, dass dieses Verbrechen überhaupt zum Thema wurde.

Als letzter Punkt sei noch die Transparenz der Verfahren angesprochen: Unser Strafgerichtshof arbeitet auf eine transparente Weise, wie es sie sonst meiner Einschätzung nach nirgendwo gibt. Zum Gerichtsgebäude gehört nicht nur der Zuhörerraum, die *public gallery*, die bei Cornelia Vismann gut beschrieben wird.[6] Dieser befindet sich hinter schusssicheren Glasscheiben, was neben Sicherheitsaspekten den weiteren Vorteil hat, dass sich die Zuschauer frei bewegen können, ohne dass das Verfahren gestört wird. Aber das Entscheidende ist, und das ist bemerkenswert, die Übertragung aller Verfahren im Internet. Das ICTY verfügt über drei Gerichtssäle, aus denen alles im Internet übertragen wird, abgesehen von den Aussagen, die zum Schutz von Beteiligten oder zur Wahrung der erforderlichen Vertraulichkeit in *closed session* abgehalten werden müssen. Die Übertragung erfolgt mit 30-minütiger Verzögerung, die dazu dient, dass nicht – und das passiert immer wieder – ein geschützter Name genannt wird, zum Beispiel von einer Person, die eine neue Identität angenommen hat und in einem anderen Land lebt. Um diesen Zeugen zu schützen, wird dann vor der Übertragung sowohl dort als auch im Protokoll, sein Name gestrichen. Dadurch wird die größte Transparenz hergestellt, die man sich vorstellen kann. Die Verfahren können auf der ganzen Welt verfolgt werden, was nach meinen Informationen im früheren Jugoslawien häufig geschieht – sowohl von Täterkreisen als auch von Opferkreisen.

Ich möchte hinzufügen, dass demgenüber die Anwesenheit des Fernsehens im Gerichtssaal eine höchstproblematische Sache ist, vor allem in einem Strafgerichtssaal. In Deutschland habe ich immer dagegen gekämpft – und würde auch weiterhin dagegen kämpfen, dass Fernsehanstalten Zugang erhalten. Diese sind nicht an der Übertragung ganzer Verfahren, also u. a. auch langweiliger Teile, oder an einer vollständigen Dokumentation interessiert: Sie brauchen das Bild vom angeklagten Kinderschänder oder Kriegsverbrecher, um dieses für ein Zwei-Minuten-Statement in den Abendnachrichten zu verwenden. Diese Praxis ist katastrophal für ein geordnetes Gerichtsverfahren, weswegen das ICTY anders vorgeht. Wir lassen keine Fernsehanstalten zu, sondern es ist das gerichts-

---

6 Vgl. Vismann: Medien der Rechtsprechung, S. 333f.

eigene System, das alles mit fünf, sechs oder sieben Kameras im Raum aufzeichnet. Die jeweilige sprechende Person ist zu sehen, manchmal auch die Totale des Gerichtssaals. Die Fernsehanstalten können sich dann aus diesem Material bedienen. Natürlich ist es zunächst einmal sehr langweilig, wenn etwa ein Militärexperte, ein Sachverständiger tagelang über seine Dokumentenanalyse oder über ballistische Feststellungen berichtet. Doch auch wenn diese Berichte für Außenstehende kaum zu verstehen sind, ist das Entscheidende, dass die Dokumentation vollständig ist. Alle unsere Dokumente, seien es Anträge, Entscheidungen oder Zwischenentscheidungen, sind im Internet einsehbar. Für jedes Verfahren gibt es einen Ordner, in dem das Material abrufbar ist.

Ich habe versucht darzustellen, dass wir eine differenzierte Wahrheitsfindung haben und nach differenzierter Gerechtigkeit streben; und dass jemand nicht schon aufgrund der Tatsache verurteilt wird, dass er angeklagt ist und in den Zeitungen schon als Täter ausgemacht wurde. Vielmehr kann nur das, was im Gerichtssaal präsentiert und als Beweismittel vorgelegt wird, zu einer Verurteilung und zu einer Feststellung der Schuld und zu Strafe führen. Damit kann wenigstens ein kleiner Beitrag zum Ende der Straflosigkeit geleistet werden. Kriege und Kriegsverbrechen werden zwar dadurch nicht abgeschafft, wie überhaupt durch Strafrecht und durch strafrechtliche Institutionen wie Strafgerichte Kriminalität nicht abgeschafft werden kann. In Deutschland werden täglich Straftaten begangen, obwohl wir ein Strafgesetzbuch und Strafgerichte haben. Aber es besteht jetzt die Chance, dass der eine oder andere von denen, die schwerste Kriegsverbrechen begehen, gefasst und zur Rechenschaft gezogen wird. Das bedeutet letztlich einen Sieg für das Recht und den Rechtsstaat.

Literatur

Hankel, Gerd/Gerhard Stuby: Die Aufarbeitung von Verbrechen durch internationale Strafgerichte, in: Petra Bock/Edgar Wolfrum (Hg.): Umkämpfte Vergangenheit. Geschichtsbilder, Erinnerung und Vergangenheitspolitik im internationalen Vergleich, Göttingen 1999, S. 247–268.

Jackson, Robert H: Grundlegende Rede, vorgetragen im Namen der Vereinigten Staaten von Amerika von Robert H. Jackson; Hauptanklagevertreter der USA beim Internationalen Militärgerichtshof zu Nürnberg, Frankfurt a. M. 1946.

Vismann, Cornelia: Medien der Rechtsprechung, Frankfurt a. M. 2011.

Internetquellen

Security Council: Resolution 808, 22. Februar 1993, http://www.un.org/ga/search/view_doc.asp?symbol=S/RES/808(1993), (letzter Aufruf: 06.05.2013).

Security Council: Resolution 827, 25. Mai 1993, http://www.un.org/ga/search/view_doc.asp?symbol=S/RES/827(1993), (letzter Aufruf: 06.05.2013).

Statut des Internationalen Strafgerichtshofs für das ehemalige Jugoslawien, http://www.icls.de/dokumente/icty_statut_dt.pdf (letzter Aufruf: 06.05.2013).

Zweiter Teil

Lokale Ungerechtigkeit, Kultur
und globales Recht: Tribunale als
Globalisierungsphänomen

Andreas Th. Müller

International Criminal Tribunals as a Phenomenon of Globalization

To say that international criminal tribunals are a »phenomenon of globalization« seems somewhat stating the obvious. By their very nature, these tribunals transcend borders and States and thus contribute to what is commonly (and cursorily) referred to as »globalization«. This becomes most visible with regard to the International Criminal Court (ICC) in The Hague which today stands, without doubt, as the epitome of international criminal law. With Côte d'Ivoire joining in February 2013, the Court has, at present, 122 Member States.[1] This represents roughly two thirds of the overall number of States of 190 and something, depending on whom one counts in. Thus, the ICC appears to provide an excellent example for a »global« organization or, at least, for an organization with global vocation and aspiration: The Court's declared goal is to cover the whole planet.[2] The whole issue seems to be a no-brainer, but it will not come not as a surprise that things are not as straightforward as that.

It is well worth looking more carefully into the question whether and to what extent international criminal tribunals in general and the ICC in particular may seriously be called a »phenomenon of globalization«. In tackling this question, we shall first make two preliminary remarks in order to delimit the scope of the analysis (I.). On this basis, we shall explore various dimensions of globalization of and through the ICC (II.). At the same time, it must be asked where and how the globalist aspirations of the ICC and international criminal justice fail with a view to identifying limitations and pitfalls of globalization in the context of international criminal tribunals (III.). This will permit to draw some conclusions as to the role and potential of international criminal tribunals as a phenomenon of globalization (IV.).

---

[1] See http://www.icc-cpi.int/en_menus/asp/states%20parties/Pages/the%20states%20parties%20to%20the%20rome%20statute.aspx (last accessed: 16.07.2013).
[2] As to the different dimensions of this claim see *infra* II.

I. Preliminary remarks

The subject-matter of the present contribution spans a wide range of questions. It is evident that, due to space restrictions, we cannot delve into them in the necessary degree here.[3] Hence, it is necessary to restrict the scope of the subsequent analysis to the core aspects of the problem and to rather give a panoramic view of the issues at stake which will, admittedly, often not do justice to the complexity and intricacies of the phenomenon. To this effect, the present article will, on the one hand, primarily focus on the ICC as the »flagship« of contemporary international criminal law. On the other hand, it will depart from a rather rough, common-sense concept of globalization, without elaborating much on the broad debate which has emerged on this subject over the last twenty years.

1. The ICC as the flagship of international criminal law

As has been said, the following remarks will be limited, for the most part, to the ICC. It is, however, well known that the landscape of international criminal tribunals is far more colorful and complex than that. This holds true in a both *diachronic* and *synchronic* perspective.

First, whilst international criminal law is a relatively young discipline, it can meanwhile look back on a non-negligible amount of history. Leaving aside (purported) historical predecessors such as the trial against Peter von Hagenbach in the late 15th century, the phenomenon of international criminal justice dates back to the beginning of the 20th century.[4] Importantly, Art. 227 of the Treaty of Versailles provided that the Allied and Associated Powers (i.e. the victorious powers in the First World War) had the »right [...] to bring before military tribunals persons accused of having committed acts in violation of the laws and customs of war«.[5] Moreover, the Allies »publicly arraign[ed] William II of Hohenzollern, formerly German Emperor, for a supreme offence against international morality and the sanctity of treaties«.[6]

While the latter tribunal never came into existence due to the Netherlands' refusal to extradite the former »Kaiser«, some twenty-five years later before the International Military Tribunal at Nuremberg, leading figures of the »German axis« were prosecuted and convicted for the Nazi aggression as well as war crimes

---

[3] See in general Müller: Der Internationale Strafgerichtshof, pp. 105 et seqq., with further references.

[4] Ibid., p. 22.

[5] Treaty of Peace between the Allied and Associated Powers and Germany of 28 June 1919, Part VII: Penalties.

[6] Ibid., Art. 228.

and crimes against humanity committed during the Second World War. Similarly, the International Military Tribunal for the Far East, the so-called Tokyo War Crimes Tribunal, charged Japanese political and military leaders with crimes of starting and waging the war in the Pacific.

Indeed, it is since the experience of Nuremberg and, to a lesser extent, Tokyo that international criminal law, both substantively and institutionally speaking, has gained sufficiently clear contours so as to qualify as paradigm or role model of contemporary international criminal tribunals in a stricter sense. Whilst the former tribunals' *substantive* heritage has been famously enshrined in the Nuremberg principles[7], on the *institutional* plane, international criminal law calls for a tribunal to have a legal basis transcending one single State, to be equipped with (at least also) international judges and prosecutors and to operate on the basis of an international law of criminal procedure. This held true in regard to both the Nuremberg and the Tokyo tribunals to a considerable extent, irrespective of their pitfalls and flaws which cannot be further addressed here.

Alas, these were *ad hoc* bodies only. In an initial phase, there were ambitious efforts to transform the moral impetus of the experience of war and dictatorship into concrete legal action for a global criminal jurisdiction. Yet, the Cold War brought these efforts to a halt. This notably became manifest in the failed attempts to agree on a definition of the crime of aggression although it was unanimously perceived as the gravest possible violation of the prohibition of the use of force as the paramount principle of the UN Charter[8] and was characterized by the Nuremberg tribunal as »the supreme international crime, differing only from other war crimes in that it contains within itself the accumulated evil of the whole«.[9]

It was only after the end of the Cold War that the paralyzed (albeit never completely dead) movement for a global codification of international criminal law and, related to it, for the establishment of a universal International Criminal Court gained new momentum. Trinidad and Tobago's initiative in the General Assembly in 1989 is well-known as the triggering event in that regard.[10] In terms of the afore-mentioned synchronic perspective, it is worthwhile emphasizing that, even though the efforts in the course of the »renaissance« of international criminal law in the early 1990ies were focused on the creation of the ICC, the decisive impetus for its creation came from a different corner – namely from its elder siblings, as it were.

---

[7] Principles of International Law Recognized in the Charter of the Nürnberg Tribunal and in the Judgment of the Tribunal, Text adopted by the International Law Commission at its 2nd session, in 1950, and submitted to the General Assembly as a part of the Commission's report covering the work of that session.

[8] See Art. 2 para. 4 and Art. 39 of the Charter of the United Nations of 26 June 1945.

[9] IMT Judgment, p. 426.

[10] See, e. g., Müller: Der Internationale Strafgerichtshof, p. 53, with further references.

By *fiat* of the Security Council, two so-called *ad hoc* tribunals were created in 1993 and 1994, respectively, one for the former Yugoslavia (ICTY) and the other for Rwanda (ICTR),[11] the first international criminal courts after Nuremberg and Tokyo. When creating these tribunals, the Security Council relied on its powers under Chapter VII of the UN Charter. This signifies that the tribunals were created as subsidiary bodies of the Council in order to safeguard and restore international peace and security[12]: international justice in the service of international peace, an intricate relationship, to say the least.

Without elaborating on the topic, one will have to admit that the creation of the *ad hoc* tribunals was less of a heroic story, but rather a substitute, and fig leaf, for the unwillingness of the Western powers to become involved in the Balkans and in Rwanda militarily. Nonetheless, in spite of their initial defects and various built-in limitations, the two tribunals can offer a remarkable record. For instance, the ICTY could eventually get hold of all persons accused by it, including former Yugoslav President Slobodan Milošević who died in custody, and in recent years Bosnian Serb leaders Radovan Karadžić and Ratko Mladić who are still standing trial in The Hague. For several years, the tribunals have been in a process of »phasing out« and they have been recently been complemented by the so-called International Residual Mechanism for International Criminal Tribunals[13] which will eventually replace the former tribunals once they have finally disposed of the pending cases.

Yet, the landscape of contemporary international criminal tribunals is even more variegated, as it has become populated by a considerable number of further *specialized* tribunals, generally referred to as *hybrid* or *internationalized* tribunals.[14] This relates to the fact that they are not based on Security Council authorization, but mostly on a treaty between the UN and the affected State or, alternatively, on domestic legislation. Their mixed legal basis, both in international and domestic law, is often mirrored on the procedural level by a hybrid of international and domestic procedural laws and by judges and prosecutors recruited both from the international and the domestic realm. One might mention in this context the Special Court for Sierra Leone, the Extraordinary Chambers in the Courts of Cambodia, the Special Panels for Serious Crimes in East Timor, the Iraqi High Tribunal, the War Crimes Chamber for Bosnia and Herzegovina, the International

---

[11] Security Council Resolution 827 of 25 May 1993; Security Council Resolution 955 of 8 November 1994.

[12] See Arts. 39 and 41 of the UN Charter (note 8) as well as the preambular paragraphs of the resolutions cited in the previous footnote.

[13] Security Council Resolution 1966 of 22 December 2010.

[14] See, for instance, Cassese: International Criminal Law, pp. 330 et seqq.; Werle: Principles of International Criminal Law, p. 26; Romano et al.: Internationalized Criminal Courts; Schabas: UN International Criminal Tribunals; Cohen: »Hybrid« Justice; Dickinson: The Promise of Hybrid Courts.

Judges and Prosecutors Programme in Kosovo and, most recently, the Special Tribunal for Lebanon. They would all deserve to be analyzed in their own right, even more so since when asking for their »global« character or potential, their hybrid or »semi-international« design would entail conclusions well different from the case of the ICC on which the present contribution focuses.

After all, the ICC in The Hague has certainly become the towering actor in the panorama of international criminal tribunals. In the powerful *renaissance* of international criminal law in the wake of the end of the Cold War, the drafting efforts could heavily draw upon the rich preparatory work done. Nonetheless, the Rome Conference of 15 June – 17 July 1998 leading to the adoption of the Rome Statute of the ICC[15] must be considered a huge achievement and success. The ICC is not only the product of a diplomatic inter-State conference, but of many years of negotiations – and a lot of lobbying, not the least from a well-organized network of several hundreds of non-governmental organizations in more than 150 countries[16] – in itself a remarkable manifestation of an emerging »global civil society« and in that sense of globalization. Finally, on 1 July 2002, the long longed-for Statute entered into force, and the Court came into existence. In 2010, as foreseen by the Statute, a review conference took place in Kampala, Uganda, which brought several amendments to the Rome Statute, most importantly including the perspective that the crime of aggression – which has been on the table since the early days of William II. and notably the Nuremberg Charter's »crimes against peace« – finally becomes an operative part of international criminal law.[17]

What categorically distinguishes the ICC from both *ad hoc* and hybrid tribunals is its *permanent* and *general* character. Whereas the other instances of international criminal tribunals are created to address a specific situation or conflict and a particular set of crimes, the ICC's jurisdiction in principle is neither limited in time nor in space. This testifies to a claim of universality which cannot be found with respect to the specialized criminal tribunals. In addition, while the latter are, by definition, *ex post facto* courts established after international crimes have been committed, the ICC shall, ideally speaking, become effective in an *ex ante*, i.e. preventive perspective.

In view of these particular features, the ICC presents itself as a particularly promising object for exploring whether, and in which respects, international criminal tribunals constitute phenomena of globalization. As we shall see in the following, a closer look at the ICC is prone to reveal both: remarkable potentials as well as pitfalls and limitations.

---

[15] Rome Statute of the International Criminal Court of 17 July 1998.
[16] See the website of the Coalition for the International Criminal Court; http://www.iccnow.org/?mod=coalition (last accessed: 16.07.2013).
[17] See *infra* III.1.

2. Globalization as a catchword and contrast term

Quite evidently, also the use of the term »globalization« begs for explanation. To be sure, there is no lack of attempts to define, and circumscribe, this concept which has become subject to such inflationary use in recent years. One should not expect, however, from the present article an in-depth discussion of the concept of globalization, its merits and disadvantages. Many will find it hard or even impossible to provide a comprehensive definition of the concept, but might feel tempted to take refuge to US Supreme Court Justice Potter Stewart's famous test to identify pornography: »I know it when I see it.«[18] Nonetheless, some conceptual clarifications may still be in place.

First, the concept of »globalization«— in spite of, but also precisely because of its often vague and indeterminate character – may serve as a *catchword* to cover, in the broadest sense, the manifold developments transcending the traditional and familiar framework of the nation State on such different levels as the economy, media, culture, information – and last but not least the law. In that sense, it refers more to a process than to a result. It is thus not a *static*, but a *dynamic* concept.

By relying on this concept, one does not claim, however, that there is a uniform and continuous process towards more globality. On the contrary, globalization is accompanied by, and gives rise to, multifaceted counter-dynamics and diametrical tendencies. Much has been said, for instance, on processes of localization going hand in hand with globalization,[19] and this also holds true in regard to international criminal justice; we shall come back to this aspect at the end of the present contribution.[20] Moreover, by using the concept of globalization in regard to the present world, one does not necessarily claim that there were no other times in human history with a similar or at least relevant degree of »globalization«.

In addition to being a convenient catch-all expression to describe a complex phenomenon, the term »globalization« maybe also is useful, somewhat paradoxically, in spite of and precisely because of not being a legal term of art. It is striking that in the Rome Statute the term »global« does not even appear a single time. Yet, this is far from being a weakness: It makes the concept equidistant, as it were, to concepts which are commonly used in the legal discourse and which emphasize different aspects of growing interaction transcending the limits of nation States. In this very sense, globalization may also work as a valuable *contrast term*, thus allowing to avoid alternative terms that may have the disadvantage of directing one's attention too much towards one feature of globalization at the cost of others.

Bearing this in mind, globalization may include, for instance, processes of *in-*

---

[18] Concurring Opinion in *Jacobellis v. Ohio*, 378 U.S. 184 (1986).
[19] Sometimes the term »glocalization« is used to denote this intricate relationship.
[20] See *infra* III.6.

ternationalization. They already refer to processes of transcending political, economic, social, cultural borders, but ultimately remain in the logic of traditional inter-State cooperation. In contrast, *transnationalism* leaves this corset behind and underscores the increasing importance of non-State actors such as transnational enterprises, international non-governmental organizations and social networks and the internet. Others, seeking to go even further, speak of processes of *universalization* and thus refer to genuinely universal and in that sense global values and aspirations that become – or should become – manifest in the legal context. Related to this, some legal scholars have identified a process of *humanization* of international law.[21] This does not only mean that the individual human person is increasingly seen as the normative reference point *par excellence* of international law[22], but that international law is deemed to be a project of all of humanity rather than the community of States.[23] Such dynamics correspond to the move of the human being as a mere object to a (or even the) subject of international law, as famously held in the *Tadić* case of the ICTY:

»[After] a period when sovereignty stood as a sacrosanct and unassailable attribute of statehood, recently this concept has suffered progressive erosion at the hands of the more liberal forces at work in the democratic societies, particularly in the field of human rights. [...] A State-sovereignty-oriented approach has been gradually supplanted by a human-being-oriented approach. Gradually the maxim of Roman law *hominum causa omne jus constitutum est* (all law is created for the benefit of human beings) has gained a firm foothold in the international community as well.«[24]

All of the perspectives mentioned before relate, to a greater or lesser extent, to processes and phenomena of globalization in a wider sense. However, not everything that looks global from outside, does necessarily translate into the same type of transcending borders. To make the obvious example: As an international organization based on an international treaty with now 122 Member States, the ICC is a prime example of (traditional) international cooperation. At the same time, much of the normative substance of the ICC derives from universal notions, as to be explained subsequently. It is therefore necessary to distinguish different aspects or dimensions of globalization in regard to the ICC.

---

[21] See, e.g., Meron: Humanization of International Law; idem: Humanization of Humanitarian Law; see also Teitel: Humanity's Law.
[22] See notably Peters: Humanity as the A and Ω of Sovereignty.
[23] See in particular Tomuschat: International Law, pp. 161 et seq.; Klabbers/Peters/Ulfstein: The Constitutionalization of International Law.
[24] ICTY, *Prosecutor v. Duško Tadić*, Appeals Chamber, Case No. IT-94-1-AR72, Decision on the Defence Motion for Interlocutory Appeal on Jurisdiction, 2 October 1995, 35 ILM (1996) 50, paras. 55 and 97, referring to a proverb that can be traced back as far as Hermogenianus: Iuris epitomae, Liber I, Digests 1.5.2.

II. Dimensions of »globalization« with respect to the ICC

The ICC can be said to reflect processes of globalization in view of a series of dimensions. In the following we shall notably address its aspiration for global membership (1.), the shared experience of suffering and the community of fate built thereupon as a foundational experience of the project of international criminal law (2.), globalization in terms of recognizing and agreeing to fight international crimes (3.) as well as globalization of procedural law (4.) and of legal cultures more generally (5.), as embodied in the Statute of the ICC.

1. Aspiration for global membership

A first aspect of globalization in regard to the ICC worth of being addressed is its aspiration for global membership. This becomes manifest in Art. 125 para. 3 of the Rome Statute according to which it is »open to accession by all States«. It has already been mentioned that, at present, the Court has 122 Members States which accounts for almost two thirds of the overall number of States.

Yet, in spite of the Statute's universal ambitions, it must not be forgotten that among those that have *not* joined the ICC are such powerful States as the United States, Russia, China (i.e. three of the P 5, the permanent members of the UN Security Council) as well as India, Pakistan, Indonesia, and Turkey; they stand aside or display open reservation vis-à-vis the Court (as, for instance, the US administration during the Bush junior administration). To this adds the deliberate absence of most Muslim-majority States; we shall come back to this aspect later.[25] Hence, quite strikingly, in terms of world population, more than half of humanity is located outside the territorial scope of application of the Rome Statute. The same holds true for those areas which are most prone to be affected by armed conflict and civil war, i.e. those very areas that would arguably deserve to come under the »protective umbrella« of the ICC most urgently.

Against this background, the question arises how representative the ICC actually is (or will be) of the global community and what should serve as a standard in that regard. It would be short-sighted, however, to assess the degree of globalization of, and through, the ICC exclusively or even primarily by the number and importance of its States Parties. There are numerous other aspects which seem relevant in this regard.

---

[25] See *infra* III.5.

2. *Globalization of the experience of suffering: a global community of fate*

A second characteristic aspect of the globalizing character of the ICC is the fact that it expressly grounds itself on a shared experience of suffering. This becomes manifest in a place in the Rome Statute that could hardly be more prominent, namely in the first two paragraphs of its Preamble and thus the opening fanfare or rather: the *opening lamentation* of the Statute.

»The State Parties to this Statute,

Conscious that *all* peoples are *united by common bonds*, their cultures pieced together in a shared heritage, and concerned that this *delicate mosaic* may be *shattered at any time*,

Mindful that during this century *millions* of children, women and men have been *victims of unimaginable atrocities* that *deeply shock the conscience of mankind*«.[26]

This is the logic of the argument: (a) *All* peoples – in itself a universalist claim as »the States Parties« of the ICC, being aware that they form part of the whole, invoke, and claim to act on behalf of, the entirety of the community of States and peoples – share an experience of *common bonds*. Yet, (b) this experience is intimately and inextricably linked to the experience of the *fragility* of these common bonds. The metaphor of the »delicate mosaic [that] may be shattered at any time« (obviously going back to a proposal of the representative of Andorra[27]) is a very powerful one indeed.

Even more, (c) the shared experience is not one of fragility only. It is also and particularly an experience of *actual breaking up and destruction* of those bonds, of large-scale murder, torture, rape and violence. It is quite sobering that the first truly global aspect arising from the Rome Statute is a radically *negative* one, namely the experience of suffering and destruction. This »common« experience does not so much consist in the fact that all of us have experienced certain types of suffering in our lives, i.e. toothache, illness or the loss of close relatives, i.e., a *parallel*, but not a *shared* experience. In contrast, the Preamble articulates an actually shared suffering in the sense that the overwhelming *quantitative* (»millions of ...«) and *qualitative* (»unimaginable atrocities«) character of the suffering – we shall come back to these two aspects in the following sub-section – are of a dimension to shock the conscience of humankind, i.e. of all of us.

This gives rise to an experience of *compassion* in the literal sense: suffering together, shared suffering. Most remarkably, Immanuel Kant has already expressed this idea two centuries ago in his famous essay on *Perpetual Peace* where he acknowledges that »the narrower or wider community of the peoples of the earth has developed so far that a violation of rights in one place is felt throughout the

---

[26] Emphasis added.
[27] See Bourdon: La Cour pénale internationale, p. 27.

world«.²⁸ It does not come by accident that, for Kant, this constitutes the foundational insight on which to ground the concept of *world citizenship*.²⁹ It is precisely the same logic which the ICC Preamble draws upon, and this qualifies it as an institution of world citizenship: It is part and parcel of our *conscience collective* that all human beings may, in principle, qualify both as perpetrators and victims of unimaginable atrocities, that these atrocities affect all of us, if only indirectly, and that it is our shared responsibility to eliminate and avert them. Thus, the Preamble moves beyond the traditional international law calculus of States and peoples and opens up the space of humankind and cosmopolitanism, i.e. a truly global and universal perspective.

Humanity therefore constitutes a *community of fate*³⁰, on the brink of atrocities and destruction, but also with the possibility, and responsibility, to take the future in our hands. Thus, the universally shared experience of large-scale suffering inflicted by man upon man has the potential to serve as a trigger, a catalyst. This is the Preamble's rhetoric: The initial *lamentatio* turns into the *exhortatio* for further action. Such move from reminding and assuring oneself of crimes so momentous that they affect the entire globe and all humankind, to collective worldwide action is not unique to the Rome Statute. We can find the very same idea already half a century earlier in no less a treaty than the UN Charter. Once again in a most prominent place, »We the Peoples of the United Nations« articulate their determination »to save succeeding generations from the scourge of war, which twice in our lifetime has brought untold sorrow to mankind«.³¹ The atrocities of World War II and Nazi dictatorship and the Nuremberg response thereto remain the foundational experiences for the ICC and are profoundly intertwined into the normative deep-structure of the Court.

---

28 Kant: Perpetual Peace, Third Definitive Article for a Perpetual Peace.
29 The citation continues: »[T]he idea of a law of world citizenship is no high-flown or exaggerated notion. It is a supplement to the unwritten code of the civil and international law, indispensable for the maintenance of the public human rights and hence also of perpetual peace. One cannot flatter oneself into believing one can approach this peace except under the condition outlined here.«
30 Höffe: Demokratie im Zeitalter der Globalisierung, p. 15.
31 See UN Charter, Preamble, first paragraph (note 8); see also the second and third preambular paragraphs of the Convention on the Prevention and Punishment of the Crime of Genocide of 9 December 1948: »Recognizing that at all periods of history genocide has inflicted great losses on humanity, and Being convinced that, in order to liberate mankind from such an odious scourge, international co-operation is required«.

3. Globalization in terms of recognizing and agreeing to fight international crimes

Furthermore, in the context of the ICC, the call for global action coincides with the call to put an end to *impunity*, in para. 5 of the Preamble. And in para. 4, it reads: »[T]he most serious crimes of concern to the international community as a whole must not go unpunished.«

This has two implications: First, the battle cry of international criminal justice for the end of impunity serves a double purpose: It does not only call for (backward-looking) *punishment* and thus sanctioning of the perpetrators, but also seeks (in a forward-looking manner) to *prevent* further crimes.[32] It merits mention, in this context, that the States Parties to the Genocide Convention equally undertake both »to prevent and to punish« genocide.[33] The preventive aspect becomes even more obvious when we consider the title of the famous 1984 report on the practices of forced disappearance in Argentina: »*nunca más*«, »never again«.[34]

Secondly, it is in these provisions of the Rome Statute where the universal aspirations of the ICC become most obvious: The Court is, as we have seen, called upon to address the »most serious crimes of concern to the international community as a whole«. This phrase can be found in virtually identical terms in the Preamble[35] as well as in Arts. 1 and 5 of the Statute, thus underscoring its importance. It is common knowledge that the ICC has jurisdiction for genocide, crimes against humanity, war crimes – and (since the 2010 Kampala compromise potentially also for) aggression[36], but a closer look at Art. 5 of the Rome Statute strikingly reveals that the jurisdiction of the ICC is first and foremost defined via the »most serious crimes« clause (para. 1) and only then subdivided into the four afore-mentioned crimes (para. 2).

This definition combines two elements: To begin with, there is a certain threshold of *gravity* or *seriousness*. The Court shall only deal with the »most serious« crimes. As indicated above, this seriousness can become manifest both on the *quantitative* (great numbers of victims, *large-scale* crimes) and the *qualitative* level (degree of violation of protected rights and degree of planning, *systemic* crimes), as may be seen in the definitions of the crimes themselves.[37] While no one

---

32 See the fifth preambular paragraph of the Rome Statute.
33 See Art. 1 of the Genocide Convention (note 31); as to preventative element in the Genocide Convention see notably *Application of the Convention on the Prevention and Punishment of the Crime of Genocide* (*Bosnia and Herzegovina* v. *Serbia and Montenegro*), Judgment, 26 February 2007, ICJ Reports 2007, p. 43, paras. 165 and 425 et seqq.
34 CONADEP: Nunca Más.
35 See paras. 4 as well as 9.
36 See *infra* III.1.
37 See, in exemplary fashion, the definition of crimes against humanity which mean, pursuant to Art. 7 para. 1 of the Rome Statute, »any of the following acts when committed as part of a *wide-*

will doubt that the four types of crimes enumerated in Art. 5 of the Rome Statute generally have the potential to be »most serious crimes«, it is well possible that a war crime, while still a grave violation of personal and property rights, will, under the circumstances of a case, still not reach the threshold of the crimes whose seriousness justifies their being prosecuted before the ICC. Correspondingly, the Rome Statute takes precaution that such crimes are not dealt with by the Court.[38]

In addition, the crimes falling within the jurisdiction of the ICC are those »of concern to the international community as a whole«. The phrase is evidently borrowed from, or at least inspired by, Art. 53 of the Vienna Convention on the Law of Treaties and its definition of *jus cogens*.[39] The idea behind using such phrase is that committing those crimes does not solely harm a specific community, people or social, ethnic or religious group, but affects the entire globe and all of humanity. This is most visible with regard to genocide which may be conceived of as an attack on humanity as such; it is therefore with good reason that it is addressed as the »crime of crimes«.[40]

This idea was, for instance, articulated in Hannah Arendt's *Eichmann in Jerusalem*. There, she rejects the view that murder and genocide are, in essence, the same crimes, and adds that in the case of genocide a complete different community is affected by the crime, namely the »order of humanity« is violated:

»[T]hese modern, state-employed mass murderers must be prosecuted because they violated the order of mankind, and not because they killed millions of people. Nothing is more pernicious to an understanding of these new crimes, or stands more in the way of the emergence of an international penal code that could take care of them, than the common illusion that the crime of murder and the crime of genocide are essentially the same, and that the latter therefore is ›no new crime properly speaking.‹ The point of the latter is that an altogether different order is broken and an altogether different community is violated.«[41]

---

spread or *systematic* attack directed against any civilian population, with knowledge of the attack« (emphasis added). See, in a similar vein, Art. 8 para. 1 on war crimes where the ICC shall have jurisdiction »in particular when committed part of a *plan or policy* or as part of a *large-scale* commission of such crimes« (emphasis added).

[38] See in this regard the definitions of crimes as exemplified in the previous footnote as well as the gravity threshold or the *de minimis* rule in Art. 17 para. 1 lit. d which declares a case which is »not of sufficient gravity to justify further action by the Court« inadmissible.

[39] See the definition of a so-called »peremptory norm of general international law (jus cogens)« as »a norm accepted and recognized by the international community of States as a whole as a norm from which no derogation is permitted and which can be modified only by a subsequent norm of general international law having the same character.« It is a remarkable detail that the Vienna Convention uses the wording »international community of States as a whole«, whereas the Rome Statute omits the phrase »the States« and speaks of »international community as a whole«, thus arguably taking a slightly more »universalist« approach.

[40] See, e. g., ICTR, *Prosecutor v. Jean Kambdanda*, Trial Chamber, Case No. ICTR 97-23-S, Judgment and Sentence, 4 September 1998, para. 16. See also the subtitle of the leading commentary on genocide; Schabas: Genocide in International Law.

[41] Arendt: Eichmann in Jerusalem, p. 272.

In a similar vein, Karl Jaspers criticized the Eichmann trial conducted before an Israeli court in Tel Aviv arguing that »[t]he crime against the Jews is at the same time a crime against mankind (*Verbrechen gegen die Menschheit*). Hence, judgment on this crime can only be passed by a judicial body representing mankind.«[42]

Against this background, the essence of universal crimes would then appear to be the element of *laesio humanitatis*[43], the violation of humanity or humankind – both in terms of the sum of all human beings and humanity in every single of them. It is in this very sense that Hannah Arendt critically referred to the »Nuremberg Charter's definition of ›crimes against humanity‹ as ›inhuman acts‹, which were translated into German as ›Verbrechen gegen die Menschlichkeit‹ – as though the Nazis had simply been lacking in human kindness, certainly the understatement of the century.«[44] Seen from the other side and drawing upon a venerable concept of international law, the perpetrator of such crimes makes himself a *hostis humani generis*, i.e. an enemy of humankind.[45] This also represents the cardinal point in which the common international law distinction between *universal* or *core* crimes, on the one hand, and *transnational* crimes on the other is anchored. Whereas the former group comprises the crimes discussed before, the latter group derives its name from the fact that the crimes pertaining thereto are well international in the sense that they transcend borders and single States, such as in the case of drug or human trafficking; yet, they are normally not considered universal crimes in the sense that they would affect the international community as a whole.[46] It was with such thoughts in mind that the catalogue of core crimes in Art. 5 para. 2 of the Rome Statute was restricted to the four crimes mentioned above.

The interesting consequence is – and Karl Jaspers states this very clearly – that core crimes are not thought to (exclusively) »belong« to the national or regional community where the crimes are committed, but also and in particular to humankind: »These crimes do not concern only Jews, but all and everybody, for it is mankind itself that has been attacked through the Jews.«[47] That the crimes within the jurisdiction of the ICC are in that sense *global* or *universal* crimes is certainly

---

[42] Jaspers: Who Should Have Tried Eichmann, p. 855.

[43] In analogy to the traditional *crimen laesae majestatis*; see in particular Müller: Der Internationale Strafgerichtshof, pp. 182–188.

[44] Arendt: Eichmann in Jerusalem, p. 275.

[45] As to this concept (commonly, but erroneously ascribed to Cicero) see Müller: Feindbegriff im Völkerrecht, pp. 135–137. In fact, the Roman philosopher refers to the pirate as a »common enemy of everyone« (*communis hostis omnium*); see Cicero: De officiis, III, 29, 107; as to this aspect see in more detail Müller: Piraterie als Herausforderung für das Völkerrecht, pp. 159 et seqq.

[46] See, for instance, Cassese: International Criminal Law, pp. 11–13; Werle: Principles of International Criminal Law, pp. 29 et seq.

[47] Jaspers: Who Should Have Tried Eichmann, p. 855.

an important trait of globalization which becomes manifest in the ICC. Alas, it may also give rise to tension and conflict in situations where both levels – the regional and the universal one – seek to prosecute the same crime and to indict the same perpetrator. One might only refer to the tug-of-war between The Hague and Tripolis considering Saif al-Islam Gaddafi, the son of Libyan long-term ruler Muammar Gaddafi, in this regard.[48] The Rome Statute provides for such conflicts of competence and in principle decides them in favor of the regional or local level: This is the so-called principle of *complementarity*, thus counter-balancing the global aspirations of the ICC.[49]

4. Globalization of procedural law

Apart from its jurisdiction for truly universal crimes, the ICC – and the specialized international criminal tribunals with it – also stand for a globalization of procedural law. While every domestic legal order has its own provisions on how to conduct criminal trials, it is common to group them into different legal traditions, notably the *common law* (the Anglo-Saxon tradition encompassing, for instance, the United States, the United Kingdom and the Commonwealth countries) and the *civil law* traditions (continental law tradition including, for instance, Germany, France, Italy and Spain as well as States historically influenced by them). To simplify things radically, these traditions draw on different »philosophies« of how to run a criminal trial, the so-called *adversarial* vs. the *inquisitorial* system. This has implications for the division of labor between judge and the parties, for the question who is in charge of collecting evidence, etc.[50]

It will not come as a surprise that both systems sought to shape the emerging discipline of international criminal law according to their respective ideals. And not surprisingly either, neither of the two fully succeeded in its mission. The result was a compromise: The procedural law of the international criminal tribunals is a *hybrid*, a mixture between these two traditions. And even there, we find dynamic and change: While the Nuremberg and Tokyo tribunals and still the *ad hoc* tribunals for the Former Yugoslavia and Rwanda were under strong US influence and thus also more inclined to adopt common law solutions, the ICC procedural

---

[48] Since January 2013, Saif al-Islam Gaddafi has been on trial in the town of Zintan in the northwest of Libya, see, in contrast, the recent decision of the ICC, Pre-Trial Chamber I, *Prosecutor v. Saif al-Islam Gaddafi and Abdullah al-Senussi*, Decision on the admissibility of the case against Saif al-Islam Gaddafi, ICC-01/11-01/11, 31 May 2013, rejecting Libya's challenge to the admissibility of the case against Saif al-Islam Gaddafi and thus determining the case admissible before the ICC.

[49] See notably Arts. 1 and 17 of the Rome Statute. As regards the vast amount of literature see only Stegmiller: The Pre-Investigation Stage; Müller/Stegmiller: Self-referrals on Trial, pp. 1282 et seqq., with further references.

[50] See, e.g., Cassese: International Criminal Law, pp. 353 et seqq.

law as embodied in the Statute and the Rules of Procedure and Evidence, particularly due to the structure of its membership, heavily draws on the civil law tradition. On the basis of the Rome compromise, the procedural law of the ICC is now in the hands of the judges. By bringing in and exchanging their often diverging views, they are entrusted with contributing to the formation of a truly universal criminal procedural law.

5. Globalization of legal cultures

Related to this aspect, the establishment of international criminal tribunals in general and the ICC in particular contributes to the globalization of legal cultures. According to Art. 36 para. 8 lit. a of the Rome Statute, the States Parties when selecting the judges of the ICC shall take into account the need for »the representation of the principal legal systems of the world« and »equitable geographical representation«. This provision thus functions as the institutional guarantee that the different legal traditions have their say in the everyday work of the Court. Furthermore, meanwhile there exists a host of professional international criminal lawyers who have learned through their work in the ICC and the other international criminal tribunals (as well as in law firms and academic institutions specializing on international criminal law) what it means to conduct a criminal trial in an institution with global aspirations. In addition, The Hague being the »Legal Capital of the World« hosts not only the ICC, but also the ICTY, the Special Tribunal for Lebanon, the Charles Taylor trial of the Special Court for Sierra Leone as well as the International Court of Justice, the Permanent Court of Arbitration and the US-Iran Claims Tribunal. This creates a vibrant environment in which judges and staff members of the different judicial institutions engage with each other – a phenomenon sometimes referred to as »The Hague Club« –, thus further contributing to the globalization of legal cultures, on the *human* level, as it were.

III. Limitations and pitfalls

As we have seen, the Rome Statute, as adopted in 1998, embodies potential for globalization on various levels. Since its coming into existence roughly a decade ago, it has realized a considerable amount of this potential. At the same time, however, serious problems and limitations of the ICC have become visible. In order to illustrate these, six aspects coming from very different corners of international criminal law shall be briefly addressed. They all show shortcomings of the project of international criminal law as it exists today. Some among them may have the character of a »*not yet*«, whereas others rather testify to *structural* problems which set the ICC as a »real life« institution apart from its aspirations for universality even in the long run.

1. Aggression: The supreme international crime with a rusty start

At the moment, the Rome Statute is only a *torso* as regards the crime of aggression. To be sure, Art. 5 para. 2 makes aggression a crime within the jurisdiction of the Court, but suspends the exercise of jurisdiction until a definition would be agreed by the States Parties. The already mentioned Review Conference in Kampala in summer of 2010 succeeded, after half a century, in securing a compromise formula concerning the *definition* of the crime of aggression and, even more importantly, the *modalities of the exercise* of the jurisdiction of the Court. Yet, in the best of scenarios, the new regime will become operational in 2017, subject to a further »activation« decision of the States Parties, and in view of the »opting out« clause solely for those States not preventing the Court from exercising its jurisdiction vis-à-vis their nationals or acts of aggression committed on their territory.[51] Hence, in fact, we shall only know in ten or twenty years from now whether and to what extent Kampala was a success or not. The first cautious ratifications of the Kampala aggression amendments[52] allow for some guarded optimism, but not more than that.

After all, huge tensions remain regarding the crime of aggression. On the one hand, the International Military Tribunal at Nuremberg famously declared aggression »the supreme international crime«.[53] Thus, aggression seems to be the crime affecting the global community the most – and in that sense it is the most universal of crimes. On the other hand, it is precisely in regard to this crime that the reluctance, notably of the major powers, to proceed to meaningful collective action is the greatest. They are obviously anxious to lose scope of maneuvering by running the risk of their political and military leaders being prosecuted for waging a war of aggression. A whole series of recent examples testify to the topicality of this question (e. g. the US in Iraq, the NATO in Kosovo, the Western powers in Libya, Russia in Georgia / South Ossetia and Abkhazia, etc.).

---

[51] Resolution RC/Res. 6 of the Review Conference creating the new Arts. 8*bis* as well as 15*bis* and 15*ter* of the Rome Statute; http://www.icc-cpi.int/iccdocs/asp_docs/Resolutions/RC-Res.6-ENG.pdf (last accessed: 16.07.2013)

[52] The amendment has been ratified by Liechtenstein, Samoa, Trinidad and Tobago, Luxembourg, Estonia, Germany and Botswana so far.

[53] IMT Judgment, p. 426; see already *supra* note 9.

2. Alleged or real universality of international crimes

The gist behind the crimes prosecuted and punished by the ICC is that they are universal inasmuch as they shock the conscience of all humankind and are of concern to the international community as a whole. This presupposes that those crimes ostracize acts that are, in principle, deemed criminal everywhere and by everyone on the planet.

Admittedly, there is broad and indeed global consensus on the criminal character of enslavement or torture. But even with regard to these seemingly universal prohibitions, things are not absolutely clear. One might only mention the infamous US »torture memo«[54] and the broader debate on the so-called »ticking bomb scenario« and »emergency torture«.[55] In addition, certain practices purportedly mandatory under Islamic criminal law, e.g. corporal punishment such as amputation of certain body parts are hardly reconcilable with the international law on the prohibition of torture.[56] This has led some Muslim States to raise doubts during the negotiation process, but those have only materialized to a limited extent in the Rome Statute.[57] Since Art. 120 excludes reservations to the Statute, the prohibition of torture, in its essence, seems untouched.[58] However, the examples mentioned above illustrate that global agreement on certain values is often rather a task to be achieved than an actual and secured achievement.

Moreover, when it comes to war crimes such as recruiting of child soldiers[59] things are even less clear. This crime is very much *à la mode* now with the con-

---

[54] See, e.g., US Department of Justice, Office of Legal Counsel, Memorandum for William J. Haynes II by John C. Yoo, Military Interrogation of Alien Unlawful Combatants Held Outside the United States, 14 March 2003, used to justify interrogation practices such as the so-called »waterboarding«.

[55] See notably the *Gäfgen* case before the European Court of Human Rights: *Gäfgen / Germany* (Grand Chamber), Case No. 22.978/05, Judgment, 1 June 2010; as well as the *GSS Interrogation Techniques* case: Supreme Court of Israel, Public Committee Against Torture in Israel et al. v. The State of Israel et al., HCJ 5100/94, 6 September 1999. See the analysis in Müller: Androhung von Folter, pp. 219 et seqq., pp. 224 et seqq., with further references.

[56] See, for instance, OIC Res. No. 4/10-LEG (IS), para. 2, which denounces EU criticism of »so-called inhuman punishments, practiced by a number of Member States in the course of applying the Sharia rules,« and calls for a halt of those »unjustified campaigns [...] against a number of Member States' that demand the abolishment of the Shari'a ordained punishments [...] under the ›protection of human rights‹ slogan«; see notably Baderin: A Macroscopic Analysis, pp. 289–292; as well as Langer: Law, Religious Offence and Human Rights, p. 634 in this regard.

[57] Art. 6 lit. b, Art. 7 para. 1 lit. f and Art. 8 para. 2 lit. a sublit. ii and lit. c sublit. i of the Rome Statute.

[58] See, however, the so-called »lawful sanctions clause« in Art. 7 para. 2 lit. e of the Rome Statute which is reported to have had the function of allaying the concerns of some Muslim States that certain Islamic forms of punishment should not be considered »torture« within the meaning of the Statute; see Arsanjani: Rome Statute, p. 31.

[59] Art. 8 para. 2 lit. b sublit. xxvi and lit. e sublit. vii of the Rome Statute.

viction of Mr. Lubanga in the ICC in March 2012[60] – the first verdict of the ICC at all – and the judgment against the former Liberian President Charles Taylor in the Special Court for Sierra Leone in May of the same year.[61] Some question these decisions by pointing out that recruiting and using child soldiers is a common practice in armed conflicts, notably in Africa. They tend to argue that it is so »normal« that it could not be considered a war crime in the proper sense, be it for the lack of *mens rea* or mistake of law on the part of the presumed perpetrator[62], be it for the lack of stigmatization by the relevant local communities. The criticism here is often that the purportedly universal crimes are, on closer observation, not free from ethnocentrism and »Western human rights imperialism«.[63]

3. Limitations to the globalization of criminal law: The example of duress

Challenges to the universality of the provisions contained in the Rome Statute cannot only be mounted against the definitions of the crimes, but may also affect other areas, for instance, the norms on »grounds for excluding criminal responsibility« (Art. 31). To be sure, the defenses of mental incapacity, self-defense and duress exist in virtually all legal systems on the planet. However, there may be substantial differences as to how they play out in detail.

In the case of *Dražen Erdemović*, the ICTY had to deal with a »simple« soldier.[64] On 16 July 1995, during the massacre of Srebrenica, he was part of a firing squad which summarily executed hundreds of Bosnian Muslim men in the Pilica collective farm. Mr. Erdemović confessed that, on that day, he personally killed about 70 people. At the same time, he claimed that he was threatened to be killed himself would he had refused to take part in the killings.

The Appeals Chamber of the ICTY was split on the issue: The majority of the bench embraced the traditional common law approach that the deliberate killing of innocent people cannot be accepted by the law, no matter in what circumstances. Thus, such situation of duress could only involve mitigating circumstances, but does not afford a complete defense leading to an acquittal.[65] In contrast, ICTY

---

[60] See for the verdict ICC, Trial Chamber I, *Prosecutor v. Thomas Lubanga Dyilo*, Judgment, ICC-01/04-01/06, 14 March 2012 as well as the Decision on Sentence of 10 July 2012.

[61] See Special Court for Sierra Leone, Trial Chamber II, *Prosecutor v. Charles Ghankay Taylor*, Judgement, SCSL-03-01-T, 18 May 2012 as well as the Sentencing Judgment of 30 May 2012.

[62] See Arts. 30 and 32 of the Rome Statute.

[63] See as to this aspect notably Grande: Hegemonic Human Rights; Oba: Female Circumcision; idem: New Muslim Perspectives in the Human Rights Debate.

[64] ICTY, *Prosecutor v. Dražen Erdemović*, IT-96-22 (»Pilica Farm«), Trial Chamber Sentencing Judgment, 29 November 1996; Appeals Chamber Judgment, 7 October 1997; Second Sentencing Judgment, 5 March 1998.

[65] See previous note: Appeals Chamber Judgment, 7 October 1997, para. 19. See notably the land-

President Antonio Cassese, in his Dissenting Opinion, articulated the counter-position that accepts duress also in these situations given that there was no possibility of a »real moral choice«.[66] Interestingly, the general shift of ICC law towards the civil law tradition[67] also becomes manifest in the fact that in Art. 31 para. 1 lit. d of the Rome Statute, the duress defense has been designed much more according to the »civil law approach«, thus, in principle, allowing for an acquittal even in the case of the killing of innocent persons.

Whatever the truth of the matter, the example is telling inasmuch as it manifests that we are in many areas, even fundamental ones, still a good deal away from truly global convictions and solutions. At the same time, the very negotiation process for the Rome Statute and its Art. 31 shows that compromise formulae acceptable to the major legal traditions on the planet can actually be found and agreed upon. At the same time, it becomes (sometimes painfully) obvious that the project of international criminal law is far from being concluded, but an ongoing effort.

4. The ICC and Africa

As we have seen, by its very vocation, the ICC has evidently universal aspirations. In terms of Member States, the African States are the biggest supporters of the ICC, with 34 African States having joined the Court, i.e. more than a quarter of its overall membership.

However, over the last years the relationship between the ICC and the African States has become increasingly tense. For one, it is striking that *all* eight situations the ICC is currently dealing with are African: Uganda, Democratic Republic of the Congo, Central African Republic, Darfur/Sudan, Kenya, Libya, Côte d'Ivoire, Libya, and, most recently, Mali.[68] In addition, on 7 June 2012, four ICC staff members were detained by the Libyan authorities following a visit to Saif Al-Islam Gaddafi; they were only released on 2 July 2012.[69] Moreover, a Pre-Trial Chamber of the ICC had formally declared, on 12 and 13 December 2011 respec-

---

mark case High Court of Justice (Queen's Bench Division), *R. v. Dudley and Stephens*, (1884) 14 QBD 273 DC, 4 December 1884.

[66] See ibid., Separate and Dissenting Opinion of Judge Cassese, 7 October 1997, para. 45.

[67] See *supra* II.4.

[68] See http://www.icc-cpi.int/EN_Menus/icc/Pages/default.aspx. On 16 January 2013, ICC Prosecutor Fatou Bensouda announced that she had formally opened an investigation into alleged crimes committed on the territory of Mali since January 2012; see http://www.icc-cpi.int/en_menus/icc/press%20and%20media/press%20releases/news%20and%20highlights/Pages/pr869.aspx (last accessed: 16.07.2013).

[69] See http://www.icc-cpi.int/en_menus/icc/press%20and%20media/press%20releases/news%20and%20highlights/Pages/pr820.aspx (last accessed: 16.07.2013).

tively, that Malawi and Chad had violated their obligations as Members of the ICC by not surrendering Sudanese President Omar Al-Bashir to the Court when the latter visited those countries.[70] In striking contrast, those two countries relied on a formal decision of the African Union not to cooperate with the ICC on this issue.[71] Furthermore, the African Union has harshly criticized the ICC for »targeting« the African continent in neocolonialist and discriminatory fashion, now in the new dress of »human rights imperialism«; at the same time, the Prosecution is said not to look into the crimes of Western powers in Kosovo, Iraq, Afghanistan or Pakistan. The culmination point of this development, for the time being, and a major setback for the Court, was Kenya's recent announcement to withdraw its membership from the ICC; and Uganda indicated that it might follow suit. This could be a dangerous trend indeed, notably for the universality claims of the Court.

There is therefore the claim that the ICC works with double standards, one of the most serious accusations to be mounted against a judicial institution whose very essence is to strive for impartiality – the goddess of justice is not depicted blindfolded for nothing. Alas, the criticism of the ICC as an »Africa only court« remains[72], and it has to be taken very seriously. The African States feel underrepresented within the institution. The recent appointment of Fatou Bensouda, a national of The Gambia, may be seen to offer some relief in this regard; after all, the position of Prosecutor is one of (if not) the most powerful at the ICC and directly entrusted with selecting and prioritizing the situations to be dealt with by the Court.

5. The ICC and Islam

Fatou Bensouda is not only a woman from Africa, but also Muslim. In that regard, the appointment of the ICC's new Prosecutor may also alleviate the criticism mounted vis-à-vis the Court from Islamic countries, notably in regard to the Court's activities regarding Darfur, Sudan and Libya. The numbers are rather sobering: Of the 57 Members of the Organization of Islamic Cooperation (which comprises almost a third of the overall number of States), so far only 23 States have ratified the Rome Statute and 17 States are signatories thereof. The States

---

[70] See ICC, Pre-Trial Chamber I, *Prosecutor v. Omar Hassan Ahmad Al Bashir*, Decision on the refusal of the Republic of Malawi (Chad) to comply with the cooperation requests issued by the Court with respect to the arrest and surrender of Omar Hassan Ahmad Al Bashir, ICC-02/05-01/09-139 and -140, 12/13 December 2011.

[71] African Union, Assembly of Heads of State and Government, 13th Ordinary Session, Assembly/AU/Dec. 245 (XIII), 3 July 2009, relying on Art. 23 para. 2 of the Constitutive Act of the African Union and Art. 98 of the Rome Statute to that effect.

[72] See e.g. Nyabola: Does the ICC have an Africa problem? See in this regard also Beham: Islamic Law and International Criminal Law, p. 352.

having neither signed nor ratified include Turkey, Saudi Arabia, Qatar, Pakistan, Malaysia, Libya, Lebanon, Syria, Iraq, and Indonesia, as well as Azerbaijan, Brunei, Kazakhstan, Mauritania, Somalia, Togo, and Turkmenistan.[73] In addition, the 18 judges bench of the Court includes solely one judge from Nigeria. Similarly, of the 18 judges in the ICTY, currently only two come from Muslim-majority States, namely Turkey and Pakistan, respectively.[74] This asymmetry in the participation of Muslim States may help to create, and stabilize, the perception (whether correct or not) of Western justice being imposed upon Muslim offenders.[75]

At the same time, one should not be overly pessimistic regarding one major tradition being left out from the international criminal justice movement (if this were the case, however, the globalist aspirations of the ICC would seriously be impaired). Within the realm of contemporary international law, international criminal law in general and the Rome Statute in particular present themselves as a prime example for a global platform and discourse on universally shared principles. After all, irrespective of all problems and pitfalls on the level of implementation and actual practice, is it not that genocide and torture are ostracized all over the planet?[76] In spite of all controversy as to where the exact lines are to be drawn[77], there exists a real and not so insignificant *corpus* of universally accepted norms of international law, with the lines of conflict not necessarily, or even generally, coinciding with the purported ideological and cultural rift between »Islam« and »the West«.[78]

6. The tension of global and local justice

Another rupture line that is commonly addressed in the present context, is the tension between the interests of justice on the global and local levels. For many, Libya and the case of Saif al-Islam Gaddafi have become a telling example in this regard which lets the question powerfully reemerge to whom a presumed perpetrator »belongs«.[79] In addition, even assuming that the local level is willing and able to effectively prosecute, the question remains whether the ICC should not get

---

[73] See http://treaties.un.org/Pages/ViewDetails.aspx?src=TREATY&mtdsg_no=XVIII-10&chapter=18&lang=en (last accessed: 16.07. 2013).
[74] See www.icty.org/sid/151 (last accessed: 16.07. 2013).
[75] As to this see notably Beham: Islamic Law and International Criminal Law, p. 361.
[76] See e.g. Frick/Müller: Introducing an Intricate Relationship, pp. 13 et seq., with further references.
[77] See the examples provided in the text accompanying *supra* notes 54–63.
[78] Frick/Müller: Introducing an Intricate Relationship, p. 12.
[79] See *supra* note 48.

involved in the name of guaranteeing a fair and impartial trial and the human rights of the accused.[80]

While the principle of complementarity, as already mentioned above, basically decides the question in favor of the local level, the very decision on this question lies in the hands of the ICC, and one might expect some centralizing dynamics to flow from this allocation of competence. In fact, Art. 53 para. 1 lit. c of the Rome Statute empowers the Prosecutor not to initiate an investigation (even if the other jurisdictional and admissibility prerequisites are met) if »[t]aking into account the gravity of the crime and the interests of victims, there are nonetheless substantial reasons to believe that an investigation would not serve the interests of justice«. This »interests of justice« clause has been read by some to authorize, and encourage, the ICC, i. e. the global level, not only to stand back in case of domestic prosecution (as required by the principle of complementarity), but also if the local level decides to deal with the atrocities and crimes committed in different ways, namely via amnesties, truth commission, alternative or traditional mechanisms of justice. We are not in a position here to delve into these questions apart from raising them. However, one may expect the proper balancing of the two fields of »local vs. global« and »peace vs. justice« to constitute the biggest challenge for the future of the ICC and international criminal law more generally.

IV. Conclusion

International criminal law is, as we have seen, a relatively young discipline of international law. Nonetheless, it has experienced a comet-like rise over the last two decades. Parallel to this development, international criminal tribunals have arisen as a new species among international institutions. They have become part and parcel of the »international legal culture« since then. When we talk of global law, there are a number of impressive and encouraging developments indeed – some of which I have tried to identify, and trace, in this contribution.

However, when »doing globalization«, the question is always: How much is aspiration, and how much is reality? The previous paragraphs should have clarified that this is far from being a trivial question. If the ICC falls short of its global aspirations categorically and over an extended period of time, it may jeopardize, or in the long run even forfeit, the very legitimacy on which the highly ambitious and remarkably successful start-up period of the project of international criminal justice is built. Against this background, a (self-)critical and candid analysis of the

---

[80] As to this aspect of the problem see notably Cernusca: Islamic Law and International Criminal Law, pp. 376 et seqq., with further references.

limitations and pitfalls is an equally relevant and perhaps even more important exercise, especially for those who consider themselves friends of the project of the ICC and global criminal justice.

List of references

Arendt, Hannah: Eichmann in Jerusalem. A Report on the Banality of Evil, New York 1963.

Arsanjani, Mahnoush H.: The Rome Statute of the International Criminal Court, in: American Journal of International Law, 93, 1999, pp. 22–43.

Baderin, Mashood A.: Macroscopic Analysis of the Practice of Muslim State Parties to International Human Rights Treaties. Conflict and Congruence, in: Human Rights Law Review, 1, 2001, pp. 265–304.

Beham, Markus: Islamic Law and International Criminal Law, in: Marie-Luisa Frick / Andreas Th. Müller (eds.): Islam and International Law. Engaging Self-Centrism from a Plurality of Perspectives, The Hague 2013, pp. 349–366.

Bourdon, William: La Cour pénale internationale. Le statut de Rome, Paris 2000.

Cassese, Antonio: International Criminal Law, 2nd ed., Oxford 2008.

Cernusca, Matthias: Islamic Law and International Criminal Law, in: Marie-Luisa Frick / Andreas Th. Müller (eds.): Islam and International Law. Engaging Self-Centrism from a Plurality of Perspectives, The Hague 2013, 367–389.

Cicero, Marcus Tullius: De officiis.

Cohen, David: »Hybrid« Justice in East Timor, Sierra Leone, and Cambodia: »Lessons learned« and Prospects for the Future, in: Stanford Journal of International Law, 43, 2007, pp. 1–38.

Comisión Nacional sobre la Desaparición de Personas (CONADEP): Nunca Más, Buenos Aires 1984.

Dickinson, Laura A.: The Promise of Hybrid Courts, in: American Journal of International Law, 97, 2003, pp. 295–310.

Frick, Marie-Luisa / Müller, Andreas Th.: Introducing and Intricate Relationship, in: iidem (eds.): Engaging Self-Centrism from a Plurality of Perspectives, The Hague 2013, pp. 1–28.

Grande, Elisabetta: Hegemonic Human Rights and African Resistance. Female Circumcision in a Broader Perspective, in: Global Jurist Frontiers, 4, 2004, pp. 1–21.

Höffe, Otfried: Demokratie im Zeitalter der Globalisierung, München 1999.

International Military Tribunal for the Trial of the Major War Criminals (IMT): Judgment of 30 September 1946 and 1st October 1946, in: The Trial of the German Major War Criminals, London 1946, Vol. 22, 1 (IMT Judgment).

Jaspers, Karl: Who Should Have Tried Eichmann? Interview by François Bondy, first published in: Der Monat, 13, May 1961, pp. 15–19, reprinted in: Journal of International Criminal Justice, 4, 2006, pp. 853–858.

Kant, Immanuel: Perpetual Peace. A Philosophical Sketch, Königsberg 1795.

Klabbers, Jan / Peters, Anne / Ulfstein, Geir: The Constitutionalization of International Law, Oxford 2009.

Langer, Lorenz: Law, Religious Offence and Human Rights. Defamation of Religions and the Rationales of Speech Regulation, Ph. D. thesis, Zurich 2013.

Meron, Theodor: The Humanization of Humanitarian Law, in: American Journal of International Law, 94, 2000, pp. 239–278.

Meron, Theodor: The Humanization of International Law, The Hague 2006.

Müller, Andreas Th.: Der Internationale Strafgerichtshof als Faktor der Globalisierung. Eine Annäherung aus rechtsphilosophischer und staatsrechtlicher Sicht, Frankfurt a. M. 2005.

Müller, Andreas Th.: Der Feindbegriff im Völkerrecht. Eine Standortbestimmung, in: Paul G. Ertl / Jodok Troy (eds.): Der Feind. Darstellung und Transformation eines Kulturbegriffs, Vol. 2, 2nd ed., Wien 2009, pp. 119–148.

Müller, Andreas Th.: Piraterie als Herausforderung für das Völkerrecht des 21. Jahrhunderts, in: Paul G. Ertl / Jodok Troy (eds.): Vom »Krieg aller gegen alle« zum staatlichen Gewaltmonopol und zurück? Herrschaftliche und private Gewalt in europäischer, internationaler und ideengeschichtlicher Perspektive, Frankfurt a. M. 2012.

Müller, Andreas Th.: Die Androhung von Folter als polizeiliche Verhörmethode: Das absolute Tabu?, in: Zeitschrift für Verwaltung, 2012, pp. 219–231.

Müller, Andreas Th. / Stegmiller, Ignaz: Self-referrals on Trial. From Panacea to Patient, in: Journal of International Criminal Justice, 8, 2010, pp. 1267–1294.

Nyabola, Nanjala: Does the ICC have an Africa problem? All 28 people indicted by the International Criminal Court so far are from Africa, Al Jazeera, 28 March 2012, www.aljazeera.com/indepth/opinion/2012/03/20123278226218587.html (last accessed: 16.07.2013).

Oba, Abdulmumini A.: Female Circumcision as Female Genital Mutilation: Human Rights or Cultural Imperialism?, in: Global Jurist (Frontiers), 8, 2008, pp. 1–38.

Oba, Abdulmumini A.: New Muslim Perspectives in the Human Rights Debate, in: Marie-Luisa Frick / Andreas Th. Müller (eds.): Islam and International Law. Engaging Self-Centrism from a Plurality of Perspectives, The Hague 2013, pp. 217–243.

Peters, Anne: Humanity as the A and Ω of Sovereignty, in: European Journal of International Law, 20, 2009, pp. 513–544.

Romano, Cesare / Nollkaemper, André / Kleffner, Jann K. (eds.): International Criminal Courts. Sierra Leone, East Timor, Kosovo, Cambodia, Oxford 2004.

Schabas, William A.: The UN International Criminal Tribunals. The former Yugoslavia, Rwanda and Sierra Leone, Cambridge 2006.

Schabas, William A.: Genocide in International Law. The Crime of Crimes, 2nd ed., Cambridge 2009.

Stegmiller, Ignaz: The Pre-investigation Stage of the ICC. The Criteria for Situation Selection, Berlin 2011.

Teitel, Ruti G.: Humanity's Law, Oxford 2011.

Tomuschat, Christian: International Law. Ensuring the Survival of Mankind on the Eve of a New Century, General Course on Public International Law, Recueil des Cours de l'Académie de droit international de La Haye, Vol. 281, The Hague 1999.

Werle, Gerhard: Principles of International Criminal Law, 2nd ed., The Hague 2009.

Chandra Lekha Sriram

Tribunals, Legacies, and Local Culture: Lessons from Some African Experiences with International Criminal Justice

Introduction

What does it mean to talk about tribunals, particularly international criminal tribunals, as cultural institutions or as affecting culture, or to talk about cultural representations of tribunals? As a lawyer, at one level the question seems somewhat perplexing to me, and a rather simple legal positivist response might be that tribunals simply apply the law to the facts, and that they should not attend to questions of culture or their own reception in it. However, that would be an extremely narrow view, one which is ill-suited to domestic courts and perhaps particularly ill-suited to international and internationalized courts. The latter, after all, deal with mass atrocities which may not only have affected many people in society, but have seriously damaged the social fabric. In such contexts, internationalized courts are often expected to do more than simply deliver verdicts regarding the guilt or innocence of the accused before them.

In this paper, I will focus upon the expectations that international and internationalized criminal tribunals can and should have a wider impact on conflict- and atrocity-affected societies, drawing upon my own research in Sierra Leone and Kenya. As I am not a specialist in cultural analysis, I will not focus in detail on cultural representations of atrocities, law and trials. Rather I will focus on the impact that such events and institutions are said to have, or expected to have, upon society and culture, as well as political institutions and behaviour, although it is worth noting that these are perhaps the opposite side of the same coin. I will consider both the difficulties which tribunals have in speaking to, let alone influencing, the affected societies, and the very real tensions between effecting legal justice and the expected communicative effects of tribunals.

Cultural representations of law, and law's efforts to influence culture

There is a long history of cultural representations of trials and punishments, notably Plato's treatment of Socrates in *Apology* through to Franz Kafka's *The Trial*. Of more direct relevance to the current discussion, there are a range of plays, novels, and nonfiction works which address past and current mass atrocities, and the range of ways in which societies seek to come to grips with them, including, but not limited to, trials. To name just a few salient examples, Ariel Dorfman's play *Death and the Maiden* deals with the aftermath of political repression and abuse and the often-ambiguous nature of guilt and innocence; Antjie Krog's *Country of My Skull*, while nonfiction, utilizes a variety of narrative approaches, and is as much literature as a chronicling of the South African Truth and Reconciliation Commission; films such as *Hotel Rwanda* seek to explore the genocide in Rwanda and narrate both the horrors that people can inflict on one another and the moments of bravery of which they are capable; and Michael Ondaatje's *Anil's Ghost* is the story of a forensic anthropologist in Sri Lanka investigating what appears to be a politically-motivated murder in the midst of the ethnic conflict. Each, in its own unique way, evokes the challenges for individuals, and societies, seeking to come to terms with often unspeakable abuses to individuals, often on a vast scale. It is perhaps not surprising that works of literature are deployed to play a host of roles – explanatory, pedagogic, therapeutic – which criminal trials are generally not designed to play.

However, as a lawyer and political scientist, I am not well-placed to analyse literary representations of atrocities and trials. Instead, this paper will focus upon the ways in which trials for mass atrocities, and in particular international criminal tribunals, are expected to speak to affected societies in a wider sense, rather than to »just« pursue criminal justice. In essence, I will examine the arguably unique demands that such institutions seek to influence local culture – legal, political, and social – in a constructive fashion. Here, I am using culture in a very particular (and perhaps both narrow and incorrect) sense, as participants in and analysts of these judicial institutions often do, namely as a range of practices, mores, and expectations, rather than as social practices including traditional rituals and practices, religious practices, or the arts.[1]

---

[1] Compare the discussion of culture in Young: Cultural appropriation and the arts, chapter 1, which broadly speaking accepts the concept of culture as a set of beliefs, achievements, and customs as traits which people share.

Why should tribunals seek to influence local culture after mass atrocity (or should they)?

As I have noted above, one answer to the question posed here is simply that tribunals should not seek to influence domestic culture, whether legal, social, or political. Instead, it could be argued, criminal trials are solely designed to judge the guilt or the innocence of the accused, weighing the evidence against the legal criteria. However, advocates of a wider role for and expectation of international criminal courts have sometimes argued that even ordinary domestic courts are never pure. Further, such courts, they argue, are influenced by, and with their pronouncements do influence, politics and society.[2] However, a further range of arguments for a more engaged or interventionist approach of courts to culture is regularly made in the context of societies which have experienced mass atrocity. They tend to overlap with, but can be seen as distinct from, wider arguments about the utility of trials in rebuilding or legitimating fragile post-conflict or post-atrocity states, or promoting democracy.[3] Thus the international nongovernmental organization (NGO), the International Center for Transitional Justice, argues that »[u]nlike domestic courts, transitional justice institutions are expected to assist in the transformation of post-conflict societies, or at least leave a legacy that will engender some transformation.«[4]

Advocates argue that the operation of trials for the most serious crimes must be accessible in such states because justice will previously have been, in fact, unjust, and/or invisible and inaccessible to most of the population. Further, they argue that social bonds have been severely damaged by abuses, and that trials (along with truth-telling, restorative justice, and other measures) are essential to repair those bonds and (re)build trust amongst communities generally, and amongst victims, perpetrators, and wider society as well as between the population and the state. The expectation is that trials have an extraordinary, and indeed extrajudicial, role to play in such circumstances.

I remain sceptical that criminal tribunals are particularly well-suited to these expectations. There is a danger, perhaps, that tribunals, whose origins lie in highly politicized violence and conflict resolution processes, will appear to be tainted by

---

2   This is an argument made by legal realists as well as critical legal scholars. Sociologists of law analyse this interaction without presuming such an artificial distinction. And legal advocates, whether progressive or conservative, regularly seek to deploy law to change social behaviour and social mores – we have only to consider the use of legislation and litigation regarding abortion and same-sex marriage in the United States to find evidence of this.

3   For literature seeking to assess the impact of trials and truth commissions on democracy and/or human rights records in post-atrocity states, see, e. g., Wiebelhaus-Brahm: Truth commissions and transitional societies; Olsen/Payne/Reiter: Transitional justice in balance; Sikkink: The justice cascade.

4   Suma: The Charles Taylor Trial and Legacy of the Special Court for Sierra Leone.

contemporary politics. This is a particular risk if they seek to engage political actors too directly, or justify their actions with reference to non-legal rationales, as they may undermine their own legitimacy.[5] Proper functioning of trials, including due process for the accused, may also be at odds with fully transparent efforts communication of court activities.[6] I will revisit these concerns later, but will seek first to outline the expected role of tribunals and processes by which they are expected to shape society in greater detail before turning to two specific institutions and their roles in two specific countries, the Special Court for Sierra Leone and the International Criminal Court in Kenya.

Trials as public spectacle and pedagogy

There is significant literature on the performativity of institutions of state, whether judicial or otherwise, and the ways in which they may constitute rituals, demonstrate power, and define identities.[7] This literature is largely beyond the scope of this paper. However, there are scholars of post-atrocity justice who suggest that trials can and should have pedagogical effects, and indeed function as theatre. Thus Sativa January states that »[a] war crimes trial can be considered a stadium in which conflicting myths are at rhetorical war«.[8] Specifically, those who emphasize pedagogical and even theatrical aspects argue that trials are important because they are public spectacles which compel a society to face its recent past rather than seek to forget, and to openly debate it. On this view, trials can and should do more than reach determinations of guilt and innocence in relation to specific accused individuals. They should not, therefore, simply present a single truth, but rather promote discussion.[9] Indeed, one advocate of this view argues that judges and prosecutors can and should pay closer attention to the »poetics of legal storytelling« as part of promoting a social narrative that can contribute to a society's transition.[10]

These expectations of trials are similar to expectations often placed upon truth commissions in the wake of mass atrocity, and of course may be subject to the same limitations – that rather than educating a populace and promoting genuine

---

[5] Struett: Why the International Criminal Court Must *Pretend* to Ignore Politics.
[6] January: *Tribunal Verité*.
[7] For example, Geertz: Negara, discusses how the rituals of state dramatized key aspects of culture. By contrast, Foucault: Discipline and Punish, elaborates on the role of penal institutions in societies in demonstrating power; in a related, Foucauldian vein, Scarry: The Body in Pain, elaborates on the use of torture not to extract information but to exercise power and define the tortured.
[8] January: *Tribunal Verité*, p. 208.
[9] Osiel: Mass atrocity, collective memory and the law.
[10] Ibid., p. 3.

debate and reflect, they either polarize, or allow those in distinct camps to remain so rather than challenging pre-existing beliefs.[11] They involve, generally, an expectation that such processes can project important lessons to a society or a culture which is deemed to be damaged or lacking in some regard. Often, such societies are seen to be missing respect for rule of law, a recognition of the importance of respect for core human rights, or something else, considered essential for sustainable coexistence, peacebuilding, or even reconciliation.

In such contexts, trials, whether state-led, international, or hybrid, are often expected to affect society in ways which rectify these perceived shortcomings. While advocates of this view do not necessarily embrace a top-down approach, the institutions which are expected to deliver important messages to local culture are frequently driven by the international community, national elites or transnational elites. This may mean that the processes do not easily connect with a significant portion of the population in the societies with which they are engaged. This observation is neither meant to denigrate the intentions of those promoting such processes as pedagogical, but merely to note that in affected countries, particularly those for whom the legacies of colonialism are strong and allegations of neo-colonialism are rife, such mechanisms may not be universally welcomed.[12]

International criminal tribunals and the growth of »victim-centred« approaches to justice

Advocates of what are known as »victim-centred« approaches to justice have argued that international criminal justice is about more than the accused and determinations of guilt and innocence, but that they are also about the needs of victims. Advocates promoting such approaches argue that greater attention must be paid to the needs and demands of victims to vindicate their needs and recognize their suffering, to minimize the risk of retaliation, and to enable social reconciliation.[13] The depiction of victims is also often tied to politicized, journalistic, and literary concepts of their innocence, or as Mark Drumbl describes some narratives

---

[11] On truth commissions generally see Hayner: Unspeakable Truths; on the uses and misuses of the South African commission see Krog: Country of My Skull.

[12] There is now a vibrant political and academic debate on the International Criminal Court and its role in Africa. See, e. g., Sriram / Pillay (eds.): Peace versus justice?; Mills, »Bashir is dividing us«. I am grateful to Amy Ross for drawing my attention to this wider normative point and to postcolonial literature criticizing the tendency of outsiders scrutinizing Africa, in particular, to assume that leadership, institutions, and culture do not exist where they are not recognizable, and to assume the role of speaking for »locals«. See, e. g., Finnström: Living with bad surroundings, p. 58.

[13] I discuss this in greater detail in Sriram: Victims, ex-combatants and communities.

surrounding child soldiers, »faultless passive victims«.[14] This is not the place to consider the rich discussions of the complexity of identities in situations of mass atrocities, including that of victim-perpetrators, but rather to observe that victims are expected, in such contexts, to serve narrative functions, as witnesses and now participants in criminal trials, as participants in social reconciliation, at the same time as criminal trials are expected to serve their needs.

The turn to victim-centred approaches to justice in international and internationalized criminal tribunals has brought narratives about restorative justice squarely into institutions which have traditionally been viewed as purveyors of retributive justice. Victims have been afforded the right to participate (albeit largely through legal representatives, with the option in limited cases to make personal statements beyond those made in any formal witness role) at the Extraordinary Chambers in the Courts of Cambodia (ECCC), and before the International Criminal Court (ICC).[15] Further, the ECCC can provide reparations, albeit community rather than individual reparations. The ICC can provide reparations generally to affected areas, through the Trust Fund for Victims, which receives voluntary contributions, thus far from a small number of states. It can also order that those convicted of a crime provide reparations to victims. At the ICC, however, the narrative of victimhood and exclusion becomes salient, for victims seeking to participate, or to potentially receive reparations via a court judgment, must be recognized as victims of the named accused person, not as victims of the situation. However, participation has been somewhat constrained, due to concerns about resources, efficiency and procedural fairness.[16] There remains some risk that victim participation will be less of a validation for victims of the most serious atrocities, and instead create artificial distinctions among categories of victims, who may feel something like the seeker of justice in Kafka's short parable »Before the Law,« barred by a gatekeeper whose resistance he does not understand. Tribunals such as the ICC are expected not only to do justice by, and recognize the needs of, victims, however; they are also expected to leave a wider legacy for affected societies.

---

[14] Drumbl: Reimagining child soldiers in international law and policy.
[15] Sriram: Victims, Ex-combatants and communities.
[16] SáCouto/Cleary: Victim Participation in the Investigations of the International Criminal Court.

International criminal tribunals – the demand for legacy and impact

International and internationalized criminal tribunals have also come under particular pressure to create what has been described as a »legacy« and to have an impact on the affected countries and societies. This pressure arose for a number of reasons. First, both the International Criminal Tribunal for the former Yugoslavia and the International Criminal Tribunal for Rwanda came under significant criticism for being distant, both geographically and in terms of comprehensibility, from the populations most affected by the crimes and criminals which they were trying.[17]

One of the frequent criticisms of such tribunals has been that they are very expensive, and that funds would be better spent on developing the often-damaged judiciaries of post-conflict countries.[18] As a result, both critics and advocates have called for such tribunals to have an impact, directly on domestic judiciaries through capacity-building, or to affect local rule of law by example.[19] These expectations have even been placed on the Special Tribunal for Lebanon, an internationalized criminal court dealing with a very small number of political assassinations in 2005, rather than atrocities committed during that nation's civil war.[20] In its strongest form, one scholar called for »proactive complementarity« by the International Criminal Court, or for the court to play a role in not only encouraging but assisting trials for mass atrocities. The former prosecutor of the ICC adopted a slightly more limited approach of »positive complementarity«.[21]

While much of the discourse around impact of tribunals has focused on their expected direct impact on domestic courts, i.e. the degree to which they help to build the capacity of weak, biased, or damaged domestic courts, there has also been a wider set of expectations also imposed on tribunals – that they contribute to a »culture« of rule of law and have a wider »legacy«. These expectations are often quite amorphous, failing to clarify what a *culture of rule of law* is beyond setting it in opposition to a *culture of impunity*. At times this culture appears to revolve simply around the creation of independent judicial institutions and a stable

---

17 This can be termed »externalization of justice«. See Sriram / Roth (eds.): Justice without borders?
18 Cohen: Hybrid Justice in East Timor, Sierra Leone, and Cambodia, pp. 2 et seq.
19 Burke-White: The Domestic Influence of International Criminal Tribunals.
20 Sriram: Unfinished business.
21 Burke-White: Proactive Complementarity; International Criminal Court, Office of the Prosecutor: Report on the activities performed during the first three years (June 2003–June 2006) para. 95; International Criminal Court, Office of the Prosecutor: Prosecutorial Strategy 2009–2012, paras. 16 and 17. The concept was supported in substance, although not by name, by the States' Parties at the review conference of the statute in June 2010 (Resolution RC/Res.1 Complementarity) 14 June 2010.

constitution. However, at others they seem to involve the belief (by an unspecified segment of elite, masses, or everyone) in the concept of rule of law generally, or trust in institutions of law specifically. Any of these versions of the concept of culture of rule of law may well be admirable, and worth pursuing, but precisely which is meant is often unclear, and, I would argue, exactly how internationalized tribunals help promote any of these variants is often underspecified.

Those who articulate these expectations also often have some difficulty elaborating on the precise meaning of »legacy«. Indeed, they may be seen as part of a longer history of efforts at, and arguments about, legal transplantation, dating from the law and development movement, which seek to use law as a tool of social change, often importing external models.[22] Advocacy from the outside of transplantation of legal models, and vulnerability within states to such transplants, are particularly significant in times of transition and in conflict-affected states: hence the promotion of external, particularly American, aspects of law in Eastern Europe following the creation and then the demise of the Soviet Union, including through the drafting of new constitutions.[23]

Similarly, one might argue, internationalized criminal tribunals are expected to help promote a different form of legal transplantation, through the imposition of international criminal law, both substantive and procedural, on defendants from societies often characterized (not least by those engaged in the promotion of accountability) as having been lawless and corrupt. The expectation of such tribunals, by their advocates, many participants, and often even their detractors, is that they can and should create or transplant a rule of law culture through capacity-building, but also through awareness-raising and outreach.[24]

Thus, discussions of legacy of international tribunals seem to demand a wider impact by international criminal tribunals than simply any direct effect on domestic legal institutions alone. Advocates also often expect that the work of these institutions will have relevance, or better still, a positive impact, on the wider society. It is here that the concept of outreach and the use of outreach offices comes into play. Outreach offices are expected not simply to assist tribunals in filling their direct operational functions, i.e. by raising public awareness of their operation in ways which may assist in the gathering of evidence and securing of

---

[22] To be clear, there is a self-conscious effort amongst practitioners not to engage in simple transplants which might be viewed as ethnocentric or imperialist. Hussain: Sustaining Judicial Rescues.

[23] Ajani: Chance and Prestige; LaGrand: The Impossibility of Legal Transplants; Watson: Legal Transplants; Mansell: Law as an Instrument of Revolutionary Change in a Traditional Milieu.

[24] Office of the High Commissioner for Human Rights: Rule of Law tools for Post-Conflict States, Tool on Maximizing the Legacy of Hybrid Tribunals; Hussain: Sustaining Judicial Rescues, p. 559; Wierda/Nassar/Maalouf: Early Reflections on Local Perceptions, Legitimacy and Legacy of the Special Tribunal for Lebanon. On efforts by international peacebuilding actors to promote rule of law in a more formal institutional sense, see Sriram/Martin-Ortega/Herman (eds.): Peacebuilding and rule of law in Africa.

witnesses and the accused. Outreach is expected also to raise public awareness in order to have a wider transformative effect on society, shaping perceptions about specific tribunals but also about accountability, past abuses, and future human rights and rule of law.[25]

Outreach offices as mediators of legacy and interveners in culture?

Many analysts and advocates assume that a key goal of international criminal tribunals is »to reach out to the local population and gain the latter's support«.[26] Outreach offices are expected to mitigate effects of the great distance that often separates the courts from the affected populations, to translate or clarify the often highly technical work of international criminal law, and, in some more ineffable way, speak to the affected populations in ways that garner their support for the institutions and their outcomes, and possibly for the »culture of the rule of law«. These are lofty aims indeed, possibly unachievable, and certainly a challenge in conflict-affected countries plagued by crimes, recrimination, and mistrust.

Outreach offices are a relatively late development in international criminal justice. The first outreach office, created for the International Criminal Tribunal for the former Yugoslavia, came after the tribunal had been in existence for six years; the outreach office for the International Criminal Tribunal for Rwanda was set up a year later. During that time, and indeed since the creation of outreach programmes, nationalist hardliners in the former Yugoslavia sought to control the local narrative about the tribunal as persecuting proud nations and ethnicities (which varied depending upon who was speaking).[27] The outreach programme was championed by one of the tribunal's judges, who recognized a need for the tribunal to speak to the affected population, which largely resided some 900 miles away from the tribunal. This need was perhaps all the more acute because in the early years, tribunal documents were not translated into the local languages and the proceedings were not broadcast online, as they are today.[28] The aim was to target the »grassroots« level, speaking to youth groups as well as judges, prosecutors, and journalists. Further, the goal according to advocates and practitioners was to promote peacebuilding and reconciliation, not just basic comprehension of

---

[25] Vinck/Pham: Outreach Evaluation, pp. 2, 5.
[26] Clark: International War Crimes Tribunals and the Challenge of Outreach, p. 99.
[27] Tolbert: The International Criminal Tribunal for the Former Yugoslavia, p. 11; Arzt: Views on the Ground, p. 230.
[28] Clark: International War Crimes Tribunals and the Challenge of Outreach, p. 101.

the tribunal's work.²⁹ However, analysis of the outreach programmes of the ICTY and the ICTR suggest they had limited effects. Further, in the former Yugoslavia, perceptions of the legitimacy of the ICTY remain divided along ethnic lines.³⁰

The Special Court for Sierra Leone: Outreach as the »jewel in the crown« or the »gold standard«

The Special Court for Sierra Leone (SCSL), a mixed national-international tribunal, was set up in Sierra Leone to try those who bore the greatest responsibility for serious crimes committed during that country's civil war. Thus its primary purpose was as an institution of retributive criminal justice, applying both international and domestic law. However, a secondary purpose was articulated for it from the start – that it would contribute to rebuilding the country's legal culture, and provide a legacy for the country. Indeed, the Security Council resolution supporting its establishment included in preambular language an emphasis on the need to have a »credible« system of justice which would »end impunity and would contribute to the process of national reconciliation and to the restoration and maintenance and peace.«³¹ I conducted fieldwork at the court and beyond in Sierra Leone between 2004 and 2011. As various interviewees, including the registrar of the tribunal, expressed it, the tribunal was to leave behind more than »bricks and mortar« for the country.³²

The SCSL's outreach office began far earlier than that of the ICTY, six months rather than six years after the court began its work, and it is viewed by some as a genuine success.³³ Outreach for the SCSL has been comparatively thorough, with a range of activities including travelling video presentations of trial proceedings, trainings for civil society groups, amputees, ex-combatants and victims, and the use of radio programmes. There has been an effort to make the court more accessible to the young through illustrated pamphlets on the SCSL and international law. All of these efforts self-consciously sought to reach the »grassroots« and particularly youths, through school »Accountability Now« clubs, support to school »Peace and Human Rights« clubs, and the radio programme »Kids talking to Kids«. The

---

29 Ibid., pp. 102 et seq.
30 Hussain: Sustaining Judicial Rescues, pp. 563, 565; Ait. Views on the Ground, p. 232.
31 United Nations: United Nations Security Council Resolution 1315.
32 Sriram: Wrong-sizing international justice?; Hussain: Sustaining judicial rescues, p. 570.
33 Clark: International War Crimes Tribunals and the Challenge of Outreach, p. 106, cites David Tolbert of the ICTY and now the ICTJ as referring to SCSL outreach as the »gold standard«; and Lincoln: Transitional justice, peace and accountability, p. 144, cites references to it as the »jewel in the crown«, albeit with a critical analysis of its reach.

Outreach office even created a special »jingle« explaining previous judgments and the then-imminent April 2012 judgment in the trial of Charles Taylor, in local languages Krio, Mende, and Temne.[34] Surveys conducted by a range of institutions have found that the outreach office has been surprisingly successful in reaching a significant proportion of the population, including rural illiterate populations.[35]

However, whether and if so, how that permeation has either helped to build the capacity of the local judiciary, or affected local views of the court itself or wider social understandings of the rule of law and accountability, is less clear.[36] While surveys have shown that popular support for the SCSL has been relatively high, most surveyed also seemed to have relatively little knowledge of the institution, and indeed some conflated the court with the Truth and Reconciliation Commission.[37] Many members of civil society, including human rights advocates, questioned the utility of the court given its limited focus on »those who bear the greatest responsibility« and trials of members of one fighting force, the Civil Defence Forces, viewed by many as heroes. Others criticized it as an external imposition or one serving the interests of the incumbent president.[38] In general, the desired projection of the court – a culture of rule of law over a culture of impunity – does not appear to have resonated at the grassroots or the organized civil society level. While people have embraced the concept of accountability and generally reported positive views of the presence of the court in polls, they have been more sceptical of its actual application of principles of justice, whether in reflecting on those whom it has prosecuted or those whom it has not.[39]

---

[34] Special Court for Sierra Leone Outreach Website. Its mission statement and summary of activities states:

»In implementing our mission of educating Sierra Leoneans on the rule of law and the operations of the Court, Outreach targets the general population, as well as specific groups including the military, the police, students at all levels, the judiciary, prison officers, religious leaders, civil society, and national and international NGOs. Outreach uses town-hall meetings, radio programmes, publications, video screenings of trial proceedings, seminars, and training to communicate the work of the Special Court.«

[35] Lincoln: Transitional justice, peace and accountability; Clark: International War Crimes Tribunals and the Challenge of Outreach, pp. 109 et seq.

[36] Sriram: (Re)building the rule of law in Sierra Leone.

[37] Campaign for Good Governance: An Opinion Poll of Sierra Leone Residents on the TRC and the Special Court; Sawyer/Kelsall: Truth vs. justice?

[38] Sriram: Wrong-sizing international Justice – interviewees suggested alternately that it was purely an imposition by the United States and/or the United Kingdom, or that it was »Kabbah's court«, referring to the president who requested its creation.

[39] Ibid.

The International Criminal Court and Kenya

The International Criminal Court faces a far larger challenge in the promotion of accountability or, as the preamble to its statute emphasizes, the fight against impunity. The reason for this is obvious – it is a global court with, as of this writing, 122 states parties, many of them conflict-affected countries or countries in conflict-affected regions. It currently has eight »situation« countries, many of them vast in terms of territory, population, and complexity and numbers of parties to conflicts. Even in Kenya, the situation I will focus on here, where the violence which the ICC is examining was relatively small in scale compared to other situation countries, the challenge is significant.

Given the number of situation countries and the scale of abuses in most, ICC outreach is not surprisingly a challenge. The ICC has an established outreach office whose stated mission is to engage in two-way communication with affected populations, to inform them of the activities of the court and to counter misinformation; the mission statement and strategy documents do not suggest that there is a goal at engaging local cultures more widely or leaving a legacy.[40] However, the concept of positive complementarity, championed by the office of the prosecutor of the ICC, seems to place the court in more direct interaction with affected countries' legal cultures, with the expectation that it will help encourage more national proceedings.[41] It does not, however, purport to engage more widely to promote the culture of the rule of law, or to leave a legacy for affected countries, as some practitioners at the SCSL did. And indeed, this may be a necessary approach for a court engaged in investigating and/or prosecuting crimes in eight countries, many of them quite territorially vast.

This has meant that outreach in Kenya has been extremely limited, in the official sense. The outreach office for the ICC in Kampala, Uganda, had a single officer dealing with substantive outreach for both the situation in northern Uganda and the situation in Kenya until an office was set up in Kenya in 2011. However, outreach efforts were spearheaded by that officer and an official of registry from 2009, seeking in early interactions to engage grassroots organizations and to educate media organizations about the ICC to address incorrect and biased interpretations and reports. Nonetheless, with the absence of an official outreach office, much of the ICC's public engagement with Kenya was in the person of the prosecutor, who has made a number of high-profile visits and met with members of civil society as well as government officials. As the confirmation of charges has only recently

---

[40] International Criminal Court, Assembly of States Parties: Strategic Plan for Outreach of the International Criminal Court.
[41] Sriram/Brown: Kenya in the Shadow of the ICC.

taken place, it is perhaps too early to say much about the impact of the ICC on local legal, political, or social culture, but a few observations may be instructive.

First, civil society reception of the court has been extremely positive. Organizations seeking accountability, and seeking to sideline the government's evasive manoeuvres in response to international pressure for accountability for post-election violence, rallied around the ICC as a venue. They united behind a simple call: »don't be vague: let's go to the Hague«.[42] The ICC has been the centre of the rallying cry, but its scrutiny may have also helped to open the social and political space for those seeking to keep up pressure for accountability in a country where impunity has been the norm. And the ICC has proven popular beyond civil society organizations: in 2011, a poll indicated that more than 60 % of Kenyans preferred trials before the ICC to any other venue.[43] Finally, the commission of inquiry into post-election violence, after criticising the local judiciary as incapable of addressing serious and politicised crimes, suggested either an internationalised criminal tribunal, or the ICC as an appropriate venue.

What is interesting about these examples, however, is that they suggest, not only the effects of the ICC on legal, political, and social culture in Kenya, but also the active engagement by that culture with the ICC. Various NGOs in the country have sought to use the institution to respond to endemic challenges and what has repeatedly been called a culture of impunity. In interviews in Kenya in April 2012, I found civil society organizations generally positive about the ICC as a mode of undermining the culture of impunity directly – by challenging the virtual »deity« status of many established politicians by prosecuting two leading presidential contenders. In particular, they pointed to the public televising of the first appearance of the six individuals against whom the prosecutor sought to bring charges, viewed in parks and other public spaces such as bars as well as homes, as an event which transfixed Kenyans and challenged the apparent inviolability of the accused. They generally evinced the view that the ICC had helped promote discussion about accountability, and hope that for once, the powerful would face justice. Notably, however, they almost invariably did not see the ICC as essential for local justice reform, a process which was initiated through the process of constitutional reform, leading to the new constitution inaugurated in the summer of 2010.[44]

It is worth recognizing that the publicity surrounding the court also has a potential downside. Two of the politicians issued summonses to appear by the court, Uhuru Kenyatta and William Ruto, travelled to the Hague in April 2011, and re-

---

[42] Although it should be noted that the same cry was enunciated by some politicians who only advocated ICC involvement because they expected it would not be swift, and who hoped to forestall local or hybrid trials.
[43] Brown/Sriram: »The big fish won't fry themselves«.
[44] Interviews not for attribution, Nairobi, April 2012.

turned to a heroes' welcome and fanfare from supporters.⁴⁵ This raises the spectre that the men, both presidential candidates in the next election, could seek to rally support by claiming to resist a foreign intervener, the court. Nonetheless, the confirmation of charges hearings in fall 2011 were followed closely by Kenyans on television, and the announcement that charges had been confirmed against four individuals, including Kenyatta and Ruto, passed peacefully. Thus the impact of the court's engagement on official political discourse as well as wider societal narratives in Kenya remains to be seen.

Politics, power and communication

Much of the foregoing discussion has taken as a given, much as the majority of the literature on internationalized criminal tribunals to date has done, that the tribunals are projecting downwards to the effected populations, victims, and perpetrators a specific set of messages, both legal and political. These messages, where tribunals and other international justice processes sit at great remove from the affected populations, are also essentially projected outwards to them, rather than operating in visible range.⁴⁶ I have argued elsewhere that such top-down and distant approaches are problematic for a range of reasons, as have others, and will not repeat those arguments here.

However, there are two further potential causes for concern. The first is that international criminal tribunals and international criminal justice processes more generally operate in highly politicized environments. They involve serious crimes committed largely by state-sanctioned actors or opposition forces seeking to remove state leadership. They often follow controversial peace agreements or military victories, or more recently involve referral to the ICC by the United Nations Security Council. In short, these processes are deeply embedded in domestic, regional, and even global political struggles, and can easily be viewed as pawns of powerful political actors. This perception was evident in many of my interviews in Sierra Leone, heightened by a reasonable distrust of judicial and other institutions, given the history of corruption and poor governance in the country.

In such a context, where judicial institutions are presumed to be politically manipulable, it may be difficult to gain public trust, not least because political leaders themselves may be seeking to turn the involvement of international justice processes to their own advantage. This was arguably the case with efforts by President Museveni of Uganda, for example, to refer only the situation in Northern

---

⁴⁵ Odula: Hero's Welcome for Kenya's Int'l Court Suspects.
⁴⁶ See, e.g., Sriram: Universal Jurisdiction.

Uganda and crimes committed by the Lord's Resistance Army to the ICC, while hoping to exclude crimes committed by the national army.[47] The Special Court for Sierra Leone, as I have noted, came under criticism for its indictment of Chief Sam Hinga Norman, its failure to indict President Ahmad Tejan Kabbah, and in some instances as a tool of the West. Real or apparent politicization (and the fact that the legal and the political can never be purely separated) can have significant effects on the legitimacy of such institutions.[48] Further, communicative efforts may not alleviate suspicions. As January notes, in Sierra Leone, there remains deep suspicion of media and other forms of communication, with a strong view held by many that truth remains hidden in what she refers to as an »erratic labyrinth of perception and power«.[49]

Finally, while advocates of the theatrical and pedagogical benefits of trials make strong arguments, it remains unclear how well tribunals can deliver on them. First, trials are not primarily exercises in truth-telling, but largely adversarial processes in which the guilt or innocence of an accused for a specified crime is in dispute. Second, trials are not always very transparent: protection of victims and witnesses means details about them may be significantly obscured in proceedings, and due process for defendants may similarly circumscribe the nature of evidence which can be introduced into proceedings.[50] At the same time, defendants, particularly politicians and charismatic figures, may have the capacity to subvert any message regarding rule of law and accountability which might be hoped for with their own »counter-theatrical« behaviour, condemning the legitimacy and legality of the courts and appealing to their constituents, as Slobodan Milošević, Saddam Hussein, and Radovan Karadžić sought to do.[51] Finally, and relatedly, trials often actually make very poor spectacles, or at least ones which are not easily digestible. They involve often-opaque legal proceedings and dense legal language, and in internationalized processes both may be foreign to the affected country, with much lost in translation, both literally and conceptually.[52] Of course, there may be particular communicative power and a special form of theatre in the apparently technical and rational language of law, which outreach might better convey.[53]

---

[47] Franceschet: The International Criminal Court's Provisional Authority to Coerce, p. 96.
[48] Struett: Why the International Criminal Court Must *Pretend* to Ignore Politics, p. 90.
[49] January: *Tribunal Verité*, p. 209.
[50] Creta: The search for justice in the former Yugoslavia and beyond; Chinkin: Due process and witness anonymity.
[51] I thank Jan Christoph Suntrup for this important point, as well as the term used, »counter-theatrical«.
[52] Hoffman: Lost in Translation, in a different context, emphasizes that the conveyance of meaning involves more than simple transliteration.
[53] I am grateful again to Suntrup for this point.

Conclusion

International courts and tribunals dealing with serious international crimes increasingly navigate a difficult dialectic: between expectations that they will be »purely« legal and apolitical, and expectations that they not only will, but should, have an impact upon individuals, societies, and the politics of the states in which the crimes which they have adjudicated occurred.[54] The multiplicity of roles assigned to courts by their advocates, beneficiaries, and in many cases even their detractors, involves adjudication, pedagogy, reparation and restoration, and in many cases reconciliation and long-term transformation of social narratives. Yet, as this short essay has discussed, such courts face a variety of challenges in fulfilling such myriad roles. They face not only the apparent tension between speaking to socio-political realities of affected countries and of maintaining real and perceived neutrality, but of translating their often politicized and sometimes unpopular work to affected populations. Much of the work of communicating the purpose, activities, and decisions of tribunals is thus devolved to outreach offices, with (as I have argued here) variable meaning for culture generally and specific persons in affected societies.

List of references

Ajani, Gianmaria: Chance and Prestige. Legal Transplants in Russia and Eastern Europe, in: The American Journal of Comparative Law, 43, 1995, pp. 93–117.

Arzt, Donna E.: Views on the Ground. The Local Perception of International Criminal Tribunals in the Former Yugoslavia and Sierra Leone, in: The Annals of the American Academy of Political and Social Science, 603, 2006, pp. 226–239.

Brown, Stephen/Sriram, Chandra Lekha: »The big fish won't fry themselves.« Criminal accountability for post-election violence in Kenya, in: African Affairs, 111, 2012, pp. 1–17.

Burke-White, William W.: Proactive Complementarity. The International Criminal Court and National Courts in the Rome System of International Justice, in: Harvard International Law Journal, 49, 2008, pp. 53–108.

Burke-White, William W.: The Domestic Influence of International Criminal Tribunals. The International Criminal Tribunal for the Former Yugoslavia

---

[54] Rodman: Why the ICC Should Operate Within Peace Processes, characterizes the former as a »law above politics« view.

and the Creation of the State Court of Bosnia and Herzegovina, in: Columbia Journal of Transnational Law, 46, 2007–2008, pp. 279–350.

Campaign for Good Governance: An Opinion Poll of Sierra Leone Residents on the TRC and the Special Court, 2002 (on file with current author).

Chinkin, Christine: Due process and witness anonymity, in: American Journal of International Law, 91, 1997, pp. 75–79.

Clark, Janine Natalya: International War Crimes Tribunals and the Challenge of Outreach, in: International Criminal Law Review, 9, 2009, pp. 99–116.

Cohen, David: Hybrid Justice in East Timor, Sierra Leone, and Cambodia. »Lessons Learned« and Prospects for the Future, in: Stanford Journal of International Law, 43, 2007, pp. 1–38.

Creta, Vincent M.: The search for justice in the former Yugoslavia and beyond. Analyzing the rights of the accused under the statute and the rules of procedure and evidence of the International Criminal Tribunal for the former Yugoslavia, in: Houston Journal of International Law, 20, 1997–1998, pp. 381–420.

Drumbl, Mark: Reimagining child soldiers in international law and policy, Oxford 2012.

Finnström, Sverker: Living with bad surroundings. War, history and everyday moments in Northern Uganda, Durham, NC 2008.

Foucault, Michel: Discipline and Punish. The Birth of the Prison, New York 1979.

Franceschet, Antonio: The International Criminal Court's Provisional Authority to Coerce, in: Ethics and International Affairs, 26, 2012, pp. 93–101.

Geertz, Clifford: Negara. The Theatre State in Nineteenth-Century Bali, Princeton, NJ 1980.

Hayner, Priscilla: Unspeakable Truths. Confronting State Terror and Atrocity, New York 2001.

Hoffman, Eva: Lost in Translation, New York 1990.

Hussain, Varda: Sustaining Judicial Rescues. The Role of Outreach and Capacity-Building Efforts in War Crimes Tribunals, in: Virginia Journal of International Law, 45, 2004–2005, pp. 547–583.

International Criminal Court, Assembly of States Parties: Strategic Plan for Outreach of the International Criminal Court, ICC-ASP/5/12 (29 September 2006), at http://www.icc-cpi.int/NR/rdonlyres/FB4C75CF-FD15-4B06-B1E3-E22618FB404C/185051/ICCASP512_English1.pdf; last accessed 21.1.2013.

International Criminal Court, Office of the Prosecutor: Prosecutorial Strategy 2009–2012, (1 February 2010), paras. 16 and 17, http://www.icc-cpi.int/NR/rdonlyres/66A8DCDC-3650-4514-AA62D229D1128F65/281506/OTP Prosecutorial Strategy20092013.pdf; 26 August 2010; last accessed 22.1.2013.

International Criminal Court, Office of the Prosecutor: Report on the activities performed during the first three years (June 2003 – June 2006) 12 September

2006, para. 95, http://www.iccnow.org/documents/3YearReport%20_06Sep14.pdf; last accessed 3.1.2013.

January, Sativa: *Tribunal Verité*. Documenting Transitional Justice in Sierra Leone, in: International Journal of Transitional Justice, 3, 2009, pp. 207–228.

Krog, Antjie: Country of My Skull, London 1999.

LaGrand, Pierre: The Impossibility of Legal Transplants, in: Maastricht Journal of European and Comparative Law, 4, 1997, pp. 111–124.

Lincoln, Jessica: Transitional justice, peace and accountability. Outreach and the role of international courts after conflict, London 2011.

Massell, Gregory J.: Law as an Instrument of Revolutionary Change in a Traditional Milieu: The Case of Soviet Central Asia, in: Law & Society Review, 2, 1968, pp. 179–228.

Mills, Kurt: »Bashir is dividing us.« Africa and the International Criminal Court, in: Human Rights Quarterly, 34, 2012, pp. 404–447.

Odula, Tom: Hero's Welcome for Kenya's Int'l Court Suspects, in: Associated Press (11 April 2011) at http://abcnews.go.com/International/wireStory?id=13345510; last accessed 22.1.2013.

Office of the High Commissioner for Human Rights: Rule of Law tools for Post-Conflict States, Tool on Maximizing the Legacy of Hybrid Tribunals, Geneva 2007.

Olsen, Tricia D./Payne, Leigh A./Reiter, Andrew G.: Transitional justice in balance. Comparing processes, weighing efficacy, Washington, DC 2010.

Osiel, Mark: Mass atrocity, collective memory and the law, New Brunswick, NJ, 1997.

Rodman, Kenneth A.: Why the ICC Should Operate Within Peace Processes, in: Ethics and International Affairs, 26, 2012, pp. 59–71.

SáCouto, Susana/Cleary, Katherine: Victim Participation in the Investigations of the International Criminal Court, in: Transnational Law and Contemporary Problems, 17, 2008, pp. 73–105.

Sawyer, Edward/Kelsall, Tim: Truth vs. justice? Popular Views on the Truth and Reconciliation Commission and the Special Court for Sierra Leone, in: Online Journal of Peace and Conflict Resolution, 7, 2007, pp. 36–68.

Scarry, Elaine: The Body in Pain. The Making and Unmaking of the World, Oxford 1985.

Sikkink, Kathryn: The justice cascade. How human rights prosecutions are changing world politics, New York 2011.

Special Court for Sierra Leone Outreach Website, at http://www.sc-sl.org/ABOUT/CourtOrganization/TheRegistry/OutreachandPublicAffairs/tabid/83/Default.aspx; last accessed 27.3.2012.

Sriram, Chandra Lekha/Brown, Stephen: Kenya in the Shadow of the ICC. Complementarity, Gravity and Impact, in: International Criminal Law Review, 12, 2012, pp. 1–26.

Sriram, Chandra Lekha/Roth, Brad R. (eds.): Justice without borders? Externalizing criminal punishment for past atrocities, (special issue) Finnish Yearbook of International Law, XII, 2001, pp. 3–189.

Sriram, Chandra Lekha/Martin-Ortega, Olga/Herman, Johanna (eds.): Peacebuilding and rule of law in Africa. Just peace?, London 2011.

Sriram, Chandra Lekha/Pillay, Suren (eds.): Peace versus justice? The dilemma of transitional justice in Africa, Durban 2009.

Sriram, Chandra Lekha: (Re)building the rule of law in Sierra Leone: Beyond the formal sector?, in: Sriram, Chandra Lekha/Martin-Ortega, Olga/Herman, Johanna (eds.): Peacebuilding and rule of law in Africa. Just peace?, London 2011, pp. 127–141.

Sriram, Chandra Lekha: Unfinished business. Peacebuilding, accountability, and rule of law in Lebanon, in: Sriram, Chandra Lekha/García-Godos, Jemima/Herman, Johanna/Martin-Ortega, Olga (eds.): Transitional justice and peacebuilding on the ground. Victims and ex-combatants, London 2012, pp. 121–138.

Sriram, Chandra Lekha: Universal Jurisdiction. Problems and Prospects of Externalizing Justice, in: Finnish Yearbook of International Law, XII, 2001, pp. 47–70.

Sriram, Chandra Lekha: Victims, excombatants, and communities. Irreconcilable demands or a dangerous convergence?, in: Safferling, Christoph/Bonacker, Thorsten (eds.): Victims of International Crimes. An Interdisciplinary Discourse, The Hague 2013 (forthcoming).

Sriram, Chandra Lekha: Wrong-sizing international justice? The hybrid tribunal in Sierra Leone, in: Fordham International Law Journal, 29, 2006, pp. 472–506.

Struett, Michael J.: Why the International Criminal Court Must *Pretend* to Ignore Politics, in: Ethics and International Affairs, 26, 2012, pp. 83–92.

Suma, Mohamed: »The Charles Taylor Trial and Legacy of the Special Court for Sierra Leone« (International Center for Transitional Justice, September 2009) at http://ictj.org/sites/default/files/ICTJ-SierraLeone-Special-Court-2009-English.pdf; last accessed 22.1.2013.

Tolbert, David: The International Criminal Tribunal for the Former Yugoslavia. Unforeseen Successes and Foreseeable Shortcomings, in: Fletcher Forum of World Affairs, 26, 2002.

United Nations: United Nations Security Council Resolution 1315, UN Doc. S/RES/1315 (14 August 2000).

Vinck, Patrick/Pham, Phuong N.: Outreach Evaluation: The International Criminal Court in the Central African Republic, in: International Journal of Transitional Justice, 2010, pp. 1–22.

Watson, Alan: Legal Transplants, Athens, GA 1993.

Wiebelhaus-Brahm, Eric: Truth commissions and transitional societies. The impact on human rights and governance, London 2010.

Wierda, Marieke / Nassar, Habib / Maalouf, Lynn: Early Reflections on Local Perceptions, Legitimacy and Legacy of the Special Tribunal for Lebanon, in: Journal of International Criminal Justice, 5, 2007, pp. 1065–1081.

Young, James O.: Cultural appropriation and the arts, London 2008.

Joachim J. Savelsberg

Tribunals, Collective Memory, and Prospects of Human Rights[1]

Introduction: Consequences of Human Rights Trials and Memory Interventions

Innovative scholarship suggests it matters that impunity is no longer the common response to offenses against humanitarian law and gross violations of human rights. Political scientist Kathryn Sikkink has recently provided crucial arguments and empirical evidence in her book on the »justice cascade«.[2] Sikkink introduces her readers to a new Transitional Trial Data Set that allows for a statistical analysis of a large number of transitional justice situations. Her results challenge opponents of interventions, showing that prosecutions of human rights perpetrators, including high level actors, do not systematically produce counter-productive consequences. To the opposite, they are associated with improved subsequent human rights and democracy records. More research is needed to make sure that the relationship between transitional justice, trials and truth commissions, and positive outcomes is not explained by third factors such as a country's past practice of the rule of law.[3]

Here I am concerned with another follow-up question. Accepting for the moment the causal nature of the link between human rights trials and improved democracy and human rights records, we need to better understand the underlying mechanisms. Sikkink focuses on the deterrence function of criminal punishment, but she concedes that cultural or socialization mechanisms may also be at work. Her finding that the statistical relationship between trials and positive outcomes is especially strong when trials are accompanied or preceded by truth commissions indicates that the cultural mechanism may be especially effective. The construction of collective memories of evil by way of transitional justice thus warrants special examination.

Collective memory, human rights, and law are linked in complex ways. Daniel

---

[1] Segments of this text are based on Chapter 3 (»Constructing and Remembering the My Lai Massacre«) of Savelsberg/King: American Memories. I thank Ryan D. King and two student assistants, Rajiv Evan Rajan, and Lacy Mitchell, for their contributions to that project.
[2] Sikkink: Justice Cascade.
[3] Cf. Meierhenrich: Legacies of Law.

Levy and Natan Sznaider think of human rights trials as »transformative opportunities, where memories of grave injustices are addressed in rituals of restitution and renewal ... Justice itself becomes a form of remembrance.«[4] These authors also join others who attribute causal power to memories.[5] They argue that the memory of failed group protection regimes, one outcome of World War I and the negotiations of Versailles, propelled the idea of individualized human rights and its enactment toward the end of World War II.

Simultaneously, trials are sites of memory production.[6] Hope that they will serve a history writing function and contribute to the establishment of protective memories was expressed by political and judicial actors toward the end of World War II. Justice Robert Jackson, the American chief prosecutor at the International Military Tribunal expressed his hope with often cited words: »Unless we write the record of this movement with clarity and precision, we cannot blame the future if in days of peace it finds incredible the accusatory generalities uttered during the war. *We must establish incredible events by credible evidence.*«[7] President Franklin Delano Roosevelt thought along similar lines. As his confidant, Judge Samuel Rosenman noted: »[Roosevelt] was determined that the question of Hitler's guilt – and the guilt of his gangsters – must not be left open to future debate. The whole nauseating matter should be spread out on a permanent record under oath by witnesses and with all the written documents.«[8]

Collective memory was obviously at stake, and courts were to play a role in establishing it – with the goal of securing future peace. Collective memory is here understood in the tradition of Maurice Halbwachs, Emile Durkheim's student (and himself a victim of the Buchenwald concentration camp), as knowledge about the past that is shared, mutually acknowledged and reinforced by a collectivity. Tools include symbols such as flags, plaques and medals and rituals such as national memorial days and holidays – and what Savelsberg and King called »applied commemorations,« including legislative sessions and trials at which historical themes are articulated or processed.[9]

Here, we are primarily concerned with a specific kind of collective memory: that of horrific pasts and calamitous events, captured in the more recent concept of *cultural trauma*.[10] Berkeley sociologist and psychoanalyst Neil Smelser defines cultural trauma as »a memory accepted and publicly given credence by a relevant

---

[4] Levy/Sznaider: Human Rights and Memory, p. 19.
[5] Cf. Karstedt: Legal Institutions; Savelsberg/King: Law and Collective Memory; Savelsberg/King: Institutionalizing Collective Memories; Savelsberg/King: American Memories.
[6] Osiel: Mass Atrocities.
[7] Quoted in Landsman: Crimes of the Holocaust, pp. 6 et seq.; emphasis by JJS.
[8] Ibid., p. 6.
[9] Savelsberg/King: Institutionalizing Collective Memories.
[10] Cf. Alexander et al.: Cultural Trauma.

membership group and evoking an event or situation that is a) laden with negative affect, b) represented as indelible, and c) regarded as threatening a society's existence or violating one or more of its cultural presuppositions.«[11] Jeffrey Alexander, head of Yale's Center for Cultural Sociology, adds that cultural trauma »is anchored in Durkheim's classical idea of ›religious imagination‹ that forms »inchoate experiences, through association, condensation, and aesthetic creation, into some specific shape.«[12] In other words, what once was diffuse and chaotic in the minds of those who were exposed to horrific events begins to take shape, to become focused and organized. It is only after such transformation that groups are capable of communicating effectively about terrifying experiences, potentially »sharing them« with others who were not directly involved. In line with Smelser's definition quoted above, one of the qualities of cultural trauma, in contrast to individual trauma, is its communicability. How then might criminal courts, trials and tribunals contribute to the construction of collective memories and cultural trauma?

Empirical Research on the Representation of Atrocities through Trials

More guarded than the optimism expressed by scholars such as Kathryn Sikkink and practitioners such as Robert Jackson are conclusions suggested by a recent and growing body of empirical research on representations and memories produced by court proceedings against grave human rights violations. Historian Devin Pendas, for example, wrote an impressive study on the *Frankfurt Auschwitz Trial*, at which a group of perpetrators from the Auschwitz concentration and annihilation camp were tried between 1963 and 1965.[13] Pendas guides the reader from the indictment, via the opening moves, the taking of evidence, the closing arguments and the judgment to public reactions. The content is purposefully organized along the trial's procedural steps. Without losing sight of the political context and extrajudicial forces, Pendas shows that there is reason to take »law on the books« seriously even while studying »law in action.« The former might directly or indirectly provide the strategic frame within which actors apply tactics to advance their goals.

Pendas' subtitle speaks to the »limits of law.« A more precise sub-title would have referred specifically to the limits of *German* criminal law. In 1956 the German government had annulled Control Council Law No. 10 with its criminal cat-

---

[11] Smelser: Psychological Trauma and Cultural Trauma, p. 44.
[12] Alexander: Theory of Cultural Trauma, p. 9.
[13] Pendas: Frankfurt Auschwitz Trial.

egories such as »crimes against humanity« and its sentencing guidelines (including the death penalty). The Basic Law (*Grundgesetz*), while acknowledging the supremacy of international law, prohibited ex post-facto prosecutions. »Genocide« could thus only be prosecuted for future cases. The Frankfurt court consequently relied on standard German criminal law, created with crimes in mind that differed radically from the genocidal acts of the Holocaust. Given its pronounced subjective orientation and its distinction between perpetrator and accomplice (the latter considered a tool rather than an autonomous actor in the execution of the crime), this type of law was ill-suited for covering the complex nature of genocidal crimes and the organizational processes through which they were executed. Instead of highlighting the agency of those engaged in the systematic annihilation of millions, prosecution was successful only in particular cases of especially atrocious actions, such as brutal acts of torture during interrogations, in which malicious intent could be documented and where defendants could not present themselves as tools of the will of others. Historian Michael Marrus shows similar limitations for the Nuremberg »Doctors' Trial« conducted by American authorities under occupation law, indicating validity of Pendas' insights beyond German law.[14]

Legal constraints thus limited the trial's representational and juridical functions, frustrating the pedagogical intent with which Fritz Bauer, Prosecutor General of the state of Hessen, had advanced these collective proceedings against 22 defendants. Inspired by the Eichmann trial in Jerusalem, he sought a large, historical trial that would stir the collective conscience, increase awareness and instill in the collective memory of Germans the horrific nature of the Nazi crimes. He partly succeeded, but only within the limits of the law. While Nazi crimes came to a public and terrifying display, the trial paradoxically helped Germans to distance themselves from these crimes. Perpetration appeared, in the logic of the Auschwitz trial, as either the outgrowth of sick minds or executed in the context of a machinery, set up by Nazi leadership, in which ordinary Germans acted without or even against their own will.

The German case thus illustrates with particular clarity what Bernhard Giesen has called the »decoupling« function of criminal law.[15] While his argument applies to criminal law generally, Pendas shows how the specifics of law matter. That lesson is further brought home in Tomaz Jardim's study on the Mauthausen trial of spring 1946, the most prominent of 462 American military trials held at the site of the former Dachau concentration camp.[16] The trial lasted only 36 days, and on May 27, 1947 the first of 49 men condemned to death at that trial was hanged in the Landshut prison. Mauthausen of course was the notorious principle concen-

---

[14] Marrus: Doctors' Trial.
[15] Giesen: Trauma of Perpetrators.
[16] Jardim: Mauthausen Trial.

tration camp in Austria, set up right after the »*Anschluss*« of March 1938, with its 49 sub-camps. The cruel conditions at Mauthausen were in line with the Nazis' »extermination through work« program, which here was supported by a gas chamber and mass shootings. In total, some 100,000 inmates perished in this camp.[17]

Jardim's message that matters in this context is about the effect the trial's particular circumstances had on the story it told about the atrocities committed at Mauthausen. The investigation started in the camp itself, immediately following its liberation, conducted by poorly equipped and staffed groups of American investigators, and with the assistance of some of the hundreds of camp inmates (including the famous Simon Wiesenthal), who remained in the camp, eager to provide eyewitness testimony and to handing over crucial documentary evidence. An important product of the investigation, essential for the prosecutors' work was the »Cohen report« named after Major Eugene S. Cohen and based on his compilation of evidence between May 6 and June 15, 1945. The report was nearly 300 pages long and drew on 143 witness statements and a wealth of documentary evidence. While erroneous in some basic conclusions, the evidence reflected the input of former prisoners and provided a narrative inspired by the urgency of those who had endured the brutalities of everyday life in the camp. During the trial, the prosecutors relied on this report and on an innovative strategy of Lieutenant Colonel William Denson, leader of the prosecutorial team, who used the »innovative charge of participating in a common design to commit war crimes [which] had allowed him to prosecute large numbers of concentration camp personnel in a single trial …«[18] Being thus free from the procedural constraints of the German court at Frankfurt, and benefitting from the immediacy of victim-witness testimony, delivered just days and weeks after liberation, the nature of the evidence allowed the prosecutor to draw attention to the everyday operation and organization of camp activity. Where the Nuremberg trials had focused on a small group of leaders, and where the Frankfurt trial had directed attention to specific cruelties, here the narrative captured the organized nature and routine brutality of standard operating procedure of the concentration camp system.

On the other hand, the Mauthausen story did not reach the public attention that the IMT in Nuremberg evoked, or the American subsequent Nuremberg trials, or the Frankfurt Auschwitz trial of the 1960s. In fact, the third path of criminal justice pursued at Dachau, through American military commission courts, using established military law to prosecute nearly 1,700 war crimes suspects in a relatively short period, is barely remembered. The stories these trials told are far less sedimented in the public mind. In light of the scarcity of systematic evidence regarding the public perception of war crimes trials, we can only speculate that

---

[17] For more detailed analyses of death rates see Jardim: Mauthausen Trial, p. 56.
[18] Ibid., p. 88.

this amnesia may be due to an interaction of the immediacy of the trial conducted in turbulent times, the relatively low rank of many of the defendants and the context of a foreign military court. These conditions were reflected, according to Jardim, by a mostly empty court room. The public and the press were largely absent.

Comparing findings of historians such as Pendas and Jardim thus demonstrates how the law under which trials are held, and their social context, affect both: the nature of representations and narratives trials produce and the chances that these narratives become sedimented in collective memory.

Toward Sedimentation of Representations in Collective Memory

Despite profound insights into the shaping of narratives by criminal trials, few studies explore the long-term effects of trials on collective memory. This deficit in the literature is not accidental. Empirically assessing such effects is most challenging. In this section I report one case study from research in which my collaborators and I have attempted to do so.[19] The case concerns the My Lai massacre, committed by an American company during the Vietnam War. It allowed us to at least approximate the measurement of collective memories as produced by a trial in a war crimes case.

The My Lai massacre was culturally processed in three distinct institutional contexts, each with its own rules and logics, and each producing a distinct narrative of the occurrence. The first is the famous journalistic work by Seymour Hersh, resulting in a Pulitzer Prize-awarded book.[20] The second is a report issued by an administrative Army commission, the Peers Report, named after General Peers who led the investigation.[21] The third is a criminal trial against a number of defendants involved in the massacre.

Historians agree on some of what occurred in My Lai, a hamlet in the village of Son My on the coast of central Vietnam. Several hundred innocent Vietnamese civilians, mostly women, children and old men, were killed by members of an American infantry brigade on March 16, 1968, during the peak of the Vietnam War. Historian Kendrick Oliver provides the following concise description in the introduction of his book, *The My Lai Massacre in American History and Memory*:

»On the morning of 16 March 1968, the men of Charlie Company, 11th Light Infantry Brigade, Americal Division, US Army, entered the hamlet of Tu Cung [which includes the

---

[19] Savelsberg/King: American Memories.
[20] Hersh: My Lai 4.
[21] Goldstein et al.: My Lai Massacre.

subhamlet of My Lai 4], in the village of Son My ... The Company was assigned to a temporary battalion-sized unit named Task Force Barker, and it was led by Captain Ernest Medina. In charge of the company's 1st Platoon was Lieutenant William Calley. Inside Tu Cung, the company encountered no enemy forces, no opposing fire of any kind. Its only casualty was self-inflicted. Nevertheless, by early afternoon, well over 300 residents of the hamlet lay dead. Those killed were, predominantly, either women, old men or small children. For a number of the women, rape had preceded death.«[22]

Despite today's consensus among historians, the three dominant accounts of My Lai, produced within the first three years after the massacre, varied with regard to several issues, including the number of victims, those responsible and their state of mind.

The My Lai Massacre: Three Institutions and three Narratives

The Peers Report, a rather thorough investigation of the My Lai incident, summarized the events as follows, addressing various dimensions of organizational and individual behavior:

»1. During the period March 16–19, 1968, U.S. Army troops of TF [Task Force] Barker, 11th Brigade, Americal Division, massacred a large number of noncombatants in two villages of Son My Village, Quang Ngai Province, Republic of Vietnam. The precise number of Vietnamese killed cannot be determined but was at least 175 and may exceed 400.

2. The massacre occurred in conjunction with a combat operation which was intended to neutralize Son My Village as a logistical support base and staging area, and to destroy elements of an enemy battalion thought to be located in the Son My area.

3. The massacre resulted primarily from the nature of the orders issued by persons in the chain of command within TF Barker ...

5. Prior to the incident, there had developed within certain elements of the 11th Brigade a permissive attitude toward the treatment and safeguarding of noncombatants which contributed to the mistreatment of such persons during the Son My operation.

6. The permissive attitude in the treatment of Vietnamese was, on 16–19 March 1968, exemplified by an almost total disregard for the lives and property of the civilian population of Son My Village on the part of commanders and key staff officers of TF Barker.

7. On 16 March, soldiers at the squad and platoon level, with some elements of TF Barker, murdered noncombatants while under the supervision and control of their immediate superiors.

8. A part of the crimes visited on the inhabitants of Son My Village included individual and group acts of murder, rape, sodomy, maiming, and assault of noncombatants and the

---

[22] Oliver: My Lai Massacre, p. 1.

mistreatment and killing of detainees. They further included the killing of livestock, destruction of crops, closing of wells, and the burning of dwellings in several subhamlets ... [for points 9–18, see the Peers Report in Goldstein et al., eds. 1976, pp. 314–16] ...

19. At every command level within the Americal Division, actions were taken, both wittingly and unwittingly, which effectively suppressed information concerning the war crimes committed at Son My Village ...«[23]

The summary entails additional sections on the inadequacy of reports, investigations and reviews, policies, directives and training, and on the actions of individuals involved in the massacre. The report only covers the period between March 16, 1968 and March 29, 1969, the date on which Ronald Ridenhour, a Vietnam veteran, sent a letter to the President, Pentagon officials, and members of the U.S. Congress that revealed information he had gathered on the massacre and the cover-up. Due to the secrecy of the Commission's work, Ridenhour believed that the cover-up was continuing. His subsequent contact with journalist Seymour Hersh resulted in Hersh's 1970 book, *My Lai 4,* which drew considerable public attention to the case. This journalistic account adds graphic detail to the Commission report, as the following excerpt illustrates:

»The killings began without warning ... [One witness reports he saw] ›some old women and some little children — fifteen or twenty of them — in a group around a temple where some incense was burning. They were kneeling and crying and praying, and various soldiers ... walked by and executed these women and children by shooting them in the head with their rifles.‹

There were few physical protests from the people; about eighty of them were taken quietly from their homes and herded together in a plaza area ... [First Platoon commander Lt.] Calley left [subordinates] Meadlo, Boyce and a few others with the responsibility of guarding the group. ›You know what I want you to do with them‹, he told Meadlo. Ten minutes later ... he returned and asked, ›Haven't you got rid of them yet? I want them dead.‹ Radioman Sledge who was trailing Calley, heard the officer tell Meadlo to ›waist them.‹ Meadlo followed orders: ›We stood about ten to fifteen feet away from them and then he [Calley] started shooting them. Then he told me to start shooting them. I started to shoot them. So we went ahead and killed them ... Women were huddled against their children, vainly trying to save them ...‹

By this time there was shooting everywhere ... Brooks and his men in the second platoon to the north had begun to systematically ransack the hamlet and slaughter the people, kill the livestock and destroy the crops. Men poured rifle and machine gun fire without knowing — or seemingly caring — who was inside ...

Carter testified that soon after the third platoon moved in, a woman was sighted. Somebody knocked her down, and then, Carter said, [Commander of Company C, Captain] ›Medina

---

[23] Goldstein et al.: My Lai Massacre, pp. 314 et seqq.

Tribunals, Collective Memory, and Prospects of Human Rights 125

shot her with his M16 rifle. I was fifty or sixty feet away and saw this. There was no reason to shoot the girl.‹ The men continued on, making sure no one was escaping. ›We came to where the soldiers had collected fifteen or more Vietnamese men, women and children in a group ... Medina said: ›Kill every one. Leave no one standing.‹ A machine gunner began firing into the group. Moments later one of Medina's radio operators slowly ›passed‹ among them and finished them off.«[24]

The events captured and narrated in the Peers Commission report and in Hersh's book were ultimately accompanied by a third narrative – the criminal trial. Initial investigations of about 30 individuals resulted in formal charges against more than half of them.[25] The court proceedings addressed two types of behavior. The first covered a large number of »spontaneous« rapes and killings of individuals during the »mop-up« operation for which Lieutenant LaCross' third platoon was largely responsible. According to Hersh:

»Le Tong, a twenty-eight-year-old rice farmer, reported seeing one woman raped after GIs killed her children. Nguyen Khoa, a thirty-seven-year-old peasant, told of the thirteen-year-old girl who was raped before being killed. GIs then attacked Khoa's wife, tearing off her clothes. Before they could rape her, however, Khoa said, their six-year-old son, riddled with bullets, fell and saturated her with blood. The GIs left her alone.«[26]

Such »unofficial« reports of spontaneous atrocities were not backed by the same hard evidence as the ordered mass killing executed by the First Platoon under the command of Lt. Calley, on which the charges were based. Calley stood trial for 102 of the killings he had ordered and in which he had participated. He pleaded, in his defense, that his actions were in line with superior orders. Yet, as the court-martial argued, and as the judge confirmed in his instructions to the jury, »... the obedience of a soldier is not the obedience of an automaton. A soldier is a reasoning agent, obliged to respond, not as a machine, but as a person. The law takes these factors into account in assessing criminal responsibility for acts done in compliance with illegal orders.«[27] A jury of combat veterans eventually convicted William Calley of premeditated murder of not less than 22 persons. The conviction was based on witness testimony, confirming that Calley had ordered and participated in the mass executions, witnessed by members of the platoon and by a helicopter crew. Legal proof was too weak to link the massacre to orders from superiors, especially since LTC Frank A. Barker, the immediate superior of Company C's leader, was killed in action shortly after the Son My massacre. Captain Ernest L. Medina, the commander of Company C, who had given the orders for the attack

---

[24] Hersh: My Lai 4, pp. 49–54.
[25] Kelman/Hamilton: Crimes of Obedience.
[26] Hesh: My Lai 4, p. 72.
[27] Kelman/Hamilton: Crimes of Obedience, p. 209.

on Son My on March 15, 1968, was not found guilty. Neither were other members of the Company, nor those who engaged in spontaneous atrocities, nor direct subordinates of Lieutenant Calley who participated in the mass executions. Rules of evidence allowed, in the eyes of the court, only for the conviction of one participant in the massacre.[28] And even this conviction was challenged in the public sphere, and politicians proved receptive to such challenges. President Nixon reduced the life sentence to twenty years, and Secretary of Defense Callaway further reduced it to ten years in 1974. It is conceivable, of course, that the public uproar was a protest against the individualizing (or decoupling) function of criminal law.[29]

We thus find a distinct difference between the accounts of the Peers Commission and the journalistic report by Seymour Hersh on the one hand, and the trial narrative on the other.

- The Commission and the journalistic report find that responsibility for the massacre and the cover-up rests with the many members of Company C, including its commander, and with military personnel above the Company level, which was not a conclusion reached by the court.
- The commission and journalistic accounts address the organized massacre and »spontaneous« rapes and killings, whereas the verdict focuses on the organized mass execution.
- The number of victims as estimated by the Peers Commission was from 175 to possibly more than 400. Hersh exceeds the upper end of the Peers' estimate (450–500).[30] The court, constrained by evidentiary rules, charged Captain Medina with the murder of 102 civilians, but in the end only Lt. Calley was found guilty of at least 22 killings.

Methodologically, the availability of three narratives, each produced in a different institutional context, including a criminal court, allows us to examine which of these social constructions of reality settle in American collective memory. In the absence of survey data on this issue, my collaborators and I measured information entailed in those sources from which many Americans learn about historic events: textbooks about American history used in high schools (8th through 12th grades) throughout the United States and reports and commentary in one prominent American newspaper over the decades.

---

[28] Randall Collins: Violence, offers a recent and distinct depiction of My Lai as a »forward panic.« For critiques and expansions of Collins's micro-sociological approach see Cooney: Collins's Violence; Savelsberg: Crime and Human Rights, Chapter 5. For local memories and reconstructions in Vietnam see Kwon: After the Massacre. These representations were not available in the 1970s United States and could thus not have affected the American collective memory of the trial. They are noteworthy as they inform us that the three narratives depicted here are not the only possible constructions of the massacre but are shaped by historical, national, and institutional contexts.

[29] See Kelman/Hamilton: Crimes of Obedience, p. 210.

[30] Hersh: My Lai 4, p. 75.

My Lai in Collective Memory – News Media and Textbook Proxies

Court trials reach a broader public primarily through the mass media. In addition, history textbooks are potential carriers of information about historical trials, suited to build repertoires of knowledge about the past in a younger, impressionable audience. Textbook production is driven, of course, by its own institutional rules and its own logic in which peculiar markets play a central role. Decisions on the acquisition of textbooks in the United States are typically made by elected school boards based on recommendations from adoption committees. In some states, such as Texas and California – massive customers that textbook publishers seek to satisfy – decisions are made at the state level. Guidelines that speak to the desired content of textbooks are typically taken seriously by publishers who make enormous investments in each textbook and are eager to see returns. Diverse lobby groups guard carefully over these guidelines and the production to make sure that no »offensive« content will appear in the books.[31] Books are thus likely to privilege state certified views of history and not to offend powerful constituents. As we examined American history textbooks we thus asked how much coverage existed of the My Lai massacre and which of the three narratives described above dominate.

As we conducted content analysis of a sample of 105 history text book, we catalogued several types of information that speak to the aforesaid narratives.[32] For instance, does the chapter (or passage) highlight individual or organizational responsibility? Are upper ranks of the military implicated? How are perpetrators and victims described? And is there mention of a cover-up?

We then used a similar coding scheme to assess how My Lai was discussed in news reporting in *The New York Times* between 1969 and 2006.[33] The articles were located and coded in a manner consistent with the procedure applied to the examination of history textbooks. This dataset resulted in 676 news articles, nearly 90 % of which appeared in the 1970s.

The findings from our content analysis of textbooks are revealing. For one, and despite the grand conjecture immediately after the massacre about My Lai being a watershed event on par with the Kennedy assassination, this mass killing of women and children only appears in a minority of American history text-

---

[31] Ravitch: Language Police.
[32] To compile a sample of high school history textbooks, we first searched diverse databases (EBSCO: Academic Search Complete; JSTOR) to establish a list of all scholarly journal articles that utilized content analysis on U.S. high school history textbooks published after 1979. We performed a search for the same keywords on the OCLC WorldCat FirstSearch database and compiled an additional list of articles and also of appropriate books. We also performed an internet database search using Google Scholar and gained additional book and articled sources. Last, we performed a simple internet search, using Google, for the same keywords from which we gained one website as a valuable source. For more information see Savelsberg/King: American Memories, pp. 42 et seq.
[33] Here we used Lexis Nexis to identify articles discussing My Lai.

books. In our sample of 105 textbooks, 61 % (N=64) made no mention of My Lai. All textbooks contain substantial chapters on the Vietnam War, and some mention damage caused to the Vietnamese countryside or the unintentional bombing of civilians. Still, the majority of textbooks avoided any explicit reference to the My Lai massacre.

Our data further indicate, that even when My Lai is addressed in history textbooks, such utterances are typically very brief, sometimes utterly fleeting. Only few books include lengthier passages that detail the minutiae of the massacre, but the »modal description« of the My Lai massacre – when one is found at all – is both terse and generic.[34] The event is often characterized as either a microcosm of combat stress that overtook soldiers after North Vietnam's Tet offensive (42 %) or as an episode that contributed to changing attitudes about Vietnam on the home front (47 %).

Second, and most pertinent here, the textbooks and the newspaper articles reflect the trial narrative more than the Commission and Seymour Hersh's accounts. Beginning with the history textbooks, we see evidence of the legal narrative in multiple places. We find no direct mention of the Peers Commission Report, and we encounter only four explicit references to Hersh's Pulitzer Prize-winning journalistic book. References to the trial, however, are more frequent. For instance, one of the earliest books in our sample to mention My Lai includes the following:

»For many in the nation the disclosure of American atrocities committed against North Vietnamese at My Lai were gruesome evidence of both the nature and futility of that war. *These revelations came out mainly in the trial of Lieutenant William Calley* [author's emphasis]. He was found guilty by a military court for allowing and encouraging troops under his immediate command to shoot at unarmed and helpless men, women, and children.«[35]

Lt. Calley was explicitly mentioned in nearly 60 % of the books noting the My Lai incident. Almost all of these books also make a general reference to »U.S. troops«; one refers to »a U.S. Army Officer« (likely Calley), yet few other soldiers are personally implicated. The only other name explicitly mentioned is Captain Ernest Medina, the leader of Company C (one mention), who was court martialed but found not guilty in the My Lai massacre. In addition, the trial made scant reference to the cover-up or the plausible culpability of military members of superior rank to Captain Medina. This omission is particularly striking in contrast to the Peers Commission report and Hersh's book. In the textbook analysis we count

---

[34] In a few cases there were references to some of the more graphic details of the My Lai incident, but these were in the strong minority. For example, in Cayton: America: Pathways to the Present, there is a graphic quote from Private Meadlo, who states: »We huddled them up. We made them squat down ... I poured about four clips [about 68 shots] into the group ... The mothers kept hugging their children ... Well, we kept right on firing ...«.

[35] Leinwand: Pageant of American History, p. 646.

only 13 mentions (about a third of cases mentioning My Lai) of a cover-up, eight of which appear after 1990. Nine books (less than one quarter) implicate higher ranks. Although the books are hardly monolithic in their coverage of My Lai, we see evidence that the trial narrative more strongly affects textbook accounts than the two competing sources.

The *Times* analysis corroborates these findings. For instance, our analysis deemed articles to fit a »script« (i.e., those of Peers, Hersh, or the court martial) if the source itself was cited specifically by name in an article. A multiple response analysis[36] shows that, when a script was mentioned, it was overwhelmingly that provided by the military trial. Forty-three percent of articles made reference to the trial, compared to two percent that mentioned Hersh's investigation and seven percent that referred to the Peers inquiry.

A similar multiple response analysis was employed for alleged perpetrators in the massacre. In all, nearly 70 different names or groups appear in the 676 articles. As with the history textbooks, the modal category is again Lt. Calley (180 mentions). A general reference to »U.S. Troops« came in a distant second (84), followed by Colonel Oran Henderson (72)[37] and Captain Medina (65). This pattern is particularly evident after the court martial and conviction of Calley. Prior to 1971, the *Times* articles often made reference to »U.S. Troops« as perpetrators at My Lai (21% of articles in our sample). Also, in this early stage, ending three years after the massacre and during the year in which the trial concluded, Henderson was mentioned fewer than two percent of the time, Medina less than four percent, and Calley in eighteen percent of articles. After the trial ended, the My Lai culprits moved in the direction from the general (e.g., »U.S. troops«) to the particular (e.g., Calley, Medina). In the post-trial period, Calley is mentioned in thirty-one percent of cases, Henderson in fifteen, and Medina in thirteen percent. Hence, much like law enforcement can apotheosize an individual within a larger struggle, law can also defile individuals and render them symbols of a sinister crime.[38] In the process, we encounter a collective forgetting of the larger milieu of circumstances surrounding the event. This sentiment is largely consistent with Oliver's recent conjecture. As Oliver writes,

»That the legal process emphasized the agency of a small number of individuals no doubt reinforced the inclination of the media to adopt what was in any case a common news practice when engaging with events as complex and enigmatic as those which had oc-

---

[36] Articles in *The New York Times* could discuss multiple scripts per article, and hence multiple response analysis was used for the *Times* sample.

[37] Henderson was in charge of the 11th Brigade and the highest ranking officer to be tried for the My Lai massacre.

[38] On ways in which Rosa Parks and her arrest became the symbol of the Montgomery, Alabama, bus boycott and the civil rights movement more generally, despite the heroic contributions by many others, see Barry Schwartz: Oneness, and his arguments on the symbolic power of oneness.

curred at My Lai (4): to gain narrative and analytical traction by reducing the frame of reportage focusing upon the fate of one or two actors. This was most evident with regard to William Calley.«[39]

Finally, we examined the discussion of victims in both the history textbooks and the *Times* articles. Compared to the other aspects of our inquiry, the issue of victims revealed a greater variety of depictions. Textbooks published in the early years of our study period stay rather close to the trial narrative. Prior to 1980, only two books mention body counts that do not align with the trial narrative. Beginning in the 1980s, a substantially higher proportion of textbooks mention the number of victims as exceeding 200.

The New York Times articles tell a comparable story, although these articles appear to stay closer to the trial narrative. When we isolate our analysis to general articles (omitting obituaries, op-ed essays and letters to the editor), about forty-two percent made no reference to the number of casualties, mentioning only »civilians« or »women and children.« More than one third, however, report a number of causalities that seems to reflect the trial narrative. Precisely forty percent of general articles in our sample cite the number of civilian deaths as somewhere between 10 and 125. These numbers are close to either the number of charges (for 102 deaths) or convictions (not less than 22) achieved in the trial. Only about ten percent of articles mentioned civilian deaths consistent with Hersh's investigation (350–400) or the Peers Report (175; perhaps as many as 400).

Clearly, textbook and media narratives that do account for the My Lai massacre focus on Lt. Calley, the one convict in the My Lai trial, the offenses committed directly under his command, and the number of victims killed directly through the mass execution he ordered. Competing narratives from the Peers Commission report and Seymour Hersh's journalistic book are underrepresented for most of our analytic categories. While they indicate how law as a constitutor of history must compete with other institutions, law's dominant position is confirmed in the case of My Lai.

Conclusions: Trials in Collective Memories

Our case study on the My Lai massacre and its cultural processing adds to insights provided by historians who explore how the institutional logic of criminal trials affects the narratives about war crimes and other mass atrocities they produce. We too find that trials tell the history of mass killings selectively. The attribution of guilt is individualized. Organizational failure is underemphasized. Crimes com-

---

[39] Oliver: My Lai Massacre, pp. 55 et seq.

mitted as standard operating procedure find less attention than specific atrocities committed by individuals who go beyond the demands of their superiors. Atrocities committed by lower ranked actors are privileged, and higher ranks are spared.

Some of these selectivities are yet more pronounced in the Vietnam case than in the NS cases, possibly reflecting broader patterns that emerge when we compare trials against grave violations of human rights: The Mauthausen trial was conducted by victorious occupying powers and under military law. The Frankfurt Auschwitz trial was conducted by a domestic court of a nation that had to face its dark past in order to regain a place in the community of nations. The My Lai trial instead was conducted by a domestic military court of a country that saw little need to justify itself toward a broad international audience.[40]

Importantly, the My Lai study goes beyond previous research to empirically demonstrate that trials leave traces in a nation's collective memory – at least as indicated by such carriers as its textbook writers and journalists and their publishers. In the My Lai case, the intensity of memory falls short of the hopes some have articulated in other contexts. We are lacking the counterfactual tough and do not know how much My Lai would be remembered had there not been a trial. We do, however, discover in the collective memory traces of the trial, the narrative it produced and the institutional logic under which it was conducted. This may be interpreted as a sign for the awareness heightening effect of the trial. But it simultaneously tells us that primarily the trial's scaled down narrative gets preserved in collective memory.

Memories have consequences. While our data do not permit attributing later patterns and events to the memories of My Lai, we do note that, according to data provided by the International Social Survey Programme, the brutalities of the Vietnam War have certainly not inflicted any enduring damage to the standing of the American military in public opinion or of national pride generally.[41] While the American population is a world leader in national pride, domain-specific data show that part of this position is due to the population's pride in the armed forces. Lessons from My Lai also seem to have little effect on the mindset of many in the American military. A report released by the U.S. Army in the fall of 2006 shows that more than one third of soldiers fighting in Iraq believe that torture should be allowed if it helps gather important information about insurgents – despite the illegality of torture in international law. Two thirds of Marines and half of Army troops respond that they would not report a team member for mistreating a civilian or for destroying civilian property unnecessarily.[42]

---

[40] Savelsberg/King: American Memories, Chapter 10.
[41] Cf. Smith: National Pride.
[42] Mental Health Advisory Team (MHAT) IV, Operation Iraqi Freedom 05-07, 2006.

In short, Durkheimian notions of trials as rituals that engrave messages into the collective conscience are partly confirmed. While the public and media were largely absent at the Mauthausen trial, and the trial is barely remembered, the legal proceedings of the more public and publicized Frankfurt Auschwitz and My Lai trials have left marks on the public consciousness and memory. Findings also suggest though that in cases in which trials focus on selected low-level frontline agents, the ritual potency of law in the formation of collective memory is at least weakened.

Weberian insights into the specific logics of distinct institutional spheres, here the law, are confirmed. And more: Legal logics and the narratives they produce color collective memories. In the My Lai case, the analysis of history textbooks and media reports reveals memories of the massacre that more often than not reflect the historic account as established by judicial proceedings. The decoupling function of trials leaves the collective's reputation unharmed as suggested by Americans' national pride in the military and military attitudes toward the breaking of international humanitarian law. The path dependency of collective memory, never letting go of the trial's construction, appears to be at work.[43] This does not exclude that memory's path is simultaneously affected by powerful mnemonic entrepreneurs, in line with presentist arguments that Maurice Halbwachs, the father of the sociology of collective memory, taught us long ago.[44]

Can trials then produce collective memories suited to end cycles of violence and advance human rights protections? Yes, they can – in some cases and within limits!

List of references

Alexander, Jeffrey C.: Toward a Theory of Cultural Trauma, in: Jeffrey C. Alexander / Ron Eyerman / Bernhard Giesen / Neil J. Smelser / Piotr Sztompka: Cultural Trauma and Collective Identity. Berkeley, CA 2004, pp. 1–30.

Alexander, Jeffrey C. / Eyerman, Ron / Giesen, Bernhard / Smelser, Neil J. / Sztompka, Piotr: Cultural Trauma and Collective Identity, Berkeley, CA 2004.

Cayton, Andrew et al.: America: Pathways to the Present, Englewood Cliffs, NJ 2000.

Collins, Randall: Violence: A Micro-sociological Theory, Princeton, NJ 2008.

Cooney, Mark: The scientific significance of Collins's »Violence«, in: British Journal of Sociology, 60, 2009, pp. 586–594.

---

[43] Cf. Olick: Genre Memories.
[44] Halbwachs: On Collective Memory.

Giesen, Bernhard: Triumph and Trauma, Boulder, CO 2004.

Goldstein, Joseph / Marshall, Burke / Schwartz, Jack: The My Lai Massacre and its Cover-up: Beyond the Reach of Law? The Peers Commission Report with a Supplement and an Introductory Essay on the Limits of Law, New York, NY 1976.

Halbwachs, Maurice: On Collective Memory, edited, translated and with an Introduction by Lewis A. Coser, Chicago, IL 1992.

Hersh, Seymour M.: My Lai 4, New York 1970.

Jardim, Tomaz: The Mauthausen Trial: American Military Justice in Germany, Cambridge, MA 2012.

Karstedt, Susanne (ed.): Legal Institutions and Collective Memory, Oxford 2009.

Kelman, Herbert C. / Hamilton, V. Lee: The My Lai Massacre: Crimes of Obedience and Sanctioned Massacres, in: M. David Ermann / Richard J. Lundman (eds.): Corporate and Governmental Deviance: Problems of Organizational Behavior in Contemporary Society, Oxford 2002, pp. 195–221.

Kwon, Hoenik: After the Massacre: Commemoration and Consolation in Ha My and My Lai. Berkeley, CA 2006.

Landsman, Stephan: Crimes of the Holocaust: The Law Confronts Hard Cases, Philadelphia, PA 2005.

Leinwand, Gerald: The Pageant of American History. Boston, MA 1975.

Levy, Daniel / Sznaider, Natan: Human Rights and Memory, University Park, PA 2010.

Marrus, Michael R.: The Nuremberg Doctors' Trial and the Limitations of Context, in: Patricia Heberer / Jürgen Matthäus (eds.): Atrocities on Trial, Lincoln, NE 2008, pp. 103–122.

Meierhenrich, Jens: The Legacies of Law: Long-run Consequences of Legal Development in South Africa, 1652–2000, Cambridge 2008.

Mental Health Advisory Team (MHAT) IV – Operation Iraqi Freedom 05-07. 2006. Final Report of November 17, 2006. Office of the Surgeon, Multi-national Force-Iraq, and Office of the Surgeon General, United States Army Medical Command, Washington, DC 2006.

Olick, Jeffrey: Genre Memories and Memory Genres: A Dialogical Analysis of May 8, 1945, Commemorations in the Federal Republic of Germany, in: The American Sociological Review, 64, 1999, pp. 381–402.

Oliver, Kendrick: The My Lai Massacre in American History and Memory, Manchester 2006.

Osiel, Mark J.: Mass Atrocities, Collective Memory, and the Law, New Brunswick, NJ 1997.

Pendas, Devin O.: The Frankfurt Auschwitz Trial, 1963–65: Genocide, History, and the Limits of Law, Cambridge 2006.

Ravitch, Diane: The Language Police: How Pressure Groups Restrict What Students Learn, New York, NY 2003.

Savelsberg, Joachim J. 2010. Crime and Human Rights: Criminology of Genocide and Atrocities, London 2010.

Savelsberg, Joachim J./King, Ryan D.: Institutionalizing Collective Memories of Hate: Law and Law Enforcement in Germany and the United States, in: American Journal of Sociology, 111, 2005, pp. 579–616.

Savelsberg, Joachim J./King, Ryan D.: Law and Collective Memory, in: Annual Review of Law and Social Science, 3, 1997, pp. 189–211.

Savelsberg, Joachim J./King, Ryan D.: American Memories: Atrocities and the Law, New York, NY 2011.

Schwartz, Barry: Collective Forgetting and the Symbolic Power of Oneness: The Strange Apotheosis of Rosa Parks, in: Social Psychology Quarterly, 72, 2009, pp. 123–142.

Sikkink, Kathryn: The Justice Cascade: How Human Rights Prosecutions are Changing World Politics, New York, NY 2011.

Smelser, Neil J.: Psychological Trauma and Cultural Trauma, in: Jeffrey C. Alexander/Ron Eyerman/Bernhard Giesen/Neil J. Smelser/Piotr Sztompka: Cultural Trauma and Collective Identity. Berkeley, CA 2004, pp. 31–59.

Smith, Tom W.: National Pride in Comparative Perspective, in: Max Haller/Roger Jowell/Tim W. Smith (eds.): The International Social Survey Programme, 1984–2009: Charting the Globe, New York, NY 2009, pp. 197–221.

Interludium
Documenting war crimes

Podiumsdiskussion mit Rob Lemkin, Ali Samadi Ahadi, Werner Gephart
und Annette Wieviorka im Anschluss an die Vorführung des Dokumentarfilms
»Enemies of the People«
Moderation: Alexander Glodzinski

Interludium

Documenting war crimes

Discussion with Rob Lemkin, Ali Samadi Ahadi, Werner Gephart and Annette Wieviorka subsequent to the screening of the documentary film *Enemies of the people*
Moderation: Alexander Glodzinski

Annotation: *Enemies of the people* is a ground-breaking documentary about the mass murders committed in Cambodia under the regime of the *Khmers rouges*. The Cambodian journalist Thet Sambath, who lost his own family in the killing fields, succeeds after many years of persistent investigative work in persuading the perpetrators of the massacres to give an account of their crimes. During his many conversations with Sambath, Nuon Chea aka ›Brother Number Two‹, who constituted together with Pol Pot the executive top of the *Khmers Rouges* state, confesses for the first time how they ordered the systematic murder of party members whom they considered ›enemies of the people‹. Moreover, Sambath manages to illuminate the actual dynamics of the killing fields by convincing a group of ordinary people in the province who were part of the execution of this murderous policy to talk about their traumatic past. Thus, this film forms an invaluable document of historiography, but also of the aesthetic means to deal with crimes that are hardly representable. Evidently, such an artistic approach must differ from the legal coping with the massacres as it is practised in the current *Khmers rouges* tribunal (the ›Extraordinary Chambers in the Courts of Cambodia‹).

Enemies of the people was screened during the conference about ›Tribunals. Literary representation and means of legally processing war crimes in a global context‹ that was hosted by the Käte Hamburger Centre for Advanced Study ›Law as Culture‹ and the University of Bonn's Institute for German Studies, Comparative Literature and Cultural Studies from April 25 to 27, 2012. In the subsequent discussion, that is reproduced here, Rob Lemkin, co-director and co-producer of the documentary, talked about the genesis and the aim of this film, accompanied by comments by cultural sociologist Werner Gephart, historian Annette Wieviorka and filmmaker Ali Samadi Ahadi.

ALEXANDER GLODZINSKI:
This film was just the beginning of a project which is still ongoing and which hopefully will keep ongoing for many years to come and bring out much more

truths out to the surface. Certainly, this truth differs from the truth that is revealed at the tribunal in Phnom Penh at the moment. The interesting approach that Thet Sambath is following here, and in which this film appears just as one piece in a bigger project, is to create an archive. He wants to inspire other people all over Cambodia to do the same work, to keep on with the research in other parts of Cambodia. So for Sambath, this is the beginning of a bigger process. It's a process that tries to answer certain questions: ›Why did all this happen? Why was my family killed?‹

The history of Cambodia was for many years a black box and the black box just started to be opened. One thing the film achieved in Cambodia was that it initiated a dialog between victims and perpetrators in the country. There were heavy reactions, not least on the victims' side because they were so happy that finally some of the perpetrators were speaking out, were giving them answers that they had been longing for for three decades. And this discourse is still going on.

Of course, doing research in a country, in which some of the politically involved people are still in power, are still in high ranking positions, is not easy. Thet Sambath had to endure some critical situations but he keeps on working in the same field.

One of the most interesting points brought up by this film is a certain contradiction between justice and truth. On the one hand there is the tribunal trying to establish justice, and on the other hand there is a certain kind of truth brought forward by the film, which is definitely not the same. At the beginning, the tribunal used parts of *Enemies of the people* to show to the jury what Nuon Chea had already stated in the film, and they were hoping that he might repeat the plea of guilty in the tribunal. He didn't do that so far. The Court also asked you, Rob, to hand them over the raw-material, these thousands of hours of interview, especially the ones with Nuon Chea, because they might have been helpful for the accusation of him. But Thet Sambath and you refused to hand over this raw-material, certainly because you were on a different mission than the tribunal. It is a hybrid tribunal of which nobody really knows where it is heading at the moment, if it is going to be successful and who is holding the political strings. Maybe you could explain: Why did you refuse to hand over the material?

Rob Lemkin:
When the film was first shown, the investigating judges wanted to use it as a part of their evidence. It was going to be used to frame an *intime conviction*, as it is called in French, a special civil law procedure. In other words, the two judges, the French judge, who is not in place anymore, and the Cambodian judge were looking to decide: Was Nuon Chea and were three other former members of the central committee of the Communist Party of Cambodia, were they guilty of these big

crimes? And so they wanted to use this film as part of their evidence they were going to consider.

At that time the film was not particularly present in the public domain, because a film like this seeps into the public domain rather gradually. At that time, it had just been shown at the Sundance Film Festival.

At that time, we were put in a position where we were being asked to give them material to use as part of their criminal investigation, which put us in contradiction with the position we have always had. Thet Sambath made our point of view clear in the film: We are not working for the court. We let the people we talked to know that their stories were to pass into the public domain and then events would take their course. So we made it clear that the court might use our material and that our interlocutors might be obliged to account for their stories. But we did not want to hand over the material these persons talked to us about directly to the investigators. We are not agents of the court. We are not part of that process. And so we decided not to give them the material. In fact, the court used the material very early on – because it did come into the public domain. But at the time when they framed their *intime conviction* they were not able to use it as a result of us. And they made a lot of complaints about it. There were various criticisms directed to me particularly and Thet Sambath for this decision.

Another reason for our choice, aside from the kind of ethical reason that I stated just now, was a practical reason. This film is just ninety minutes long and it is a distillation of around two hundred hours of material. Many dimensions to the story of the killing fields have not made their way into this film. When we completed the film we felt that there were many aspects that needed further investigation. Thus, we continued our work and we are actually making a second film at the moment, a dangerous film to make. If we had handed material of the first film over to the court, we would have no credibility when going to the people out in villages, in the countryside and saying: ›We would like to talk to you. Tell us everything that you know. Tell us everything that you did. Try to remember people you worked with back in those terrible days, if you can just remember things.‹ These people would certainly refuse to share their knowledge because they would consider us agents of the court. So we would have not been able to continue that work, and not just us, but probably any other investigators, researchers or journalists who wanted to do this story – and I hope that this work of inquiry will be taken on by all sorts of different people over the years that are left. Obviously, the people who were participants in the killing fields do not have that many years left on this earth, but maybe there is another ten or twenty years in which some of this information can still be got. And this attempt would have been compromised, so that we still think we have come to the right decision.

COMMENT FROM THE AUDIENCE:
As long as there is a court, people will be suspicious anyway.

LEMKIN:
That is true. Every day, in the tribunal's procedure people are being cross-examined for the taking of evidence. Of course they are always concerned if they are liable to prosecution and are inclined to stop talking. Even the court, even the judges are not able to give assurances to the people who are coming into the court about what may happen. Duch, the supervisor of the infamous prison camp S-21, who has already been convicted and sentenced to life in prison, even he was concerned about his situation. This is a man who knows he will never leave prison, but he was concerned whether he was going to incriminate himself. And no lawyers and no judges in the court could assure him about whether he was not actually going to be prosecuted in some other dimension.

So who are we? We are very humble people, we just have no power to do anything.

GLODZINSKI:
In Duch's case, it is not clear why they put the charge against him up and down. It might have political reasons.

LEMKIN:
Yes, perhaps they had given him a sentence that was regarded as too light earlier on and there was a lot of outrage about that. This sentence might have been possibly due to the fact that the tribunal is dependent on his knowledge. Duch has evidence, which he has always told other people, that Nuon Chea told him to kill 300 people in January 1979. This terrible images of the corpses and skulls at the end of the film were recorded in S-21, the former Tuol Sleng High School which was used as a prison. They were filmed by the camera crews of the Vietnamese military after coming into Phnom Penh. Duch's evidence is that a week before these images were recorded he was told by Nuon Chea to kill all of the 300 people who were still in this prison. According to him, he was horrified by this statement, which is slightly strange because he had already been convicted of killing 12 500 people, so why 300 more would be so disturbing to him is not comprehensible. It certainly raises some questions about the nature of his evidence. But the prosecution needs him because actually there is no actual ›smoking gun‹, if that's the right phrase, for Nuon Chea, aside perhaps from the kind of things he says to Thet Sambath in our film.

GLODZINSKI:

If you look at people like Duch and Nuon Chea who are actually speaking to an audience, either through this film or in court, and who are telling their own perspective on the things they have been doing: I believe in the whole history we do not have these comparable statements from perpetrators. Could it change our view on history?

ANNETTE WIEVIORKA:

Actually, we have a lot of statements. For example, during the Nuremberg Trials there was a man called Otto Ohlendorf. He was sure that he was so bright and marvellous that the Americans and the British were going to use him to build a new Germany after the war. So he spoke a lot, and when he testified during the Nuremberg Trial he was very talkative and he explained a lot of things. At the end of the trial, he was condemned to death and executed.

There are a lot of testimonies of perpetrators. You got them from the trials. And for the historian trials are very important documents. But we also get information from other sources, from people who wrote their own memoirs and from filmmakers who did what Rob Lemkin and Thet Sambath do. For example Claude Lanzmann in *Shoah* and other filmmakers.

LEMKIN:

There is one particular interrogator from S-21 who was interviewed in the trial and was beginning to tell. I have read pretty much most of the evidence from that trial and I did not really learn too much, because most of the facts we already knew. But this one man came in and began to reveal details about the institution and functioning of S-21. He was then, however, reminded in the issue of self-incrimination. And the judges asked him if he wanted to have a legal advisor, which the man affirmed. So when he came back after meeting his legal advisor, they asked him the same kind of questions again and he stated that he had been advised not to comment. This raises quite a big issue: Can criminal justice procedures like these get to the truth of what happened? Obviously the truth of what happened is immense and probably too much to put into words. But the people who suffered during that time and the population of the country that has to live with the legacy of that history, they do want to know: ›Why did this violence happen? Why did all of this happen to them 30 years ago?‹. I think a criminal justice procedure like the trial in Phnom Penh has difficulties in actually being able to find answers to these questions. Vast amounts of time, not to say millions of dollars are spent dealing with legal arguments, of which it is obvious that they are not understood by the people. I think at the moment in Phnom Penh not many people attend the hearings because they feel that it is a rather arcane process. Of course people will show up at the time of the verdict when they get the answer. But if the answer is simply that Nuon Chea is guilty, many people will still feel dissatisfied with that. For one person going to prison for the remaining five or six years of his life does not tell them why this thing happened. But this is the question that they need an answer for.

Question from the audience:
Have you found an answer to this question during your work?

Lemkin:
We are making a second film to illuminate the very specific case in Cambodia. What happened in the killing fields was, in very broad terms, a civil war between two parts of the communist movement. The Cambodian communist party was split into two parts. Both of those parts were trying to take control. Pol Pot and Nuon Chea formed one group and the other group consisted also of people on the central committee, and many of those people were finally executed in S-21. Other members of this second group came into power in 1979, on the occasion of the Vietnamese invasion, and they are the people who are still in power, individuals that are not in the communist party movement anymore but are still in power.

This history has never really been investigated because it is not in the interest of the current ruling party, the Cambodian People's Party, to have this kind of thing unearthed. It is much easier for them to convey the story of Pol Pot and Nuon Chea sitting in their evil headquarters, stroking their cats and sending out the directions to massacre the population left, right and centre. This is not the reason why the violence happened, and the people know that and want an explanation they are not going to get.

All the problems that the tribunal has in terms of its efficacy are of a political nature, problems that are put in its way by the government of Cambodia which is really not very keen on this kind of information coming out. This government has not permitted the screening of our film in Cambodia. It is only shown in a kind of samizdat independent style in a German owned cinema in Phnom Penh. Very few Cambodians can see it. There are many cinemas in Phnom Penh, in Battambang, in Siem Reap that wanted to show the film. These are big cinemas where hundreds of people can just come and watch films for very little money. The government did not allow it to be shown, and they still do not allow it.

Question from the audience:
What is the relationship between the tribunal and the kind of investigation Thet Sambath is doing? At the end of the film he stated that he was sad that Nuon Chea was going to be tried in the tribunal. Could you tell us about what Thet Sambath is looking for in his work?

LEMKIN:
I do not think Sambath has been really looking for Nuon Chea or any other people to be punished. Probably Sambath would be more in favour of a truth and reconciliation style commission, if something like that could be done. But of course the state, the government, the ruling party would not be an honest broker in this process. So whereas the African National Congress Party was big enough to do that in South Africa, the CCP in Cambodia is certainly not big enough, morally or politically strong enough to do that. But that would be Sambath's wish and that is what Sum, one of the interviewees, says at one point in the film. He wants these interviews and confessions to be shown all around the country so that the people like him can come out and talk about it and younger generations can know about it.

There is also an argument that the Prime Minister Hun Sen has been producing for the last ten years, namely the refusal to expose history to public scrutiny in any kind of way. He is saying that for the reasons I have just eluded to. Maybe a truth and reconciliation commission will be possible after the trial has finished. At the moment the working of the tribunal is rather unsatisfactory.

WERNER GEPHART:
Do you think that Sambath's method could be recommended to the Cambodian society? It was the most impressive feature of this film to see that for ten years he worked with the man who was responsible for the killing of his family. I cannot imagine how this is possible on a psychological level and recommendation for this method in general would certainly be a little bit problematic. But could we understand how it was possible to him? Obviously, there had been a close personal relationship as a condition to make Nuon Chea speak. This would explain at the same time that Sambath had feelings of regret at the moment when Nuon Chea was taken to the tribunal. The situation brought Sambath into an insoluble moral trap. This is one of the messages of this film, at least for me, and this is why it is so moving. Did you understand Sambath's personality?

LEMKIN:
I think you are right that Sambath sees everybody he works with, not just Nuon Chea, in a very human way. He is just meeting them as people, he is not making any accusation, he is not making any allegation. Of course he is also a bit deceptive because he is not identifying himself to Nuon Chea as a personal sufferer under the *Khmers Rouges* regime. But he comes to all these people in a very human way and his relationship with them is as human and as sincere as he can make it. The divulging of information on their part is part of that relationship. What is more, he is offering all of these people a chance to tell the truth that they wanted to tell. Particularly the low-level killers want to talk about it. They have been keeping it secret for the last thirty years, they do not even tell their wives. The woman

who is in silhouette in the film, has not told her husband about what she was involved in. She was responsible for thirty thousand deaths. Not physically, but she was ticking the lists of very large numbers, ten thousands of people. They want to talk about it because nobody feels good about it. In some senses they need to talk about it because this unspoken-about thing translates to their children and future generations.

They know more about it in America where the Cambodian-American audience has been the one that I have been able to relate to more. You can see there that lots of people, younger people, are talking to their parents in a way that they have not been able to do before. There are sometimes also negative reactions when some people are saying that they had better not seen this film. But by and large the reactions are more positive, and certainly amongst younger people who feel that this film has been able to open the possibility of dialogue.

About a year after the film was first finished, some Californian Cambodian refugees from the killing fields actually had a video conference with the people in this film – not Nuon Chea, because he is in prison, but several *Khmers Rouges* executioners. It was quite interesting to see that both the victims and the perpetrators talked about the nightmares that they had all together. They actually found a common human bonding, even though they were on different sides of this incredible violence. In fact, one of the people in the Cambodian community in Long Beach who facilitated this and particular was able to persuade a lot of the older generation to come to this video conference is a man who was very close to becoming an executioner himself. He was in the *Khmers Rouges*, he was a militia person and his boss had been asked to do loads and loads of killing in a particular village that he was at and he just happened to be ill that day and was not able to come to that meeting and so he did not. There is not one origin to this killing; this is a war you have to think of as a civil war going on inside a completely sealed society. There are things happening very randomly. He just missed it by not much. So the difference between victim and perpetrator, as he put it himself in this interview, is reed-thin as the grass.

There was a sense in which all of these people felt really much that this is terrible shared history, and the talking about it was certainly a positive thing.

WIEVIORKA:
What is your meaning of writing history? I am not sure that History with a big ›H‹ can be written just by oral testimonies or by films. And the problem with the *Khmers Rouges* is that we do not have many archives and if we stress S-21, it is for two reasons: There was a big propaganda campaign from the Vietnamese and the footage we saw in your film is one part of the propaganda of the Vietnamese when they arrived in Phnom Penh. We have the archives and the only history which is now written from the archives is those of S-21. I think that you are right

in alluding in your film to the influence of the Chinese, the Cultural Revolution on the *Khmers Rouges*: Same outfit, same hat.

Claude Lanzmann and the great American historian Raul Hilberg said: We are not asking the question of ›why?‹, we are asking the question of ›how?‹. I think we have to ask the question of ›why‹. But to answer the question of ›how‹ is quite a big task and I do not think that there is one answer to the ›why‹. And I do not think that the perpetrators themselves have the answer of ›why‹. In your film, what is great, they explain how. But we are still discussing – ›we‹, that means philosophers, lawyers, historians – about the ›why‹ of the holocaust. And we still have no complete and very satisfying answer.

LEMKIN:
I do not think that any single piece of work could answer why. You could write a million, billion or trillion words and you still would not have necessarily explained ›why?‹. However, the reason why we need to know ›why?‹ is because people live with this history and they live with the possibility that this kind of history can come back again. We were not trying to find out ›why?‹ because we were interested in Pharaonic rule from Egypt 3000 years ago. We are talking about people who are living with the direct results of this previous generation of violence.

There are strong reasons for being involved in that process in an as open way as possible. The criminal justice process is a very well worked-out process and I think I just raised from my own very own humble position, and Sambath would agree, the topic that this is a process that possibly cannot really be won in a sense that people are able to go forward with in a liberating way. Because the results are going to nail the criminalization of the regime in a way that suits the current power plays and does not really answer many of the emotional questions that the people have. They experienced manifold forms of violence and they have different needs. So I think, whatever process is being worked on, they need to service all these needs.

ALI SAMADI AHADI:
In every conflict and every historical momentum things are so different. It depends on so many aspects how you solve the situation, but one thing is very clear: A trial cannot be the answer of a social treatment or historical treatment, a trial has a different function.

The truth commission in South Africa and all the other institutions and instruments in Chile, Spain and elsewhere were different attempts to solve this extremely high violence in these societies. The basic question was always how to deal with that in a long term situation when the victims and the perpetrators are alive and have to get along with each other. And there is no single clear answer to all these problems, but there is a mixture of all of them. We have to find a clear balance.

I think that there is a need to have a trial. I made a film called *Lost Children* about child soldiers in Uganda. And when the International Criminal Court asked me to support them to go to Uganda and start their researches, I tried to help them to find the right people and to get in contact with them. For me it was very clear: They have to do their job, they have to get access to the people there. It is a very personal point of view. Filmmakers are so different. It is always a very personal decision

QUESTION FROM THE AUDIENCE:
I have a suggestion how to understand what the film is doing. May it be the case that the film is showing how a certain impossibility becomes real? The film explains how the impossible confession as a confession of the impossible is becoming possible and even real. Maybe that is the key or the core process you are showing: becoming the impossible real in this process of public confession.

LEMKIN:
The term ›public confession‹ raises a really interesting point because that is what it ends up being in terms of this film. It did not start as public confessions. Nuon Chea and all of the people that Sambath met were not talking to him. He did not even have a notebook and was just talking to them face-to-face. And then after about four years he said to Nuon Chea and also to other people but particularly to Nuon Chea: ›Do you mind if I just take some notes?‹ And then after a year after that he said: ›Do you mind if I just record the conversation?‹ And then just before I met him he had started to videotape. But when Nuon Chea was talking about Pol Pot and the decisions that they have made, I could not film this material because Nuon Chea would not talk about it in my presence. So this started off as a very private confession one to one ... that shows the human side of it. Sambath devoted his life to it, which probably not many people would do. And for him it is therapy. He is not really dealing with the emotional trauma of his life. As a child he was holding his mother's hand when she died. She had been forced to marry a *Khmers Rouges* cadre who was actually involved in the killing of his father. But we did not put that in because we tried to keep the film simple.

COMMENT FROM THE AUDIENCE:
It sounds like a tragedy.

LEMKIN:
It is a tragedy. There are millions of tragedies all over the world almost every day. This is something that Sambath was doing because he needed to do it. He did not

want to lie on a couch and have therapy. He wanted to be in his car, just going off and talking to people, getting on his motorbike and going off into the forest to find someone there. And in between he went back to his work and his ›normal‹ life with his wife and his two children. Sambath was driven to live like this. This commitment to some kind of truth was what the perpetrators responded to and they start of responding personally and then gradually the process of the film opens up to the point where it becomes pretty public.

GLODZINSKI:
From this argument I would like to come back to one point discussed earlier: collective identity. You have different reactions of people reacting to trials, to court rulings, to personal testimonies. What is the biggest aim? Is it reconciliation or is it justice? And what brings us closer to the biggest aim that makes living together possible? Perpetrators and victims have to deal with each other.

LEMKIN:
The biggest aim for Sambath, and I was with him on this project, was and still is reconciliation. That is to answer it very simply.

COMMENT FROM THE AUDIENCE:
I think it is a remarkable film. That is the second time I saw your film, the first time was at the Walter Read Festival where your film was shown. My sense is that what comes out very clearly is that the interviewer that you were filming found out what worked for him. Sambath is evidently a traumatized person. You can see this in the beginning of the film when he does not say goodbye to his own family. And there are so many signs of trauma when he is spending every weekend with this weird relationship where he can commune in a way with his missing family. It is remarkable because someone can spend a lifetime searching for what will help us and many people probably in this room have histories that relate to this issue.

On the level of the society, I am very uncomfortable with the idea that there will be a rule or a principle about what a society in the first part of transitional moment needs. There must at some time be a vote if there should be a trial or if they should better postpone it when there are further looking goals or when the justice system is compromised.

Victims are all different and very often the needs of victims are in conflict with the political goals and purposes of societies in the immediate transition. Thirty years later, it is a different politics. I doubt that there is a one-line-conclusion about those different goals and very often the society does not take care of victims because their needs are neglected in comparison to other social goals. Maybe that is what you are seeing with respect to the trial in Cambodia. The trials are necessary, but often they serve certain goals of the current political establishment and the needs of the victims are seen to be represented elsewhere or satisfied elsewhere.

Gephart:
We should not forget about the emphatic dimension of the film. The image of the bubbling water you, Rob, used in your film, is very impressive because it alludes to the violence. That is a great effort, to represent in a scaring way the atrocity without showing the atrocity.

Lemkin:
That is why I put in lots of that black and white images at the end because throughout the whole film you have heard talking these people about these atrocities and perhaps some of you may have started to almost feel sorry for these people, for the perpetrators, certainly some people in the audience feel sorry for some of these people. We just have to remember all we are looking at is propaganda footage, but then: everything is propaganda, isn't it?

Glodzinski:
I would like to close the session by a little story from myself. When I went to Cambodia last year I had heard about this film before. And I was actually on the move of going to the Phnom Penh Post to meet Thet Sambath to see: ›Who is this guy, who made this film and what is he actually working about‹? And I realized that not many people in Cambodia are really talking about these issues, that it is very, very difficult to unearth the black box which was dug in by the Prime Minister Hun Sen. In my opinion, these films will be some very important historical documents to the future generations because they get an easier access to the history of their own parents. I am glad that films like these are made and that the history is being dug out. And I hope that people learn a lesson from Thet Sambath in Cambodia and all around the world.

Dritter Teil
Recht sprechen: Tribunale als
theatralische Erscheinung

Dževad Karahasan

Tribunal, Theater und das Drama des Rechts

Werden Tribunal, Theater und das Drama des Rechts zu einem Thema verbunden, stellen sich mir zwei zentrale Fragen: Als erstes wäre die Frage nach der Technik der literarischen Darstellungsweise von Verbrechen und Unrecht zu nennen. Zum anderen stellt sich die Frage nach der Bedeutung und Einordnung der jeweiligen Darstellungsweise. Dabei geht es mir nicht nur um das Verbrechen, das, vor das Tribunal gekommen, zum literarischen Thema wird. Vielmehr geht es mir allgemein um die Darstellung des Bösen, des Feindes, all dessen, was das Paradigma des Feindlichen und in ethischer Hinsicht negativ Besetzten ausmacht.

Zwei verschiedene Darstellungsformen des Bösen möchte ich vereinfacht vorstellen. Die erste ist eine klassische, die auf der Überzeugung gründet, dass die Literatur eine wichtige Erkenntnisform (griech. *mathema*) darstellt. Bei den Griechen galt die Tragödie im Besonderen, die Literatur allgemein als eine *mathema*, eine zentrale Form des Erkennens. Johann Wolfgang von Goethe lässt seinen Teufel Mephistopheles in seiner Tragödie *Faust* in Form eines Pudels erscheinen und erklären, er sei ein Teil jener Kraft, die stets das Böse will und stets das Gute schafft. Etwa zwanzig Jahre später erklärt Charles Baudelaire in *Der freigebige Spieler* diese Entscheidung: Die größte List des Teufels liege darin, dass er es verstehe, als naiv und nett zu erscheinen, oder sogar darin, dass er imstande sei, seine Opfer zu überzeugen, dass es ihn überhaupt nicht gebe. Warum ist der Teufel bei Goethe ein Pudel? Warum erscheint der Teufel als ein nettes, liebes Tier, das erst in seinen Handlungen seine teuflische Natur zeigt? Weil es Goethe darum geht, das Böse, den Teufel zu erkennen und zu verstehen. Er teilt offensichtlich Überzeugung, die Platon in *Theaithetos* formuliert: »Das Böse nun kann niemals verschwinden – es kann aber auch nicht etwa bei den Göttern seinen Wohnsitz haben. Sondern in unserer irdischen sterblichen Natur zieht es notwendigermaßen umher und in unseren Gegenden.«

Etwas Ähnliches zeigt sich bei Fjodor Dostojewski. All seine Verbrecher, Mörder – und davon gibt es in den Romanen Dostojewskis eine ganze Menge – sind konsequent von innen aus gesehen. Als Figuren sind sie sorgfältig und bruchlos gezeichnet. Dostojewski versucht, den Verbrecher zu verstehen, seine Neigungen, seine Gründe, seine Taten von innen zu sehen, zu begreifen, zu erkennen. Er bemüht sich, auch das Andere zu verstehen, wenn er in *Die Brüder Karamasow* Smerdjakow, den Stinkenden, von innen darstellt und einen ganz und gar menschlichen Teufel bei Iwan zu Besuch erscheinen lässt.

Diese Darstellungsweise, die von der Möglichkeit der Nachvollziehbarkeit des Bösen und Anderen ausgeht, findet sich bereits bei Aischylos. Sein Drama *Die Perser* ist unmittelbar nach dem Krieg zwischen Hellas und Persien verfasst worden, und zwar aus der Sicht der Perser. Aischylos entscheidet sich, die große Epopöe seines Landes aus der Sicht des Feindes darzustellen. Sein literarischer Impetus scheint die Überzeugung zu sein, dass die Literatur, die Kunst den Feind erkennen und verstehen muss, ihn nicht vorschnell verurteilt ins Abseits stellen darf. Denn seiner wahren Natur nach ist der Feind ein Mensch, wie ich, unsere Gleichartigkeit ist notwendig und gesetzmäßig, während unsere Feindschaft akzidentiell ist.

Was nun impliziert diese klassische Darstellung des Bösen, des negativ Besetzten, in der Literatur? Sie zeigt, dass es keine mechanische Trennung zwischen Freund und Feind, zwischen Ich und Du, zwischen Plus und Minus gibt. Stattdessen ist von einer Dreistelligkeit des Verhältnisses auszugehen: Es gibt ein Ich, (m)einen Feind und etwas, das uns verbindet, uns gemeinsam ist. Gerade diese dreistellige Konstellation erlaubt die *mathema*: Aufgrund des Gemeinsamen ist die Erkenntnis des Feindes möglich. Mephistopheles hat Eigenschaften, die ihm und Faust gemein sind. Mephistopheles ist sozusagen ein Teil des komplexen Wesens von Faust. Aufgrund dieser Dreistelligkeit in der Darstellung entsteht zwischen mir und meinem Feind, zwischen Plus und Minus, eine gute dramatische Spannung – eine Spannung, kein Konflikt. In dieser Darstellungsform wird der Gegensatz zwischen mir und meinem Feind nicht aufgehoben. Wir bleiben Feinde. Aber wir sind Feinde, die sich verstehen, die sich erkennen können. Möglicherweise wird der Gegensatz zwischen uns aufgehoben werden, aber das muss nicht geschehen.

Die zweite Darstellungsform möchte ich als eine ideologisierte Darstellungsform bezeichnen, die zwischen Gut und Böse scharf trennt. Beispiele kann man erst in den Literaturen der monotheistischen Religionen finden. Die griechische Literatur kennt keine Beispiele für diese Darstellungsform des Feindes, des Bösen. Als Beispiel für die klare Trennung wäre Dante zu nennen, der in *Die Göttliche Komödie* die Seiten aufteilt in Gott/Beatrice/ich einerseits, Satan/Vergil/Platon andererseits. Dante schickt sogar seinen großen Lehrer Vergil in die Hölle. Diese scharfe Trennung zwischen Paradies und Hölle als Orte für das Gute und das Böse gelingt dann, wenn alles Böse nur von außen gesehen wird.

In dieser Darstellungsform des Bösen gibt es eine metaphysische Trennlinie zwischen dem Guten an sich und dem Bösen an sich, denn Zugehörigkeit entscheidet darüber, ob man gut oder böse ist. Für Dante war es klar: Man ist katholisch oder verdammt, tertium non datur. Auch wenn Zugehörigkeit nicht mit metaphysischem Prinzip gleichzusetzen ist, hat sie offensichtlich eine metaphysische Dimension, denn sie ist durch das metaphysische Prinzip bestimmt. Etwas Ähnliches findet sich bei William Shakespeare in *Richard III*: Richard ist das Böse schlechthin, hässlich, invalid, ein Monster, ein Mörder. Er will kämpfen, er will morden, aber nicht die Gegenseite erkennen. Bei Shakespeares Schüler Friedrich Schiller findet sich Ähnliches: In seinem Drama *Die Räuber* ist Franz Moor das Ungeheuer schlechthin. Er wird als kompromisslose Figur gezeichnet: Da gibt es nichts zu erkennen, nur etwas zu erledigen. In dieser Darstellungsform gibt es keine Spannung, nur Konflikt. Insofern ließe sich hier nicht von einer dramatischen, sondern von einer ideologischen Darstellung sprechen. Zwischen Ich und Du, zwischen Plus und Minus gibt es nichts Gemeinsames.

Diese Darstellungsform der scharfen Trennung ist nicht zuletzt deshalb eine moderne, weil sie digital verfährt: auf der Differenz zwischen 0 und 1 bzw. hier: Plus und Minus basierend. Dieses konsequente Denken und Handeln, diese konsequente Trennung ist in einer virtuellen Welt möglich. Denn virtuelle Welten sind per definitionem konsequent und absolut genau, weil darin weder Leben noch Körper existieren, nicht existieren können. Zwei plus zwei macht immer vier in der Arithmetik, weil in der Arithmetik weder Körper noch Leben möglich sind. In einer Welt der materialisierten körperhaften Formen, in einer Welt, in der Leben möglich ist, ergeben zwei plus zwei manchmal fünf, am häufigsten leider nur drei, gelegentlich meinetwegen auch vier.

Ebenso wie die mathematische Abstraktion mit exakten Differenzen arbeitet, so rechnet die ideologische Darstellungsform mit einer exakten Trennung und metaphysischen Bestimmung von Gut und Böse. Dabei steht – das kennzeichnet die von Ideologie geprägte Darstellungsform – das Ich selbstverständlich auf der Seite des Guten. Diese Darstellungsform hat nicht zum Ziel, das Böse oder allgemeiner: das Andere zu erkennen. Sie verurteilt es einfach in der Überzeugung, dass das Böse gar nicht zu erkennen, geschweige denn zu verstehen ist. Es ist etwas seinem Wesen nach völlig anderes. Dabei ist sehr wichtig zu betonen, dass dieses Andere sehr selten, beinahe niemals, etwas Exotisches ist. Exotik ist etwas anderes, aber darüber wäre an anderer Stelle zu reden.

Als Theaterpraktiker kann ich sagen, dass diese als ideologisch bezeichneten Darstellungsformen des Bösen im Theater große Probleme machen. Wie sollte man etwa Othello von Shakespeare inszenieren? Dort gibt es eine Figur, die eben böse an sich, böse schlechthin ist: Jago. Besetzt man Jago mit einem Schauspieler, der ein schiefes Gesicht und kleine Augen hat und immer schlecht gelaunt spricht, wird es eine schlechte Aufführung, weil Othello nicht als ein tragischer Held, sondern als ein Idiot erscheinen muss. Jago muss man immer mit dem schönsten Schauspieler besetzen, der zur Verfügung steht, mit einem Schauspieler, der ein Mondgesicht hat und naiv, nett und vertrauenswürdig erscheinen kann. Jago muss einer sein, dem man vertraut. Nur in dem Fall kann Othello als tragischer Held erscheinen.

Diese dramentheoretischen und theaterpraktischen Ausführungen zum Bösen und zum Verbrechen auf der Bühne können den Kontext bilden für ein anderes

›Schauspiel‹, das mich die Logik des ideologischen Auffassens des Feindes am eigenen Leib spüren ließ: Als im Jahre 2008 Radovan Karadžić verhaftet wurde, habe ich meinem Freund Hannes Hintermeier für die Zeitung FAZ ein Interview gegeben und versucht, eine wichtige Tatsache zu betonen: dass Radovan Karadžić leider mein Bruder Mensch ist. Vielleicht ist er ein hervorragender Arzt. Möglicherweise ist er ein liebevoller Vater, ein netter Nachbar. Vielleicht ist er ein zarter, wunderbarer Liebhaber. Und schließlich ist er ein Massenmörder und Verbrecher. Denn der Mensch ist weder ein Prinzip noch ein Begriff, demzufolge kann er nicht an sich rein gut oder rein böse sein. Nur der Mensch ist der menschlichen Ethik verpflichtet – niemand verurteilt einen Tiger, wenn er mordet. Wer einen Verbrecher zum Monster stilisiert und ihm Menschlichkeit abspricht, der spricht den Täter frei, denn für ein unmenschliches Wesen gilt die menschliche Ethik nicht. Auch Gesetze gelten nicht für dieses Wesen; einen Tiger stellt man nicht vor Gericht. Nach dem Erscheinen des Interviews – ich lebte damals in Berlin – haben mich dutzende Menschen angerufen und verwundert gefragt, wieso ich Karadžić verteidige. Ein Jahr später wurde dieses Interview in Sarajevo übersetzt und in einer Zeitung abgedruckt. Man veranstaltete in dieser Zeitung eine mehrere Monate andauernde Hetze gegen mich. Alle wurden aufgerufen, sich über mich auszulassen. Die Wut, mit der manche Menschen in Sarajevo auf die Behauptung reagiert haben, Radovan Karadžić sei einfach ein Mensch, kann ich in ihrer Leidenschaft noch nachvollziehen, die merkwürdige Reaktion meiner Freunde in Deutschland, die dachten, ich verteidigte Karadžić, kann ich eigentlich nicht nachvollziehen, denn sie hatten mit Karadžić keine Erfahrungen gemacht.

Ist es die digitale Kultur, die uns eine Denkweise der scharfen Trennung aufgedrängt hat, und dies auch in unseren ethischen Entscheidungen? Geht nicht gerade aufgrund dieser Digitalisierung das ethische Vermögen verloren? Denn ich würde mich nicht eine Sekunde lang mit Karadžić beschäftigen, wenn ich nicht wüsste, dass er auch etwas über mich aussagt, dass er ein Mensch ist, so wie ich ein Mensch bin. Es gibt nichts, was uns davor schützt, selbst zu Verbrechern zu werden. Ich bin herzensfroh, im bosnischen Krieg auf der Seite der Opfer gestanden zu haben. Gott sei Dank. Aber nichts kann mich sicher machen, mich in einem möglichen künftigen Krieg wieder auf die Seite der Opfer zu schlagen. Das einzige, was mich einigermaßen davor schützen kann, zum Täter zu werden, ist mein ethisches Gefühl. Dieses Gefühl lehrt uns weder die Wissenschaft noch die digitale Welt, sondern – das ist meine Überzeugung – nur die ästhetische Erkenntnis des Bösen.

Die erste theatralische Darstellung eines Gerichtsverfahrens waren die *Eumeniden* von Aischylos. Darin führt die *Anagnorisis*, das Erkennen und Wiedererkennen, zur Verwandlung der Erinnyen, der Rächerinnen, in Eumeniden, die Gnädigen, Milden. Dürfen wir hoffen, dass etwas Ähnliches auch heute und in Wirklichkeit möglich ist? Davon träumen dürfen wir allemal.

Gerade weil die wirkliche Erkenntnis des Bösen eng mit dem Verständnis, der Nachvollziehbarkeit des Bösen zusammenhängt, bin ich ein Befürworter der klassischen Darstellungsform des Bösen. Ich plädiere dafür, das Böse, das Verbrechen, den Feind, alles negativ Besetzte möglichst zu verstehen. Unsere Aufgabe ist es, das Andere, auch das Böse zu verstehen. Zwar sind wir auch aufgefordert, es zu beurteilen, dann aber sollten wir uns dessen bewusst sein, dass es möglicherweise ein Teil von uns ist.

(Wir danken Dževad Karahasan für die Erlaubnis, seinen frei gehaltenen Vortrag hier abdrucken zu dürfen.)

Jürgen Brokoff

Übergänge. Literarisch-juridische Interferenzen bei Peter Handke und die Medialität von Rechtsprechung und Tribunal

I.

Die Beobachtung von Gerichtsverfahren ist eine gängige juristische Praxis. Das sogenannte *Monitoring* soll insbesondere bei internationalen Prozessen durch die Anwesenheit von Prozessbeobachtern die Rechtsstaatlichkeit der Verfahren überwachen, die Angeklagtenrechte sicherstellen helfen, eine gerechte Verurteilung von Straftätern, insbesondere bei Menschenrechtsverletzungen, gewährleisten und den Blick der Öffentlichkeit für die Verfahren der Rechtsprechung und die möglichen Probleme des Rechtssystems schärfen.[1] In Deutschland wird das *Monitoring*, dessen Kommunikationsform der Bericht (*Monitoring Report*) ist, mittlerweile auch im nationalen Rahmen praktiziert. So hat etwa das Forschungs- und Dokumentationszentrum für Kriegsverbrecherprozesse (ICWC) in Marburg die Prozessbeobachtung institutionalisiert und in die juristische Ausbildung integriert.[2]

Monitoring betreibende Prozessbeobachter, ob sie in juristischer Ausbildung befindlich sind oder nicht, werden im Rahmen ihrer Tätigkeit aber nicht nur mit rechtlichen Fragen und historisch-politischen Hintergründen des verhandelten Falls konfrontiert, sondern auch mit medialen Bedingungen und kommunikativen Umständen. Sie stoßen ungeachtet der nach wie vor konstitutiven Sprachförmigkeit einer jeden Gerichtsverhandlung zunehmend auf Monitore. Von einer solchen Konfrontation mit Monitoren berichtet jedenfalls ein Prozessbeobachter, der beim Verfahren gegen Slobodan Milošević am *Internationalen Strafgerichtshof für das ehemalige Jugoslawien* (ICTY) zum wiederholten Male als Zuschauer anwesend war. Der österreichische Schriftsteller und ehemalige Jurastudent Peter Handke, der sich seine alte Liebe zu »Gerichts- und Zellenfilme[n]«[3] (mit Angeklagten und Einsitzenden als Protagonisten) bewahrt hat, beschreibt den Ver-

---

[1] Vgl. mit weiterführenden Literaturhinweisen Safferling et al.: Das Monitoring-Projekt des Forschungs- und Dokumentationszentrums für Kriegsverbrecherprozesse.
[2] Vgl. ebd., S. 569 ff.
[3] Handke: Rund um das Große Tribunal, S. 11.

handlungsraum, in dem der Prozess gegen Milošević stattfand, im Sommer 2002 wie folgt:

»Und wieder der tageslichtlose Gerichtssaal Nr 1 im ersten Stock, bildgenau wie vor vier Jahren. Aber hat es auch damals schon, links und rechts oben im durch Panzerglas vom Verhandlungssaal getrennten Zuschauer- und Journalistenteil, die Übertragungsbildschirme gegeben? Jedenfalls wußte ich dann beim Prozeßbeobachten oft nicht, wohin schauen: auf die Vorgänge hinter der Scheibe, sozusagen in Totale, oder auf einen der ›Fernseher‹ über mir, wo in der Regel jeweils nur eine Einzelperson erschien, vor allem der Angeklagte, immer viel näher zu sehen als in Natur, halbgroß, und zudem, in einem völlig anderen Winkel, eher von vorn, statt im Profil. [...] Und wer wohl bestimmte den Kamerablickwinkel? Und wer wohl, vor allem, bestimmte, wer von den Akteuren im Gerichtssaal jetzt groß ins Bild gerückt werden sollte, und wie lange er jeweils so zu sehen wäre? Warum wurde immer wieder der Angeklagte derart gezeigt, auch wenn er nicht sprach, sondern bloß zuhörte und stumm reagierte, oder auch nicht reagierte? Die Einstellungen auf dem Bildschirm, die ›Schnitte‹, deren Rhythmus insbesondere suggerierten mir dermaßen einen Spielfilm, daß sie einen Sog erzeugten weg vom direkten und unmittelbaren Zuschauen.«[4]

Die Umlenkung des direkten und unmittelbaren Zuschauerblicks auf das TV-Bild ist Kennzeichen eines medialen Vermittlungsprozesses, den Handke schon früher als Tendenz zur bloßen »(Fern-)Sehbeteiligung«[5] kritisiert hat und der grundsätzliche Fragen nach der Bildregie und nach dem Bildregime aufwirft: Wer bestimmt, was gesehen wird? Die 2010 verstorbene Medienwissenschaftlerin Cornelia Vismann ist dieser Frage in ihrem Buch *Medien der Rechtsprechung* auf erhellende Weise nachgegangen.[6] Für sie belegen die auf dem neuesten technischen Stand befindlichen Übertragungsmedien des Jugoslawientribunals, dessen Bilder zeitversetzt im Internet als Stream veröffentlicht werden, die Entwicklung der internationalen Strafgerichtsbarkeit hin zu einer »Fern-« bzw. »Online-Justiz«[7]. Eine der Thesen von Vismanns Buch ist, dass diese medientechnisch induzierte Entwicklung erhebliche Auswirkungen auf die Form der juristischen Verfahren hat, die in ihrer Tragweite bislang kaum berücksichtigt wurden. Die eingesetzten technischen Medien dienen nicht einfach nur dem audiovisuellen Transport und der Verbreitung von Informationen, sondern sie erhalten laut Vismann »faktische Verfahrensautonomie«[8], indem sie etwa die räumliche Anordnung und Ausstattung des Verhandlungssaals und damit letztendlich die Form des Verfahrens selbst bestimmen.

Eingebettet ist diese These über die »Fern-Justiz« des Jugoslawientribunals in

---

4   Ebd., S. 35 f.
5   Handke: Eine winterliche Reise, S. 56; vgl. dazu Brokoff: Srebrenica.
6   Vgl. Vismann: Medien der Rechtsprechung.
7   Ebd., S. 333, 361.
8   Ebd., S. 341.

eine historische und systematische Analyse der Medialität der Rechtsprechung. Vismann fragt in diesem Kontext unter anderem nach der prekären Unterscheidung von Gericht und Tribunal. Dabei geht es nicht um eine idealtypische Gegenüberstellung von ordentlichem Gericht und außerordentlicher Tribunalgerichtsbarkeit, sondern um die Hervorhebung der dominanten Aspekte in beiden Formen der Rechtsprechung. Wenn Vismann die Rechtsprechungsform ›Gericht‹ von einem theatralen Dispositiv bestimmt sieht, das in geschlossenen Räumen unter der Ägide von Richtern im Zuge einer Versprachlichung aus dem strittigen Ding eine zu verhandelnde Sache werden lässt,[9] und wenn sie in der Rechtsprechungsform ›Tribunal‹ ein agonales Prinzip ausmacht, bei dem unter freiem Himmel ohne die Dazwischenkunft neutraler Richter und unter Beteiligung von Zuschauern der Kampf um die Wahrheit offen zum Austrag kommt,[10] dann ist dies mit der Überlegung verbunden, dass diese beiden Formen der Rechtsprechung nur als »Mischformen«[11] existieren. Pointiert gesagt, geht es um zwei Entwicklungsprozesse, die zur Ausprägung dieser »Mischformen« geführt haben und bei denen zwei unterschiedliche Konzepte von Öffentlichkeit eine Rolle spielen. Weil in jedem Gericht das Tribunal latent vorhanden ist, besteht die Möglichkeit einer *Tribunalisierung des Gerichts*, die auf die Ausweitung der Öffentlichkeit in einem unbegrenzten und überrechtlichen Maßstab abzielt. Und weil in jedem Tribunal das Gericht latent vorhanden ist, besteht die Möglichkeit einer *Vergerichtlichung des Tribunals*, die auf die Begrenzung und Kontrolle der Öffentlichkeit im Sinne einer »Gerichtsöffentlichkeit«[12] abzielt. Das Jugoslawientribunal ist in dieser Perspektive sowohl Gericht als auch Tribunal oder, wie Vismann an einer Stelle hervorhebt, keines von beiden richtig.[13] Es ist Gericht, weil es in geschlossenen Räumen unter der Ägide von Richtern individuelle Schuld feststellt, und es ist Tribunal, weil es per Internet die Gerichtsöffentlichkeit überschreitet und ein Forum überrechtlicher Wahrheitsfindung ist. Im Folgenden soll diese »Mischform« von Gericht und Tribunal nicht in abstrakter und allgemeiner Hinsicht interessieren. Vielmehr ist in einem ersten Schritt am Beispiel von Handkes Tribunalsschriften die Thematisierung der theatralen und der agonalen Dimension des Jugoslawientribunals genauer zu betrachten (II.). In einem zweiten Schritt wird die Frage zu erörtern sein, ob sich Handkes Tribunalsschriften, die das bedeutendste Zeugnis einer literarischen Auseinandersetzung mit der Thematik darstellen, auf die Funktion einer Prozessbeobachtung beschränken lassen oder ob sie die Grenze dieser Beobachtung überschreiten (III.). Gehen Handkes Texte selbst zu einer gerichtlichen Form der Rede über, werden sie selbst zu einer Art Tribunal?

---

9   Vgl. ebd., S. 19–37, 146–183.
10 Vgl. ebd., S. 72–84, 146–183.
11 Ebd., S. 153.
12 Ebd., S. 148.
13 Vgl. ebd., S. 355.

II.

Ähnlich wie in der eingangs zitierten Schrift *Rund um das Große Tribunal* von 2003 geht Handke auch in der Tribunalsschrift *Die Tablas von Daimiel* von 2005 von einer persönlichen Erfahrung aus, die das Nachdenken über die Medialität und Theatralität der Rechtsprechung des Tribunals in den Mittelpunkt rückt. Konstatiert der Filmliebhaber Handke in der Schrift *Rund um das Große Tribunal* einen Paradigmenwechsel in der Darstellung der Angeklagtenfigur, der in TV-Serien jeder Kredit zugunsten der heldenhaften Vertreter der Legalität entzogen werde, und sieht er, wichtiger noch, diesen Paradigmenwechsel in der filmischen Gerichtsrealität des Haager Jugoslawientribunals bestätigt, so stellt er in der Schrift *Die Tablas von Daimiel* eine andere Medienreflexion an. In dieser zweiten Tribunalsschrift berichtet Handke von einer eigenen Verhaltensweise, die immer dann einsetzt, wenn er sich vor einem anderen »ins Recht zu setzen«[14] trachtet, wenn er diesen anderen schuldig sprechen will. In diesem Fall kommt es zur Einrichtung einer »Bühne«[15] in Handkes »Innerem«[16], zu einer »theatralischen Inszenierung«[17] des Anklagens, zu einem »Schuldspruch-Theater«[18]. Dieses sich im Inneren vollziehende »Schuldspruch-Theater« bedient sich, wie Handke mehrfach betont, einer Vielzahl von »Redefiguren«[19]. Es findet ein »pausen- wie lückenloses Verbalisieren, Dialogisieren, Rhetorisieren und vor allem Plädieren und Fingieren«[20] statt, und am Ende steht jedesmal die Feststellung der Schuld des anderen. Dieses »Bewußtseinstheater«[21], so Handke am Ende seiner kritischen Selbstreflexion, fährt deshalb so viele Begründungen auf, weil ihm »der Grund fehlte«[22].

Es gehört nun seinerseits zur Rhetorik von Handkes Text, dass er die Vorstellung vom durchgängig rhetorischen »Bewußtseinstheater« von innen nach außen stülpt und von der Selbstreflexion zur Fremdbeschreibung rechtlicher Einrichtungen übergeht:

»Gewiß hat jede Gerichtsinstitution etwas von solch einem in die Tat-Wirklichkeit übertragenen Bewußtseinstheater, mehr oder weniger. Auf dieses Mehr oder Weniger kommt es aber an.«[23]

---

[14] Handke: Die Tablas von Daimiel, S. 17. – Erstveröffentlicht wurde der Text 2005 in der Zeitschrift *Literaturen*. Zitatnachweise fortan nach der Buchausgabe.
[15] Ebd.
[16] Ebd.
[17] Ebd.
[18] Ebd., S. 18.
[19] Ebd., S. 17.
[20] Ebd.
[21] Ebd., S. 18.
[22] Ebd.
[23] Ebd., S. 18.

Auf der Grundlage der Bestimmung dieses »Mehr oder Weniger« entwickelt Handke ein interessantes Differenzmodell, das zentrale Aspekte der Unterscheidung von Gericht und Tribunal zu erhellen vermag. Je stärker ein Gericht und dessen Amtssitz an den »Ort«[24] bzw. die »Gegend«[25] gebunden ist, in der die vom Gericht betroffene Gesellschaft ansässig ist und lebt, desto schwächer ist das »Bewußtseinstheater« dieses Gerichts ausgeprägt. Es handelt sich in diesem Fall um ein »lokalbezogenes«[26] und »sach(en)bezogenes«[27] Rechtsinstitut. Je »grenzüberschreitender, überlokaler, ›internationaler‹«[28] und »abgesetzter von der [...] Gesellschaft«[29] dagegen ein Gericht ist, desto stärker ist es auf die Inszenierungskünste des »Bewußtseinstheaters« angewiesen. Durch »Imponiergehabe, [...] Rhetorik, Sprechen in höherem und höchstem Namen«[30] versucht es, die fehlende Ortsgebundenheit und den Mangel an Sachbezug zu überdecken. Wird das Gericht mit schwach ausgeprägtem »Bewußtseinstheater« von der »Inszenierung«[31] lediglich »begleitet«[32], wird dasjenige mit stark ausgeprägtem »Bewußtseinstheater« von solcher »Inszenierung« »bestimmt«[33]. Arbeitet ersteres »wie ein normales Gericht«[34], ist letzteres ein Tribunal im negativen Wortsinne.

Zur Ortsungebundenheit und zur mangelnden gesellschaftlichen Verflechtung kommt als ein weiteres Merkmal des Tribunals die mögliche Überdehnung des Geltungsanspruchs und der Zuständigkeit hinzu. Das Jugoslawientribunal leistet nach Handke überall dort überzeugende Arbeit, wo es den Angeklagten der unteren Befehlsebene konkrete strafbare Handlungen nachzuweisen versucht, und es wird immer dann unglaubwürdig, wenn es vor den Augen der Öffentlichkeit »Welttribunal spielt«[35] und »moralische, humanitäre [...] Kategorien«[36] geltend macht. Handke rührt hier, über die Frage der Performanz und Performativität hinaus, an einen heiklen Punkt, denn in der Tat ist der genaue Geltungsanspruch des Tribunals nicht so einfach bestimmbar. Ist der Gerichtscharakter des Tribunals in der richterlichen Feststellung und Bestrafung von individueller Schuld zu sehen, so geht sein »humanitärer« Anspruch darüber hinaus.[37] Vismann spricht

---

24 Ebd.
25 Ebd.
26 Ebd., S. 18 f.
27 Ebd., S. 19.
28 Ebd.
29 Ebd.
30 Ebd.
31 Ebd.
32 Ebd.
33 Ebd.
34 Ebd., S. 20.
35 Ebd., S. 19.
36 Ebd., S. 23.
37 Die Internationalität des humanitären Völkerrechts ist dabei das Strukturelement eines »Übergangsrechts«, das unter den Bedingungen einer »postnationalen Konstellation« (Jürgen Habermas) an Bedeutung gewinnt; vgl. dazu Teitel: Transitional Justice; dies.: Humanity's Law, S. 73–104.

in diesem Kontext von »Anklage nach außerrechtlichen Kategorien«[38] und davon, dass das Jugoslawientribunal »Gerichtsverfahren plus Geschichtslektion, Täterbestrafung plus Opferforum«[39] sein will und sich damit möglicherweise selbst überfordert. Ein Vertreter des internationalen Strafrechts führt in diesem Kontext die in der Forschung weit verbreitete Ansicht ins Feld, »that trials involving genocide and crime against humanity are less about judging a person than about establishing the truth of the events.«[40] Die Umfunktionierung tribunalförmiger Gerichtsverfahren zur »Geschichtslektion« hatte schon Hannah Arendt in ihrem Buch über den Jerusalemer Eichmann-Prozess kritisiert. Arendts harsche Kritik an dem von Generalstaatsanwalt Gideon Hausner geführten »Schauprozeß«[41] (mit Premierminister David Ben Gurion als Regisseur und Richter Moshe Landau als Widerpart) ist dabei nicht als Forderung zu verstehen, zur regionalen oder lokalen Gerichtsbarkeit zurückzukehren, sondern fordert explizit einen Ausbau des noch unzureichenden Völkerstrafrechts. Im Gegensatz zu Handke plädiert Arendt nicht für weniger, sondern für mehr Internationalität.[42]

Handkes Kritik am »Welttribunal«[43] impliziert zwei weitere Aspekte. Der Begriff »Welttribunal« soll erstens deutlich machen, dass die am Jugoslawientribunal arbeitenden Richter »im Sold der ›Weltgemeinschaft‹«[44] stehen und deshalb von dieser Weltgemeinschaft abhängig sind. Handkes Äußerung, dass das Jugoslawientribunal »von Anfang an, von Grund auf, schon in seinem Ursprung Partei ist«[45], spielt darauf an, dass die Einrichtung des Tribunals auf eine Resolution des UN-Sicherheitsrats zurückgeht, also jenes Organs, in dem die Mächte tonangebend waren und sind, die 1999 im Kosovo ohne UN-Mandat einen »Krieg an der Grenze zwischen Recht und Moral«[46] führen. Handkes Äußerung über die »schon im Ursprung« vorhandene Parteilichkeit erinnert dabei ebenso wie die Formulierung, dass Begründungen vor allem dann erforderlich seien, wenn »der Grund

---

[38] Vismann: Medien der Rechtsprechung, S. 163.
[39] Ebd., S. 335.
[40] Koskenniemi: Between Impunity and Show Trials, S. 3.
[41] Arendt: Eichmann in Jerusalem, S. 71.
[42] Im *Epilog* ihres Eichmann-Buches führt Arendt aus, dass »die physische Ausrottung des jüdischen Volkes ein Verbrechen gegen die Menschheit war, und daß nur die Wahl der Opfer, nicht aber die Natur des Verbrechens aus der langen Geschichte von Judenhaß und Antisemitismus abgeleitet werden konnte. Insofern die Opfer Juden waren, war es nur recht und billig, daß das Verfahren [gegen Eichmann; J. B.] vor einem jüdischen Gerichtshof stattfand; aber insoweit das Verbrechen ein Verbrechen an der Menschheit war, hätte es eines internationalen Tribunals bedurft, um in dieser Sache Recht zu sprechen.« Ebd., S. 391f.
[43] Handke: Die Tablas von Daimiel, S. 19.
[44] Handke: Rund um das Große Tribunal, S. 21.
[45] Handke: Die Tablas von Daimiel, S. 28.
[46] Habermas: Bestialität und Humanität.

fehlte«, an Überlegungen, die der Philosoph Jacques Derrida in seiner Schrift *Force de loi* über die Grundlosigkeit rechtsetzender Gewalt angestellt hatte.[47]

Zweitens soll Handkes Begriff des »Welttribunals« darauf hinweisen, dass sich unter der Überschrift »Welt«[48] eine Gemeinschaft versammelt, bei der Richter und Ankläger in Übereinstimmung mit Journalisten handeln. Handke spricht von einer »Symbiose«[49] zwischen Strafjustiz und Journalismus. Das Ergebnis dieser Symbiose ist eine »Weltöffentlichkeit«[50], die an der Vereinheitlichung der öffentlichen Meinung über die zu verhandelnden Sachverhalte arbeitet. Es ist vor allem diese Annahme einer uniformen, über die Weltöffentlichkeit »lückenlos herrschend[en]«[51] Meinung, die Handke mit Vehemenz gegen das Jugoslawientribunal anschreiben lässt. Dabei treten die von Handke zuvor geleisteten begrifflichen Differenzierungen wieder in den Hintergrund. Wenn der österreichische Schriftsteller schreibt, dass das in Den Haag tagende Welttribunal »nichts taugt«[52], »falsch ist und falsch bleibt«[53] und der »Idee des Rechts scheußlichsten Hohn spricht«[54], und wenn er die Diskussion über die problematische Rechtsgrundlage des Tribunals vorab zur Aussage zuspitzt, dass dessen Errichtung »keinerlei Rechtsbasis«[55] habe, dann dürfte der umfassende Anspruch von Handkes Kritik deutlich sein: Das Jugoslawientribunal ist »das falsche Gericht«[56].

In Handkes drastischer Wortwahl wird die emotionale Spannung erkennbar, von der seine Tribunalstexte gekennzeichnet sind. Zugleich lässt sich an ihr eine rhetorische Strategie ablesen, die eine Verbindung zur *stratégie de rupture* des französischen Rechtsanwalts Jacques Vergès nahelegt. Derrida hatte die von Vergès ursprünglich ausgehende »Faszination«[57] damit erklärt, dass dieser in seinen spektakulären Fällen das Recht in Anspruch nimmt, der Rechtsordnung ihr Recht streitig zu machen. Handke lobt in seiner zweiten Tribunalsschrift ausdrücklich die »große Leistung«[58] des Anwalts Vergès. Dessen Vorgehen bei Gericht lässt sich in den Worten von Vismann als »Tribunalisierung der Justiz«[59] bezeichnen. Mit dieser »Tribunalisierung« ist nicht die Verteidigung oder Rechtshilfe des französischen Anwalts für die Angeklagten Khieu Samphan und Milošević im Rahmen der Sondertribunale in Phnom Penh (ECCC) und Den Haag (ICTY)

---

[47] Vgl. Derrida: Gesetzeskraft, S. 28 ff.
[48] Handke: Rund um das Große Tribunal, S. 12.
[49] Handke: Die Tablas von Daimiel, S. 23.
[50] Ebd., S. 52; vgl. auch Handke: Eine winterliche Reise, S. 64.
[51] Handke: Rund um das Große Tribunal, S. 65.
[52] Handke: Die Tablas von Daimiel, S. 30.
[53] Ebd.
[54] Ebd.
[55] Ebd., S. 12.
[56] Ebd., S. 30.
[57] Derrida: Gesetzeskraft, S. 74.
[58] Handke: Die Tablas von Daimiel, S. 11.
[59] Vismann: Medien der Rechtsprechung, S. 181.

gemeint, sondern die Überführung der Rechtsfälle in eine außergerichtliche Öffentlichkeit und der Versuch, Richter und Ankläger als Interessenvertreter einer nur unzureichend legitimierten, »grund-los[en]«[60] Staatsgewalt zu erweisen, der der Angeklagte allein gegenübersteht. Abgesehen davon, dass eine solche von Verteidigerseite vorgenommene Tribunalisierung etwas anderes ist als die Tribunalisierung durch die das Tribunal einsetzende Macht – es gibt also zwei Arten der Tribunalisierung –, wirft die von Handke selbst hergestellte Verbindung zu Vergès die Frage auf, welches Ziel Handkes Tribunalsschriften im genaueren Sinne verfolgen. Es wurde ausgeführt, dass Handke eine scharfe Tribunalkritik formuliert und gegenüber dem Tribunal ein »normal« arbeitendes Gericht eindeutig favorisiert. Handke ist also, juristisch gesehen, der Befürworter einer De- oder Enttribunalisierung. Zugleich aber lässt sich sagen, dass er durch seine Kritik, dass Richter und Strafverfolger interessengebunden und voreingenommen handeln, durch sein Beharren darauf, dass es eine andere Wahrheit als die im Gerichtsverfahren verhandelte gibt, und durch die Adressierung seiner Texte an eine außergerichtliche Öffentlichkeit auf nichtjuristischem Feld das zu tun versucht, was der Rechtsanwalt Vergès im Verhandlungssaal tut. Handke ist, literarisch gesehen, der Befürworter einer Tribunalisierung, die das Hauptmerkmal des Tribunals, den offen ausgetragenen Kampf um die Wahrheit, reaktiviert und reaktualisiert.

III.

Im Folgenden sollen deshalb jene Aspekte im Vordergrund stehen, die die Performanz von Handkes Texten bestimmen. Als was treten diese Texte eigentlich auf und wie funktionieren sie als Ganzes? Dass Handke in seinen Prozessberichten zum Jugoslawientribunal auch Aussagen des Angeklagten Milošević wiedergibt, ist kaum überraschend. Diese Wiedergabe nimmt allerdings nur einen geringen Teil der beiden Texte ein. So zitiert er in der Schrift *Rund um das Große Tribunal* die Rede des Angeklagten Milošević über »Clinton, mit seinem Genozid gegen die Serben«[61]. Und in der Schrift *Die Tablas von Daimiel* berichtet er darüber, wie Milošević ihm im Gefängnis seine Sicht der Dinge über die Ereignisse in Kosovo Polje 1987 und die Amselfeldrede von 1989 mitteilt.[62] Deutlich mehr Raum nimmt dagegen in Handkes Texten der Bericht über Zeugenaussagen ein. Dies

---

60 Derrida: Gesetzeskraft, S. 29.
61 Handke: Rund um das Große Tribunal, S. 39.
62 Vgl. Handke: Die Tablas von Daimiel, S. 36ff.

betrifft insbesondere die Aussagen von »Zeugen der Anklage«[63] im Milošević-Prozess. Handke gibt diese Zeugenaussagen wieder und stellt sie zugleich in einen bestimmten Kontext. Das erste Beispiel hierfür ist im Text *Rund um das Große Tribunal* ein »junger Amerikaner aus New York«[64], der Mitglied der Organisation *Human Rights Watch* ist und im Kosovo wissenschaftliche Feldforschung betrieben hat. Handke referiert zunächst die Aussage des Zeugen, dass die Tötungen der albanischen Zivilbevölkerung planmäßig und unter Einbindung paramilitärischer Einheiten geschehen sei und dass andererseits für die gezielte Tötung der serbischen Zivilbevölkerung durch NATO-Bomben keine ausreichenden Beweise gesammelt werden konnten. Aufschlussreich ist das textuelle Umfeld, in dem Handke sein Zeugenreferat platziert. Unmittelbar vor dem Zeugenreferat karikiert er einen Menschenrechtsbeobachter derselben Organisation, der am Prozess als Zuschauer teilgenommen hat. Laut Handke hielt dieser auf den Stufen des Gerichtsgebäudes nach Mikrofonen Ausschau und begab sich für anstehende Interviews »in Positur«[65]. Am Ende des Zeugenreferats bezweifelt Handke dann das Expertentum des Zeugen, indem er diesen Zeugen einen vollständig banalen Satz über die geografischen Gegebenheiten vor Ort sagen lässt: »›Die Drenica ist eine hügelige Gegend‹, ›Drenica is a hilly region‹«[66].

In noch stärkerem Maße erscheint der zweite von Handke präsentierte Zeuge in einem zweifelhaften Licht. Es handelt sich um einen jungen Albaner, der Zeuge des Massakers von Račak gewesen ist, bei dem im Januar 1999 45 Albaner getötet wurden und das für die Intervention der NATO-Streitkräfte eine wichtige Rolle spielte. Handke berichtet, dass der Zeuge die von Milošević vorgebrachten Zweifel an seiner Aussage »in Grund und Boden«[67] gelacht, durch »Weglachen«[68] erledigt habe, und fährt dann fort:

»Völlig unabgekartet wirkte es, als der junge Mensch sich erbot, dem Gericht zu einem jeden einzelnen der Toten von Račak nicht nur dessen Vor- und Zunamen und Daten, sondern auch die Geschichte zu erzählen; [...].«[69]

Interessant ist die Rhetorik des Aussagetyps »Völlig unabgekartet wirkte es ...«. Sie manifestiert sich auch in einer Aussage Handkes über die Unterbringung des albanischen Zeugen. Der Zeuge wohnt in einem »Vier-Sterne-Kasten«[70], »wohl zwei Kategorien über dem, wo ich vor über vier Jahren den Serbenzeugen gese-

---

63 Handke: Rund um das Große Tribunal, S. 43.
64 Ebd.
65 Ebd., S. 42.
66 Ebd., S. 45.
67 Ebd., S. 46.
68 Ebd.
69 Ebd.
70 Ebd., S. 47.

hen hatte«[71]. Der Prozess- und Zeugenbeobachter Handke gerät über diesen Umstand auch angesichts des selbstbewussten Auftretens der albanischen Zeugen als »Sippe«[72] ins Grübeln:

»Undenkbar wohl die Bevorzugung der albanischen Zeugenschaften durch das große Tribunal: waren also die Finanzmittel des Gerichts im Lauf der Zeit derart angewachsen?«[73]

Dass die Zeugenaussage abgekartet ist, also einer Absprache oder, inszenatorisch gesprochen, einem Drehbuch bzw. Skript folgt, und dass das Tribunal die Zeugen je nach ethnischer Zugehörigkeit ungleich behandelt, wird nicht direkt behauptet, sondern indirekt, auf einem sprachlichen Umweg, den Lesern nahegebracht, diesen ans Herz gelegt. Das rhetorische Mittel, das Handke hier und an anderen Stellen seiner Texte einsetzt, ist die Insinuation, die auch einen juristischen Aspekt impliziert: Im römischen Recht bedeutete Insinuation die förmliche Eingabe einer Sache vor Gericht. Der rhetorische Einsatz der Insinuation wird hier nicht deshalb angeführt, um Handke auf moralischer Ebene zu kritisieren, sondern um sein Verfahren sprachlich und rhetorisch zu erhellen. Dieses Verfahren besteht auf einer ersten Stufe darin, die Glaubwürdigkeit der »Zeugen der Anklage« zu erschüttern. Dies ist klassischerweise die Aufgabe eines Verteidigers bei Gericht.

Auf einer zweiten Stufe geht es Handke dann um die Präsentation eigener Zeugen. Dies kann auch ein aus Sicht der Verteidigung zu Unrecht Angeklagter sein, der die ihm zur Last gelegte Straftat nicht selbst begangen hat, sondern nur am Tatort war und sie bezeugen kann. Genau dies ist nach Handkes Aussage beim Angeklagten Novislav Djajić der Fall, der im Juni 1992 im Dorf Trnovače bei Foča als Wachmann und Angehöriger der jugoslawischen Armee an der Erschießung von vierzehn Muslimen auf der dortigen Drinabrücke beteiligt war und vom Bayerischen Obersten Landesgericht in München wegen Beihilfe zum Mord zu fünf Jahren Haft verurteilt wurde. Auch wenn dieser Fall nicht am Jugoslawientribunal in Den Haag verhandelt wurde, kommt Handke auf ihn in seinem Text *Rund um das Große Tribunal* ausführlich zu sprechen. Zunächst wird der Tathergang in Form einer Geschichte erzählt: »An einem Abend im Juni 1992 war der bosnische Serbe Novislav Djajić Teil einer militärischen Eskorte [...].«[74] In dieser Geschichte schildert Handke, dass der Angeklagte unfreiwillig Zeuge des Mordes wird, dass der Mord auf das Konto einer paramilitärischen Einheit geht und dass der Angeklagte angesichts der eigenen Unschuld von einem »Glücksgefühl«[75] bestimmt gewesen sei. Erzählt wird diese Geschichte im Modus interner Fokalisierung, der Erzähler nimmt also die Geschehnisse aus der Perspektive der Figur

---

[71] Ebd.
[72] Ebd., S. 49.
[73] Ebd., S. 50.
[74] Ebd., S. 52.
[75] Ebd., S. 54.

wahr, die sie erlebt hat. Beglaubigt wird diese Darstellung durch den zweifachen Hinweis, dass der Angeklagte Handke die Geschichte persönlich, außerhalb des Gerichts erzählt habe.[76] Doch es bleibt nicht bei dieser Darstellung durch den Autor Handke. Im Anschluss fügt er in seine Schrift einen etwa zwei Druckseiten umfassenden Bericht ein, der aus der Feder des Angeklagten selbst stammt und der das Unbeteiligtsein und die Unschuld des Erzählenden noch einmal unterstreicht. Handke kommentiert diesen eingeschobenen Text, der »bisher nicht veröffentlicht«[77] ist, wie folgt:

»[W]o in der Welt gab es Richter, Journalisten, Gerichtspsychologen, die ihm [dem erzählenden Angeklagten; J. B.] eine solche Geschichte abnähmen? die mit solch einer Geschichte etwas anfangen könnten? denen solch eine Geschichte einleuchtete? für die solch eine Geschichte Beweiskraft hätte?«[78]

Die von Handke und vom Angeklagten zweifach erzählte Geschichte hat offenbar keine juristische Relevanz, was auch heißt, dass sie im Gerichtsverfahren unberücksichtigt geblieben ist, als Beweismittel nicht zugelassen wurde. Andernfalls hätte es aus Handkes Sicht keine Verurteilung des Angeklagten geben dürfen. Mit der »Veröffentlichung« der Geschichte des Novislav Djajić eröffnet Handke die bereits abgeschlossene Gerichtsverhandlung in gewisser Weise noch einmal neu. Aus dem rechtskräftig verurteilten Angeklagten wird ein Zeuge, der das eigenständige Vorgehen paramilitärischer Einheiten bei den sogenannten ethnischen Säuberungen bestätigen soll. Dieses eigenständige Vorgehen aber war ein überaus wichtiger Aspekt im seinerzeit noch unabgeschlossenen Milošević-Prozess, und von daher erklärt sich die zunächst willkürlich erscheinende Aufnahme des Münchner Falls in Handkes Tribunalsschrift. Die Umwandlung des Angeklagten in einen Zeugen wird bei Handke durch das (zweifache) Erzählen einer Geschichte, das heißt mit den Mitteln der literarischen Sprache erreicht. Die Bühne für die Neueröffnung der Gerichtsverhandlung ist die Literatur, deren Sprache im Gegensatz zur »Sprache der Journalisten und der anderen Voraus-Verurteiler«[79] einer anderen Wahrheit als der des Gerichts Gehör und Geltung verschafft.

Die Rede von der literarischen Bühne, auf der nach Maßgabe einer anderen Sprache eine andere Wahrheit verhandelt werden soll, ist dabei ganz wörtlich zu nehmen. Handke hat Zeugen seiner Tribunalsschriften, die reale Personen in realen Gerichtsverfahren waren, in einem Theaterstück auftreten lassen und damit auf einer dritten Stufe den Übergang vom Gericht auf die Theaterbühne vollzogen. In seinem Drama *Die Fahrt im Einbaum oder das Stück zum Film*

---

76 Vgl. ebd., S. 53, 54.
77 Ebd., S. 54.
78 Ebd., S. 56.
79 Ebd.

vom Krieg von 1999, das Claus Peymann am Wiener Burgtheater inszeniert hat, tritt unter anderem der von einem Angeklagten in einen Zeugen umgewandelte Djajić auf.[80] Der bosnische Serbe steht, mit eindeutigen Erkennungszeichen versehen, hinter der Dramenfigur des »Wald- oder Irrläufers«[81], was Handkes Stück zu einem Werk der Schlüsselliteratur macht. Die Figur des Waldläufers gibt den tragischen Helden des Stücks ab, bei dem zwei Filmregisseure in einem Provinzhotel im »tiefsten oder innersten Balkan«[82] ein Casting für den geplanten Film vom Krieg durchführen. Der Waldläufer ist die zentrale Figur innerhalb einer Reihe von Figuren, deren Auf- und Abtritte von einem Ansager kommentiert werden. Der Zuschauer des Stücks erfährt dabei Einzelheiten aus dem Leben des Waldläufers, die auf Djajić und seine Verurteilung in Deutschland Bezug nehmen. Vor allem aber wird im Stück die skizzierte These von der Zeugenschaft des Verurteilten schärfer gefasst als in der Schrift *Rund um das Große Tribunal*. Wenn die Figur des »Ansagers«[83] die »Geschichte eines jungen Mannes«[84] als filmreifen *Plot* ankündigt und sie sogleich zu erzählen beginnt, dann wird im Stück aus der Beihilfe des Angeklagten nicht nur ein unschuldiges Unbeteiligtsein wie in der Tribunalsschrift, sondern, mehr noch, ein aktives Sich-dazwischen-Stellen »zwischen die einen und die andern«[85]. Wie der Ansager erklärt, will der Waldläufer »nicht aufhören, Zeuge zu spielen. Aber warum greift er nicht ein? Die Antwort: sein Dabeistehen und Aufnehmen hält er bereits für ein Eingreifen«[86].

Dass die Umdeutung der Passivität des Zeugen über den Begriff des Dabeistehens läuft, ist einigermaßen irritierend. Der Waldläufer wird im Anschluss an die eben zitierte Stelle dreimal im positiven Sinne ein »Dabeisteher«[87] genannt, eine recht auffällige Wortbildung, deren Semantik zumindest im Englischen einen historisch-politischen Resonanzraum besitzt. ›Bystander‹ ist im Rahmen der historischen Aufarbeitung der Shoah ein besetzter Begriff für diejenigen, die dem Völkermord an den europäischen Juden tatenlos zugesehen haben. Zu verweisen ist etwa auf Raul Hilbergs Buch *Perpetrators, Victims, Bystanders*.[88] In welchem Umfang Handkes Stück den Begriff »Dabeisteher« im positiven Sinne umwerten will, bleibt eine offene Frage.

Abgesehen davon ist Handkes Stück im doppelten Wortsinne eine Vorführung der internationalen Akteure, die im Umfeld des Jugoslawienkriegs tätig sind: Vorführung als (theatralische) Aufführung und als Bloßstellung. Die schlicht

---

80 Vgl. Handke: Die Fahrt im Einbaum.
81 Ebd., S. 8.
82 Ebd., S. 9.
83 Ebd., S. 8.
84 Ebd., S. 48.
85 Ebd., S. 49.
86 Ebd., S. 50.
87 Ebd., S. 51, 52.
88 Vgl. Hilberg: Perpetrators, Victims, Bystanders.

»Internationale«[89] genannten Figuren werden als lautstark auf die Bühne preschende »Bergradfahrer«[90] theatralisch vor Augen gestellt, um sich zu blamieren und lächerlich zu machen. Mit Sätzen wie »Wir müssen das Weltgericht sein.«[91], »Wir sind die Welt. Wir sind die Macht. Wir schreiben die Geschichte.«[92] und »Wir sind die Sprache.«[93] soll der allumfassende Geltungsanspruch dieser »Internationalen« ad absurdum geführt werden. In erster Linie zielt dieser Angriff, der im Zeichen der Groteske steht, auf das »IFSUG«[94], das »Internationale Friedens- und Strafgericht«[95], das »Allvölkergericht«[96], mit dem unzweifelhaft das Jugoslawientribunal gemeint ist. Dass dieser Angriff dramaturgisch weitgehend misslingt, ist zweitrangig und soll hier nicht weiter interessieren. Wichtiger ist der Umstand, dass Handke neben den skizzierten rhetorischen (Schreib-)Verfahren auch die Theaterbühne nutzt, um über das Jugoslawientribunal literarisch zu Gericht zu sitzen. Der emotionale Kern der rhetorisch-theatralischen Unternehmung ist dabei in einer Verletzung zu sehen, die darin besteht, dass Handke die Leidensgeschichte Serbiens in und nach dem Zweiten Weltkrieg nicht angemessen berücksichtigt sieht. Im Drama *Die Fahrt im Einbaum* äußert sich dies an der Stelle, wo ein aus dem Kreis der »Internationalen« ausgescharter Ex-Journalist über Tribunale nach dem Zweiten Weltkrieg spricht und die Aussage des allerersten Zeugen, der am Jugoslawientribunal über die an Serben begangenen Kriegsverbrechen sprechen darf, gewürdigt sehen will:

»Tribunale da und dort – keinmal aber ein Zeugnis aus dem Volk, das in jenem Krieg [im Zweiten Weltkrieg; J. B.] mit am stärksten dezimiert worden war, und keinmal so auch ein Bewusstwerden der Welt für eine der bittersten Schmerzgeschichten Europas – nichts, nirgends. Und dort also vor dem Dünentribunal endlich der erste aus dem Volk, welcher euch, der Welt, eine Vorstellung hätte geben können, einen Schimmer!«[97]

Die Verwendung des Irrealis »hätte geben können« zeigt an, dass der Sprecher davon ausgeht, dass niemand dem Zeugen zugehört hat. Aus diesem Nichtzuhören der Welt, das den Aussagenden zu einem »stimmlosen«[98] Zeugen macht, bezieht Handke die Legitimation seines Sprechens. Es ist ein Sprechen für andere, ein Sprechen im Namen der anderen.[99]

---

[89] Handke: Die Fahrt im Einbaum, S. 56.
[90] Ebd.
[91] Ebd., S. 76.
[92] Ebd., S. 87.
[93] Ebd., S. 95.
[94] Ebd., S. 63.
[95] Ebd.
[96] Ebd., S. 88.
[97] Ebd., S. 90.
[98] Handke: Rund um das Große Tribunal, S. 22.
[99] Zum (rhetorisch-forensischen) Konzept der Fürsprache vgl. Campe: An Outline for a Critical History of *Fürsprache*.

IV.

Vor dem Hintergrund der skizzierten Überlegungen zur Unterscheidung von Gericht und Tribunal und der Analyse von Handkes Texten stellt sich die Frage, was der österreichische Schriftsteller in seinen Tribunalsschriften und darüber hinaus in seinem Theaterstück vollzieht. In gewisser Weise stülpt er das »Bewußtseinstheater«[100], das im Inneren stattfindet und das – »in die Tat-Wirklichkeit übertragen«[101] – auch jede »Gerichtsinstitution«[102] kennzeichnet, vor allem deshalb nach außen, um die ambivalente Struktur des Jugoslawientribunals zu erklären. Diese ambivalente Struktur, die zwischen der Arbeitsweise eines »normalen Gerichts«[103] und der Inszenierungsmacht eines »Welttribunals«[104] oszilliert, hat durchaus etwas von jener »Zweideutigkeit«[105], die Walter Benjamin 1921 in seiner berühmten Kritik der Rechtsgewalt diagnostiziert hat. Doch erschöpft sich Handkes Vorstellung vom »Bewußtseinstheater« nicht in dieser Erklärung und Grundsatzkritik rechtlicher Institutionen. Er stülpt das »Bewußtseinstheater« auch deshalb nach außen, um es in seinen eigenen Texten zu materialisieren, damit es in diesen literarische Gestalt gewinnt. Die behandelten Texte Handkes zum Jugoslawientribunal sind sein eigenes literarisches »Schuldspruch-Theater«[106]. Die Anklage dieses Schuldspruch-Theaters ergeht, um noch einmal Handkes Drama zu zitieren, an »die internationale Gemeinschaft«[107]: an »die Öffentlichkeit«[108], an »die Welt«[109].

---

[100] Handke: Die Tablas von Daimiel, S. 18.
[101] Ebd.
[102] Ebd.
[103] Ebd., S. 20.
[104] Ebd., S. 19.
[105] Benjamin: Zur Kritik der Gewalt, S. 199.
[106] Handke: Die Tablas von Daimiel, S. 20.
[107] Handke: Die Fahrt im Einbaum, S. 55.
[108] Ebd.
[109] Ebd.

Literatur

Arendt, Hannah: Eichmann in Jerusalem. Ein Bericht von der Banalität des Bösen, München 1998.

Benjamin, Walter: Zur Kritik der Gewalt, in: Gesammelte Schriften, Bd. II/1, Frankfurt a. M. 1991, S. 179–203.

Brokoff, Jürgen: »Srebrenica – was für ein klangvolles Wort«. Zur Problematik der poetischen Sprache in Peter Handkes Texten zum Jugoslawien-Krieg, in: Carsten Gansel/Heinrich Kaulen (Hg.): Störungen. Kriegsdiskurse in Literatur und Medien von 1989 bis zum Beginn des 21. Jahrhunderts, Göttingen 2011, S. 61–88.

Campe, Rüdiger: An Outline for a Critical History of *Fürsprache*: *Synegoria* and *Advocacy*, in: Deutsche Vierteljahrsschrift für Literaturwissenschaft und Geistesgeschichte, Jg. 82, H. 3, 2008, S. 355–381.

Derrida, Jacques: Gesetzeskraft. Der »mystische Grund der Autorität«, Frankfurt a. M. 1991.

Habermas, Jürgen: Bestialität und Humanität. Ein Krieg an der Grenze zwischen Recht und Moral, in: Die Zeit vom 29. April 1999.

Handke, Peter: Eine winterliche Reise zu den Flüssen Donau, Save, Morawa und Drina oder Gerechtigkeit für Serbien, in: Ders.: Abschied des Träumers vom Neunten Land, Eine winterliche Reise zu den Flüssen Donau, Save, Morawa und Drina, Sommerlicher Nachtrag zu einer winterlichen Reise, Frankfurt a. M. 1998, S. 33–161.

Handke, Peter: Die Fahrt im Einbaum oder das Stück zum Film vom Krieg, Frankfurt a. M. 1999.

Handke, Peter: Rund um das Große Tribunal, Frankfurt a. M. 2003.

Handke, Peter: Die Tablas von Daimiel. Ein Umwegzeugenbericht zum Prozeß gegen Slobodan Milošević, Frankfurt a. M. 2006.

Hilberg, Raul: Perpetrators, Victims, Bystanders. The Jewish Catastrophe 1933–1945, New York 1992.

Koskenniemi, Martti: Between Impunity and Show Trials, in: Max Planck Yearbook of United Nations Law, Jg. 6, 2002, S. 1–35.

Safferling, Christoph: Das Monitoring-Projekt des Forschungs- und Dokumentationszentrums für Kriegsverbrecherprozesse (ICWC), Marburg, in: Zeitschrift für Internationale Strafrechtsdogmatik, Jg. 7, 2011, S. 564–572.

Teitel, Ruti G: Transitional Justice, New York 2000.

Teitel, Ruti G: Humanity's Law, New York 2011.

Vismann, Cornelia: Medien der Rechtsprechung, Frankfurt a. M. 2011.

Svjetlan Lacko Vidulić

Geteilter Erinnerungsort? Der Internationale Gerichtshof für das ehemalige Jugoslawien als Topos regionaler Erinnerungskulturen

»Dies wird nicht vergessen bis ins zehnte Glied.«¹

Den Haag ist bekanntlich eine Stadt an der Nordsee, Regierungssitz der Niederlande, königliche Residenzstadt und Hauptstadt der Provinz Südholland; seit dem 20. Jahrhundert ein Zentrum der internationalen Politik und Gerichtsbarkeit. Im Raum des ehemaligen Jugoslawien steht der Name der Stadt, metonymisch reduziert auf eine ihrer zahlreichen internationalen Institutionen, für das Erbe eines Krieges, für gesühnte und ungesühnte Verbrechen, für Kriegshelden in Not.² *Haag* ist das Kürzel für ein diskursives Feld, in dem das Tagesgeschäft des Gerichtshofs untrennbar ist von der Frage nach historischer Gerechtigkeit und historischem Unrecht, nach der Würde oder Schande eines Krieges, einer Heldenriege, einer Nation. Scheveningen ist folglich weniger ein Stadtteil von Den Haag oder ein »geschichtsträchtiger Seekurort mit historischem Kurhaus« (Lexikon), sondern vielmehr der Ort, an dem sich das Untersuchungsgefängnis für mutmaßliche Kriegsverbrecher befindet, ein Ort, an dem Objekte innenpolitischer Tauziehen und außenpolitischer Erpressung in Gewahrsam landen, um schließlich – und mit manchen von ihnen symbolisch ganze Führungseliten und politische Doktrinen, ganze Staaten und Nationen – in den Gerichtsstand einer juridischen Macht zu treten, die je nach Perspektive als zynisch und politisch manipuliert oder, trotz aller Kontroversen und Widersprüche, als Katalysator von Befriedung und Aufarbeitung gilt.

---

1 »Ovo će biti upamćeno do našeg desetog koljena.« Schlusssatz im Kommentar der Bosnierin Munira Subašić (*Frauen Srebrenicas*) zum Freispruch für General Momčilo Perišić, in einer Sendung von *Al Jazeera Balkans* am 28.02.2013; http://balkans.aljazeera.net/vijesti/haski-tribunal-oslobodio-momcila-perisica; Zugriff auf diese und alle weiteren angeführten Internetquellen: 01.03.2013.
2 Einer globalen Sprachpraxis entsprechend (vgl. http://en.wikipedia.org/wiki/Hague_Tribunal) wird der Internationale Strafgerichtshof für das ehemalige Jugoslawien im Alltags- und Mediendiskurs des betreffenden Raumes meistens als Haager Tribunal (»Haški tribunal« usw.) bzw. metonymisch als »Haag«/»Hag« bezeichnet. In der derzeit umfassendsten Datenbank digitalisierter Zeitungsartikel zum Thema Kriegsverbrechen aus der kroatischen Tages- und Wochenpresse des Zeitraums 02.04.1996–18.07.2011 (s. Database of digitized newspaper articles) sind von den 50.546 Beiträgen 12.403 mit »Haag« verschlagwortet, 10.889 mit »ICTY«.

Als Standort internationaler Gerichtshöfe entwickelt die südholländische Stadt eine Bedeutung und eine symbolische Ausstrahlung, die eine gewisse Verwandtschaft mit der Stadt Nürnberg aufweist. Nürnberg allerdings war nicht nur Standort der Kriegsverbrecherprozesse 1946–1949, sondern zugleich – als Stätte der NS-Reichsparteitage, die an die alten Nürnberger Reichstraditionen anknüpfen sollten – ein exemplarischer Tatort. Nürnberg steht somit für die Selbstzerstörung einer Kultur, für die politischen und juridischen Konsequenzen und für die langfristige Aufarbeitung der Vergangenheit; Nürnberg spielt in der Folge eine markante Rolle in der deutschen und gesamteuropäischen Erinnerungskultur.[3] Die politische Bedeutung, vor allem aber die symbolische Aura Den Haags als Sitz des Tribunals für Jugoslawien (seit 1993) und für Ruanda (seit 1994) sowie des Internationalen Strafgerichtshofs (seit 2002) entfaltet sich hingegen vor allem im jeweiligen Zuständigkeitsbereich dieser Gerichte: an fernen Tatorten, in unterschiedlichen Gesellschaften und Kulturen. *Haag* ist im vorliegenden Fall der Brennpunkt einer geografisch *fernen* Kontroverse um die Deutung der *nahen* Vergangenheit; Brennpunkt in einem Deutungskonflikt, der mit zentralen Gehalten regionaler Erinnerungskultur und kollektiver Identitätsstiftung zusammenhängt. Entwickelt sich *Haag* somit zu einem postjugoslawischen Erinnerungsort?

Eingeführt von der französischen Historikerschule um Pierre Nora als neuer Zugang zur Erforschung der Nationalgeschichte, hat sich das Konzept der Erinnerungsorte als »das international einflussreichste Konzept« im Rahmen der kulturwissenschaftlichen Gedächtnisforschung seit den 1980er Jahren erwiesen.[4] Der Kritik an der Unschärfe des Leitbegriffs und den theoretischen Prämissen des Konzepts steht eine beachtliche Wirkungsgeschichte gegenüber: Noras Projekt wurde zum Vorbild für eine Reihe nationaler und regionaler Nachfolgeprojekte. Die Herausgeber der *Deutschen Erinnerungsorte* bestimmen Erinnerungsorte als »langlebige, Generationen überdauernde Kristallisationspunkte kollektiver Erinnerung und Identität, die in gesellschaftliche, kulturelle und politische Üblichkeiten eingebunden sind und die sich in dem Maße verändern, in dem sich die Weise ihrer Wahrnehmung, Aneignung, Anwendung und Übertragung verändert«[5]. Das Konzept der Erinnerungsorte geht also von ihrer Einbettung in bestimmte Kollektive und Erinnerungskulturen, ihrem Wandel im Lauf der Zeit, ihrer netzartigen Verbindung aus. Wenn *Haag* als potenzieller postjugoslawischer Erinnerungsort betrachtet wird, stellt sich die Frage, von welchem Trägerkollektiv und welchem Netzwerk auszugehen wäre.

---

[3] Vgl. Kosfeld: Nürnberg.
[4] Erll: Kollektives Gedächtnis, S. 13. Zur Kritik des Konzepts vgl. ebd., S. 25; Schmidt: Zwischen Medien und Topoi.
[5] François/Schulze: Deutsche Erinnerungsorte, Einleitung, S. 18.

»[D]ie Gesellschaften des ehemaligen Jugoslawien«, konstatiert Wolfgang Höpken in einer Studie über postsozialistische Erinnerungskulturen, stehen »[v]or ganz besonderen Schwierigkeiten im Umgang mit der Vergangenheit«. Diese Gesellschaften seien »mit einem dreifachen ›Erbe der Vergangenheit‹ konfrontiert«, mit einer dreifachen Gedächtnisrevision befasst: mit der postkommunistischen Pluralisierung, mit der postjugoslawisch-nationalstaatlichen Neuorientierung und mit der Verarbeitung der Kriegserfahrung.[6] Am auffälligsten im öffentlichen Raum war seit Mitte der 1980er Jahre der ethnonationale Aspekt der Revision (eingebettet in je unterschiedliche historische und aktuelle Zusammenhänge in den einzelnen Republiken), da er zugleich den dominanten Gehalt der postkommunistischen Pluralisierung darstellte und in der posttitoistischen kollektiven Paranoia, mehr noch im anschließenden Krieg, der Existenzsicherung im Rahmen der ›limitischen Aufrüstung‹ der Konfliktparteien zu dienen schien.[7]

Die radikale Abwertung der jugoslawischen Vergangenheit im Zeichen aufgewerteter nationalgeschichtlicher Narrative wie auch der undifferenzierte Blick auf diese »Kultur der Lüge«[8] führten zum Trugbild eines Kahlschlags um 1990, einer mnemonischen ›Stunde Null‹, in der eine Totalrevision der jugoslawischen Geschichte die Geburtsstunde der Nationen einzuleiten schien. Die mnemonischen Extremisten beider Couleurs, die Nationalisten wie die »Post-Jugoslawen«[9], verdrängen gerne die Linien der Kontinuität. Eine solche ist in der Entwicklung der jugoslawischen Föderation seit den 1960er Jahren zu erkennen, geprägt von den widersprüchlichen Aspekten eines »Ethno-Sozialismus«[10], der die nationale Frage durch ein Gleichgewicht zwischen nationaler Selbstbehauptung und jugoslawischer Integration zu lösen trachtete.[11] Dazu gehörte eine Geschichts- und Erinnerungspolitik, die die nationalen Überlieferungen weiterhin als solche institutionell tradierte, in bestimmten Kontexten allerdings in ein supranationales und sozialistisches Masternarrativ integrierte, um ihr Konfliktpotenzial zu bändigen.

Nicht anders als im Fall französischer, deutscher oder dänischer Erinnerungsorte ist eine Rekonstruktion kroatischer, bosniakischer oder serbischer Topoi denkbar, die von der sozialen Konstruktion einer entsprechenden kollektiven Erinnerung und Identität ausgehen kann, deren maßgebliche Entwicklungsgeschichte mit den Nationsbildungsprozessen im 19. Jahrhundert einsetzt. Mehr noch und

---

6   Höpken: Post-sozialistische Erinnerungskulturen, S. 16.
7   Als ›limitische Aufrüstung‹ bezeichnet Jan Assmann (Das kulturelle Gedächtnis, S. 156) in typologischer Perspektive sinngemäß jene Abgrenzungsprozesse, die im jugoslawischen Fall die durchgehend ›starken‹ ethnischen Identitäten Jugoslawiens von der ›latenten‹ zur ›manifesten‹ Form überführt haben; zu dieser Deutung vgl. Banovac: Etničnost i regionalizam, S. 250f.
8   Ugrešić: Die Kultur der Lüge.
9   Ebd., S. 146.
10 In der überspitzten Formulierung von Enver Kazaz: Tranzicijska etnokulturna pustinja, S. 83.
11 Zur allgemeinen Entwicklung vgl. Calic: Geschichte Jugoslawiens, S. 237ff.; Ramet: Tri Jugoslavije, Kapitel 8 und 10.

anders als die *Deutschen Erinnerungsorte* oder die Untersuchungen zur zentraleuropäischen Region würde eine solche Rekonstruktion allerdings von einer offenen Konzeption, von bi-, multi- oder transnationalen Perspektiven profitieren, die die Differenzen und Verflechtungen der regionalen Erinnerungskulturen zum Ausdruck bringen würden.[12] Neben den allgemeinen Aspekten supra- und subnationaler Vielfalt und Verflechtung, die das norasche »Netz von materiellen und immateriellen Erinnerungsfäden, das das nationale Bewußtsein in einem ungenau bestimmbaren, aber sehr profunden Sinne zusammenhält«[13], als essenzialistische Stilisierung und starke Reduktion kollektiver Gedächtnisbestände erscheinen lassen, liegen hier offenbar besondere regionale Bezüge vor. Der jeweilige landestypische Stil in der Beziehung zur Vergangenheit, der nach Nora den Gegenstand der Rekonstruktion nationaler Erinnerungsorte darstellt,[14] dürfte aufgrund geteilter Geschichte und geteilter Kontexte gewisse zentraleuropäische, südosteuropäische und postjugoslawische Aspekte aufweisen.[15] Außerdem scheinen Profilierung und Bedeutungswandel vieler nationaler Topoi mit regionalen Transferprozessen zusammenzuhängen, deren Effekte zwischen Übernahme oder Synergie auf der einen, Abgrenzung und Konflikt auf der anderen Seite liegen. Dies gilt sowohl für die exklusiven nationalen Symbole[16] als auch für die gemeinsamen und die geteilten Erinnerungsorte,[17] in der breiten Palette von Topoi einer gemeinsamen Alltagskultur mit veränderbarer nationaler Identitätsrelevanz bis zu den Topoi einer verwobenen politischen Geschichte – den Brennpunkten der kollektiven Erinnerung und Identifikation, deren Entwicklung sich zwischen den Polen einer exklusiv nationalen und einer transnationalen Kodierung und Instrumentalisierung bewegt.[18]

Kriege haben eine »Schlüsselfunktion [...] für das kollektive Gedächtnis und die Erinnerungskultur einer Gesellschaft«, da sie im individuellen wie im kollektiven Maßstab Erfahrungs- und Erinnerungsbrüche darstellen und im Rückblick als

---

12 Vgl. François/Schulze: Deutsche Erinnerungsorte, Einleitung, S. 19; Csáky/Stachel: Die Verortung von Gedächtnis.
13 Nora, zit. nach François/Schulze: Deutsche Erinnerungsorte, Einleitung, S. 16.
14 Vgl. ebd.
15 Zu den strukturellen Parallelen der postjugoslawischen Erinnerungskulturen seit dem Staatszerfall vgl. Sundhaussen: Jugoslawien und seine Nachfolgestaaten; Höpken: Post-sozialistische Erinnerungskulturen; umfassend, allerdings unter weitgehender Ausblendung der Differenzen Kuljić: Umkämpfte Vergangenheiten.
16 Vgl. Žanić et al.: Nationale Symbole.
17 Gemeinsame, geteilte und parallele Erinnerungsorte unterscheidet Hans Henning Hahn im Rahmen einer Typologie binationaler Erinnerungsorte; vgl. Wierzcholska: Tagungsbericht.
18 Die Entwicklungsdynamik der geteilten Erinnerung, im doppelten Sinn von Gemeinsamkeit und Trennung und in Verbindung von Alltagskultur und politischem Wandel seit 1980, kann bspw. an der Wahrnehmungsgeschichte des Tito-Kults beobachtet werden; vgl. Škrbić Alempijević/Mathiesen Hjemdahl: O Titu kao mitu; Kuljić: Sećanje na titoizam.

»Schleusen der Erinnerung« wirken.[19] Dass Kriege zu dramatischen Deutungs- und Erinnerungsdifferenzen in den Gesellschaften der ehemaligen Kriegsparteien führen können und dass Episoden, Schauplätze, Protagonisten des Krieges in besonderem Maße dazu tendieren, Fixpunkte verwobener und opponierender Erinnerungsprozesse zu werden, liegt auf der Hand. Das langfristige Konfliktpotenzial des Kriegserbes haben die Desintegrationsprozesse in Jugoslawien eindringlich vor Augen geführt: Eine eskalierende Wirkung entfaltete seit den 1980er Jahren – in einer durch das Oktroi der jugoslawischen Erinnerungskultur frustrierten und infantilisierten Gegenöffentlichkeit – die pluralistische Revision des offiziellen anational-antifaschistischen Narrativs zum Zweiten Weltkrieg. Dabei setzten sich im öffentlichen Raum vor allem die konträren (in je unterschiedliche historische und aktuelle Zusammenhänge eingebetteten) nationalistischen Narrative und eine entsprechende Umkodierung der zentralen Erinnerungsorte der Weltkriegs- und Nachkriegszeit durch.[20] Der Trugschluss einer kausalen Verbindung und Kontinuität zwischen den offenen Rechnungen des Zweiten Weltkriegs und den sogenannten jugoslawischen Erbfolgekriegen gehört bis heute zu den Spätfolgen einer verfehlten Aufarbeitung der Vergangenheit.

Zu den Zielen und Ansprüchen des 1993 zur Ahndung der postjugoslawischen Kriegsverbrechen gegründeten Ad-hoc-Tribunals der UNO gehört die strafrechtliche Verfolgung der Täter und Verantwortungsträger ohne Rücksicht auf Rang und Status, die Faktensicherung als Weg zur Aufarbeitung und als Mittel gegen Leugnung und Revisionismus sowie die Förderung eines dauerhaften Friedens. Der vom Tribunal angeblich erreichte »Triumph der Gerechtigkeit«[21] wird von seinen Vertretern zudem als Beitrag zu den Versöhnungsprozessen in der Region gewertet.[22] Der besondere Charakter und Anspruch des UNO-Tribunals, die Schwächen in der Entwicklung entsprechender Formen der Vermittlungs- und Öffentlichkeitsarbeit in der Region und die Besonderheiten der regionalen Deutungskonflikte haben im Zusammenhang jedoch überwiegend Wirkungen entfaltet, die im auffälligen Widerspruch zu den Zielen des Tribunals stehen.[23]

Die Vorstellung vom Tribunal als Medium überfälliger Aufarbeitung der Vergangenheit, gar des Schiedsspruchs in kontroversen Deutungs- und Erinnerungs-

---

19 Speitkamp: Einleitung, S. 9.
20 Vgl. Sundhaussen: Jugoslawien und seine Nachfolgestaaten.
21 John Hocking, Sekretär des Tribunals, schließt die Video-Vorstellung des Tribunals mit den Worten: »Bringing war criminals to justice was our mandate, the triumph of justice is our legacy.«; http://www.icty.org/sections/AbouttheICTY.
22 Zum Selbstverständnis des Tribunals vgl. die offiziellen Internetseiten, bes. das Kapitel *About the ICTY;* http://www.icty.org/sections/AbouttheICTY. Von Versöhnungseffekten ist auch in öffentlichen Vorträgen (vgl. Del Ponte: The Role of International Criminal Prosecutions) sowie in einzelnen Prozessdokumenten die Rede, bspw. im Zusammenhang mit Schuldeingeständnissen.
23 Zu dem begrenzten Beitrag des Tribunals zu den Versöhnungprozessen vgl. Clark: The ICTY and the Challenges of Reconciliation. Entsprechende Befunde liegen auch zu anderen Kriegsverbrecherprozessen und -tribunalen vor, vgl. Kardov et al.: Suočavanje s prošlošću, S. 92 f.

gehalten, ist in der Öffentlichkeit der Nachkriegsgesellschaften eine im Sinne der Breitenwirkung marginale Position, auch wenn sie mittlerweile als offizieller Standpunkt etwa der aktuellen links-liberalen Regierung in Kroatien gilt. Im Mittelpunkt der öffentlichen Wahrnehmung stehen die unübersehbaren politischen Implikationen von Prozessen, bei denen höchste Vertreter der damaligen oder gar der aktuellen Führungs- und Militärelite mit Inkriminierungen wie ›Genozid‹ oder ›gemeinsames kriminelles Unterfangen‹ konfrontiert werden; und zwar vor einem Tribunal, dessen Anspruch auf Gerechtigkeit und Faktensicherung im Rahmen seines exklusiven Zuständigkeitsbereichs, paradoxerweise aber auch das von ihm angewendete Prinzip der Individualisierung der Schuld, zu dem naheliegenden Trugschluss führen, die Summe seiner Urteile ergäbe ein analytisches Gesamturteil über die Verteilung von Verantwortung, Schuld und erlittenem Leid auf die einzelnen Nationen und Staaten – oder könnte von der internationalen Gemeinschaft zumindest in diesem Sinne verstanden werden. In der bisher dominierenden Perspektive erscheint das Tribunal daher als Institution, deren Tätigkeit – so sie nicht diesem oder jenem politischen Kalkül der internationalen Gemeinschaft, sondern der Wahrheit dient – das quasi einzig wahre, nämlich das jeweilige nationale Vergangenheitsnarrativ bestätigen und einen entsprechenden »Triumph der Gerechtigkeit« herbeiführen müsste; womit die anderen, konkurrierenden nationalen Narrative und Gerechtigkeitsvorstellungen in dem Nullsummenspiel der Wahrheit entschieden widerlegt sein müssten. So gesehen leitet das Tribunal die Geschicke der jeweiligen Nation und webt maßgeblich an der internationalen Deutung der regionalen Geschichte. Damit erreicht *Haag* jene »maximale Bedeutungsdichte bei geringster Zeichenmenge«, die Nora den ›Lieux de mémoire‹ attestiert,[24] und scheint als geteilter, quadrilateraler (bosnischer, kroatischer, serbischer und kosovo-albanischer) Erinnerungsort das Potenzial für einen »langlebigen, Generationen überdauernden Kristallisationspunkt«[25] der kollektiven Erinnerung und Identität aufzuweisen.

Den Widerspruch zwischen Anspruch und Wahrnehmung, Intention und Wirkung des Tribunals soll die öffentliche Resonanz jenes Gerichtsverfahrens illustrieren, das ohne großes prognostisches Risiko als besonders bedeutsam für *Haag* als kroatischen Erinnerungstopos und seine anzunehmende Entwicklung in den nächsten Jahren bezeichnet werden kann.[26] Das Urteil in letzter Instanz im Verfahren *Gotovina et al. (IT-06-90)* »*Operation Storm*«[27] am 16. November 2012 ist aufgrund seiner Wirkung im Kontext des dominanten Erinnerungsnarrativs ein

---

[24] Nora: Between Memory and History, S. 15.
[25] François / Schulze: Deutsche Erinnerungsorte, Einleitung, S. 18.
[26] Ausführlich zur Wahrnehmung des Tribunals in Kroatien Pavlaković: Better the Grave than a Slave; Kardov et al.: Suočavanje s prošlošću.
[27] Die Dokumente des Verfahrens sind zugänglich unter: http://www.icty.org/case/gotovina/4.

Schlüsselereignis der kroatischen Nachkriegsgeschichte. Das Gerichtsverfahren hatte elf lange Jahre die innen- und außenpolitische Szene in Aufruhr versetzt. Die Anklageschrift von 2001, die Fahndung nach dem untergetauchten General Gotovina und seine Inhaftierung auf Teneriffa 2005, das Tauziehen um die Lieferung zentraler Beweisstücke an das Tribunal und schließlich das Urteil in erster Instanz von 2011, das auf 24 und 18 Jahre Haft für die Angeklagten lautete: Höhepunkte in einem Verfahren, das drei national-konservative und zwei linksliberale Regierungen sowie drei Staatspräsidenten[28] unter wechselnden Umständen in Bedrängnis brachte und die Beitrittsverhandlungen des Landes mit der Europäischen Union aufgrund der Koppelung an die Zusammenarbeit mit dem Tribunal um Jahre verzögerte.

Der außenpolitische Druck und die innenpolitischen Kontroversen rund um die Zusammenarbeit mit dem Tribunal seit dem Ende des autoritär-nationalistischen Jahrzehnts (1991–1999), besonders aber die an die heimischen Gerichte abgetretenen Prozesse haben die institutionelle Bereitschaft zur Aufarbeitung ›eigener‹ Kriegsverbrechen ohne Zweifel gefördert und die öffentliche Leugnung notorischer Verbrechen allmählich in einen Nischendiskurs verdrängt. Dies konnte in dem Maße gelingen, in dem die Schattenseiten der Kriegsführung als individuelle Entgleisungen gedeutet werden konnten, mit deren Eingeständnis die Heldenriege zwar um einige Namen gekürzt, das dominante, den Krieg verherrlichende heroische Erinnerungsnarrativ jedoch nicht grundsätzlich infrage gestellt werden musste. Im Fall der *Operation Sturm* waren Individualisierung der Schuld und Ausgliederung der Schuldigen aus dem herrschenden Erinnerungsnarrativ nicht möglich, da die Anklage die Kernelemente dieses Narrativs infrage stellte. Aus dem entscheidenden Befreiungsschlag in dem zum Gründungsmythos stilisierten ›Heimatkrieg‹ wurde in der Anklage von 2006 und dem Urteil von 2011 ein »gemeinsames kriminelles Unterfangen, dessen Ziel die dauerhafte und zwangsweise Entfernung der serbischen Zivilbevölkerung« gewesen sei, begleitet und gefolgt von Morden, Brandschatzungen, Plünderungen und einer diskriminatorischen Staatspolitik; als Anführer des »kriminellen Unterfangens« erschienen die Spitzen der nationalen Heldenriege.[29]

---

28 Der erste dieser Reihe, Franjo Tuđman (1991–1999), wurde erstmals 2000 als (verstorbenes) Ermittlungsobjekt des Tribunals genannt und im Urteil gegen Gotovina et al. als Anführer des »gemeinsamen kriminellen Unterfangens« identifiziert. Der zweite, Stipe Mesić (2000–2010), war angeblich für die Lieferung des Schlüsselbeweisstücks gegen Gotovina et al. aus dem Archiv seines Amtsvorgängers verantwortlich (Brioni-Transkripte) und fundierte damit sein Image als Landesverräter bzw. Pazifist. Der dritte, Ivo Josipović (seit 2011), hatte im Fall Gotovina et al. zwischen seinen Überzeugungen als linksliberaler Experte für internationales Strafrecht und einem patriotischen Pragmatismus zu jonglieren.

29 IT-06-90, Judgement Summary, S. 4f. – Die im Zusammenhang mit der *Operation Sturm* verübten Verbrechen an den kroatischen Serben in der Krajina und die anschließende diskriminatorische Politik werden in dem 1.377 Seiten starken Urteil in erster Instanz ausführlich dokumentiert

Parallel zu der im linken Bereich und im Zentrum des politischen Spektrums wachsenden Bereitschaft zur Aufarbeitung der heimischen Verbrechen bewirkte der Gerichtsfall *Gotovina et al.* im national-konservativen Mainstream eine zunehmende Profilierung des heroischen Narrativs und dessen Fokussierung auf die eine, zunehmend sakralisierte Schlacht sowie auf den einen, zunehmend auratisierten Befehlshaber. Abzulesen ist diese Entwicklung exemplarisch an Erklärungen des kroatischen Parlaments zwischen 1999 und 2006, die – angesichts heftiger innenpolitischer Kontroversen und drohender Regierungskrisen im Zusammenhang mit der Zusammenarbeit mit dem Haager Tribunal – das dominante Narrativ zum offiziellen Geschichtsbild erheben und dadurch stabilisieren sollten.[30] Die Höhepunkte der Serie sind die *Deklaration über den Heimatkrieg* (Oktober 2000), die seinen Charakter klarstellen, seiner »Kriminalisierung« entgegenwirken und seiner »Würde« dienlich sein will,[31] sowie die umfangreiche *Deklaration über die Operation Sturm* (2006) – den »entscheidende[n], ruhmreiche[n], siegreiche[n] Kampf des Heimatkrieges, der zum Bestandteil der kroatischen ›nützlichen Vergangenheit‹ für zukünftige Generationen werden wird«[32]. Seit 2001, dem Jahr der ersten Anklageschrift gegen seine Befehlshaber, ist diesem Kampf ein Staatsfeiertag gewidmet.[33]

Als am Morgen des 16. November 2012 die Urteilsverkündung in letzter Instanz im Fall *Gotovina et al.* erwartet wurde, stand für Millionen Menschen viel auf dem Spiel. Für die in Kroatien kaum wahrgenommenen serbischen ›Sekundäropfer‹ ging es um Sühne für persönlich Erlittenes. Für die ebenso unsichtbaren Mörder, Brandstifter und Plünderer von 1995 ging es um das steigende Risiko strafrechtlicher Verfolgung und den gefährdeten Glanz ihrer biografischen Narrative. Für die kroatischen ›Erstopfer‹ und Landesverteidiger ging es – in dem Nullsummenspiel der Narrative – um die Relativierung *ihrer* Leiden und die Herabwürdigung von Heldentaten. Für das national-konservative Milieu insgesamt ging es darüber hinaus um die endgültige ›Kriminalisierung‹ der Landesverteidigung; um eine empfindliche Niederlage in dem globalen antikroatischen ›Geheimkrieg‹; um den Zahltag für den EU-Beitritt, erkauft mit der Ausliefe-

---

und nachgewiesen. Weiterhin kontrovers bleibt die Deutung des im Vorfeld und während der Operation erfolgten Exodus der nahezu gesamten Restbevölkerung der Krajina (150.000–200.000), die nach den Vertreibungen der nicht-serbischen Bevölkerung 1991–1995 fast ausschließlich aus Serben bestand. Ausführlich (979 Seiten) zu dem Gesamtkomplex der serbischen Sezession und den Umständen von 1995 aus soziologischer Perspektive Žunec: Goli život.

[30] Ausführlich zu den Texten und Kontexten der Resolutionen und Deklarationen Koren: Korisna prošlost.

[31] Deklaracija o Domovinskom ratu, in: Koren: Korisna prošlost, S. 150f.; auch in: Narodne novine 102/2000, http://www.nn.hr.

[32] Deklaracija o Oluji, in: Koren: Korisna prošlost, S. 155; auch in: Narodne novine 76/2006, http://www.nn.hr.

[33] »Dan pobjede i domovinske zahvalnosti« – »Tag des Sieges und des Heimat-Dankes« (5. August).

rung der Helden.³⁴ Aber auch eine breite kroatische Mitte trauerte dem gefühlten historischen Unrecht einer Gleichstellung von Angriffs- und Verteidigungskrieg, systematischen Verbrechen und reaktiven Entgleisungen sowie dem Triumph des serbischen Mainstreamnarrativs und dessen Propaganda entgegen. Im linksliberalen Milieu begegnete man dem erwarteten Effekt der Schuldnivellierung eher gelassen, traf er doch vor allem die nationalistischen Eliten und damit auch den politischen und ideologischen Gegner im eigenen Land.³⁵

Doch das Unerwartete geschah. Eine Hand mehr in dem fünfköpfigen Gremium in Den Haag³⁶ – und der Bannspruch des ›kriminellen Unterfangens‹, das Stigma der staatlich organisierten Kriegsverbrechen im Herzen des Gründungsmythos, der Aufwind für die feindliche Propaganda und die internationale Verschwörung lösten sich in nichts auf. Die Kriegsverbrecher von gestern flogen noch am selben Tag quasi als Helden mit UNO-Plazet in Zagreb ein und wurden herumgereicht in einem Sturm der Erleichterung und des patriotischen Paroxysmus, wie er seit der »entscheidende[n], ruhmreiche[n], siegreiche[n]« Operation vom Sommer 1995 nicht mehr da gewesen war. Die Opfer dieser Operation – in Serbien in einem Sturm der Entrüstung und Wut von offizieller Stelle als »größter Pogrom nach dem Zweiten Weltkrieg« bezeichnet, dessen Ergebnisse »die Kroaten nun legitim feiern« könnten³⁷ – schienen in Kroatien als Kollateralschaden des Befreiungskrieges in einer Fußnote der ›nützlichen Vergangenheit‹ zu versinken. Im Haupttext der großen Erzählung erschien das Tribunal plötzlich als Stütze des patriotischen Narrativs: Mit dem jüngsten Urteil aus Den Haag wurde auch der ›juridische Sturm‹ zum Sieg, galt die Landesverteidigung auch offiziell als ›rein‹, war der Krieg für Kroatien ›beendet‹.³⁸

---

34 Zur These vom ›Geheimkrieg‹ vgl. das Diskurs-Konzentrat von Neva G. Mihalić: Snaga nacije, Vijenac, 15.11.2012, S. 2; und dies.: Slom specijalnog rata protiv Hrvatske, Vijenac, 29.11.2012, S. 3. Die These vom politischen Verkauf des Generals Gotovina findet einen symbolischen Aufhänger in seinem Namen, der (bei anderer Akzentuierung) ›Bargeld‹ bedeutet.

35 Entsprechend titelte die auflagenstärkste Tageszeitung *Jutarnji list* voreilig (vor der Urteilsverkündung) in der Onlineausgabe, offenbar in Fühlung mit den links-liberalen Regierungskreisen: »Tudmans Kroatien ist verurteilt« (»Osudena Tudmanova Hrvatska«; kolportierte Information; die Formulierung ist erhalten geblieben in einem Zwischentitel vom 16. November 2012, vgl. http://www.jutarnji.hr/template/article/article-print.jsp?id=1066716 sowie die Internetadresse der aktualisierten Titelstory, s. Anm. 38).

36 Wesentliche Entscheidungen, die in Konsequenz zum Freispruch führten, traf die Berufungskammer mit einer 3:2-Mehrheit; vgl. u. a.: »[…] the Appeals Chamber, Judge Agius and Judge Pocar dissenting, […] reverses the Trial Chamber's finding that a JCE existed to permanently remove the Serb civilian population from the Krajina by force or threat of force.« Appeals Chamber Judgement Summary, S. 4f.

37 Aussage des serbischen Präsidenten Nikolić am 16. November 2012 (übertragen in zahlreichen Medien), dabei anknüpfend an eine gängige rhetorische Praxis, vgl. Pavlaković: From Conflict to Commemoration, S. 14.

38 Diese Schlagworte benutzte am 16. November 2013 als Erster der freigesprochene Gotovina; vgl. http://www.jutarnji.hr/sudac-meron-danas-ce-procitati-konacnu-presudu-hrvatskoj-dr--franje-tudmana/1066689/. Die links-liberale Staatsführung mahnte zwar mit deutlichen Worten eine über-

Die unmittelbare Wirkung im Kontext der jeweiligen politischen Konstellationen und Erinnerungskonflikte in den Nachkriegsgesellschaften endet mit der für 2016 vorgesehenen Schließung des Tribunals. Die unmittelbare Wirkung – die erzwungene Aufarbeitung der Vergangenheit, die tagespolitische Instrumentalisierung der Urteile, die Verschärfung der heroisch-monumentalen Narrative – ist der laute ereignisgeschichtliche Auftakt einer bevorstehenden stilleren Wahrnehmungsgeschichte. Entscheidend für die Haltbarkeit der These vom geteilten Erinnerungsort ist allerdings die offene Frage, ob und auf welche Weise das Tribunal – auch nach der stufenweisen Überführung seiner Rolle an den MICT[39] und die nationalen Gerichte – ein Bezugspunkt national kodierter Erinnerungsnarrative bleibt. Voraussehbar ist die anhaltende, negativ besetzte Bedeutung des Erinnerungstopos *Haag* im Rahmen der monumentalen Narrative, vor allem im Zusammenhang mit der Opfer- und Verschwörungssemantik. In diesem Rahmen könnten auch die zunächst als nationale Sternstunden erlebten Freisprüche – wie der skizzierte Fall Gotovina für das kroatische Narrativ, der Fall Haradinaj für das kosovo-albanische und der Fall Perišić für das serbische (auf andere Weise auch das Völkermord-Urteil des Internationalen Gerichtshofs für das bosniakische Narrativ) – im Rückblick als Ergebnisse einer politisch motivierten Äquidistanz der internationalen Gerichtsbarkeit erscheinen und damit viel von ihrem anfänglichen Glanz verlieren.

Ein anderer Strang der Wahrnehmungsgeschichte des Tribunals ist in alternativen, kritischen Narrativen angelegt, die eine umfassende Aufarbeitung der Vergangenheit als konstitutiv für die kollektive Erinnerung und Identität erachten, wobei dem Tribunal und seinem Erbe die Rolle eines unentbehrlichen Katalysators zukommt. Sollten diese Narrative jemals die Nische verlassen, die vorläufig von Menschenrechtsorganisationen, Kleinparteien, kritischen Einzelstimmen und dem konjunkturabhängigen Diskurs der politischen ›Linken‹ dominiert wird,[40] so könnten die Archive des Tribunals, derzeit Speichergedächtnis einer ortsfremden Gerichtsbarkeit, zum Funktionsgedächtnis einer offenen Erinnerungskultur im postjugoslawischen Raum werden.[41] Die Archivbestände des Tribunals könnten

---

fällige Aufarbeitung der im Urteil dokumentierten Verbrechen an, kapitalisierte aber ansonsten den unerwarteten Freispruch im Sinne eines pragmatischen Einheitsnarrativs, unter Einbeziehung des Nationalhelden Gotovina und seiner überraschend zurückhaltenden, der links-liberalen Staatsführung gegenüber betont loyalen Aussagen. Dem Einheitsnarrativ entsprechend erwähnte *Jutarnji list* nach der Urteilsverkündung nicht mehr »*Tuđmans* Kroatien« (vgl. Anm. 35; Hervorhebung von mir), sondern titelte in der Printausgabe vom 16. November 2013: »Kroatien ist unschuldig: Gotovina und Markač sind frei!« (»Hrvatska nevina: Gotovina i Markač slobodni!«).

[39] Mechanism for International Criminal Tribunals, vgl. http://unmict.org/index.html.
[40] Zum Verhältnis von Sozialstruktur und Vergangenheitsbewältigung in Kroatien vgl. Kardov et al.: Suočavanje s prošlošću, bes. S. 30.
[41] Die Bereitstellung seiner Archive für die Aufarbeitung der Vergangenheit vor Ort gehört zu den Ansprüchen des Tribunals (vgl. die Selbstdarstellung: http://www.icty.org/sections/Aboutthe

in das »Museum der Schande des ehemaligen Jugoslawien« überführt werden, das vorläufig nur als Vorschlag des serbischen Soziologen Todor Kuljić existiert.[42]

Das Eingeständnis der in *jedem* Krieg generierten Gewaltspirale und des daraus sich ergebenden größeren oder geringeren schändlichen Erbes *aller* Kriegsparteien, das *ohne* gegenseitige Aufrechnung zu verwalten ist; und das Eingeständnis der supranationalen Wirksamkeit identischer Mechanismen, die in sich bedroht fühlenden Kollektiven zur Prägung kompensatorischer Narrative führen, aus bewaffneten Männern menschenverachtende Bestien machen können usw.: Dies sind nur zwei Voraussetzungen für die Gründung des »Museums der Schande«. Eine weitere, nicht minder wichtige Voraussetzung besteht in der zeitgleichen Entwicklung ergebnisoffener und konsensfähiger Deutungen der *politischen* Geschichte der Jugoslawienkriege, verbunden mit dem Verzicht auf zwei charakteristische Vorurteilskomplexe der gängigen Erinnerungspolitik: zum einen auf die nationalen Wahrheitsmonopole; zum anderen auf jenes – in der Außenperspektive so überzeugend und friedensstiftend anmutende, dabei so kommode, Komplexität scheuende – Phantasma einer Gleichheit aller Kriegsparteien in dem scheinbaren Einheitsbrei des ›jugoslawischen Bürgerkriegs‹.

Unter diesen Voraussetzungen ist die Chance zur produktiven Hegung der regionalen Erinnerungskonflikte mit den Mitteln des Tribunals und seines langfristig gesicherten Erbes in der Tat noch lange nicht verspielt.

Literatur

Assmann, Jan: Das kulturelle Gedächtnis. Schrift, Erinnerung und politische Identität in frühen Hochkulturen, München 1992.
Banovac, Boris: Etničnost i regionalizam kao izvori identifikacijskih procesa, in: R. Čičak-Chand / J. Kumpes (Hg.): Etničnost, nacija, identitet. Hrvatska i Europa, Zagreb 1998, S. 249–262.
Calic, Marie-Janine: Geschichte Jugoslawiens im 20. Jahrhundert, München 2010.
Clark, Janine Natalya: The ICTY and the Challenges of Reconciliation in the former Yugoslavia. E-International Relations (23.01.2012), http://www.e-ir.info/2012/01/23/the-icty-and-the-challenges-of-reconciliation-in-the-former-yugoslavia/; letzter Zugriff: 01.03.2013.
Csáky, Moritz / Stachel, Peter (Hg.): Die Verortung von Gedächtnis, Wien 2001.

ICTY) und ist ein zentrales Argument der Optimisten in der Bilanz seiner Ergebnisse; vgl. Hodžić: Why the ICTY.
[42] Kuljić: Umkämpfte Vergangenheiten, S. 170.

Database of digitized newspaper articles – war crimes [Ergebnis des Projekts: »Documenting the Past in Croatia: Establishing of War Crime Database«], http://inarchive.pravo.hr; letzter Zugriff: 01.03.2013.

Del Ponte, Carla: The Role of International Criminal Prosecutions in Reconstructing Divided Communities. Public Lecture given at the London School of Economics (20.10.2003), http://dspace.cigilibrary.org/jspui/bitstream/123456789/8663/1/The%20Role%20of%20International%20Criminal%20Prosecutions%20in%20Reconstructing%20Divided%20Communities.pdf?1; letzter Zugriff: 01.03.2013.

Erll, Astrid: Kollektives Gedächtnis und Erinnerungskulturen. Eine Einführung, Stuttgart 2005.

François, Etienne / Schulze, Hagen (Hg.): Deutsche Erinnerungsorte, Bd. 1, München 2001.

Hodžić, Refik: Why the ICTY has Contributed to Reconciliation in the former Yugoslavia, in: Osservatorio Balcani e Caucaso, 20.02.2013, http://www.balcanicaucaso.org/eng/content/view/full/130374; letzter Zugriff: 01.03.2013.

Höpken, Wolfgang: Post-sozialistische Erinnerungskulturen im ehemaligen Jugoslawien, in: Emil Brix / Arnold Suppan / Elisabeth Vyslonzil (Hg.): Südosteuropa. Traditionen als Macht, Wien 2007, S. 13–50.

Kardov, Kruno / Lalić, Dražen / Teršelič, Vesna: Suočavanje s prošlošću u Hrvatskoj. Stavovi i mišljenja aktera i javnosti u poraću, Zagreb 2010.

Kazaz, Enver: Tranzicijska etnokulturna pustinja, in: Sarajevske sveske, Nr. 27/28, 2010, S. 83–102, online unter: http://www.sveske.ba/bs/broj/2728; letzter Zugriff: 01.03.2013.

Koren, Snježana: »Korisna prošlost«? Ratovi devedesetih u deklaracijama Hrvatskog sabora, in: Tihomir Cipek (Hg.): Kultura sjećanja: 1991. Povijesni lomovi i svladavanje prošlosti, Zagreb 2011, S. 123–156.

Kosfeld, Anne G.: Nürnberg, in: Etienne François / Hagen Schulze (Hg.): Deutsche Erinnerungsorte, Bd. 1, München 2001, S. 68–85.

Kuljić, Todor: Umkämpfte Vergangenheiten. Die Kultur der Erinnerung im postjugoslawischen Raum, Berlin 2010 (auch: Bonn 2010).

Kuljić, Todor: Sećanje na titoizam. Između diktata i otpora, Beograd 2011.

Nora, Pierre: General Introduction: Between Memory and History, in: Lawrence D. Kritzman (Hg.): Realms of Memory. The Construction of the French Past. Under the Direction of Pierre Nora, Bd. 1, New York 1996, S. 1–20.

Pavlaković, Vjeran: Better the Grave than a Slave: Croatia and the International Criminal Tribunal for the former Yugoslavia, in: Sabrina P. Ramet / Konrad Clewing / Reneo Lukic (Hg.): Croatia since Independence. War, Politics, Society, Foreign Relations, München 2008, S. 447–483.

Pavlaković, Vjeran: From Conflict to Commemoration: Serb-Croat Relations and the Anniversaries of Operation Storm, in: Darko Gavrilović (Hg.): Serbo-Croat

Relations: Political Cooperation and National Minorities, Sremska Kamenica 2009, S. 73–82; online unter: http://www.academia.edu/855537/From_Conflict_to_Commemoration_Serb-Croat_Relations_and_the_Anniversaries_of_Operation_Storm; letzter Zugriff: 01.03.2013.

Ramet, Sabrina P.: Tri Jugoslavije. Izgradnja države i izazov legitimacije. 1918–2005, Zagreb 2009 (dt. Ausgabe: Die drei Jugoslawien. Eine Geschichte der Staatsbildungen und ihrer Probleme, München 2011).

Schmidt, Patrick: Zwischen Medien und Topoi. Die *Lieux de Mémoire* und die Medialität des kulturellen Gedächtnisses, in: Astrid Erll/Ansgar Nünning (Hg.): Medien des kollektiven Gedächtnisses. Konstruktivität – Historizität – Kulturspezifität, Berlin/New York 2004, S. 25–43.

Škrbić Alempijević, Nevena/Mathiesen Hjemdahl, Kristi (Hg.): O Titu kao mitu. Proslava Dana mladosti u Kumrovcu, Zagreb 2006.

Speitkamp, Winfried: Einleitung, in: Helmut Berding/Klaus Heller/ders. (Hg.): Krieg und Erinnerung. Fallstudien zum 19. und 20. Jahrhundert, Göttingen 2000, S. 9–13.

Sundhaussen, Holm: Jugoslawien und seine Nachfolgestaaten: Konstruktion, Dekonstruktion und Rekonstruktion von »Erinnerungen« und Mythen, in: Monika Flacke (Hg.): Mythen der Nationen: 1945 – Arena der Erinnerungen, Bd. 1, Berlin 2004, S. 373–426.

Ugrešić, Dubravka: Kultura laži (Antipolitički eseji), Zagreb/Beograd 2002 (dt. Ausgabe: Die Kultur der Lüge, Frankfurt a. M. 1995).

Wierzcholska, Agnieszka: Tagungsbericht HT 2008: Kollektives Gedächtnis und Beziehungsgeschichte. Binationale Erinnerungsorte im deutsch-polnischen Verhältnis, in: H-Soz-u-Kult, 20.11.2008, http://www.h-net.org/reviews/showrev.php?id=28344; letzter Zugriff: 01.03.2013.

Žanić, Ivo/Kebo, Ozren/Čolović, Ivan: Nationale Symbole zwischen Mythos und Propaganda, in: Dunja Melčić (Hg.): Der Jugoslawien-Krieg. Handbuch zu Vorgeschichte, Verlauf und Konsequenzen, Wiesbaden 2007, S. 286–311.

Žunec, Ozren: Goli život. Socijetalne dimenzije pobune Srba u Hrvatskoj, Zagreb 2007.

Vierter Teil
(Post-)Jugoslawien:
Theater und Literatur der Gegenwart

Andrea Schütte

Peter Handkes Literatur der Fürsprache

Seit Publikation von Peter Handkes *Eine winterliche Reise* ist dessen Engagement für Serbien im Feuilleton harsch und in der Literaturwissenschaft nicht weniger heftig kritisiert worden. Die wechselseitigen Beschuldigungen sind bekannt: Formen der politischen und militärischen Einflussnahme und der öffentlichen Berichterstattung aufseiten des Westens werden von Handke geschmäht; die westliche Öffentlichkeit wiederum kritisiert Handkes literarische und außerliterarische Parteinahme für Serbien und dessen prominenteste Kriegsverbrecher: Er trifft sich mit Radovan Karadžić noch vor dessen Verhaftung und trinkt Schnaps, besucht serbische Kriegsverbrecher im Gefängnis in Den Haag und in Serbien, hält eine Grabrede bei Slobodan Milošević' Beerdigung. Die wechselseitigen Beschuldigungen eröffnen eine Art Tribunal, in dem um die Rechtmäßigkeit von Verhalten und Position gestritten wird. Die Verhandlungen konzentrieren sich dabei auf Fragen der moralischen Angemessenheit von Engagement. Dabei verschärfen die Verhandlungen, die literarische Konstruktion mit außerliterarischem Engagement, verallgemeinertes Ethos mit individueller Wertbestimmung, Neutralität mit Affekt mischen, das kritisierte Ausgangsverhalten und die wechselseitigen Anklagen nur noch. Aber auch der Diskurs, der eine Tribunalisierung von Handkes Einsatz verhindern will und darum diese Aspekte scharf voneinander trennt – so z. B. eine Literaturwissenschaft, die Handkes Einsatz ignoriert und sich auf die poietische Qualität seiner Texte zurückzieht –, führt ebenso wenig weiter. Dagegen scheint es angebracht, sich mit der Tatsache der Parteinahme auf eine Weise auseinanderzusetzen, die zum einen nach ihren Motiven fragt, die Handkes Texte selbst nahelegen, zum anderen nach deren Steuerungskraft für die Textgestaltung.

1. Engagement und Literatur

Parteinahme ist für Handke ein genuin sprachliches Unternehmen. Sie artikuliert sich als *Fürsprache*, die einen des Rechtsbeistands Bedürftigen unterstützt und ihm zur Wiederherstellung seines Rechts verhilft, und sie hat ihren Ort in der Sprache. In diesem Sinne ist es naheliegend, wenn Handke seine Parteinahme für Serbien auch literarisch verarbeitet. Sein sogenanntes Serbienbuch ist Restitution von Gerechtigkeit, Wiederherstellung eines Rechts, das einem Land genommen wurde, wie der Titel ankündigt: *Eine winterliche Reise zu den Flüssen Donau, Save, Morawa und Drina oder Gerechtigkeit für Serbien*. Bezeichnend ist allerdings, dass für Handke auch die inverse Formulierung gilt: Literatur ist Fürsprache. Dies gilt uneingeschränkt für sein ganzes Werk, insofern Handke mit seiner viel gerühmten Beobachtungs- und Beschreibungssprache auch den kleinen Dingen der Welt Ausdruck und Leben, ja: Geltung verleiht. Es gilt im Besonderen für die literarischen Produktionen der letzten Jahre, in denen sich Handke immer wieder mit (Ex-)Jugoslawien auseinandersetzt und vor allem *für* Serbien und Slowenien *spricht*. Programmatisch entfaltet Handke den Zusammenhang von Literatur und Parteinahme in seiner Rede *Wut und Geheimnis* anlässlich der Verleihung der Ehrendoktorwürde der Universität Klagenfurt am 8. November 2002.

Diese Rede ist eine Würdigung der Partisanenliteratur. Vier erwähnte Bücher empfiehlt er den Zuhörern zur Lektüre, davon drei zum kärntnerisch-slowenischen Widerstand in Österreich im Zweiten Weltkrieg.[1] Würde für Würde. Partisanentum versteht er dabei in seiner engeren und weiteren Bedeutung: »Partisan kommt von ›partigiano‹, vom italienischen ›Teil‹, bedeutet also erst Anteilnehmen und dann die Partei einer Sache zu werden«[2]. Entsprechend ist seine Rede nicht nur Lektüreempfehlung von Berichten des politischen Widerstands, sondern zugleich Aufruf zur grundsätzlichen Anteilnahme. Diese grundsätzliche Anteilnahme ist eng verquickt mit der Literatur, hat ihren Ort in der Literatur, selbst da, wo Literatur aufgrund der besonderen Umstände scheinbar keine besonders wichtige Rolle haben kann: Die erwähnten kärntnerisch-slowenischen Partisanen stammen aus kleinbäuerlichem Milieu, kämpfen in den Wäldern entbehrungsreich ums Überleben – und brauchen Literatur: »und die Leute, die Monate und Monate auf der Saualpe waren, die haben nicht nach Würsten gefragt oder nach Brot, die haben gesagt: ›Bitte, wo ist Literatur?‹ Die wollten Geschriebenes, die Kämpfer.«[3] So, wie die Partisanen Literatur brauchten, so braucht die Anteilnahme eine Artikulation; so, wie die Partisanenliteratur als Literatur besonderer Güte herausgestellt wird, so soll – ließe sich schließen – die Sprache Fürsprache sein, Literatur Anteilnahme bis hin zur Parteinahme. Wer ein solches Literaturverständnis hat, verlängert den Widerstand in die Gegenwart. Dies zumindest deutet sich an, wenn Handke die Universität Klagenfurt sicher zu vollmundig bezeichnet als »vielleicht die einzige Universität im deutschen Sprachraum, die in der Lage ist, Widerstand zu leisten«, was Handke an den »wissenschaftlichen Ergebnissen, an Büchern, Übersetzungen« festmacht.[4] Wäre es zulässig, das

---

[1] Karel Prušnik-Gašper: Gemsen auf der Lawine; Lipej Kolenik: Für das Leben, gegen den Tod; Andrej Kokot: Das Kind das ich war; René Char: Zorn und Geheimnis.
[2] Handke: Wut und Geheimnis.
[3] Ebd.
[4] Ebd.

Widerständige der Universität Klagenfurt nicht eher darin zu sehen, dass sie mit Handke einen umstrittenen Widerständigen ehrt, was 2006 dann im Rahmen der Verleihung des Heinrich-Heine-Preises der Stadt Düsseldorf nicht gelungen ist, weil Handke aufgrund der Proteste des Stadtrats den Preis ablehnte? Dann wäre es Handke als Widerständiger, der sich in die Widerstandsliteratur einschreibt und sich gewissermaßen zum Partisanen macht. In der Klagenfurter Rede wird deutlich, wie behutsam, aber überzeugt Handke sich in die Partisanenliteratur zumindest hineinliest:

»Diesmal habe ich neu gelesen, und würde Sie, alle gutwilligen Menschen hier in diesem Saal, ersuchen, dieses Buch als Zeugnis des Widerstands im österreichischen oder deutschsprachigen Raum, in Kärnten, zu lesen: eines kämpferischen Widerstands, eines tragischen Widerstands. Ich war die ganze Zeit erschüttert, als ich es wieder gelesen habe. [...] Wie die Partisanen [...] nicht sofort und nicht mit einer Gewalt-Idee in die Wälder und in die Berge gingen, wie langsam. Was für ein schwerer Prozess es war, überhaupt zu verschwinden, von den Eltern wegzugehen, die Kinder allein zu lassen.«[5]

Die Innigkeit seiner Lektüre wird zur Inständigkeit seiner Buchempfehlungen:

»Ich bitte euch, ich ersuche euch – wenn ich schon hier bin –, diese drei herrlichen, gewaltigen, geschichtsöffnenden und für die Versöhnung der Leute [...] essentiellen Bücher Wort für Wort und Satz für Satz und ohne Voreingenommenheit, langsam und mit möglicher Erschütterung und vor allem Offenheit euch zu Gemüte zu führen.«[6]

Was Handke hier trotz aller Offenheitsmaßgaben propagiert, ist, sich in den Sog der Partisanenliteratur (und des Partisanentums) zu begeben. Er selbst ist nicht nur in seiner Rezeption dieser Bücher darin, sondern richtet auch seine literarische Produktion danach aus. Vor allem sein Vortragstitel macht das augenfällig: Mit *Wut und Geheimnis* schreibt er sich an das Werk *Zorn und Geheimnis* des französischen Dichters und Résistance-Kämpfers René Char heran. Damit definiert er sein Verständnis von Partisanenliteratur: Es geht um die Koppelung von kämpferischem Widerstand und poetischem Ausdruck, um das Getriebenwerden zu einer Reaktion und um Dichtung. Beides, »krude Tatsachengeschichten« und »das dichterische Sich-Ausdrücken«, gehört zusammen:

»Beides sollte und muss zusammen gelesen werden. Und beides – ›Fureur‹, das heißt ›Wut‹ oder ›Treiben‹ oder ›Wahnsinn‹, und ›Mystère‹ ›Geheimnis‹ – können Sie auf Deutsch in *Zorn und Geheimnis* von René Char wunderbar nachlesen. Beides gehört zusammen, und zugleich denke ich natürlich: Vielleicht ist das eine Illusion.«[7]

---

[5] Ebd.
[6] Ebd.
[7] Ebd.

Wo aber die kruden Tatsachengeschichten des Widerstandskampfes im dichterischen Ausdruck erscheinen, das eine im anderen aufgeht, findet eine Verdichtung statt, die Affekte auslöst. Einer der Affekte ist die Erschütterung – Handke erinnert seine Lektüre: »Ich war die ganze Zeit erschüttert«. Ähnliches legt er seinen Zuhörern als Rezeptionshaltung nahe: »[I]ch ersuche euch, diese [...] Bücher [...] mit möglicher Erschütterung zu lesen«[8]. Widerstand als Partisanentum ist Erschütterung der (Kriegs-)Ordnung, und Lektüre der Widerstandsliteratur erzeugt Erschütterung des Affekthaushalts. Ähnliches geschieht mit dem Affekt Wut: Von der Antriebsenergie zum Widerstand wandelt sie sich zum Ton, der in der eigenen Sprache herrscht. Fürsprache ist nicht leise Anteilnahme, sondern leidenschaftliche Parteinahme. Parteinahme bedeutet Wut.

2. Wut und Fürsprache

Ein solches Verständnis von Advokatur, das die eigenen Emotionen nicht zurückhält, sondern sie bewusst einsetzt, weil es sie sogar für konstitutiv hält, würde im gerichtlichen Kontext irritieren. Schaut man sich aber die ersten Theorien zur Fürsprache vor Gericht an, ist der Affekt tatsächlich konstitutiv für den Rechtsbeistand. Rüdiger Campe hat dies minutiös und kenntnisreich in seiner Studie zu einer kritischen Geschichte der Fürsprache gezeigt. Als Beleg für die Verwobenheit von Fürsprache bzw. Rechtsdiskurs und Affekten zitiert Campe Aristoteles' *Rhetorik*. Wie alle antiken Rhetoriken geht auch die aristotelische zentral von der Gerichtsrede aus. Die Gattung der Gerichtsrede nimmt Bezug auf eine Rechtsinstitution der Fürsprecher im antiken Griechenland. Diese unterstützen eine Partei im Rechtsstreit, indem sie deren Rede (Verteidigung oder Anklage) schreiben, aber nicht halten.[9] Der Betroffene vertritt sich selbst. Der griechische Rhetor, so Campe, spreche nicht *anstelle von*, sondern *mit* der Partei (dafür ist der Terminus *synegoria: sprechen mit* reserviert), mache deren Stimme hörbar, die Betonung klarer, das Argument effizienter.[10] Die Rhetorik lehrt den Synegoros, wirkungsvoll und effizient vorzugehen, wofür die Kenntnis von Affekten unerlässlich ist:

»Da aber die Kunst der Rede auf Entscheidung abzielt [...], so hat man nicht nur darauf zu sehen, daß die Rede beweisend und überzeugend sei, sondern man muß auch sorgen, sich selbst und den Beurteiler in eine bestimmte Verfassung zu bringen. [...] Der Eindruck vom

---

8 Ebd.
9 Die Synegoroi sind keine Anwälte, die die Rechtsparteien repräsentieren, sondern ihre Reden sind immer zusätzlich zur Verteidigungs- oder Anklagerede, selbst dann, wenn sie die Hauptrede darstellen; vgl. Rubinstein: Litigation and Cooperation.
10 Vgl. Campe: An Outline for a Critical History of *Fürsprache*, S. 371.

Redner ist wichtiger für die Ratsrede, die Stimmung des Zuhörers für die Gerichtsrede, da unsere Ansicht nicht unbeeinflußt bleibt von Liebe und Haß, von Zorn und Friedfertigkeit, sondern entweder vollständig oder doch dem Grade nach sich ändert.«[11]

Auf diese Stelle folgt eine Diskussion des Zorns. Fürsprache als *synegoria* und Zorn rücken ganz eng aneinander. Zorn definiert Aristoteles als »leidvolles Streben nach sichtbarer Vergeltung wegen sichtlicher Geringschätzung seiner Belange oder seiner Person, ohne daß man diese verdient hätte«[12]. In dieser Definition steckt eine ganze Geschichte: Man fühlt sich von jemandem missachtet, von dem man Wertschätzung erwartet hätte, und diese Diskrepanz erzeugt im Innern der Person eine Reibung, die sich im Zorn entlädt. Zorn als Gefühlseruption zeugt von einer Energie, die aufgebracht wird, um das Missachtungsverhältnis umzudrehen und seine eigene Überlegenheit in der Kränkung des anderen zu spüren. Doch neben dem Lustgefühl, das sich nach Aristoteles in der Rache kundtut, ist es vor allem ein Unlustgefühl, die Trauer, die den Zorn auslöst.

Trauer über Missachtung löst sich in Wut auf, die auch stellvertretend zum Ausdruck kommen kann, wenn sie nicht vom Missachteten selbst geäußert wird. Das entwickelt nicht nur Aristoteles in seinen Aufzeichnungen zur Gerichtsrede, sondern auch Handke in seinem Roman *Die Wiederholung* (1986). Der Protagonist Filip Kobal wird von einem gleichaltrigen Kind bis zur Unerträglichkeit nachgeäfft:

»Kein übliches Zungezeigen, Spucken, Beinstellen. Der Kindfeind erklärte sich nicht, war nur feindselig da, und seine Feindschaft brach dann aus als ein Überfall. [...] Wenn ich irgendwo ging, sprang er zum Beispiel aus dem Gebüsch und bewegte sich in meiner Haltung, die Füße gleichzeitig aufsetzend, die Arme im selben Rhythmus schwingend, neben mir her. Lief ich los, lief auch er; blieb ich stehen, stoppte auch er; zuckte ich mit den Wimpern, zuckte auch er. [...] Der andere wurde allgegenwärtig – auch wenn er nicht in Person neben mir war. War ich einmal froh, verlor ich sofort die Freude, weil sie sich in Gedanken von meinem Feind geäfft und damit bestritten sah. Ebenso war es mit sonstigen Lebensgefühlen – Stolz, Trauer, Zorn, Zuneigung: Im Schattenspiel verloren sie auf der Stelle ihre Echtheit. Und wo ich mich am lebendigsten fühlte, in der Versenkung, da drängte sich nun der Widersacher schon bei der geringsten Annäherung zwischen mich und den Gegenstand [...]. Mörderischer konnte sich kein Haß ausdrücken als in solch ständigem, wie unter lautlosen Peitschenhieben erfolgendem Nach-Stellen. [...] Als ich ihn dann zum ersten Mal anschrie, wich er nicht etwa zurück, sondern horchte auf: Der Schrei war das Zeichen, auf das er gewartet hatte. Und wer schließlich tätlich wurde, das war ich. Ich wußte, zwölf Jahre alt, im Gedränge mit dem andern, nicht mehr, wer ich war; das hieß: Ich war nichts mehr; und das hieß: Ich wurde böse.«[13]

---

[11] Aristoteles: Rhetorik, II, 1, S. 104.
[12] Ebd., S. 106.
[13] Handke: Wiederholung, S. 26–29. Roland Borgards weist in seiner Dissertation auf diese Stelle hin; vgl. Borgards: Sprache als Bild, S. 214.

Er, der vorher keine Schläge kannte, wird »böse«, und das heißt: zornig, wütend.[14] Es schlägt aus ihm heraus, als sein »Todfeind« ihm sein Gesicht hinzuhalten scheint.

»Von diesem Tag an war ich, vor aller Augen, sozusagen ›sein Schläger‹. Er hatte jetzt den Grund und das Recht, mich nie mehr in Frieden zu lassen. Unsere bis dahin verborgene Feindschaft war übergegangen in einen Krieg, und der mußte offen ausgetragen werden, ohne eine andere Ausgangsmöglichkeit als unser beider gemeinsamer Höllensturz.«[15]

Die Demütigung kann nicht größer sein. Man wird nachgeäfft, jede Regung wird registriert und nachgeahmt, was sie insofern entleert, als sie keine Gültigkeit aus ihrer Situationsbezogenheit beanspruchen kann. Jede Regung wird sinnfrei, zur Disposition gestellt, entleert, würdelos. Filip ist absolut würdelos, und dies wird noch gesteigert, weil er auch noch Täter wird: Provoziert vom Nachäffer, diesen zu schlagen, entehrt er als Letztes auch noch sich selbst, seine Würde. Er, der nie geschlagen wird, schlägt den, der täglich zu Hause geschlagen wird.

Wechselseitige Entehrungen finden auch zwischen Filip Kobald und seinem Lieblingslehrer statt, deren Verhältnis zunächst von wechselseitiger Verehrung gekennzeichnet ist. Filip genießt die Beachtung:

»Ich war keinen Moment geschmeichelt – es war etwas ganz anderes: Ich fühlte mich erkannt. Nach Jahren des Übersehenwerdens wurde ich endlich wahrgenommen, und das war geradezu eine Erweckung. Und ich erwachte im Überschwang.«[16]

Doch als Filip einmal vonseiten des Lehrers »ein großer Blick der Freude, ja Bewegtheit traf«, zieht Filip »eine fürchterliche Grimasse, die lediglich von mir ablenken sollte, den jungen Lehrer aber, ich fühlte es im gleichen Moment mit ihm, ins Herz traf. Er erstarrte, verließ dann die Klasse und kehrte in dieser Stunde nicht mehr zurück.«[17]

Der Lehrer reagiert mit Liebesentzug:

»Mit dem Lernen war es vorbei. Der Lehrer bewies mir jeden Tag, daß ich nichts wußte, oder daß, was ich wußte, nicht ›verlangt‹ war. […] Ich […] war allein mit der schwarzen Wolke in mir. Unvorstellbar, sie könnte sich auflösen; sie wurde schwerer, breitete sich aus, stieg in den Mundraum, die Augen, verschlug mir Stimme und Blick […]. [I]n der Schule wurde ich […] bald weder gefragt noch überhaupt wahrgenommen. In dieser Zeit erfuhr ich, was es heißt, die Sprache zu verlieren – nicht nur ein Verstummen vor den andern; auch kein Wort, kein Laut und keine Geste mehr vor sich selber. Eine solche Stummheit schrie nach Gewalt; ein Einlenken war nicht denkbar. Und die Gewalt konnte sich, zum

---

14 Ich identifiziere hier beide Begriffe miteinander, wissend um eine nötige Trennschärfe in anderen Zusammenhängen.
15 Handke: Wiederholung, S. 29 f.
16 Ebd., S. 35.
17 Ebd., S. 37.

Unterschied von dem kleinen Feind, nicht nach außen kehren; der große Feind, er lastete im Innern, auf der Bauchhöhle, dem Zwerchfell, den Lungenflügeln, der Luftröhre, dem Kehlkopf, dem Gaumensegel, versperrte die Nüstern und die Gehörgänge, und das von ihm eingeschlossene Herz in der Mitte, es schlug, klopfte, pulste, pochte, schwirrte und blutete nicht mehr, sondern tickte, scharf, spitz und böse.«[18]

Wieder geht es um die Würdelosigkeit des Nicht-(mehr-)wahrgenommen-Werdens, die gewaltbereit macht, wenn sie hier zunächst auch als autoaggressive Gewalt erscheint, und wieder ist es die Schmach, sich selbst als Entwürdigender eines anderen zu erleben, Selbstachtung nicht nur durch den anderen, sondern aufgrund eigenen Verhaltens zu verlieren. Doch was hier als autoaggressive Gewalt erscheint, wird vom sich anschließenden Bild korrigiert: Eine Zeitbombe scheint in Filip zu ticken, die irgendwann zum Ausbruch kommen wird. Das Herz »tickte, scharf, spitz und böse« – und bereitet den Zornausbruch vor.

Von beiden »Todfeinden«[19], Mitschüler und Lehrer, errettet ihn beide Male die Mutter mit entschiedenen Handlungsanweisungen, denen er sich nicht widersetzt:

»Die Stimme der Mutter war die einer Rechtsprecherin. Sie wußte von mir, was zu wissen war; sie war für mich zuständig; sie bestimmte; und sie verfügte meine unverzügliche Freilassung.«[20]

Die Mutter errettet aus den selbstverschuldeten Qualen, die zum Rückschlag bereit wären. Sie handelt unverzüglich und setzt sich für das Wohl ihres Sohnes ein. Sie holt zusammen mit einem Nachbarn ihren Sohn aus dem Internat und singt mit dem Nachbarn auf der Rückreise *Partisanen*lieder.[21] Sie nimmt handelnd Anteil am Schicksal ihres Sohnes und spricht ihrem Sohn sein Recht zu. Ähnlich hat sie schon reagiert, nachdem die Situation zwischen Filip und seinem »Todfeind« eskaliert war zu regelmäßig ausgeübter Gewalt – nach seinem Wutausbruch schlägt Filip seinen »Todfeind« regelmäßig, woraufhin ihn der Vater des »Todfeinds« aus Wut ebenso regelmäßig schlägt.

»Die Mißhandlung löste mir die Zunge, und ich konnte der Mutter (ja, ihr) von dem Feind erzählen. Jene Erzählung begann mit einem Befehl: ›Hör zu!‹, und schloß mit einem andern Befehl: ›Tu etwas!‹ Und die Mutter wurde, wie immer in der Familie, die Handelnde.«[22]

Selbst weder Täterin noch Opfer, solidarisiert sie sich mit ihrem Sohn und handelt stellvertretend, in die Regularitäten des ›Kabinettkriegs‹ zwischen Filip und Feind bzw. Feindesvater eingreifend. Bezeichnend ist, dass Filips »Erzählung«

---

18 Ebd., S. 38f.
19 Ebd., S. 22.
20 Ebd., S. 40.
21 Ebd.
22 Ebd., S. 30.

hier nicht erzählt wird, sodass über das Wie seiner Darstellung der Sachlage nicht geurteilt werden kann. Das mag andeuten, dass es bei der Parteinahme nicht in erster Linie auf die Einschätzung der Sachlage ankommt. Der persönliche Einsatz beruht auf der Überzeugung von einer *justa causa*. Es kommt auf den ermächtigenden Imperativ an, der ein Sichverwenden für die Interessen eines anderen bewirkt. Parteinahme gründet sich hier auf die Beziehung zwischen zwei Menschen. Man handelt aufgrund eines ethischen Imperativs, ob er nun vom als Opfer verstandenen Subjekt ausgesprochen wird oder nur vom Engagierten gehört wird, der aufgrund der Bindung ein bestimmtes Rollenverhalten einnimmt. Dieses parteiliche Handeln erfolgt allein aufgrund der eigenen Einschätzung von der Schutzbedürftigkeit des anderen bzw. weitergehend: aufgrund von Empathie angesichts dessen, was der andere in den eigenen Augen erleidet. An diesem Verständnis von Parteinahme wird deutlich, dass das Engagement wohl ein Maß für das Erleiden einer anderen Person hat, und zwar ein besonders fein erspürtes, aber weniger Wert auf die Angemessenheit der Sachlage und das Maß des eigenen Handelns legt.

Das steht in einer Linie mit dem römischen Fürsprachemodell. In *De Oratore* schildert Cicero, dass der *advocatus* Antonius, auf die Wahrhaftigkeit seiner Rede vor Gericht hin befragt, diese nicht mit dem Rekurs auf Wahrheit, also die Konvergenz von Wörtern und Dingen, begründet, sondern mit einem Rekurs auf die Konvergenz von Diskurs und Gefühlen:[23] Er müsse doch wahrhaftig sprechen, damit die Gefühle, die er beim Richter auszulösen beabsichtige, tatsächlich ausgelöst werden, und zwar nicht nur bei dem Richter, sondern auch bei ihm, dem Fürsprecher, selbst. Anstelle von Wahrheit der Sache steht also Wahrhaftigkeit der Rede, statt sachlicher Richtigkeit emotionale Richtigkeit, die durch Selbst- und Fremderregung erreicht wird.

Auf Handkes Parteinahme für die von Österreich fast vergessenen[24] kärntnerisch-slowenischen Partisanen trifft das zu: Er selbst ist erschüttert bei der Relektüre der Partisanenbücher, wie sich gezeigt hat, und er empfiehlt seinen Zuhörern ebendiese Erschütterung als Lektürehaltung. Er möchte sie gar »beschwören«[25], die Partisanenliteratur erschüttert zu lesen. Obwohl diese Formulierung sofort relativiert wird zum »einfach nur vorschlagen, ganz leise vorschlagen«, kann diese Ergänzung den ursprünglichen Ton des Bedrängens nicht eliminieren. Der Ton von Handkes Fürsprache ist unmissverständlich und beauftragt in gewisser Weise seine Zuhörer eindeutig. Tatsächlich fällt noch ein mobilisierender oder erzieherischer Imperativ: Ähnlich wie Filip zu seiner Mutter sagt: »Tu etwas!«,

---

23 Ich folge und referiere hier Campe: An Outline for a Critical History of *Fürsprache*, S. 375.
24 Vgl. Handke: Wut und Geheimnis.
25 Ebd.

fordert Handke seine Zuhörer auf: »Lesen Sie gefälligst!«[26], und er meint natürlich Partisanenliteratur im engeren Sinne, Fürsprachetexte vielleicht im weiteren.

Dieser Imperativ, der sich und die anderen von der Notwendigkeit von Parteinahme überzeugen und Handeln befördern will, spricht sich noch viel stärker in der Wut aus. Die von Wut zeugenden sprachlichen Entgleisungen, die sowohl bei Handke als auch bei diversen anderen zu verzeichnen sind, die sich in dieser Angelegenheit zu Wort gemeldet haben, sind allzu bekannt.[27] Wenn die Frage nach der Herkunft dieser Wut an dieser Stelle auch nicht beantwortet werden soll oder kann, so lässt sich zumindest schließen, welche Funktion sie in diesem Diskurs hat.

Mit der Wut greift Handke auf eine der vitalsten Kräfte zu, die nicht nur das Geschehen, sondern auch dessen Darstellung im Text in Produktion und Rezeption steuern können. Zorn diktiert die Richtung des Handelns, weiß Sloterdijk,[28] und dieses Handeln ist unmittelbar, direkt, unverzüglich. Es geht in diesem Literaturmodell der selbstaffizierten Fürsprache, den von Zorn in Bewegung gesetzten Texten, um ein Schreibmodell, das imperativisch ist. Seine Heftigkeit und Direktheit erlauben kaum ein Ausweichen, zwingen die Rezipienten zum Zuhören, die Wörter zu den Dingen. Damit wird eine Form der Unmittelbarkeit und Kraftfülle des Redens erzeugt. Die Berührung durch den selbst berührten Redner erfolgt in der absoluten Gegenwart, ohne Verzug durch Repräsentation. Der Kämpfer für die gerechte Sache kämpft zwar in Texten, aber die befinden sich nach Maßgabe der *energeia* im Jetzt, ohne Aufsparung. Damit wird eine »totale Expressivität«[29] erreicht. Sloterdijk entwickelt diesen Gedanken in seiner Lektüre von Homers *Ilias*, wenn auch in anderer Absicht:

»Beim reinen Zorn [...] gilt der Grundsatz, das Innere des Akteurs solle ganz manifest und öffentlich, ganz Tat [...] werden. Dem aufwallenden Zorn ist es eigentümlich, in seinem verschwenderischen Ausdruck restlos aufzugehen; wo die totale Expressivität den Ton

---

[26] Ebd.
[27] Handke beschimpft bekanntlich in der *Winterlichen Reise* die *Frankfurter Allgemeine Zeitung* als »zentrale(s) europäische(s) Serbenfreßblatt« und als »Organ einer stockfinsteren Sekte«; Handke: Winterliche Reise, S. 125 und S. 127. Den Schriftsteller Peter Schneider, der zwei Jahre zuvor Sarajevo bereist hatte und sich für die bosnische Seite einsetzte, beschuldigt er, einen »mechanischen, feind- und kriegsbildverknallten, mitläuferischen statt mauerspringerischen Schrieb [...] für das Eingreifen der Nato gegen die verbrecherischen Bosno-Serben« verfasst zu haben; ebd., S. 132. Schneider reagiert darauf mit einem Artikel in *Der Spiegel*: »In weiten Teilen dieser Intervention [gegen die westliche Berichterstattung; A. S.] liest man nichts als Meinung: Insinuationen, Wutausbrüche«. Handke bediene eine Sprache, die »einen beachtlichen Killerinstinkt zur Entfaltung kommen« lasse. Schneider sieht die »historische Dummheit von Handkes Intervention« darin, »daß er in seinem überschäumenden, sich heilig wähnenden Zorn gegen die internationale Journalistenverschwörung wieder nur von ›den Serben‹« spreche und die serbischen Kriegsherren kleinrede; Schneider: Der Ritt über den Balkan.
[28] Vgl. Sloterdijk: Zorn und Zeit, S. 18.
[29] Ebd., S. 21.

angibt, ist von Zurückhaltung und Aufsparung keine Rede. Natürlich wird auch immer ›um etwas‹ gekämpft, vor allem aber dient der Kampf der Offenbarung der kämpfenden Energie an sich [...].«[30]

Der Zorn ist der Versuch, die Unhintergehbarkeit der Repräsentation zu verhindern und zur absoluten Übereinstimmung zu kommen: von Wörtern und Sachen, von berührtem Autor und zu berührendem Rezipienten, vom Autor mit sich selbst.

Dieser letzte Aspekt weist auf eine Rekursion hin, die schließlich erwähnt werden muss: Der Parteinehmende legt mit seiner Wut nicht nur die Schande derjenigen offen, denen ungerechtfertigt ihr Recht genommen worden ist,[31] und richtet die Blicke darauf aus, sondern er offenbart sich auch selbst und stellt sein eigenes Reden aus. Die Unmittelbarkeit und Kraftfülle des Redens kommen nicht nur der *justa causa* zu, sondern auch dem Autor, ob sie diesen beiden Instanzen nun dienlich sind (Miterregung des Rezipienten durch den Affekt) oder nicht (Ablehnung des Affekts durch den Rezipienten). Wenn im römischen Fürsprachemodell davon ausgegangen wird, dass der Advokat *in eigener Person* spricht, und zwar selbsterregt, dann spricht er nicht mehr nur für den anderen, sondern zugleich über und zu sich selbst.

Dies hält noch an, wenn der Primäraffekt der Wut verschwunden ist und dem dahinter verborgenen Affekt der Trauer Platz gemacht hat. An Handkes Artikel in der österreichischen Tageszeitung *Die Presse* vom 5. August 2011 wird dies deutlich: Er erzählt hier »Die Geschichte des Dragoljub Milanović«, des Leiters des serbischen Fernsehsenders, der damals schon seit zehn Jahren in Serbien inhaftiert ist, weil er angeblich seine Mitarbeiter nicht aus dem Sendergebäude abzog, obwohl die NATO das Bombardement des Senders angekündigt hatte. Handke beginnt den Artikel so:

»Es ist hier eine Geschichte zu erzählen. Nur weiß ich nicht, wem. Mir scheint, es gebe keinen Adressaten für diese Geschichte [...]. Und trotzdem ist es eine dringende Geschichte. Der Meister Eckhart spricht einmal von seinem Bedürfnis zu predigen, das so stark sei, daß er, fände er für seine Predigt kein Gegenüber, seine Predigt [...] notfalls auch an einen ›Opferstock‹ richten würde. Hier handelt es sich um keine Predigt, sondern, wie gesagt, um eine Geschichte. Aber auch die wäre notfalls einem Holzstoß oder einem leeren Schneckenhaus zu erzählen oder gar, wie im übrigen nicht zum ersten Male, mir hier ganz allein.«[32]

Aus der letzten Formulierung mag eine Frustration zu hören sein, dass niemand seiner immer wieder anhebenden Fürsprache für Serbien mehr zuhört, aber sie erlaubt auch die Deutung, dass der Erzähler sich seine Geschichten selbst erzählt,

---

[30] Ebd.
[31] Aristoteles bestimmt Zorn als eine Reaktion, die dann eintritt, wenn ein anderer »diejenigen geringschätzig behandelt, denen nicht zu helfen eine Schande ist«; Aristoteles: Rhetorik, II, 2, S. 111.
[32] Handke: Die Geschichte des Dragoljub Milanović.

der Autor seine Texte für sich selbst schreibt. Das ist kein narzisstisches Projekt, sondern ein ethisches, insofern die affektgetriebene Fürsprache nicht nur den geschmähten Dritten zu ihrem Recht verhilft, sondern auch den Autor selbst mit in die Reihe der beschädigten Kreaturen stellt:

»So höre, Schuhband, zerschlissenes. Hör zu, verrosteter Nußknacker. Hör zu, krumme Nähnadel. Höre, verstaubtes Stofftier. Höre, mein abgewetzter Fußabstreifer. Hör zu, Spiegelbild.«[33]

Der Fürsprecher restituiert die Würde der Beschädigten, zu denen auch das eigene Spiegelbild gehört. Er adressiert die Entwerteten und hebt sie mit den Kräften der Sprache und des Affekts in die absolute Gegenwart. Damit wird das ermächtigende Wort vollgültig zur Tat gemacht. Das ist das Schreibprojekt des ›Partisanen‹ und Advokaten Handke.

3. Theorie des Partisanen

Fürsprache bedarf einer Ermächtigung. Im Juridischen erfolgt die Advokatur klassicherweise durch einen Auftrag dessen, der seine Rechte durch einen Stärkeren, einen Rechtsexperten, vertreten sehen möchte. Im Ethischen findet oftmals nur eine implizite Beauftragung statt: Die in den Augen des Beobachters benachteiligten Personen artikulieren keine Hilfegesuche, aber der Beobachter fühlt sich aufgrund seiner Einschätzung der Verhältnisse verpflichtet, Partei für die seines Erachtens Entrechteten zu ergreifen. Unangebrachte Ungerechtigkeit der Verhältnisse ermächtigt den Fürsprecher, wobei allerdings nicht nur sein Gerechtigkeitssinn zur Tätigkeit motiviert, sondern auch Empathie: nicht nur stellvertretender Einsatz, sondern auch stellvertretendes Erleiden im Nach- oder Mitvollzug des Leidens anderer.

Doch das Fürsprachemodell bricht in der Theorie zusammen, wenn die Instanz des ungerechtfertigt Leidenden ausfällt. In Bezug auf Handkes Serbienengagement deutet sich das an, wenn die serbische Menschenrechtsaktivistin Sonja Biserko in einem Interview sagt, dass Serbien Handke nicht brauche.[34] Handkes Einsatz wird hier abgelehnt, um nationale Verantwortung für eigenes Handeln zu befördern. Das Berufen auf die eigene Souveränität bedeutet, Zuständigkeiten für die eigene Geschichte zu klären, ohne die Bindung zu Freunden zurückzuweisen. Wie kann Parteinahme aussehen, wenn die Fürsprache ihre Gül-

---

[33] Ebd.; Hervorhebung A. S.
[34] Vgl. Seibel: Serbien braucht keinen Handke, S. 89–91.

tigkeit verliert, weil niemand mehr zuhört, weil die Betroffenen keine Fürsprache wollen, weil die Bedeutung von Engagement nicht erkannt wird?

Handkes Kritik an der fehlenden Würdigung der Leistung von Partisanen (als Parteinahme im speziellen Sinne) scheint in seinen Texten immer wieder durch. In *Wut und Geheimnis* moniert er, dass der österreichische Staat der kärntnerisch-slowenischen Partisanen des Zweiten Weltkriegs nicht genügend gedenkt, obwohl sie es als einzige militärisch organisierte Widerstandseinheit waren, die Österreich nach Kriegsende dazu verholfen haben, einen souveränen Status zu erlangen. Mit seiner dramatischen Erzählung *Immer noch Sturm* schafft Handke dem kärntnerisch-slowenischen Partisanentum ein »Buch-Denkm[a]l«[35], wenn er durch die Figur, die er »Ich« nennt, zum einen die Bedeutung der Partisanen herausstellt und zum anderen deren Nichtwürdigung in der Rezeption kritisiert:

»Nie hatten sie [die Partisanen; A. S.] und ihre Vorfahren hierzulande Krieg geführt? Jetzt war er da, ihr Krieg, ja, ihr Krieg, geführt von den einheimischen ehemaligen Kirchenchorsängern, den Tenören, Baritonen, Bässen, welche als Partisanen den einzigen organisierten militärischen andauernden Widerstand innerhalb der Grenzen des Tausendjährigen Reichs leisteten, als das Heer der Partisanen, und zuletzt auch als Sieger. Fragt sich nur, was der Krieg ihnen gebracht hat, und was der Sieg, ihnen, dir und mir. Fragt sich nur, was das für ein Frieden war nach Krieg und Sieg, und ob überhaupt. Fragt sich, wo die Krieger geblieben sind, wo sind sie geblieben? Fragt sich, fragen wir, fragt ihr, fragen sie, fragt wen oder was, fragt den Himmel, fragt die SINGER-Nähmaschine, fragt den verrosteten Schlitten, fragt alle, nur nicht mich!«[36]

Nach dem 8. Mai 1945 sind die Partisanen zehn Tage lang Sieger gewesen, bevor sie als Verlierer und Unterdrückte behandelt wurden. Das Ich beklagt die ungerechte Behandlung der Partisanen durch die neuen Machthaber:

»Zehn Tage lang der warme, warme Frieden, und dann der kalte, kalte Krieg – der andauert. Der kalte Krieg, in Kraft getreten ist er, verfügt vom Westen her […]. Die Engländer, gerade noch eure, einmal weniger, einmal mehr, Verbündete in eurem Sprach- und Freiheitskampf, sind von einem Tag zum andern als eure Feinde aufgetreten. Aus ist es mit eurer Macht. Sie sind die Machthaber, das Land ist ihnen zugeteilt, und eure slawischen Brüder im Osten lassen's geschehen. Eure Sprache wird schon wieder befeindet, und ihre einheimischen Gegner, die sie und euch wie eh und je weghaben wollen, sind ein Herz und eine Seele geworden mit den Besatzern […].«[37]

Die Partisanen werden von Siegern zu Delinquenten, die bei Verstoß gegen das Versammlungsverbot ins Gefängnis gesperrt werden zusammen »mit den aus

---

[35] »Vielleicht sollte man keine Denkmäler errichten für den und den, keine steinernen; vielleicht ist das richtig. Aber was bestehen sollte, sind die Buch-Denkmäler«; Handke: Wut und Geheimnis.
[36] Handke: Immer noch Sturm, S. 74.
[37] Ebd., S. 141.

Jugoslawien geflüchteten Weißgardisten, die mit BeMu killten, und den Heimwehrleuten und Ustascha, die für AHi mordeten«[38]. Wo solch eine Vertauschung des politisch-nationalen Selbstverständnisses geschieht, können die Partisanen nur mit einer weiteren Vertauschung reagieren: des Lebens mit dem Tod. Der Partisan Gregor, Onkel des Ich, wünscht sich angesichts dieser Vertauschung der Rollen den Tod: »Ich denke an unsere Toten [...] und ich wünsche mir, bei ihnen zu sein, tot, unter meinen Toten, den Meinigen«[39]. Die Schmach, trotz der Verdienste ausgestoßen zu sein, wird vor allem in der verweigerten Kommunion deutlich. Brot und Wein werden den Partisanen vom Priester verweigert, was zugleich bedeutet, dass ihnen (nicht nur das geistliche) Leben verweigert wird: »Die gerade noch im Evangelium ›Das Leben ist erschienen!‹ verkündet haben, haben dieses Leben mit der verweigerten Kommunion wieder verschwinden lassen, für immer und ewig«[40]. Diejenigen, die sich für ihr Heimatland mit dem Leben eingesetzt haben, wollen angesichts ihrer Schmähung nach dem Krieg lieber auf die Seite des Todes, um hier Kommunion mit Gleichgesinnten zu haben.

Was Handke hier am Fall der kärntnerisch-slowenischen Partisanen des Zweiten Weltkriegs diskutiert, ist in der politischen Theorie nur allzu bekannt: die dem Politischen zugrunde liegende Frage nach der Unterscheidung von Freund und Feind. Carl Schmitt erläutert seine *Theorie des Partisanen* (1963) anhand des Feindschaftsbegriffs: Während der konventionelle Staatenkrieg ein Kabinettskrieg ist, in dem es definierte Feinde, eine definierte Kriegsordnung, einen definierten Sieg, zuletzt eine definierte Behandlung der Verlierer gibt, verändert das Partisanentum die Kriegsführung durch Prinzipien der Irregularität. Partisanen stören die Ordnung im besetzten Gebiet, das »Rechtsinstitut der occupatio bellica«[41]. Darum ist die ambivalente Bewertung des Partisanen als Widerstandskämpfer einerseits oder Verbrecher andererseits nicht verwunderlich. Er, der definierte Feindschaft untergräbt, sie entkoppelt von offiziellen Erklärungen und an die grundsätzliche Bedrohung des Autochthonen bindet, weitet den Begriff der Feindschaft aus. Aus der konventionellen Feindschaft wird die wirkliche Feindschaft.[42] Feind ist für den Partisanen derjenige, der dessen tellurische Bindung ignoriert und das Heimatland als Ort des freiheitlichen Lebens bedroht. Gerade in der Feindschaft findet der rechtlos Gewordene sein Recht.[43]

---

[38] Ebd.
[39] Ebd., S. 142.
[40] Ebd., S. 144.
[41] Schmitt: Theorie des Partisanen, S. 32.
[42] »Der moderne Partisan erwartet vom Feind weder Recht noch Gnade. Er hat sich von der konventionellen Feindschaft des gezähmten und gehegten Krieges abgewandt und in den Bereich einer anderen, der wirklichen Feindschaft begeben, die sich durch Terror und Gegen-Terror bis zur Vernichtung steigert«; ebd., S. 17. Die wirkliche Feindschaft wird zur absoluten Feindschaft, wenn der Partisan für revolutionäre Ideologien und mit suprakonventionellen Waffen kämpft.
[43] »In der Feindschaft sucht der rechtlos Gewordene sein Recht. In ihr findet er den Sinn der

Handke führt eine solche Struktur an Filip Kobald in *Die Wiederholung* literarisch vor: Filip ist durch die Nachäffungen seines Mitschülers seiner Würde beraubt und deklariert darum seinen Nachäffer als seinen »Todfeind«. Die Benennung als Feind ist die Reaktion auf den Versuch des Mitschülers, Filips Person durch Imitation zu entleeren und seine Existenz sinnlos zu machen. Indem Filip ihn zum Feind macht, gewinnt er einen Sinn, ein Recht auf Reaktion und einen Rechtssinn, in einer Situation, in der ihm gerade sein Recht auf Personsein genommen wird. Die »verborgene Feindschaft« wird zur wirklichen, ja: absoluten Feindschaft: »Unsere bis dahin verborgene Feindschaft war übergegangen in einen Krieg, und der mußte offen ausgetragen werden.« Zwar klingt ein Bedauern aus Filips Worten, wenn er kommentiert, dass er seinen Mitschüler geschlagen hat, aber dieser Schlag ist zugleich ein Befreiungsschlag, der mit der Feindschaft auch dem eigenen Recht zur Geltung verhilft. Hier steht die Souveränität des Rechts über der Souveränität des moralischen Gesetzes.[44]

Wenn Filip Kobald seine Mutter bittet, ihm zu helfen, ließe sie sich vielleicht im weitesten Sinne in der Rolle desjenigen sehen, den Carl Schmitt als den »interessierten Dritten« bezeichnet. Ihn braucht der Partisan als fremden Unterstützer, nicht nur, weil er ihm technische Ausrüstung beschafft (in *Immer noch Sturm* beschreibt Handke, wie die Engländer als interessierte Dritte den Partisanen Schreibmaschinen bereitstellen), sondern auch, weil er ihm politische Anerkennung gibt, derer er bedarf, um sein Handeln nicht als illegal deuten zu müssen.[45] Zwar hat Filips Mutter hier eher die Rolle der Schützenden, zu der er fliehen kann, die in die schwierigen Situationen ihres Sohnes tätig eingreift, aber sie wird von Filip auch als »Rechtsprecherin«[46] bezeichnet, die ihm zu seinem Recht verhilft. Wohlgemerkt: Es geht hier nicht darum, die Positionen von Partisan, offiziellem Feind und Freund und interessiertem Dritten auf die Romanfiguren zuzurechnen, sondern vielmehr darum, Motivationen für Anteilnahme aus der Logik der Struktur des Partisanenmodells zu beziehen. Handke weiß um die Bedeutung des Dritten, wenn er die Mutter in Filips Kampf tätig werden lässt, Partisanenlieder singend, und Entsprechendes ließe sich auch in Bezug auf sein Serbienengagement sagen: Indem er Partei ergreift, als Dritter sich einmischt (hier gehen die Funktionen von Partisan und interessiertem Dritten ineinander über), stärkt er die Position der in seinen Augen insgesamt Entrechteten und sorgt für deren Anerkennung. Mit dem partisanenorientiertem Modell von Anteilnahme

---

Sache und den Sinn des Rechts, wenn das Gehäuse von Schutz und Gehorsam zerbricht, das er bisher bewohnte, oder das Normengewebe der Legalität zerreißt, von dem er bisher Recht und Rechtsschutz erwarten konnte«; ebd., S. 92.

[44] Schmitt benutzt die Gegenüberstellung von Souveränität des Rechts und Souveränität des Gesetzes, von Legitimität und Legalität, zur Beschreibung des Falls Salan; vgl. ebd., S. 85f.

[45] Vgl. ebd., S. 78.

[46] Handke: Wiederholung, S. 40.

übernimmt er ein besonderes Differenzierungsmodell: Es geht nicht um die Differenzierung von Täter und Opfer innerhalb der Serben, so, wie es der juridische und der ethische Diskurs der westlichen Öffentlichkeit fordern, sondern um ein vollständiges Sich-Verwenden für eine Fraktion, die eine tellurische, autochthone Bindung hat – und das gilt sowohl für serbische Opfer wie für serbische Täter. Die Grenze zwischen Freund und Feind ist keine strafrechtliche, sondern eine nationale: zwischen Serben und Nichtserben. Damit befördert Handke natürlich die Abgründigkeit der blutigen ethnischen Kämpfe. Das ist nicht zu entschuldigen – es ist hier nur anzumerken, dass es sich bei Handke dabei wohl weniger um eine genuin völkische Position handelt als um eine Radikalisierung von Anteilnahme, die pauschale Feindzuschreibungen bestätigt und dabei in Kauf nimmt, selbst diskriminiert zu werden. Alle, die für die *justa causa* kämpfen, sind wirkliche Freunde, und alle, die im Dienste anderer Interessen stehen, auch einer anderen Gerechtigkeit, werden zu wirklichen Feinden. Das ist die Logik des anteilnehmenden Kriegs.

4. Immer noch Sturm

Handkes Stück *Immer noch Sturm* von 2010 *ist* das Buch-Denkmal des Partisanenkampfes. Ein »Ich« begegnet seiner Familie mütterlicherseits auf dem Jaunfeld: Die vom Ich schon als gestorben gewussten Familienmitglieder treten auf der Bühne des heimatlichen Jaunfelds in Kärnten auf. Sie erzählen dabei die eigene, sehr private Geschichte des Zweiten Weltkriegs: Die Großeltern erleben erneut den Tod zweier Söhne an der Front; zwei weitere ihrer Kinder, Gregor und Ursula, schließen sich den kärntnerisch-slowenischen Partisanen an; die Mutter des Ich bekommt ein uneheliches Kind mit einem Deutschen, das heranwächst zum erwachsenen Ich, sodass das Ich auf dem Jaunfeld sich selbst als Kind begegnet.

Das Stück ist Buch-Denkmal für das Partisanendasein in zweierlei Hinsicht. Die zentrale Auseinandersetzung mit der Rolle von Tante und Onkel des Ich, die zu den Partisanen gehen und von der eigenen Familie darin unterstützt werden, steht für die enge, buchstäbliche Deutung des Partisanentums.[47] Die weitere Hinsicht bezieht sich auf das Verständnis von Partisanentum als Anteilnahme: Das Stück ist eine Familienaufstellung, in der das Ich die Gelegenheit bekommt, seine

---

[47] Liest man das Stück biografistisch, so beteiligt Handke hier seine Familie am aktiven Widerstand und realisiert damit das, was sich in ihm in einem Traum vorbereitet hat: Am 13. Januar 1963 schreibt Handke seiner Mutter, dass er geträumt habe, sein Onkel Gregor sei im Zweiten Weltkrieg desertiert, ebenso auch dessen Bruder Hans, und im Traum sei er Gregor gewesen. Die Handke-Biografik stellt diesen Traum als ein zentrales Erlebnis Handkes heraus, das an zahlreichen Stellen in sein Schreiben eingehe; vgl. Bieringer: Spuren der Liturgie bei Peter Handke, S. 702.

Familienmitglieder in ihrem Familienverbund in Distanz anzuschauen, ihre jeweiligen Konflikte mit der Familie wahrzunehmen, die Stärke der familiären Bindung im Positiven wie im Negativen zu erkennen, den Sog des Verbunds zu erleben, das gemeinsame Schicksal der Familie zu affirmieren und den Familienmitgliedern und sich neu zu begegnen. Es ist ein Stück, das um den Modus von Anteilnahme kreist, um soziale Systemzwänge und freies Sich-verbunden-Fühlen.

Die Anlage des Stücks lässt die Assoziationen mit der Familienaufstellung, entwickelt als therapeutisches und organisationspsychologisches Verfahren, zu: Der Auftritt der Familienmitglieder folgt nicht nur der Logik eines dramatischen Stücks, sondern auch ebenjenem der Familienaufstellung:

»Und was sehe ich nun? Meine Vorfahren nähern sich von allen Seiten, mit dem typischen Jaunfeldschritt, deutlich von einem Fuß auf den andern tretend. Einzeln kommen sie daher, ausgenommen das Großelternpaar, [...] jeder auf einem eigenen Weg, oder Nicht-Weg. [...] Einzeln steuert ein jeder auf den ihm scheint's vorgegebenen Ort oder Stehplatz zu [...]. [...] Sie sind es nicht, weder in Aussehen noch Haltung noch Mienen. Und zugleich sind sie es. Sie sind es! Und dazu paßt es, daß sie mich jetzt auf meinem Platz ausfindig machen und mich erkennen, einer nach dem andern, erschrocken, erfreut, verdrießlich, gleichgültig, still, laut. Ein mehrstimmiges: ›Hallo! Da schau her. Ach herrje. Der also. Du hier!‹ ergibt das, gefolgt von dem familien- und sippenüblichen einstimmigen Seufzerchor und dann einem ein- oder zehnstimmigen ›Komm, Nachzügler. Aufgesprungen auf den Familienzug, Nachfahr. Der einzige, der uns noch träumt. Ach, daß uns doch jemand anderer träume! Jemand Sachgerechter. Einer, der uns denkt, und bedenkt – und nicht dein ewiges Gedenken, dein immerwährendes Heraufbeschwören. Mit einem Wort: ein Dritter! Kannst du uns nicht endlich in Ruhe lassen? Aber da du schon einmal hier bist: Her mit dir, Letzter, ins Bild mit uns.‹«[48]

Die *Mise en Scène* arbeitet auch mit Positionswechseln je nach Qualität der Beziehung der Familienmitglieder untereinander: Man tritt zur Seite, gruppiert um, bildet einen Halbkreis um das Ich:

»Diese gemeinsame Bewegung hat mich freilich nicht geängstigt: Ich bin zuletzt meinen Leuten entgegengekommen und habe ihnen nacheinander die Hand gereicht (eine andere Berührung kam ja, oder kommt, bei unsereinem kaum in Betracht). Nur vor der Mutter dann habe ich im Abstand innegehalten, und habe gesagt: ›Da seid ihr nun, Vorfahren. Die längste Zeit schon habe ich auf euch gewartet. Nicht ich lasse euch nicht in Ruhe. Es läßt mich nicht in Ruhe, nicht ruhen. Ihr laßt mich nicht in Ruhe, nicht und nicht.‹«[49]

Die prekäre Rolle, die das Ich im Familiensystem hat, ist damit klar umrissen: Es steht auf der Grenze der Zugehörigkeit, ist Dritter und auch nicht. Als uneheliches Kind mit deutschem Vater, der die Familie verlassen hat, gehört es nur halb

---

[48] Handke: Immer noch Sturm, S. 8f.
[49] Ebd., S. 10.

zum Verbund, wird missachtet und respektiert zugleich. Es darf aufspringen auf den Familienzug, weil es zumindest eines ist, das diese Familie denkt (wenn auch im falschen Modus des »immerwährende[n] Heraufbeschwören[s]«). Es ist seine Rede, die es zum Familienzugehörigen macht, und zwar nicht nur seine Slowenischkenntnisse, nicht nur die familieneigenen Sprachspiele, sondern eben auch sein heraufbeschwörendes Sprechen. Auch daran erkennt die Mutter ihren Sohn:

»Auch ich habe dich nicht gleich erkannt. Und bevor du ins Reden kamst, war ich – unsicher. Aber so weiß ich, du bist es, mein Sohn. Mein Sohn, der nie zu uns hier, zur Familie, zur Sippe gehören wird, Vaterloser du, der du Ersatz, Halt und Licht suchst bei deinen Vorfahren.«[50]

Genetische Verhältnisse stellen das Ich außerhalb der Sippe. Es wird ein Schulddiskurs geführt, der dem Vater des Ich anlastet, ein deutscher Soldat zu sein und seine Frau mit dem gemeinsamen Kind im Stich gelassen zu haben. Diese Schuld lastet auf dem Ich und wird von ihm fortgeführt: »und wie der Vater, so der Sohn, mehr ist darüber nicht zu sagen«[51]. Gerade weil die Familie dem Ich ein hohes Schuldpotenzial explizit oder implizit zuweist, zieht es das Ich paradoxerweise umso stärker hinein in den Familienverbund. Hier sucht es den eigenen Verlust an sinnvoller Bindung zu kompensieren, doch zugleich bedeutet die duldende Anerkennung durch die Familie die Vergrößerung der eigenen Schuld, insofern das Ich nun in ihrer Schuld steht. Liebe und Schuldzuweisung sind die barmherzig-unbarmherzigen Mechanismen, mit denen die Familie ihre Sippe organisiert. An Ursulas Schicksal wird die Verquickung von Familienliebe und Familienschuld besonders deutlich. Sie stellt sich als diejenige dar, die von der Familie gehasst und ausgegrenzt wird, und zugleich kann sie nicht aus der Familie heraustreten, in der sie ihren Platz zugewiesen bekommt.

Es ist der Großvater als *pater familias*, der strukturell derjenige ist, der ein Platzfinden der Familienmitglieder auch außerhalb der Familie verhindert. Er wacht über die Grundordnung der Familie: Er bestimmt, dass das Wort ›Liebe‹ in seinem Haus nicht benutzt werden darf,[52] dass Fremdwörter ausgeschlossen sind,[53] dass niemand sein Haus und Hof anders bezeichnen darf.[54] Die Ordnungen der Verpflichtungen sind klar:

»Der Vater: ›Was für eine Sprache du sprichst, Sohn. So hat noch niemand in unserer Sippe geredet.‹ – Die Mutter: ›So laß ihn, Vater. Nie hast du die deinigen lassen können.‹«[55]

---

50 Ebd., S. 12.
51 Ebd., S. 15.
52 Ebd., S. 133.
53 Ebd., S. 22.
54 Ebd., S. 108.
55 Ebd.

Der Großvater hat das Bestreben, das System zu erhalten. Es ist nicht nur die gemeinsame Sprache des kärntnerischen Slowenisch, die miteinander verbindet, sondern die Sippe ist bis in ihre phatische Kommunikation hinein erkennbar: im sogenannten Sippenjammer, den »sippeneigenen Laute[n]«[56], die das ganze Geschehen auf dem Jaunfeld immer wieder unterbrechen und gestalten. Massiver wird die gebotene Zusammengehörigkeit im großväterlichen Einschwören auf das »Wir« als Kollektivsingular:

»Der Vater: ›Früher bin ich euch Kindern ein jedesmal über den Mund gefahren, wenn ihr ›ich‹ gesagt habt, weißt du noch?‹ – Jonathan: ›Wie denn nicht, Vater? ›In diesem Haus kein Ich!‹ Und obwohl es in unsrer lieben Sprache normal kein eignes Wort gibt für ›ich‹ […], hast du uns seinerzeit in Haus und Hof sogar die versteckte Ich-Form austreiben wollen, kein ›ich fühle‹, kein ›ich denke‹, kein ›ich möchte‹, und wie erst die betonte, ›*ich* meine‹, ›*ich* denke‹, ›*jaz* menim‹, ›*jaz* mislim‹ … ›In unserem Haus ist Platz einzig für wir und uns!‹ hast du gesagt …‹«[57]

Was in seiner Zeit als pädagogische Maßnahme den Sinn hatte, zur Bescheidenheit zu erziehen, wird zugleich zur Beförderung eines »kontraautonomen Überich«[58], das das Verhalten der einzelnen Familienmitglieder reguliert, ohne dass ein aktiv und selbstständig differenzierendes Ich die Chance auf Mitgestaltung hätte.

Dieses kontraautonome Überich führt ein Familienschuldkonto, indem es die Verpflichtungen der Mitglieder in ständiger Erinnerung hält, Verdienste belohnt, Gegenleistungen einfordert und damit die familieninterne Gerechtigkeitsbilanz immer wieder ins Gleichgewicht zu bringen bemüht ist. Das familiäre Beziehungssystem ist konservativ, auf Erhalt angelegt, und kaum etwas kann Bindung so fest im Griff halten wie ein Schuldzusammenhang, der ständig aufgerufen wird. Nur so kann die Verletzung verstanden werden, mit der Ursula, die sich geschmäht fühlt, ihren Neffen als Baby schmäht:

»›Daß ich mich zeitweise im Wald nach dem Kind der Schwester gesehnt habe: seltsam. Nach dem Wechselbalg mit dem fremdländischen Geschau, den Grottenmolchhänden, den Haaren, die wie nasse Hühnerfedern riechen, der Haut, die auch nach dem Entwöhnen die Muttermilch riecht. Als ob nach all dem, was sich zugetragen hat, nur der Anblick eines unschuldigen Kindes einen reinigen könnte, sogar eines, das schon am Tag seiner Geburt gar nicht so unschuldig gewirkt hat …‹ Ich habe den Kopf gehoben, um mich ihr bemerkbar zu machen. Aber sie ist schon verschwunden, so unversehens, wie sie gekommen ist.«[59]

Das unschuldige Baby hat keine Chance, seiner Schuld zu entkommen, die Teil des Familienschicksals ist. Sein Onkel Gregor gar diktiert ihm, dem Kind, die

---

56 Ebd., S. 158.
57 Ebd., S. 105 f.
58 Boszormenyi-Nagy / Spark: Unsichtbare Bindungen, S. 23.
59 Handke: Immer noch Sturm, S. 114 f.

Familiengeschichte (»schreib mit, Patenkind, wörtlich!«[60]), damit sie, »unsere Leidensgeschichte«[61], »[i]m Buch unseres Lebens«[62] notiert ist, ins gemeinsame Gedächtnis eingeht und hier wachgehalten wird. Dieses Erbe ist eingeschrieben und macht sich bis in die Träume des Ich bemerkbar:

»Aber zurück zu meinen Vorfahrträumen: Wie habe ich gesagt – daß die wirklicher sind als sonstwas? Nein, wirksamer. – Schönes Wort übrigens: wirksam. – Inwiefern wirksam? Gebieterisch. Inwiefern gebieterisch? Ich soll. Was soll ich? Die Altvorderen überliefern? Zu großes Wort, und außerdem falsch. Nein, es gibt keine großen Wörter, nur welche am falschen Platz, im falschen Moment. Die Ahnen hochhalten? Das tue ich ohnedies, aber darum geht es nicht. Ihnen nachspüren? Sie zu Wort kommen lassen? [...] Weiß nicht, weiß nicht, weiß nicht. Was ich weiß: ich soll. Ein schlechtes Gewissen beschert ihr mir, von Zeit zu Zeit jedenfalls, Leute. Schlechtes Gewissen weshalb? Wegen meiner Undankbarkeit. Ganz schön lästig seid ihr mir, Leute, von Zeit zu Zeit. Andererseits: wenn ihr dann eine Zeitlang nicht auftretet, weder tagsüber noch im Traum, bekomme ich wieder mein schlechtes Gewissen, dann allerdings so: Was habe ich bloß falsch gemacht, daß ihr mir nicht mehr erscheint?«[63]

Der Familienverbund reguliert, ja diktiert das eigene Verhalten: »Ich soll.« Über das schlechte Gewissen, das die Familie bewusst oder unbewusst dem Nachfahren beschert, stellt sie die Bindung an das eigene System sicher.[64] Für den Nachfahren ist die Zugehörigkeit und Treue zum System wichtiger als das eigene selbstbestimmte Leben ohne diese Familie. Er kommt aus dem Sog der genetischen Verhältnisse, die zugleich eine Ordnung von Verpflichtungen vorgeben, nicht heraus. Man gehört, im wörtlichen Sinne ›auf Gedeih und Verderb‹, zur Familie.

Diese Dynamik ist umso stärker, je mehr sich eine Familie als Verbund stabilisieren und nach außen schützen muss, je mehr Leiden sie in ihrer Geschichte erfahren hat und mit sich trägt. Je mehr »Leidensgeschichte«[65], umso stärker der Drang nach innen, um hier mit einem Maximum an Fürsorge und Anteilnahme das zu kompensieren, was die Mitglieder bzw. die Familie als ganze geschwächt hat. Das ist die heilvolle und zugleich heillose Logik des Familiensystems, die Crux der unmittelbaren, differenzlosen Anteilnahme.

---

[60] Ebd., S. 129.
[61] Ebd., S. 22.
[62] Ebd., S. 122.
[63] Ebd., S. 45 f.
[64] Ein weiteres besonderes Beispiel für die Schuldzuweisung stellt die gnadenlose Frage der Mutter an ihren Sohn dar: »Aber du, Sohn: bist du bei uns geblieben? Wirst du bei uns bleiben? Hast du uns nicht immer abtun wollen? Uns loswerden? So bleib du mit uns. Hast du denn nicht gemerkt, daß du nicht anders kannst, du Obstgartenflüchtling? Daß wir, ob du willst oder nicht, dich führen? Daß wir dich bestimmen, und nicht nur, wie du zeitweise gemeint hast, zu deinem Unglück, du Piaukel?«; ebd., S. 43.
[65] Ebd., S. 22.

5. Freund und Feind der Familie

An dieser Dynamik, die die Familie als Beziehungssystem bestimmt, wird deutlich, wie im gesellschaftlichen Kleinstverband Zugehörigkeiten organisiert werden. Letztlich ist das Familiengeschehen in dieser Radikalität eine Demonstration der Unterscheidung von Freund und Feind. Der Feind war von der Familie immer klar definiert als ein politischer: all jene, die das Slowenischsein in Kärnten gefährden. All jene, die es unterstützen, die Partisanen, ihre Unterstützer in der Bevölkerung, die Engländer als interessierte Dritte, zählen zu den Freunden, den »Unsrigen«[66]. Feind ist, wer sich den Unsrigen entgegenstellt, und sei er nur unwirtlich wie die winterliche Drau (»Drau? [...] Als meinen Feind betrachte ich sie«[67]). Die Feindeszone weitet sich unaufhörlich aus. Die Verbündeten werden zu Feinden,[68] und dies trifft nicht nur auf die Engländer zu: Weitaus gefährdender, zersetzender ist die Ausweitung des Feindes auf die eigene Familie. Mutter und Sohn, das Ich, erkennen, dass der wirkliche Feind nicht der von außen Kommende ist, nicht der deutsche Vater des Ich:

»Derjenige, welcher, den ich mir dort drüben aus dem Bauch geredet habe, das war kein Feind. Es handelt sich zwar um jemand Tiefbösen. Aber ich erlebe ihn nicht als unseren Gegenspieler. Er taugt dazu nicht. Er ist unserer Geschichte nicht würdig. Ja, richtig gehört: nicht würdig!«[69]

Wirklicher Feind kann nur der sein, der auch Freund sein kann, und das heißt: der aus den Reihen der eigenen Familie kommt. Und so ist es weniger die Schuld des deutschen Verehrers bzw. Vaters, die Mutter und Sohn in die eigene Familie hineintragen, sondern die eigene Schuld. Mutter und Sohn sind die Feinde der Familie. Das ist nicht nur das dramaturgische Gesetz der Aufführung auf dem Jaunfeld (»Schon die längste Zeit fehlt mir in unserer Geschichte ein Gegenspieler. Einer, der aufmischt und durcheinanderbringt«[70]), sondern auch die radikale Logik des schicksalhaft geschwächten und darum umso mehr auf Schulterschluss setzenden Familiensystems. Die Mutter ahnt das Aufkommen des Feindes, der Gegenspieler:

»Und mir schwant, daß sie aus unseren eigenen Reihen kommen werden, aus unserem eigenen Stamm, womöglich aus unserm eigenen Haus. [...] Kann sein, daß auch ich selber mich eines gar nicht fernen Tages auf der Gegenseite finde [...]. Möglich, daß ich jetzt und hier gerade auf dem Sprung zum Feindwerden bin [...]. Der Feind der Sippe, des Stamms, des Volkes von hier: ich?«[71]

---

[66] Ebd., S. 45.
[67] Ebd., S. 120.
[68] Ebd., S. 141.
[69] Ebd., S. 59.
[70] Ebd., S. 57.
[71] Ebd., S. 58 f.

Selbst das ungeborene Kind wird zum Feind, der den Tod des Onkels im Krieg zu verantworten hat, wenn der Großvater es im Bauch seiner Mutter verflucht:

»›Und verflucht sei der Liebeswurm in deinem Liebesbauch. Verflucht sei die Frucht deines Leibes. Der Herr hat's gegeben, der Herr hat's genommen, verflucht sei der Name des Herrn in Ewigkeit!‹ Und er hat dabei ausgeholt wie zum Schlag, und ich auf der Bank – habe ich mich geduckt? bin ich zurückgezuckt? Und meine Mutter? Hat sich nicht von der Stelle gerührt, hat nicht mit der Wimper gezuckt.«[72]

Auch der sanftmütige Onkel Gregor erklärt den Säugling zum Feind:

»Es geht mir ja selber gegen den Strich, daß ich sogar in dem käsigen Säugling da den Feind sehe. Aber so ist es, so ist es gekommen. Da liegt er, [...] winkt mir in einem fort zu mit seinen Schlackeröhrchen, durchsichtig und fettig wie Butterpapier – Feind hört mit. Ja, den Feind stellt er mir dar, den Kuckuck, der uns Heimische bis auf den letzten Piepser und Flaum aus dem Nest wird schmeißen. Winzling, Vorform des großen Feindes, des Usurpators. Familienfeind – Volksfeind. Heraus aus der Wiege – in die Hundehütte mit dem Bankert.«[73]

Am radikalsten wird die Feindzuweisung, wenn derjenige, der den Familienzusammenhalt befördert, die Familie selbst als Feind sieht und selbst zum Feind wird. Gregor, der das Slawentum seiner Familie hochhält, ist es, »der den Sturm sät zwischen uns, den hitzigen, herz- und kopfkrankmachenden Südsturm, [...] den Krieg«[74], er ist es, der beschließt, Feind zu werden.[75] Was sich hier noch auf seinen Entschluss bezieht, zu desertieren und Partisan zu werden, weitet sich später aus auf eine allgemeine Feindschaft: »Ein Menschenfeind bin ich geworden«[76]. Wenn Carl Schmitts Theorie des Partisanen eine Ausweitung von Feindschaft zur absoluten Feindschaft bei den revolutionären Ideologien feststellt, so zeigt sich hier eine andere Form der absoluten Feindschaft: der selbstzerstörerische Mechanismus des Sich-selbst-zum-Feind-Machens. Gregor leidet unter seiner entstehenden Idiosynkrasie: »Der Teufel steckt in mir, tausend Teufel stecken in mir«[77]. Der Feind in ihm zeigt sich in Form des Ekels, der zum einen ein Familienekel ist, weil er die Familienmitglieder verbindet:

»Der Ekel, der ›Eckel‹, unseres toten Benjamin, über die Milchhaut auf dem Kaffee, über die Maden im Käse, über alle Gummibänder in Form einer liegenden Acht, über die Nudeln in Form eines S ist scheint's in mich gefahren als Ekel, als Eckel, vor den Jetztmenschen jetzt«[78].

---

[72] Ebd., S. 67f.
[73] Ebd., S. 79f.
[74] Ebd., S. 40.
[75] Ebd., S. 79.
[76] Ebd., S. 156.
[77] Ebd., S. 158.
[78] Ebd.

Zum anderen ist es ein Ekel, der auch in Verbindung stehen könnte mit dem Bindungsdiktat der Familie, insofern nicht nur die Geschichte Gregor zum Menschenfeind macht, sondern auch die Familiengeschichte. Denn Weltgeschichte und Familiengeschichte sind für die Familienmitglieder meist in eins gewendet: Weltkrieg ist Familienkrieg und vice versa.[79]

Darum scheint es als Befreiung, dass der dem Ich vererbte Rock des toten Benjamin auf dem Körper des Ich zerreißt und zerfällt,[80] vielleicht mit ihm auch der Ekel seines früheren Trägers. Intuitiv bilden Gregor und Ich neue Verbindungen, die sie mit ihrer Heimat als Ort der Familie assoziieren: »Jaunfeld: Motten und Blutegel. Blei und Glimmer. Wasserläufer und Kuhmist. Meßkelch und Hühnerleiter ...«[81] Diese Wörter mögen ein weiteres Beschwören der Heimat sein, sie können allerdings auch für ebendiese andere Form der Verbindung stehen, die Gegenständliches mit einer schlichten Kopula aneinanderfügt und nicht Subjekte aneinanderkettet. Diese Form der lockeren Verbindung ist es auch, die zum Schluss dem Ich als Familienbande vorschwebt: ein ›In-den-Hintergrund-Geraten‹ der Familienmitglieder, von anderen ›auseinandergewürfelt‹, aber noch in gemeinsamem Kontakt stehend über »Handzeichen, mit denen wir einander noch zuwinken«[82]. In der Vision der lockeren Verbindung, die die Familienmitglieder untereinander haben, kann eine Bindung und eine Anteilnahme gelebt werden, die frei ist von impliziten Aufträgen und Zuständigkeitszuweisungen des Familienschicksals. Es geht um einen Modus der Anteilnahme, der frei ist von Übernahme.

6. Literatur als Fürsprache

Es verwundert nicht, dass Handke Partisanentum und Familiengeschichte derart eng miteinander verzahnt. In der Anteilnahme findet sich das Bindeglied zwischen zwei zunächst einander fremd erscheinenden Systemen. Handkes Familienaufstellung zeigt, wie die in der Theorie des Partisanen entwickelten Strukturen und Funktionen eines Unterscheidungsmodells (Freund- und Feindzuschreibungen, Bindungsformen, Anerkennung durch einen interessierten Dritten, Disziplinierung und Störung von Ordnung, eigene Rechtsprechung, Gerechtigkeit) ins Familiäre transportiert und hier mit einem Bindungsmodell gekoppelt werden können. Denn die hier dargestellte Familie scheint nach strukturähnlichen Prinzipien organisiert zu sein: In- und Exklusion, Einschwören auf die gemeinsame

---

[79] Ebd., S. 18.
[80] Ebd., S. 160 f.
[81] Ebd., S. 161.
[82] Ebd., S. 166.

Familientradition als Bindemittel und Disziplinierungsmaßnahme, partielle Integration eines Dritten (sofern er das familieneigene System nicht gefährdet, sondern es bestätigt), familieneigene Ordnung von wechselseitigen Verpflichtungen, familieneigene Gerechtigkeitsbilanz.

In Handkes Stück *Immer noch Sturm* werden diese strukturellen Verzahnungen erkennbar, die auf ein Modell von Unterscheidung und Bindung hinweisen, das für Handkes Schreiben grundlegend zu sein scheint. Denn es geht in den besprochenen Texten um eine *andere* Form von Unterscheidung und eine *andere* Form von Bindung an ein Unterschiedenes, die den als ›normal‹ apostrophierten Rechts- und Gerechtigkeitsvorstellungen widersprechen. Die Theorie des Partisanen liefert dabei das Unterscheidungsmodell von Freund und Feind, und die Theorie der Familie ergänzt sie um das Bindungsmodell von unbedingter Loyalität. Da gerade die psychologische Theorie der Familiendynamik, wie sie sich in der Familienaufstellung zeigt, auf die emotionale Ordnung hinweist und sie deutet, vermag sie einen Schlüssel anzubieten für die Erklärung von Emotionen, die in ebendiesen besprochenen Texten zutage treten. Das bedeutet schließlich, dass jede Äußerung, auch jede Gefühlsäußerung, im Lichte von Handkes radikalem Unterscheidungs- und Bindungsmodell daraufhin zu befragen wäre, ob sie auch zu verstehen sei als eingebunden in und motiviert durch unsichtbare Systemkräfte des (Schicksals-)Verbunds. Sie wäre zu befragen, ob sie auch zu verstehen sei als kontraautonome, intuitive Äußerung, die stärker ist als das vorhandene Differenzierungsvermögen der Reflexion.

Für den Zorn in seiner ganzen Energie der unmittelbaren Äußerung kann das zutreffen. So erhält beispielsweise Gregors Zorn als heftige Leidenschaft seine notwendige Kehrseite, die der handkeschen ›Logik des anderen‹ entspricht: »[A]uf einmal wird er der leibhaftige Zorn, zugleich ein Zorn so sanft und hilflos, wie ich ihn noch keinmal erlebt habe«[83]. Zorn ist eine Artikulation von Sanftheit und Hilflosigkeit, Wut ist nicht nur destruktiv in seiner Wirkung, sondern zeugt auch von Fürsorge für ein zu schützendes Gut, Diskriminierung des Gegners ist das Ergebnis einer Solidarisierung mit dem Opfer. Entsprechend muss man auch die jaunfeldtypischen Sprachspiele in ihrer scheinbaren Negativität und Destruktivität dialektisch verstehen: Wenn die Karawanken als »Totschlägerberg«, »Teufelsschlucht« und »Mammutfurzklamm«[84] bezeichnet werden, deutet das Sprachspiel auf seine gegenteilige Interpretation, denn die Karawanken verweisen auf die (Sprach-)Heimat Slowenien, wo Gregor für die Familie deren Wurzeln gefunden hat.[85] In die Heimat zu kommen bedeutet für Benjamin, »heim in den Stall zu den seichenden, furzenden, scheißenden Tieren« zu kommen.

---

[83] Ebd., S. 156.
[84] Ebd., S. 13.
[85] Ebd., S. 30.

Ursula wird von ihrem Vater als »Saudirn«, »uns-Jauche-in-die-Ohren-Tropferin, Herrgottswinkelverpesterin«[86], von ihrem Bruder Benjamin als »Übelheid und Ekeltraud«[87] bezeichnet und zugleich doch geliebt, und dies nicht nur für ihre Partisanentätigkeit. Auf die Nachricht von Benjamins und Valentins Tod reagieren deren Eltern, indem sie sich gerade Benjamins und Valentins Ungeschicklichkeiten in Erinnerung rufen. All die Schimpftiraden und Unfreundlichkeiten sind – perverserweise – als Artikulation von Hilflosigkeit und Zärtlichkeit zu verstehen, als inverse Formen der Artikulation von Anteilnahme und Fürsorge.

Die Anwendung einer solchen Lektüreanweisung, gerade die heftigen Formulierungen immer auch gegen den Strich zu lesen, ist nicht unproblematisch. Für die fiktionalen Texte mag sie ihre Berechtigung und Gültigkeit haben. Aber dort, wo die Person Handke in deutlichen Autorkommentaren in heftiger Leidenschaft und in politischer Absicht mit explizitem Serbienbezug spricht, mag man dies nicht nur als Artikulation von Fürsorge deuten. Damit droht das, was als Erklärungsmodell konzipiert ist, zur Verteidigungsrede, zur Fürsprache für Handke zu werden. Dann kommt man allerdings aus der Tribunalisierung der *Causa Handke* nicht heraus. Dagegen kann eine Lektüre, die um die Kräfte weiß, die die sprachlichen Äußerungen steuern, weil man die Mechanismen eines Kräftehaushalts aus anderen Beziehungsgefügen kennt, den Sturm um diese sprachlichen Äußerungen, ob er immer noch ist oder nicht, ergründen und beruhigen. Sie mag erklären, wie es zu Handkes Einsatz für einen anderen kommt, was ihn motiviert, sich an dessen Seite zu stellen. Wenn das Ich auf dem Jaunfeld feststellt, dass hier »alles paarweise« geschieht[88] und dass das Slowenische eine eigene grammatische Form für die Zweiheit hat, den Dual[89], dann ließe sich das auf Handkes Text- und Literaturverständnis beziehen: Literatur ist unbedingte Fürsprache und artikuliert sich immer im Dual.

---

[86] Ebd., S. 37.
[87] Ebd., S. 39.
[88] Ebd., S. 7.
[89] Ebd., S. 93.

Literatur

Aristoteles: Rhetorik, II, 1, 2, hg. und übertragen von Paul Gohlke, Paderborn 1959.

Bieringer, Andreas: Spuren der Liturgie bei Peter Handke, in: Internationale Zeitschrift Communio, 39, 2019, S. 701–708.

Borgards, Roland: Sprache als Bild. Handkes Poetologie und das 18. Jahrhundert, München 2003.

Boszormenyi-Nagy, Ivan / Spark, Geraldine M.: Unsichtbare Bindungen. Die Dynamik familiärer Systeme, aus dem Amerikanischen übersetzt von Suzanne A. Gangloff, Stuttgart 1981 (amerik. 1973).

Campe, Rüdiger: An Outline for a Critical History of *Fürsprache*: *Synegoria* and Advocacy. In: Deutsche Vierteljahrsschrift für Literaturwissenschaft und Geistesgeschichte, Jg. 82, H. 3, 2008, S. 355–381.

Handke, Peter: Die Wiederholung, Frankfurt a. M. 1986.

Handke, Peter: Eine winterliche Reise zu den Flüssen Donau, Save, Morawa und Drina oder Gerechtigkeit für Serbien, Frankfurt a. M. 1996.

Handke, Peter: Immer noch Sturm, Frankfurt a. M. 2010.

Handke, Peter: Die Geschichte des Dragoljub Milanovic, in: Die Presse vom 05.08.2011, http://diepresse.com/home/spectrum/zeichenderzeit/683784/Die-Geschichte-des-Dragoljub-Milanovi; letzter Zugriff: 17.04.2012.

Handke, Peter: Wut und Geheimnis, online unter: http://www.uni-klu.ac.at/home/unisono/Handke_Klagenfurter_Rede.pdf; letzter Zugriff: 20.03.2013.

Rubinstein, Lene: Litigation and Cooperation. Supporting Speakers in the Courts of Classical Athens, Stuttgart 2000.

Schmitt, Carl: Theorie des Partisanen. Zwischenbemerkung zum Begriff des Politischen, Berlin 1963.

Schneider, Peter: Der Ritt über den Balkan, in: Der Spiegel, 3, 1996, http://www.spiegel.de/spiegel/print/d-8871151.html; letzter Zugriff: 12.04.2012.

Seibel, Andrea: Serbien braucht keinen Handke. Interview mit Sonja Biserko, in: Tilman Zülch (Hg.): Die Angst des Dichters vor der Wirklichkeit. 16 Antworten auf Peter Handkes Winterreise nach Serbien, Göttingen 1996, S. 89–91.

Sloterdijk, Peter: Zorn und Zeit. Politisch-psychologischer Versuch, Frankfurt a. M. 2006.

Andrea Schütte

Imaginäres Interview mit der kroatischen Autorin Dubravka Ugrešić[1]

A. S.: Dubravka Ugrešić, Sie sind 1949 in Jugoslawien, im heutigen Kroatien, geboren, waren lange Jahre Dozentin für Literaturtheorie an der Universität in Zagreb und hatten bereits in Jugoslawien als Autorin von Kurzgeschichten und einem Roman einen Namen. 1993 haben Sie Kroatien verlassen und leben seitdem, unterbrochen von Gastdozenturen in den USA, in den Niederlanden. Wie sehen Sie Ihre Rolle als Exilantin, die ihr früheres Heimatland beobachtet, den damaligen Krieg und die Konflikte, die jetzt noch dort ausgetragen werden?

D. U.: Ich [...] habe kaum Illusionen. Ich bin eine von etwa 4 Millionen Ex-Jugoslawen, eine aus dem Stamm, dessen Mitglieder heute über die ganze Weltkarte verstreut sind. Ich bin eine Obdachlose, Heimatlose, Exilantin, ein Flüchtling, ein Nomade, alles auf einmal, eine Person mit dem Pass eines neuen europäischen Kleinstaats. [...]
  Ich schreibe meine Trümmer-Seiten, nervös drängen sich die Wörter, jedes vermehrt nur die Hilflosigkeit oder sogar Verlogenheit, wie vor langer Zeit der Exilant Theodor W. Adorno geschrieben hat. Dennoch lasse ich nicht nach, ich frage bis zur Erschöpfung. Ist wirklich Hass der Urheber von allem? Wenn es so ist, wo liegt das Herz dieses Hasses? In der Angst. Wenn es so ist, wo ist das Herz dieser Angst? Ich frage weiter wie in dem Märchen, in dem der Held über sieben Berge und Täler geht, um den Drachen zu besiegen. Aber die Kraft des Drachens weicht ständig aus, mal ist sie in dem einen, mal in dem anderen, mal ein Fisch, mal ein Vogel ... (KL 297)

A. S.: Sie meinen, die Macht des ›Bösen‹, die den Krieg entfacht und befeuert hat, zeige sich überall und sei doch nirgend zu fassen? Ist das nicht zu einfach? Sie benennen in Ihren Texten doch auch Milošević, Mladić und Karadžić als Kriegsverbrecher, die sicher zu Recht am ICTY angeklagt worden sind. Und Sie beschreiben auch die bedenkliche Rolle der Volksvertreter, der Medien, der Intellektuellen ...

---

[1] Alle Antworten der Autorin sind ihrem Buch *Die Kultur der Lüge* entnommen, das ihre Essays aus den Jahren 1991–94 versammelt: Dubravka Ugrešić: Die Kultur der Lüge, aus dem Kroatischen übersetzt von Barbara Antkowiak, Frankfurt a. M. 1995 (im Folgenden zitiert mit der Sigle KL).

D. U.: Die großen Manipulatoren, die *transformers*, demontierten das alte System und erbauten ein neues aus *denselben* Teilen! Und dann ruhten sie aus von allen ihren Werken, aber siehe, das Land war immer noch ganz. Also machten sie sich an die Demontage des Landes. Die wohlausgerüsteten Teams (Schriftsteller, Soziologen, Politologen, Psychiater, Philosophen und Generale) begannen mit der Produktion von Hass, Lügen und Wahnsinn. Um sich die Demontage des so multinationalen, so multikulturellen Landes zu erleichtern, offerierten die Großen Manipulatoren und ihre Teams die wirksamste Formel, eine neue Utopie: DIE NATION. Und um das eingeschläferte Nationalbewusstsein wachzurufen, mussten schnell Unterschiede definiert werden: wodurch sind WIR anders (d. h. besser) als SIE. In den Teams zum Aufbau der schlummernden, verlorenen, »repressierten« nationalen Identität arbeiten einmütig die Kollegen: Universitätsprofessoren, Linguisten, Journalisten, Schriftsteller, Historiker, Psychiater ... (KL 60)

A. S.: Die Nation als wirksame Formel, die kollektivbildend ist – ist es also doch die anonyme Masse, das Milieu, das für den Drachen steht, der hinter den sieben Bergen zu suchen ist?

D. U.: [D]as Milieu, das ist die Obrigkeit, das sind die Institutionen, die Polizei, die Minister, die Kollegen, die nächsten Nachbarn, das Milieu sind WIR alle. Diesem Milieu etwas Unangenehmes zu sagen, zu sagen, dass etwas *blutbesudelt, verbrecherisch und moralisch krank* ist, würde bedeuten, sich selbst auszuschließen, zum nackten, individuellen ICH zu werden. [...] VATERLAND, INSTITUTION, WIR, das sind die schützenden Zauberformeln, die vor der Gefahr des individuellen Handelns bewahren. Und wo es kein individuelles Handeln gibt, gibt es auch keine Verantwortung. Der wird sicher nicht vor Scham sterben, sagt man im Volksmund von jemandem mit unterentwickeltem Gefühl für moralische Normen. Die Bürger des Landes, das nicht mehr existiert, sterben durch Kugeln, Messer, Bomben, aber kein einziger von den mehr als zwanzig Millionen Menschen des gewesenen Landes ist vor Scham gestorben und wird es auch nicht. Denn Scham ist eine zutiefst individuelle Empfindung. Wenn ich gefragt werde, WER IST AN ALLDEM SCHULD, sage ich voller Scham: ICH! Und ich meine es ernst: ich bin schuld, weil ich nichts getan habe, um den Krieg aufzuhalten. [...] Meine Aktionen sind unbedeutend, sie waren meist schriftlicher Natur. Zu spät und zu flau habe ich mein Milieu durch das geschriebene Wort aufgestört. Es ist mir nicht einmal gelungen, vor Scham zu sterben. Dass es auch anderen nicht gelungen ist, rechtfertigt mich nicht. Ja, ich bin schuld ... (KL 262 f.)

A. S.: Dann hat die Frau Recht, die in Kopenhagen aus dem Publikum Ihnen die Frage gestellt hat, was Sie als Schriftstellerin und Intellektuelle für Kroatien getan hätten (und sie meinte damit: was Sie getan hätten, um den Krieg zu verhindern)?

D. U.: Der Krieg hat unter anderem den musealen Beruf des *Intellektuellen* wiedererweckt. Wieder erwacht sind die schon vergessenen Phrasen vom *politischen Engagement des Intellektuellen*, von der *Rolle der Verantwortung des Intellektuellen in der Geschichte* usw., usf. Der Krieg hat den moralischen Puls des intellektuellen Europa beschleunigt. Wieder toben verbale Schlachten *pro* und *contra*, die Intellektuellen werden beschuldigt, sie beschuldigen einander, sie kämpfen um *falsch* und *richtig*, um das *wahre* intellektuelle Image, sie wollen dem Beruf des Intellektuellen die verlorene Würde wiedergeben. Der Intellektuelle ist bei den Medien eine gefragte Ware, man fragt ihn wieder, was er über all das *denkt*, er selbst lässt keine Gelegenheit aus, sich über all das *Gedanken zu machen*, ja er ist überzeugt, dass das seine *Pflicht* sei. [...] Dabei wird unser Intellektueller weder von den *Tätern* noch von den *Opfern* gebraucht. [...] Aber sofern er sich engagiert, und sein Engagement ist immer eine BOTSCHAFT, muss er darüber nachdenken, WOHER er seine Botschaft sendet und AN WEN. [...] [U]nser Jugo-Intellektueller [richtet] seine Botschaft meist ans Ausland. Die Ausländer sind die einzigen, die ihn offenbar brauchen oder ihm wenigstens aufmerksam zuhören. Außerdem ist seine Botschaft draußen wenigstens für eine Zeit vor Manipulationen geschützt. Aber dafür geht sie noch offensichtlicher ins Leere. Unser engagierter Intellektueller spielt seine Rolle am falschen Platz, er kämpft weitab vom Schlachtfeld. Und unser Intellektueller wird nolens volens zu einer Art Vorzeigeobjekt. Er wird gern eingeladen, er nimmt die Einladungen immer öfter an, er redet immer öfter und immer autoritärer, ohne zu bemerken, dass er seine Botschaft an die Kollegen richtet. So wird er zum moralischen Psychotherapeuten für seinesgleichen. Sie üben gemeinsam Standpunkte ein, vermehren die Missverständnisse, recken die Fäuste, und alle sind fest überzeugt, gegen das Böse zu fechten. [...] All die ausländischen Kollegen – die Promotoren fremden Unglücks, die Verfechter der Gerechtigkeit auf fremden Terrain [...] – sie alle kommen ihm auf einmal gleichermaßen verloren vor. Der Strudel des Krieges hat sie in seinen Schlund gezogen [...]. Unser Jugo-Intellektueller glaubt sich auf einmal von demselben Albtraum umgeben, vor dem er geflohen war, er sieht dieselben Stereotypen (kann er etwas Besseres anbieten?) über die Entstehung des Krieges, über die Gründe, über die Schuld. Er glaubt, die Kriegsrufe wiederzuerkennen, die Wandlung von Klischees in allgemeingültige Wahrheit, die Wandlung der Wahrheit zum Klischee ... Er hört die Stimmen seiner *Landsleute (Ich habe schon 19... vor alldem gewarnt!)*, denen das Copyright auf die eigene Erklärung wichtiger ist als das Unglück selbst. Unser *goodie* befragt sein Gewissen. *(Wieso habe ich nichts gesehen? [...])* Unser Intellektueller sieht plötzlich, wie leicht aus menschlichem Unglück ein intellektualistischer und künstlerischer *Porno* gemacht werden kann, er sieht die Kollegen Wahrheitsapostel im Kampf um ihre Mediensekunde (ihren *sound bite*), in dem sie das, was noch zu retten ist, retten und (oder) nebenbei das eigene mediale Image auffrischen werden. [...] Und unser Jugo-Intellektueller grübelt, quält sich, mur-

melt in Hamlet-Manier ... Was tun? Reden? Schreiben? Mit Lektüren über den Krieg die Tränendrüsen des Publikums massieren? Für immer verstummen und durch das Schweigen den Krieg verlängern? [...] Dann glaubt unser Jugo-Intellektueller endlich zu wissen, was er tun soll. Ja, er ist überzeugt, dass es das einzige ist, was zu tun lohnt. Ja, er muss sich der Technik des schnellen und lauten *sound bite* anpassen! Und unser Intellektueller kauft sich einen Revolver und schießt ...
... schießt auf Radovan Karadžić! Zuerst auf ihn, und danach kommen alle die anderen an die Reihe ... In der Sekunde, da er das Geschoss abfeuert, ist unser *goodie* fest davon überzeugt, durch seine Tat die lange Kette des Bösen zu zerreißen. Sein nächster Gedanke ist, dass es damit überhaupt nicht getan ist, er setzt den Lauf langsam an die eigene Schläfe und drückt ab. (KL 249–255)

A. S.: Sie kommentieren an einer Stelle eine Karikatur aus dem *New Yorker* vom 22.11.93, worin der Unterhaltungswert der ständigen Kriegsnachrichten vom Balkan herausgehoben wird. Auch hier sprechen Sie davon, dass »die Manager der Todespornographie« (KL 209) das eigene Unglück weiterverkaufen, dass auf dem Balkan die Kunst des Sterbens gezeigt und es mit zunehmender Häufigkeit zum Provinzspektakel würde. Sie schreiben: »Je mehr von uns sterben, desto langweiliger werden wir für die Welt. Nun sind wir Witzfiguren, leblose Materie, aber wir haben es weit gebracht: wir stehen im *New Yorker*« (KL 210). Ist das nicht zynisch? Kommt man mit der Diagnose von Albernheit, Karikatur und Gute-Nacht-Geschichte an die Brisanz des Themas, an – wie Sie es nennen – das »Herz der Angst«?

D. U.: Hätte ich Gelegenheit, die schrecklichen Szenen des 20. Jahrhunderts zusammenzustellen, käme die Fernsehaufzeichnung einer Sitzung des serbischen (restjugoslawischen) Parlaments sicher in die engere Wahl. Da saßen angejahrte, beleibte Männer, die meisten mit gedunsenen Gesichtern, alle etwas ungepflegt, verschwitzt, mit gelockerten Krawatten und halboffenen Hemden. Plötzlich erlaubte sich der am Rednerpult Stehende die UNART, mit einem zerknüllten Zettel nach einem anderen, im Publikum Sitzenden zu werfen. Ein unsichtbarer Magnet zog alle Gesichter in eine Richtung. Dutzende Männer blickten in die Kamera und grinsten. Sie *mussten wissen*, dass ihre Soldaten seit Monaten Sarajevo beschossen, dass sie vergewaltigten, töteten, brandschatzten; sie *mussten wissen*, dass mit ihrem Segen Kroatien und Bosnien zerstört wurden. Es waren die demokratisch gewählten Vertreter derjenigen, die töteten, aber auch derjenigen, die Abfalltonnen nach etwas Essbarem durchwühlten oder eben die Leichen ihrer Söhne begruben. Der *Führer* grinste, und die Abgeordneten grinsten, und alles war auf einmal so lustig. *Mamaaa, sieh mal, was ich gemacht habe*, frohlockten diese Gesichter, denn ALLE hatten *gemacht* und sahen keinen Grund, sich einzeln zu schämen, weil sich nur erwachsene Menschen schämen. (KL 172)

A. S.: Sie schildern hier die serbischen Volksvertreter sarkastisch als kleine Jungs mit Unarten. Wie steht es mit den anderen, mit der Rolle der internationalen Gemeinschaft auf dem Balkan?

D. U.: Slobodan Milošević sprach 1987 auf einem Treffen den historischen Satz: *Von nun an darf euch niemand schlagen!* Mit dem Instinkt des geborenen Führers hat Milošević den infantilen Puls seines Volkes erfühlt. Und die KINDER (die Jungs) stürmten los in der Gewissheit, dass ihnen die UNART namens Krieg verziehen würde. Denn nur erwachsene Menschen sind für ihre Taten verantwortlich.

Das ist natürlich nur ein Blick auf die Dinge. Der nirgends akzeptiert wird. Denn was machen wir dann mit den internationalen Unterhändlern, politischen Foren und Institutionen; was mit der künftigen Geschichte der Nationen; was mit den Gefallenen, den Helden und den vielen Opfern; was mit der Struktur der künftigen Staaten?! Nein, aus Unarten entsteht keine Geschichte. Alle werden eher einem anderen Blick auf die Dinge zuneigen und behaupten, an einer schweren und verantwortungsvollen HISTORISCHEN Aufgabe gearbeitet zu haben. (KL 180 f.)

A. S.: Sie kritisieren die serbischen Jungs, die kroatischen Intellektuellen u. a., alle »Jugos«, die sich von der Idee der Nation haben verführen lassen. Sie kritisieren, so scheint es, auch die internationale Gemeinschaft, die sich von ihrer eigenen Bedeutung als Vermittlerin im Krieg zwischen den Nationen hat verführen lassen. Die Kriege und die Friedensverhandlungen auf dem Balkan scheinen in dieser Perspektive eine durchweg narzisstische Angelegenheit gewesen zu sein?

D. U.: Bisweilen scheint mir, die Balkanvölker führten einen obsessiven, erniedrigenden Kampf um den Nachweis der eigenen Identität, sie sind besessen vom Blick in den Spiegel, von einem Zwangsnarzissmus, vom mühsamen Aufbau der eigenen Absurdität. Aber im Spiegel sehen wir uns nicht selbst, sondern immer jenen ANDEREN, unser Ebenbild, er folgt uns wie ein Schatten. Die unablässige Sorge um das nationale Ego ist eine ermüdende Arbeit, ist Produktion von mythischem Nebel. Nach gewisser Zeit ermatten die Völker, legen die Waffen nieder, versöhnen sich für etwas fünfzig Jahre, und dann beginnt alles von vorn ... (KL 298 f.)

A. S.: Das klingt nach Fatalismus, nach Relativierung, nach Resignation.

D. U.: In allen Teilen Jugoslawiens wird derzeit ein postmodernes Chaos gelebt. Man lebt GLEICHZEITIG Vergangenheit, Gegenwart und Zukunft. Im Mischmasch der Zeiten ist plötzlich alles, was wir wussten, und alles, was wir wissen werden, aufgekeimt und hat sich seine Daseinsberechtigung erkämpft. Nach genau 50 Jahren (1941–1991), fast nach teuflischer Symmetrie, hat wieder der zweite

Weltkrieg begonnen: oft sind es dieselben Dörfer, die niedergebrannt wurden, viele Familien haben symmetrische Schicksale erlebt, viele Kinder und Enkel das Schicksal ihrer Väter und Großväter. Selbst die Waffen sind bisweilen dieselben: in der Not aus den lokalen »Revolutionsmuseen« gestohlene [...] Waffen. [...]

Auf dem Territorium des zerfallenden Jugoslawien wird zugleich auch die Zukunft gelebt, jene postapokalyptische, die den anderen vielleicht noch bevorsteht. [...] Die Gegenwart, in der gestorben wird, gleicht einem permanenten Abspulen von Filmen aus der Vergangenheit und solchen aus der Zukunft. [...] Durch die ständige Wiederholung in den Medien haben Anklagen und Lügen ihre grausame Realität verloren. Die Menschen sehen auf dem Bildschirm ihren eigenen Tod, sie wissen nur nicht, ob das Geschoss, das sie treffen wird, von der Straße oder aus dem Fernsehgerät kommt. Was ohnehin egal ist, denn wir sind im Grunde schon alle tot. *Oder wir sind schon tot, nur dass wie bei Toten unsere Nägel noch wachsen, zu Krallen werden*, schrieb der Dichter Abdulah Sidran aus Sarajevo. Die Wiederholung des Schreckens entwertet den Schrecken, die Wiederholung des Bösen entkleidet es seiner Schwere. Schließlich und endlich ist ja gar nichts geschehen, wenn das, was geschieht, nur ein Zitat dessen ist, was bereits geschehen ist, und wenn das, was geschieht, nur das ist, was geschehen wird. (KL 128 ff.)

A. S.: Sie sprechen die Rolle der Medien in der Kriegsberichterstattung an, die ja in Deutschland im Zuge von Peter Handkes Medienschelte heftig diskutiert worden ist. Welchen Anteil haben die Medien an der Kriegsführung?

D. U.: Können die Medien einen Krieg auslösen? Ich gestatte mir die These, dass der Krieg in Jugoslawien vor einigen Jahren vom Gesäß eines unschuldigen serbischen Bauern ausgegangen ist. Bis heute erinnere ich mich an seinen Namen: Martinović. Der bedauernswerte Bauer, der angeblich mit einer Flasche im After gefunden wurde, war monatelang das Thema vieler jugoslawischer, vor allem serbischer, Zeitungen und Fernsehstationen. Die einen behaupteten, Martinović sei von Albanern mit einer Bierflasche vergewaltigt worden, die anderen, Martinović sei pervers und habe sich mit der Flasche selbstbefriedigt. Die dritten hingegen, Serben hätten Martinović vergewaltigt, um den Albanern die Schuld zuzuschieben. Die vierten, gründlicheren, errechneten anhand der Verletzung, Martinović müsse vom Baum auf die Flasche gesprungen sein. Die vielköpfige und leidgeprüfte Martinović-Familie zeugte zugunsten ihres Oberhaupts, Ärzteteams stritten öffentlich um die verschiedenen Möglichkeiten der Verletzung oder Selbstverletzung. Vom Klinikbett aus schickte Martinović den besorgten TV-Zuschauern ein schwaches Lächeln. Die Medien machten aus seinem After ein politisches Spektakel im balkanischen Geist. So bekräftigte der Fall Martinović den Glauben des serbischen Volkes, dass der Entschluss von Slobodan Milošević – unter Bruch der jugoslawischen Verfassung die Autonomie des Kosovo und der Vojvodina aufzuheben – mehr als gerecht sei! So gewöhnten sich die Massen daran, leidenschaftlich und im Kollektiv an der unglückseligen und geschmacklosen Medienstory teilzunehmen. (KL 109 f.)

A. S.: Das disqualifiziert die einheimischen Medien als glaubwürdige, verantwortungsvolle Berichterstatter und macht sie zu Spielbällen des plebejischen und auch parlamentarischen Populismus. Sind die Medien, zugespitzt formuliert, dumm? Ist der Medienkonsument genauso Spielball der Medien, auch in Westeuropa?

D. U.: Der Führer der bosnischen Serben und unbezweifelbare Kriegsverbrecher Radovan Karadžić ist ein bei vielen westlichen Medien beliebtes Thema. Wenn es um ihn geht, arbeiten diese Medien aus unbekannten Gründen meist mit Großaufnahme. Vielleicht, damit Karadžić (der gelernte Psychiater) besser mit seinen »Klienten« im Westen kommunizieren kann. Ich stelle mir einen westlichen Leser / Zuschauer im bequemen Sessel vor. Zuerst empfindet er heimliche Genugtuung, weil er Gott sei Dank nicht in diesem schrecklichen Land lebt [...]. Dann betrachtet er den dicken Kopf des »Heiducken« aus den bosnischen Urwäldern und gibt sich für einen Moment romantischen Phantasien über einen Gangster hin, der die ganze Welt an der Nase herumführt. Danach verscheucht er die ungehörigen Phantasien und entsetzt sich aufrichtig über den Vandalismus der »Heiducken«. Schließlich schaltet er den Fernseher aus, faltet die Zeitung zusammen. Mein fiktiver westlicher Medienkonsument ist dabei irgendwie erleichtert. Er ahnt nicht, dass der dunkle Schatten von Karadžić bereits in seinem Sessel sitzt und ihn, den Besitzer von Sessel und Zeitung, in den Händen hält! (KL 127)

A. S.: Wenn ich zum Ende unseren Interviews zusammenfasse, was Sie als kroatischstämmiger »Niemand« (KL 299) im Exil (denn das möchten Sie ja sein) und als bedeutende Autorin, die ihr Herkunftsland kritisch beobachtet, entfaltet haben, ergibt sich ein eigentümliches, ja paradoxes Bild – etwas verkürzt gesprochen: Sie suchen die Quelle des Hasses und zerstreuen sie überall; sie individualisieren und personalisieren Schuld und finden sie zugleich im Kollektiv und seinen vereinheitlichenden Konzepten und Beschwörungsformeln; Sie reden von Schuld und Verantwortung und von Jungenstreichen; Sie trauen dem Intellektuellen viel und nichts zu; Sie banalisieren und dramatisieren; Sie sind fatalistisch und fragen nach der Verantwortung und der Freiheit des Einzelnen; Sie virtualisieren und holen das Virtuelle in die unentrinnbare reale Gegenwart; Sie kritisieren das Ausland und können nur dort leben; Ihnen bleibt angesichts der Dummheit der Medien das Lachen im Halse stecken und Sie warnen vor der Klugheit der Medien. Besteht die ›Wahrheit‹ bzw. etwas weniger pathetisch: die Herausforderung, die diese Kriege in Jugoslawien (wie ja auch jeder andere Krieg) uns stellen, darin, die Dinge von zwei Seiten zu betrachten? Muss das Sprechen über den Krieg einem Palindrom gleichen, das von zwei Seiten, vorwärts und rückwärts, von Westen nach Osten, von oben nach unten (und immer vice versa) gelesen werden kann und muss? Sie deuten das in Ihrem Essay über den Palindrom-Skandal an, in dem das von einer kroatischen Autorin namens Dubravka Oraić 1981 verfasste Palindrom, das eine für 1991 vorausgesehene Apokalypse zum Thema hat, sich 1991 als Wahrheit entrollt: Die Apokalypse bricht tatsächlich mit dem Kriegsbeginn herein.

D. U.: Im Poem von Dubravka Oraić ereignet sich die Apokalypse im Jahr 1991, dem Jahr, das vor- und rückwärts gleich lautet. [...]. Die Wirklichkeit hatte sich binnen eines Jahrzehnts so entrollt, wie es ihr eingerolltes Palindrom diktierte. [...] Das Kunstwerk war zur Wahrheit geworden. [...] In dem Augenblick, da sie ihr eigenes Poem wie ein Horoskop liest – dessen Voraussagen eingetroffen sind bis auf das Ende, für das noch Zeit ist –, wünscht sich Dubravka Oraić nur eins: dass die Wirklichkeit verschwindet, dass das Poem bleibt, was es war – ein Spiel, ein künstlerisches Werk. Der Geist des Palindroms ist schon aus der Flasche befreit, es ist zu spät. In diesem Augenblick, da sie die blutige Realität liest wie das eigene Poem, wünscht sich Dubravka nur eins: dass das Poem zu dem wird, was es ursprünglich war – zu einer eindeutigen Sprache, der Sprache Einer Wahrheit, weil es nur Eine Wahrheit geben kann.

Denn ihr in der kleinen kroatischen Sprache geschriebener Palindrom-Rosenkranz – ein unbekanntes, verkanntes Meisterwerk kroatischer Literatur – liest sich von links ebenso wie von rechts, in kroatischer Sprache, aber auch in serbischer, in lateinischer Schrift, aber auch in kyrillischer, die Wahrheit des Palindroms ist hier, auf der linken Seite, aber wie behauptet wird, auch dort, auf der rechten, von Westen und Osten liest sich alles gleich!

In der Wirklichkeit sprechen die tödlich verfeindeten Seiten des gequälten Landes kroatisch, aber auch serbisch, und gestorben wird auf beiden Seiten. Die Wahrheit ist auf unserer Seite – ruft es von links nach rechts. Die Wahrheit ist auf unserer Seite – ruft es von rechts nach links. Aber man tötet uns! tönt es von links nach rechts. Aber man tötet uns! tönt es von rechts nach links. *O Jugo! O gujo!* (O Jugoslawien! O Schlange!) [...]

Die Sprache des Palindroms ist freigelassen wie der Flaschengeist. Die Wahrheit verwandelt sich wie ein Wüstenphänomen in zwei gleiche! Zwei Wahrheiten sind zwei Wahrheiten, sind zwei Lügen, zwei Wahrheiten sind eine Lüge. Eine von beiden ist Lüge ...

Diese bittere, schreckliche Farce hatte niemand vorausgesehen. Vorausgesehen hatte sie das Palindrom.

Der Geist des Palindroms, aus der Flasche befreit, kriecht rückwärts seinem Ende, seinem Anfang entgegen, er schlingt sich um unseren Hals wie eine Schlange, würgt uns, nimmt uns den Atem.

O Jugo! O gujo! (KL 40–45)

Miranda Jakiša

Postdramatisches Bühnen-Tribunal: Gerichtstheater rund um das ICTY[1]

In der erstmals 2010 auf die Bühne gebrachten Aufführung *Kukavičluk* (dt: *Feigheit*) des Theaterregisseurs Oliver Frljić wird einer strittigen Fragen der politischen und gesellschaftlichen Gegenwart Nachjugoslawiens, der Frage nach der Schuld und dem Umgang mit Srebrenica, mit Formen des *Gerichtstheaters* begegnet. Theater und Gericht als kulturelle Praxis und performatives Geschehen gehen auseinander hervor. Der gemeinsame Ursprung von Theater und Gericht hat die Kulturwissenschaften in den letzten Jahren ebenso beschäftigt wie die postdramatische Theorie und Praxis, vor deren Hintergrund die hier behandelte Aufführung entsteht.

Der Frankfurter Theaterwissenschaftler Hans-Thies Lehmann beschreibt in seiner paradigmatischen Studie *Postdramatisches Theater* das *theatron* der griechischen Antike als Orientierungs- und Fluchtpunkt der re-politisierten theatralen Praxis der Gegenwart. Das antike Theater und das antike Gericht teilten sich als produktive Begegnungs- und öffentliche Verhandlungsstätte ein und denselben Schauplatz, der allen Anwesenden Partizipationsmöglichkeiten einräumte. Das postdramatische Theater stellt an sich den Anspruch, im Sinne dieses antiken Vorbilds das theatrale Geschehen zu demokratisieren und den im Guckkastenprinzip des (bürgerlichen) dramatischen Theaters zur Passivität verdammten Zuschauer in seine ›Verhandlungen‹ wieder einzubinden. In postdramatischen Theaterformen, die gerade südslawische Bühnen zur Zeit entscheidend prägen, offenbart sich ein verändertes Verhältnis des Theaters zum öffentlichen Raum[2] wie auch der Wunsch der Theatermacher, den Zuschauer wieder selbst über gemeinschaftliche Fragen »urteilen«[3] zu lassen.

Wie eng Theaterspielen und Gerichthalten auch aus der Warte des Gerichts miteinander in Wechselbeziehung stehen, hat Cornelia Vismann eindrücklich als »theatrales Dispositiv« des Gerichthaltens in ihrer Studie *Medien der Recht-*

---

[1] Beim vorliegenden Beitrag handelt es sich um eine geringfügig geänderte Fassung von: Miranda Jakiša: Die Evidenz Srebrenicas: Oliver Frljićs Theatergericht in *Kukavičluk*, in: Susi Frank/Schamma Schahadat (Hg.): Evidenz und Zeugenschaft. Poetische und mediale Strategien im Umgang mit dem Unzugänglichen, Wien 2012, S. 115–133.
[2] Vgl. Primavesi: Orte und Strategien postdramatischer Theaterformen, S. 9.
[3] Lehmann: Das Politische Schreiben, S. 19.

sprechung beschrieben. Die »Gerichtsbarkeit ist vollkommen den Bedingungen des Theaters angepasst«[4], hält sie fest. Das Entstehen des Gerichts aus der Versammlung um ein Ding, um eine strittige Sache also, hat »dem Gerichthalten performative Züge« aufgeprägt.[5] Die strittige Sache muss, bevor über sie entschieden werden kann, für alle Anwesenden zunächst zur Darstellung gebracht, d. h. auf der Bühne des Gerichts den Beteiligten vor Augen gestellt werden.

In der Verbindung, die Formen des Gericht-Haltens mit theatraler Praxis in *Kukavičluk* eingehen, spielen drei Ebenen des vergegenwärtigenden Vor-Augen-Stellens und damit der per öffentlichem Tribunal herzustellenden Gerechtigkeit eine Rolle. Zuallererst sind es rhetorische Verfahren der Vergegenwärtigung überhaupt, die eine (strittige) Sache vor Gericht wie im Theater zur Darstellung bringen und sie performativ aktualisieren. Es geht dann im Wortlaut der Quintilianschen Rhetorik darum, das Publikum »gleichsam gegenwärtig in den Vorgang zu versetzen«, der zur Debatte steht, und es damit qua Macht der Rede durch konkretisierende Detaillierung zum Augenzeugen zu machen.[6] Dieses Vor-Augen-Stellen der Sache gehört in die *narratio* und dient in der gerichtlichen wie theatralen Rede der plausibilisierenden, zudem im Sinne der Parteimeinung affekterregenden Ausgestaltung des Sachverhalts. In Frljić's Umsetzung wird dies mit der schlichten Evidenz Srebrenicas bewerkstelligt, für die ein Dokument, die Namensliste, in der Performanz des Verlesens zur Vergegenwärtigung selbst wird (»3. Die Evidenz Srebrenicas«).

Zweitens führt das Theater spätestens seit den historischen Avantgarden den Zuschauer als aktiven, bewussten und ermächtigten Teilnehmer der Aufführung immer wieder in Situationen vergegenwärtigter Gemeinschaftlichkeit zurück (»2. Zuschauerzeugen und Aussagepflicht«). Hier geht es nicht mehr nur um das reine Nach- und Wiedererleben des Tathergangs, es geht darum, sich gegenseitig als anwesend zu erfahren und sich, mit vernehmbaren Stimmen versehen, wechselseitig anzuerkennen. Die Theorie der Postdramatik idealisiert (theoretisch mit Rancières »Aufteilung des Sinnlichen« aufgerüstet) das antike Gerichthalten als Praxis gemeinschaftlicher Verantwortungsübernahme. Das Gerichtssetting wird zur Vorlage für das Ausgestalten des Theaterraums zum Raum der Begegnung – eine Erweiterung, die sich entlang der »Theatron-Achse«[7] zwischen Zuschauerraum und Szene vollzieht. In der Durchbrechung der Vierten Wand des dramatischen Theaters durch Vergegenwärtigungsverfahren, die die Zeugenschaft des Publikums zur bewussten, gemeinschaftlichen Erfahrung im ›Hier und Jetzt‹ machen, soll politische Mitverantwortung aktiviert und zum integralen Bestandteil des Theaters gemacht werden.

[4] Vismann: Medien der Rechtsprechung, S. 17.
[5] Ebd.
[6] Ueding: Grundriss der Rhetorik, S. 285.
[7] Lehmann: Postdramatisches Theater.

Und drittens bietet das theatrale Dispositiv des Gerichts sich durch seine Strukturparallelität von vorneherein für eine Übertragung des Gerichts ins (engagierte) Theater an (»1. Gerichtstheater/Theatergericht«). Wenn der Richter als Regisseur der Gerichtsaufführung[8]) die Rollen aller am Gericht Beteiligten kontrollieren und in Szene setzen kann, ist es dann nicht auch am Regisseur, wenn nötig, per Aufführung Gericht zu halten? In einem solchen Gerichtstheater der fingierten Augenzeugenschaft spielen sowohl der Zuschauer als Zeuge, das Publikum als Öffentlichkeit wie auch die Mittel der Darstellung bei der Beweisaufnahme und Falldarstellung erneut eine, nunmehr gedoppelte, Rolle – als Teil des Gerichts und als Teil des Theaters. Ich beginne also, die Reihenfolge umkehrend, hinten bei der wechselseitigen Vergegenwärtigung des jeweils anderen durch das Theater und das Gericht.

1. Gerichtstheater / Theatergericht

Die Theaterförmigkeit des Gerichts selbst ins Gericht zu nehmen bleibt, Cornelia Vismann zufolge, dem Theater, aus dem das Gericht hervorgeht, vorbehalten.[9] Auch lässt sich natürlich nie eindeutiger als per Gerichtsaufführung eine strittige Sache in Szene setzen und kaum direkter Anklage erheben. Heinrich von Kleists *Der zerbrochene Krug* stellt für Vismann den Prototyp für die Übertragung des Gerichts ins Theater und für die Inszenierung einer Anklage dar. An Kleists Theaterstück wurde so manches Mal exemplifiziert, dass »nichts näher [liegt], als das Geschehen von der einen auf die andere Bühne zu verlagern«[10], keinesfalls jedoch, um das bloße Verurteilen und Gerichthalten zu doppeln, sondern um das Wesen des Theaters wie das Wesen des Gerichts in der Verschiebung auszuleuchten. Auf zeitgenössischen Bühnen hat das Gericht wieder einmal Konjunktur, und zwar gerade da, wo es um das jeweilige Wesen der performativen Praxis geht, sei diese nun Performance, Postdramatisches Theater, Reenactment oder Aktion.

Oliver Frljić's Aufführung *Kukavičluk*, im Dezember 2010 in Subotica in der Vojvodina an der serbisch-ungarischen Grenze erstaufgeführt, hält nun ein Gerichtstheater ab, das offensichtlich in der verhandelten und dargestellten Sache eklatanten (im wörtlichen Sinne von éclat = Lärm, plötzlicher Krach) Klärungsbedarf reklamiert. In dem provokanten Stück, das auf dem renommierten Theaterfestival *Sterijino Pozorje* 2011 in Novi Sad mit dem Preis für die beste Aufführung und dem Preis für die beste Regie ausgezeichnet wurde, findet nicht nur ein

---

[8] Vismann: Medien der Rechtsprechung, S. 17.
[9] Ebd., S. 38 ff.
[10] Ebd., S. 38.

Gericht auf der Bühne statt (Theatergericht), die Aufführung selbst inszeniert ein regelrechtes Tribunal[11] (Gerichtstheater) im Theatron, dem erweiterten Zuschauerraum. Die Gerichtsrollen (Richter, Kläger, Angeklagter, Zeugen, Öffentlichkeit), die die Schauspieler, der Regisseur, das Publikum und die Gemeinschaft aller Anwesenden im Theater in dieser Gerichtsaufführung zugewiesen bekommen, rotieren laufend, so dass die Aufführung auch nie zur schlichten Verschiebung von einer Bühne auf die andere, zur Deklassierung also des Theaters zum Gerichtssaal gerät. Stattdessen bleibt das Theater des Gerichthaltens (Gerichtstheater) in der Aufführung durchweg mit dem Gerichthalten des Theaters (Theatergericht), die theatrale Form mit der ›strittigen Sache‹ verschränkt. Kollektive Schuld, Verantwortungsverweigerung und prekäres Erinnern, die zentralen Themen, die *Kukavičluk* antastet, lassen sich in der Aufführung, die im Wechsel Theatergericht und Gerichtstheater ist, nie von der Anklage an das Theater selbst trennen.

Mit Akzent auf das Gerichtstheater beginnt *Kukavičluk* mit der unter Tränen hervorgestoßenen Aussage einer einzelnen Darstellerin in Form eines Prologs, dass alles, was in der Aufführung gesagt werden wird, weder der Wahrheit noch der Meinung der Beteiligten entspricht. Sie und die übrigen Schauspieler seien vom namentlich genannten Regisseur, Oliver Frljić, gezwungen worden, diese Sätze auszusprechen. Die Aufführung setzt somit mit der Rahmung von Theater ein und spielt auf die postdramatische Abkehr von ›König Text‹[12] an, die Schauspieler nicht als Unbeteiligte und wortgetreu eine feststehende Textvorlage Ausagierende verstehen will. Doch die emotionale Klage deutet zugleich auch in eine andere Richtung, die, erzwungener Aussagen vor einem öffentlichen Gericht. Die a priori Problematisierung der Schauspieler-Rolle im Theater, die hier geschieht, wird nicht zuletzt dadurch, dass die Darsteller in *Kukavičluk* später auch als Zeugen der Geschehnisse in Serbien in den 1990er Jahren auftreten werden, zur Problematisierung der Rollen vor Gericht. Wenn Aussagen von der Rolle des Sprechers in der Aufführung abhängig sind, so hat auch die Zeugenaussage in der Gerichtsaufführung nicht den Wahrheitsfindungswert, den ihr das Gericht einräumt? Die Einzelstimme im Prolog setzt fort, alle stünden hier ja vor Gericht, aber kollektive Schuld »eines ganzen Volkes« könne es doch gar nicht geben. Die damit eingeführte ›Schuld Serbiens‹, die das Publikum mit einschließt (*Kukavičluk* wurde nur in der Vojvodina in Subotica und in Novi Sad aufgeführt), wird als Thema der Aufführung in der ersten Szene (nun mit dem Akzent mehr auf dem Theatergericht) deutlich herausgestellt. Weitere sieben Darsteller betreten die Bühne und wiederholen wortgetreu (brüllend und im Chor) Miloševićs berüchtigte Gazimestan-Rede. Dabei hält jede/r ein Milošević-Plakat in den Händen.

---

[11] Vom Unterschied zwischen Gericht und Tribunal wird noch zu sprechen sein.
[12] Lehmann: Just a word on a page and there is the drama.

Miloševićs Rede, die der Internationale Gerichtshof ICTY in der Untersuchung gegen den Angeklagten ins Feld führte, dient hier auch dem Gerichtstheater als Dokument der Beweisaufnahme und zugleich als Vergegenwärtigungsszenario für unliebsame gemeinsame Erinnerungen im Aufführungsraum des Theaters. In einer *translatio temporum* wird Vergangenes als Gegenwärtiges auf die Bühne geholt und die Person Miloševićs in einer Mischung aus *prosopopeia* und *fictio personae* (sprechen die Plakate oder ein re-animierter Milošević?) den Zuschauern vor Augen gestellt. Als »Katachrese des Gesichts«[13] gibt Milošević hier einem noch Unbenannten, der Schuld und der Verantwortung für Geschehenes, ein Gesicht. Am Beispiel des damaligen Staatspräsidenten, dessen Verfahren in Den Haag urteilslos eingestellt wurde musste, weil er 2006 in Gefangenschaft starb, hat auch Peter Handke die Natur der Zeugenschaft und das »außer Kontrolle geratene Schuldspruchtheater«[14] ins Visier genommen. Das Gericht um Milošević »spielte Welttribunal«[15] und hätte als inszeniertes »Großes Welttheater« »wie jedes Theater«, so Handke, bestenfalls nebenbei »diese oder jene Wahrheit mit sich«[16] gebracht. Handkes polemische Prozessbeobachtung, die er in *Rund um das Große Tribunal* (2003) und *Die Tablas von Daimiel* (2006) festgehalten hat, steht im erklärten Widerspruch zu Madeleine Albrights vielzitiertem Ausspruch anlässlich der Einsetzung des Tribunals: »This is no victor's tribunal, the only victor here is truth.«

Handke, der den Wortlaut in späteren Interviews relativiert, spricht in seinen Schriften zum Jugoslawientribunal dem ICTY, das »falsch ist und falsch bleibt«[17], jegliche Legitimität als Gericht ab (»keinerlei Rechtsbasis«[18]). Jürgen Brokoff hat an eben den Tribunal-Texten Handkes herausgestellt, dass sie die ambivalente Struktur zwischen ordentlichem Gericht und ›Welttribunal‹ vorführen. Handke setze letztlich einen doppelten Tribunalbegriff um, der einerseits das um eine außergerichtliche Öffentlichkeit erweiterte Tribunal »als das falsche Gericht«[19] ablehnt, andererseits aber Handke literarisch zum »Befürworter einer Tribunalisierung« erhebt, denn seinen Texten ginge es, wie dem Tribunal als solchem, um den Kampf um Wahrheit.[20] Brokoff folgt hier Vismanns Unterscheidung von Gericht und Tribunal, in denen jeweils das agonale oder das theatrale Dispositiv vorherrscht.

---

13 Menke: Prosopopoiia, S. 229.
14 Handke: Die Tablas von Daimiel, S. 18.
15 Ebd., S. 19.
16 Ebd.
17 Ebd., S. 30.
18 Ebd., S. 12.
19 Ebd., S. 30.
20 Vgl. dazu den Beitrag von Jürgen Brokoff in diesem Band.

Die Unterscheidung von Gericht und Tribunal, die Handke an der Trennlinie zwischen Legitimität und Selbstermächtigung entlang für Serbien zieht, ist auch für Frljićs Theatergericht von Bedeutung. Das Tribunal als adhoc-Gericht bleibt stets von einer gewissen Voreingenommenheit gebrandmarkt, die daraus hervorgeht, dass das Tribunal ›außerrechtlich‹ ist, d. h. nicht bestehendes Recht anwendet, sondern im Nachhinein Recht setzt.[21] Das Tribunal, für das eine Öffentlichkeit konstitutiv ist, will entmachten. Es weiß bereits vor jeglicher Verhandlung, wie diese auszugehen hat. Ein Tribunal – man denke nur an die Nürnberger Prozesse – macht auch »einem überwundenen Regime den Prozess«[22] und erklärt dessen Justiz selbst zum Gegenstand des Verfahrens. Und eben hier offenbaren sich zwei zentrale Überschneidungen von Tribunalorganisation und postdramatischem Theater, die *Kukavičluk* in den Fokus des Gerichtstheaters rückt: die wesenhafte Rolle der Zuschauergemeinschaft als Öffentlichkeit und die Abkanzelung eines falschen Regimes. Ging historisch das ursprüngliche Tribunal, abgehalten im Freien durch einen Tribun und die interessierte, anwesende, potentiell stets erweiterbare Öffentlichkeit in das im geschlossenen Raum stattfindende ordentliche Gericht über, so machte das Theater im 20. Jh. den entgegengesetzten Anlauf. Davor aber folgte das Theater dem Gericht und endete, von Bert Brecht und Erwin Piscator prominent kritisiert, als geschlossener Guckkasten. Das Gericht, das die Teilnahme an seinen Verhandlungen reglementiert und Zuschauer nur als Unbeteiligte (wer spricht, wird des Gerichtssaals verwiesen) zulässt, hat Ähnlichkeit mit dem Drama des bürgerlichen Theaters, das durch den Vorhang, die Beleuchtung und die Geschlossenheit seiner Abläufe den Zuschauer vom Theatergeschehen trennt. Die Postdramatik hingegen re-tribunalisiert; sie versucht eine große, partizipierende Öffentlichkeit performativ etwa durch Aufführungsorte im Freien oder durch an das Publikum gerichtete Aktivierungsstrategien zu erschaffen, die bis hin zur Bedrohung des anwesenden Publikums reichen können.

Frljićs Theatergericht erweist sich bei näherer Betrachtung tatsächlich als Gericht mit Tribunalstruktur, das einerseits die ›Tribunalisierung‹ als theaterhistorisch notwendige und willkommene Erweiterung der Mitentscheider feiert (Publikumsinvolvierung),[23] zugleich jedoch das überhebliche Welt-Tribunal und die Tribunalisierung als kollektiv (traumatische) Erfahrung einer Region theatral zur Verhandlung stellt. Die Theatralität des Internationalen Strafgerichtshofs ICTY, des International Criminal Tribunal for the former Yugoslavia, wird dabei auf eine Weise ausgestellt, dass sie auf das Urteilen im Theater zurückfällt. Das Gericht im Theater dient somit der Vergegenwärtigung der Theatralität des Ge-

---

[21] Vgl. Vismann: Medien der Rechtsprechung, S. 160–163.
[22] Ebd., S. 161.
[23] Zur Einbeziehung des Zuschauers ins Theater siehe Fischer-Lichte: Die Entdeckung des Zuschauers.

richts wie der Vergegenwärtigung des Theaters als Ort der Urteilsfindung und des Schuldspruchs. Wenn Kleist in *Der zerbrochene Krug* das Theater über die Gerichtsform verhandelt, so dient Frljić die Gerichtsform des Tribunals dazu, in *Kukavičluk* neben der postdramatischen Selbstverpflichtung zur Zuschauereinbindung auch die Grenzen dieses postdramatischen Theatron-Mantras aufzuzeigen. Ein Theater-Gericht, das sich illegitim und selbstgerecht unzulässige Freiheiten herausnimmt, kann eben selbst auch zum Tribunal verkommen.

2. Zuschauerzeugen und Aussagepflicht

Wie unangenehm Theater für den Zuschauer, die Darsteller und den Aufführungskontext werden kann, dafür steht im nachjugoslawischen Theater gerade Oliver Frljić wie kein anderer: Die Zuschauerbrüskierung ist, wie die politisch-gesellschaftliche Intervention, kalkuliert und in seinen Aufführungen weitaus vorhersehbar. Zuschauer verlassen (wegen gleichgeschlechtlicher Küsse, anti-nationalistischer Statements, pädophiler Priesterfiguren, Requisiten aus rohem Fleisch etc.) empört Frljićs Vorstellungen, seine Inszenierung von Euripides' *Bakchen* in Split wurde vom Intendanten Milan Štrljić (wenn auch nur für wenige Stunden) verboten und vom bosnischen Schauspieler und Kultusminister des Kantons Sarajevo, Emir Hadžihafizbegović, erhielt Oliver Frljić publik gewordene Drohanrufe, weil er dessen O-Ton aus den 1990er Jahren für ein Theaterprojekt verwendet hat. Während diese Art von kalkuliertem Einspruch mehr auf die Zurschaustellung ›unzulässiger‹, tabuisierter politischer und gesellschaftlicher Inhalte und Haltungen baut,[24] interessiert *Kukavičluk* zusätzlich die Frage der operablen und zulässigen Form, in der der Zuschauer zum Zeugen von im Theater ausgesprochenen ›Wahrheiten‹ gemacht wird.

Kukavičluk, das wie die meisten gegenwärtigen postjugoslawischen Aufführungen die sekundäre Augenzeugenschaft (des Theaterzuschauers) in Beziehung zur primären Augenzeugenschaft (des Zeugen historischer Ereignisse) setzt,[25] scheut sich nicht, zugleich die Begrenztheit des theatralen Bezeugens kritisch aufzugreifen, das zuletzt großen Zuspruch sowohl auf der Bühne als auch in den Theaterwissenschaften erfahren hat. »Theater schafft Zeugen«[26], schreibt Sybille Krämer und meint damit den postdramatischen Anspruch, das Theater

---

[24] Frljić hat sich mehrfach in Interviews zur Zurückgebliebenheit des kroatischen und allgemein nachjugoslawischen Publikums geäußert, dem im internationalen Vergleich kaum etwas zuzumuten sei und gerade daher zugemutet werden muss.
[25] Weitere Beispiele sind hier u. a. die Aufführungen Selma Spahićs, Dino Mustafićs, Borut Šeparovićs oder Biljana Srbljanovićs.
[26] Krämer: Zuschauer zu Zeugen machen, S. 19.

als »öffentlichen und zugleich politischen Schauplatz« und als »ereignishafte Begegnung von Akteuren und Zuschauern« wieder einzusetzen.[27]

Der Zuschauer, der zum teilnehmenden Zeugen gemacht wird, hat Mit-Verantwortung für das, was er/sie leibhaftig erfahren, mit eigenen Augen und Ohren wahrgenommen hat. Das gilt für die Theater- wie Geschichtserfahrung gleichermaßen. Frljić setzt an dieser, mittlerweile etablierten Vorstellung an, dass das Gewahr-Werden seiner selbst über den Vergegenwärtigungsprozess des Publikums auch das Theater als Spielort in die Aufmerksamkeit rückt. Das solchermaßen in den Fokus geratende Theater kann auch nicht mehr außerhalb eines gesellschaftlichen Kontextes wahrgenommen werden. Die per Partizipation fühlbar gemachte Gegenwart muss – folgt man den Diskussionen der Theatermacher und Performancekünste – im Verlauf der Aufführung dann aber ›auseinanderbrechen‹, um nicht bloße Entlarvung, nicht schlicht öffentliche Entrüstung über das Gezeigte zu sein.[28] Nur in der »Unterbrechung« seiner selbst kann das postdramatische Theater, dem Frankfurter Theaterwissenschaftler Hans-Thies Lehmann zufolge, zum wirklich Politischen finden, indem es eben nicht einfach politische Themen inszeniert, sondern die »trügerische Unschuld des Zuschauers« stört und diesen die »schwankenden Voraussetzungen des eigenen Urteilens erfahren lasse«[29]. Über das Wie der Darstellung, nicht über das Angreifen von Missständen, werde dann der »Kern der Sozialität selbst«[30] kritisch offengelegt. Diese, doch deutlich an die Brechtsche Tradition anknüpfende, Idealisierung des politischen Einflusses von Theater erfährt für nachjugoslawische Bühnen sogar noch eine Zuspitzung durch den allgegenwärtigen Anspruch an die Künste, widerständige Gegenorte zur prekären Gegenwart anzubieten.

Avanciert theoretisiert hat die Frage des Dissenses in der Kunst Jacques Rancière, auf den die Debatte im Theater stets bezogen bleibt. Im aus *Le Partage du sensible. Esthétique et politique* (2000) entwickelten Verständnis von Postdramatik als politisch und gesellschaftlich verpflichtetem Theater, verlangen Bühnen von sich, »Unrecht sichtbar zu machen«[31]. Rancière, an dem sich die komplette gegenwärtige Theatergeneration der in den 1970er und 80er Jahren Geborenen abarbeitet, macht in *Die Aufteilung des Sinnlichen* einen Unterschied zwischen »Politik« als sichtbar gemachtem Dissens und »Polizei«, die den Raum alles Sag- und Machbaren ordnet und allen Plätze in dieser Ordnung zuweist. Was gemeinhin unter Politik gefasst wird, entspricht in Rancières Terminologie der »Polizei«. Es ist eben diese »Polizei«, die der Gleichheit im erzwungenen Erhalt von Konsens Unrecht tut. Konsens erfordert schließlich stets Ausschluss. Rancière verlangt nun

---

27 Primavesi: Theater/Politik, S. 47.
28 Lehmann: Das Politische Schreiben, S. 21.
29 Ebd., S. 19.
30 Ebd., S. 21.
31 Bandi/Kraft/Lasinger: Kunst, Politik und Polizei im Denken Jacques Rancières, S. 174.

von der Kunst, die Konturierung und Verschiebung der Grenze zwischen den von der Ordnung Vorgesehenen und den von ihr Ausgeschlossenen als ständigem Prozess. Aufgabe der Kunst, die sich so verstanden nicht von Politik trennen lässt, ist es für Rancière entsprechend, nicht politisch im Sinne einer engagierten Kunst zu sein, sondern das Potential ihrer »prinzipiellen Unerfüllbarkeit« für einen kurzen Augenblick erfahrbar zu machen. Nur darin hat sie emanzipatorischen, wahrhaft politischen Charakter und setzt die fundamentale Gleichheit aller, die nicht Ziel, sondern Voraussetzung von Politik ist, stets aufs Neue wieder ein. Für Frljić stellt Rancières ›Kunst in der Verantwortung‹ einen zentralen Referenzpunkt in seiner postdramatischen Bühnenarbeit dar.[32]

Wie, fragt *Kukavičluk*, gehen die Darstellung des Prekären, der Kriegsverbrechen, der traumatischen Transformationen mit dem per Theatermittel herzustellenden Ausnahmezustand einer ästhetischen Unterbrechung Hand in Hand? Kann Theater den utopischen Verheißungsmoment prinzipieller Unerfüllbarkeit tatsächlich aufblitzen lassen, ohne zugleich auch »Polizei« zu werden? Auf welche Weise soll Theater politisch werden, ohne politische Inhalte zur Darstellung zu bringen? Und: Kann der Zuschauer überhaupt zum emanzipierten, selbstverantwortlichen Teilnehmer von Aufführungen im Sinne des postdramatischen Anspruchs gemacht werden?

Erika Fischer-Lichte hat in Ästhetik des Performativen mit dem systemtheoretischen Begriff der »autopoietischen feedback-Schleife« umschrieben, auf welche Weise ethische Kategorien über Formen der hergestellten, zugelassenen oder erzwungen Zuschauerpartizipation seit den Sechzigerjahren und vermittelt über die Performancekunst Einzug ins Theater hielten.[33] Das Publikum dynamisiert in der feedback-Schleife durch steten Rollenwechsel der Mitwirkenden das Subjekt-Objekt Verhältnis im Theater mit. Dafür muss es seiner selbst als an der Aufführung beteiligt gewahr werden; Teilnahme wird somit nicht schlicht vorgeführt, sie wird in der Präsenz erfahrbar gemacht. Gegenwart wird als ›gedehnter Augenblick‹ in der Performanz erlebbar, um dann als singuläres, unwiederholbares Ereignis vom Zuschauer bezeugt zu werden (vgl. dazu *liveliness*[34]).

Die Herstellung von Gegenwärtigkeit, von Präsenz gehört somit zu den zentralen Vorhaben und ist zugleich auch ein Effekt des Performativen und der Konzeption von Postdramatischem Theater. Auch in der Bühnenarbeit und den Theatertexten der Zagreber Theaterautorin und Dramaturgin Ivana Sajko wird deutlich sichtbar, wie das Evidenz-Potential von Theater die fiktive Augenzeugenschaft des Publikums hervorbringt und diese sekundäre Zeugenschaft selbst postdra-

---

[32] In Vorträgen und Beiträgen in Theaterzeitschriften setzt sich Oliver Frljić auch jenseits der Bühne mit der Frage des politischen Theater auseinander. Vgl. Frljić: Politicko i postdramsko.
[33] Fischer-Lichte: Ästhetik des Performativen, S. 63 ff.
[34] Lehmann: Prädramatische und postdramatische Theater-Stimmen.

matisch ›vor Augen stellt‹. Gerade darin wird die Zeugenschaft im Theater zum evidenten, zum Unzugängliches vergegenwärtigenden Mittel tatsächlicher Erfahrung und Zeugenschaft. Einerseits vergegenwärtigt die Zuschauerschaft sich selbst als verantwortliche Gemeinschaft im Theater und zugleich wird andererseits die vom Abgleiten ins Unzugängliche bedrohte Erfahrung des Einbruchs von Krieg und Ausnahmezustand im erweiterten Theaterraum aktualisiert.[35] Die Quasi-Zeugenschaft der theatralen Situation vergegenwärtigt die echte Zeugenschaft als Verdrängtes und als Vergessenes, nicht (nur), weil sie die Ereignisse anschaulich vor das *geistige Auge* holt, sondern weil sie die *location* – den Ort der ereignishaften Begegnung von Akteuren und Zuschauern – selbst zur geschauten Szene werden lässt.

Einen solchen Zuschauer, der sich selbst beim Wegsehen ertappt und somit selbst erkennt, hatte Frljić noch 2008 in der aufsehenerregenden Aufführung *Turbofolk*, einer das Anarchistische in Bild und Ton setzenden Inszenierung der postjugoslawischen, gewaltgeladenen »Stressgemeinschaft« (Sloterdijk), auf die Bühne gebracht. Unter hämmerndem Turbofolksound wird im Stück vergewaltigt, geschlagen, entbunden, gebrüllt, um am Ende der affektgeladenen Aufführung dem Publikum leere Ränge als eigenes Spiegelbild vorzuhalten. Während in *Turbofolk* noch die Einsicht produziert werden sollte, dass jene, die alles hätten sehen können, nicht ›anwesend‹ waren (und sind), rollt das Theater Frljićs in *Kukavičluk* die bekannten postdramatischen (Partizipations-)Strategien in einer Reflexion auch des eigenen Vorgehens in vorhergehenden Aufführungen von hinten her auf. *Kukavičluk*, das nicht mehr einfach beim emphatischen Aufruf zur Teilnahme stehen bleiben will, zieht verschiedene Register der Zuschauerinvolvierung. Dabei invertiert das Theatergericht den Gerichtsablauf, indem zu Beginn Schuldsprüche stehen, die Falldarstellung und das Hören der Zeugen aber erst anschließend stattfinden, um am Ende in der Srebrenica-Szene, auf die ich noch zu sprechen komme, bei der Verlesung einer Anklage stehen zu bleiben.

In *Kukavičluk* werden mehrfach Zeugen gehört, die kollektive und lokal spezifische Erfahrungen der Zuschauergemeinschaft vergegenwärtigen. So geben alle Akteure in teil-biographischen Statements Auskunft darüber, wie sie das NATO-Bombardement Serbiens erlebt haben. Auch äußern sich alle in persönlichen Zeugnissen, teilweise Geständnissen, zu Situationen, in denen sie Diskriminierungen von Ungarn in der Vojvodina erlebt oder selbst rassistische Übergriffe auf diese ausgeführt haben. Die Aussagen machen eine Palette auf, die für jeden Zuschauer aus der Vojvodina ein gewisses Wiedererkennungs- und Identifikationspotential hat. Die zentrale Botschaft hier ist, dass *wir*, das anwesende lokale

---

35 Ausführlich ist Sajkos Geschichts- und Kriegstheater dargestellt in Jakiša: Die Evidenz Srebrenicas.

Publikum, es sind, die zur Aufführung kommen, die eine Bühne erhalten, die dargestellt, aber auch zur Teilnahme aufgefordert werden.

Das Stück forciert darüber hinaus Partizipation, indem jeweils bedrängten Zuschauern ein öffentliches, politisches Statement abgerungen wird. Die vergemeinschaftende Wirkung des Theatron zeigt hier seine dunklere, unter Öffentlichkeitsdruck stellende Rückseite. Frljić lässt einen der Darsteller mit Mikrophon ausgestattet über die Ränge springen und zufällig ausgewählten Zuschauern Fragen zu ihrem favorisierten politischen Lager, zu ihren Ansichten über Homosexualität und ethnische Minderheiten oder zur Akzeptanz des Internationalen Gerichtshofs in Den Haag stellen. Die Auswahl der gestellten Fragen macht deutlich, dass es um ein plakatives Vergegenwärtigen der prekären gesellschaftlichen Gesamtverfassung in Serbien geht. Das Vorgehen erzwingt dabei die Aussagen und ruft damit das internationale Tribunal in Haag auf den Plan, das nach Ansicht der Mehrheit in Serbien allen unverhältnismäßig zu Leibe rückt, was in der Aufführung mehrfach erwähnt wird. In der Interview-Aktion werden nicht nur die befragten Zuschauer, die sich den anderen Zuschauern ausgeliefert sehen, unter Druck gesetzt, das ›Richtige‹ zu sagen, auch die Nicht-Befragten müssen sich stets sorgen, als nächste an der Reihe zu sein. Statt der sich wechselseitig anerkennenden, ermächtigenden Zuschauergemeinschaft kreiert die Aufführung an dieser Stelle eine sich gegenseitig ausgelieferte Zuschauerschaft. Dabei steht die Frage, was denn die richtige, von der Gemeinschaft akzeptierte Antwort jeweils sein könnte, mit sichtbarer Präsenz im Raum, so dass erneut der Status von Wahrheit zur Disposition steht. Antwortet man mit der von einer serbischen Mehrheit vertretenen Auffassung, die Akzeptanz beim durchschnittlichen Sitznachbarn finden könnte, die aber nicht mit einer ›politisch korrekten‹ deckungsgleich ist? Tatsächlich antwortet die Mehrheit der Befragten in diesem Sinne aufschlussreich: Sie sind für Vojislav Šešelj (bosnisch-serbischer Ultranationalist, seit 2006 in Den Haag vor Gericht) und gegen das ICTY, sie haben vorgeblich nichts gegen Kosovo-Albaner und sind in der Frage der Schwulenakzeptanz gespalten. Die u. a. an das Publikum gestellten Fragen: »Haager Tribunal – dafür oder dagegen?« und »Vojislav Šešelj oder Madeleine Albright?« werden jeweils mit »Dagegen« und mit »Vojislav Šešelj« beantwortet.[36] Die Interviewsituation macht der Zuschauerschaft die eigene doppelgesichtige Identität gewahr; sie vertreten ›serbische Durchschnitts-

---

36 Die weiteren Fragen, die dem Publikum gestellt werden, lauten: »Würden Sie die Unabhängigkeit Kosovos im Austausch für ein Gehalt von 3000 Euro anerkennen?«, »Ist das Kosovarische Szenario auch in der Vojvodina denkbar?«, »Würden Sie einen hohen Posten annehmen, wenn Sie zwischen einem Homosexuellen und einem Albaner sitzen müssten?«, »Glauben Sie, dass die Serbisch-Orthodoxe Kirche eine Hauptquelle der Macht ist?«, »Würden Sie in einem Restaurant, in dem das Bild Ratko Mladićs hängt, essen?«, »Würden Sie bei Präsidentschaftswahlen einem Kandidaten Ihre Stimme geben, mit dessen Ansichten Sie vollkommen übereinstimmen, der aber von der Nationalität her Roma ist?«, »Gehört Ceca Ražnatović [Turbofolk-Sängerin und Witwe des Kriegsverbrechers und Hooligans Arkan] ins Gefängnis?«.

ansichten‹ und sind doch zugleich eine versierte, gebildete Öffentlichkeit, die als Theaterzuschauerschaft auch unter den Druck des kultivierten ›Welttribunals‹ steht. Jene, die sich homophob oder nationalistisch äußerten, mussten sich entweder durchringen (zumindest aktiv entscheiden), eine politisch nicht korrekte Antwort öffentlich zu äußern. Oder aber, und auch dies wird fühlbar/sichtbar, sie äußern eine Meinung, die (wie zu Beginn der Aufführung angekündigt) nicht der eigenen, sehr wohl aber der einer statistischen Mehrheit entspricht. Das Auseinanderklaffen von global anerkannter und ›zurückgebliebener serbischer‹ Haltung und von eigener vs. unter Druck der Gruppe geäußerter Meinung könnte (den Anwesenden) nicht deutlicher werden.

Einzelne Zuschauer suchen sich dieser peinlichen Befragung zu entziehen, indem sie mit dem expliziten Satz: »Ich nehme an dieser Aufführung nicht teil« antworten. Diese Antwortverweigerer produzieren nun den für *Kukavičluk* entscheidenden performativen Widerspruch. Ausgerechnet diese Verweigerer sind es ja, die zuletzt das Verweigerte vollziehen,[37] die also zu wirklichen Mit-Akteuren im Theater werden. Ihre Teilnahmeverweigerung expliziert das performative Erzwingen von Zuschauerpartizipation und von Rollenwechsel im Theater. Vor allem sie beteiligen sich tatsächlich am Aushandeln von Beziehungen zwischen Anwesenden, Zuschauern und Akteuren und sie entlarven mit ihren Antworten auch die Partizipationsstrategie als das, was sie (eben auch) ist: eine anmaßende Tribunalisierung. Der Einbindung des Zuschauers, das führt *Kukavičluk* vor Augen, unterliegt ein pädagogisch-umerziehender Impetus, der der Demokratisierung des Events Theater letztlich diametral entgegensteht und vom besseren Wissen einer lenkenden Instanz, des Regisseurs und Theaterrichters, ausgeht. Mit Gewalt erzwingt dieser in der Aufführung Aussagen, die den Zuschauer zum performativ beteiligten Zeugen, hier zugleich aber auch zum Zeugen der eigenen Meinungsunfreiheit macht. Ganz im Gegensatz zum postdramatischen Theatron-Mantra steht somit plötzlich, was als Ermächtigungsschauplatz konzipiert ist, auch für ein Ohnmachtsszenario.

Die Aufführung *Kukavičluk* ringt als selbstermächtigtes Theatergericht neben den Zuschauern auch den Darstellern Zeugenaussagen ab. Dokumentarische, aus den privaten Schauspielerbiographien genommene Erinnerungen, die ausgiebig in das Theaterprojekt eingeflossen sind, lassen die Darsteller als Augenzeugen der serbischen 1990er in Erscheinung treten. Diese Erlebnisse, die das Publikum teilt und die daher identifikatorisch wirksam werden, vergegenwärtigen die unmittelbare serbische Vergangenheit auf der Bühne. Die Darsteller berichten, wie ihnen als Teenager der Einbruch des Krieges das lang ersehnte dramatische Ereignis im Leben verschafft hatte, wie die Eltern sie (ausgerechnet!) zu Verwandten nach Bosnien schickten, um sie vor den NATO-Angriffen in Sicherheit zu brin-

---

[37] Vgl. Fischer-Lichte: Ästhetik des Performativen, S. 66.

gen, wie die Deutschlehrerin den Unterricht unterbrach, weil sie zu erschüttert von den Ereignissen war, wie das Bombardement dazu führte, dass man Zeit für gemeinsame Spiele mit den Eltern fand, wie Freunde, die den Angriffen in Novi Sad ausgesetzt waren, zum Ausschlafen nach Belgrad kamen oder dass die Tante aus Dänemark anrief, um die Beschießung Belgrads anzukündigen.

Die persönlichen Erinnerungen der Darsteller werden dabei von einem laufenden Fernsehgerät begleitet, auf dem Nachrichtensendungen aus den 1990er Jahren gezeigt werden, so dass das Erinnern der Ereignisse untertrennbar mit der Berichterstattung dazu verwoben bleibt. Die Wieder-Einsetzung des Verdrängten und Vergessenen wird auch durch den Einsatz des Telefons auf der Bühne performiert. Alle Darsteller werden nach der Wiedergabe ihrer Erinnerungen von Verwandten aus der Vergangenheit angerufen. Kurz angebunden und in Panik bereden sie mit diesen die Fluchtbewegungen angesichts des kriegerischen Ausnahmezustands. Katharina Pewny hat das Telefon auf der Bühne vor dem Hintergrund der Subjektwerdung durch Anrufung, die Althusser entwickelt und Judith Butler aufgreift, interpretiert.[38] Die Telefonate geben den Abwesenden und den Vergangenen eine auf die Bühne geholte Gestalt.

Die Verlässlichkeit der Darsteller-Zeugnisse und ihrer authentifizierenden Erinnerungen wird indes dadurch im Wanken gehalten, dass die Schauspieler zuvor schon als Figuren in Erscheinung traten, die ihre Nichtidentität mit sich selbst zur Schau stellten. Unmittelbar auf die Eingangssequenz mit der Gazimestan-Rede, in der Milošević unisono zitiert wird, folgt in der Aufführung eine Gerichtsszene, in der alle beteiligten Schauspieler reihum eingefangen, vor den Richtertisch gezerrt und nach Verkündung der Anklage gegen sie jeweils dazu verurteilt werden, sich selbst zu spielen. »Dies Theatergericht klagt dich an, nicht [Name der Figur] zu sein und verurteilt dich dazu, dich selbst in dieser Aufführung zu spielen!«, heißt es in jedem einzelnen Urteilsspruch. Die Charaktere werden also für etwas vor einem theatralen Gericht und auf einer Theaterbühne verurteilt, was nicht immer ein Verbrechen im Theater war: Figur zu sein. Die Darsteller tragen dabei Namensschilder wiederum echter historischer Theaterpersonen, die sie hätten darstellen sollen, wenn ihnen kein Richtspruch dazwischen gekommen wäre. Es handelt sich um KPTG-Mitglieder und Mitwirkende an der Inszenierung Šiptar (pejorativer Ausdruck für Kosovo-Albaner gebildet nach der Selbstbezeichnung *shqiptar*), die unter der Federführung von Ljubiša Ristić 1985 in Subotica – eben jenem Theater in dem nun 25 Jahre später *Kukavičluk* aufgeführt wird – entstanden war. (*Kukavičluk* enthält direkte Zitate aus Šiptar.) Alle damals Mitwirkenden werden jeweils einzeln auf Grundlage der in Form einer Anklage vorgetragenen künstlerischen und privaten Biographie für ihr Lebenswerk ins Gericht genommen. Dabei markiert das negative Vorzeichen vor den biographischen Zusam-

---

[38] Vgl. Pewny: Das Drama des Prekären, S. 29.

menfassungen der KPTG-Personen – »Ti nisi Dušan Jovanović. Ti se nisi rodio u Beogradu prvog oktobra tridesetdevete. Ti nisi diplomirao [...]. Ti nisi osnovao [...]«[39] – den Bruch in der Vita jedes einzelnen, der mit der jugoslawischen Wende erfolgte und für den jeder von ihnen von der Aufführung angeklagt wird. Auch expliziert die Minusbiographie das Konzept der Theaterrolle und mithin, dass Darsteller nicht deckungsgleich mit den dargestellten Personen sind. So spielt der Darsteller Vladimir Grbić den slowenischen Regisseur Dušan Jovanović, der 1986 in Subotica mit *Titus Andronicus* gastierte, und der Darsteller Srđan Sekulić den Theatertexter und Gründer der gesamtjugoslawischen Theatergesellschaft KPGT (Abbreviatur für Kazalište, Pozorište, Gledališče, Teatar) Ljubiša Ristić, dessen ideologische Wende nach seiner KPTG-Zeit hier Anlass zur Anklage gegen ihn wird. Im Schuldspruch und der Verurteilung »sich selbst zu spielen« wird dem hier exemplarisch herausgestellten Darsteller ein Rückzug in die gespielte Rolle verweigert, wie auch der Figur des Ristić ihre Janusgesichtigkeit (das Zurücknehmen seiner Theateransichten aus sozialistischer Zeit) vorgehalten wird. Zugleich dürfen sich Frljić's Darsteller der Charaktere aber auch nicht entledigen: Sie tragen die Namensschilder ihres jeweiligen Alias noch in der letzten Szene!

Wenn also klar ist, dass politische und ästhetische Verantwortung im Theater übernehmen für *Kukavičluk* heißt, nicht bloßes Theater sein zu dürfen, ist ebenso klar, dass Darsteller doch Darsteller sind und bleiben und dass jede Aufführung auch im Zeichen ihr vorausgehender anderer Aufführungen steht. Zuschauer und Darsteller werden für das Geschehen mitverantwortlich gemacht und mit dem (theater-)historischen Kontext synchronisiert. Sie werden schuldig gesprochen, hinter den Schuldspruch zurück gehend noch einmal als Zeugen gehört und zuletzt mit einem uminterpretierten, von konkreter Schuld zunächst wieder befreiten Ereignis konfrontiert, das nicht mehr aus »Feigheit« verschwiegen werden darf.

3. Die Evidenz Srebrenicas

Frljić, der in der kroatischen Theaterkritik den Ruf eines »reditelj pamfleta«[40], eines Pamphlet-Regisseurs, hat, der Ärger produziert, wo Ruhe herrscht, definiert eine klare Mission der Wahrheitssuche für seine Bühnenarbeit: Die postjugoslawi-

---

[39] »Du bist nicht Dušan Jovanović. Du wurdest nicht in Belgrad am ersten Oktober Neununddreißig geboren. Du hast nicht [...] absolviert. Du hast nicht [...] gegründet.«

[40] Igor Ružić schreibt »[...] ›reditelj pamfleta‹ koji može da izazove haos i tamo gde ga nema, i gde ne bi trebalo da ga bude« (»›Pamphlet-Regisseur‹, der Chaos auch dort hervorrufen kann, wo keines ist und wo auch keines sein sollte in: *Kultura*, 24. September 2012:http://www.tportal.hr/ kultura/kazaliste/216291/Predstava-predodredena-za-uspjeh.html#.UPZwfELEcbo (letzter Zugriff

schen Gesellschaften lebten, so Frljić auf Dubravka Ugrešićs bekannten Essayband Bezug nehmend, nach wie vor in einer *kultura laži*, einer Kultur der Lüge, in der Niederlagen als Siege und Kriegsverbrecher als Helden gelten.[41] Alle jenseits dieses verlogenen Konsenses haben − hier folgt Frljić Rancières politisch-ästhetischer Theorie − keine Stimme im nachjugoslawischen Raum. Entsprechend ist Theater, mit dem Zuschauer einverstanden sind, für Frljić − in Anlehnung an Rancières Dissenskonzept − Konsenstheater, das auf Lügen basiert. Öffentliche Kritik und politische Intervention, die seinen Aufführungen widerfahren, versteht Oliver Frljić somit als Vehikel, als produktive Hilfsmittel, selbst ein Theater des Dissenses zu produzieren. Seine Theaterprojekte, unter denen *Kukavičluk*, *Zoran Đinđić* (2012) und *Pismo iz 1920* (2011) besonderes Aufsehen in Serbien bzw. Bosnien erregten, verstehen sich als dezidierte Akte von öffentlich gemachter Wahrheitsfindung, in denen eine Verschiebung der Grenze zwischen Konsensgemeinschaft und der Gruppe der Ausgeschlossenen und damit eine Sichtbarmachung von Opfer-Rechten stattfindet. Letztlich kreisen alle Theaterprojekte Frljićs um offen gebliebene Fragen der »Jugosphäre« (Tim Judah).

Die von Albrights Tribunal reklamierte und von Handke mitunter in kopfloser Serbophilie angezweifelte ›Wahrheit‹ über die Kriegsverbrechen im ehemaligen Jugoslawien wird von *Kukavičluk* in einem erneuten Akt der Wahrheitsfindung zurückgenommen, ohne sie jedoch auszustreichen. Die Aufführung, die ausdifferenziert selbst Anklage gegen vieles führt und darin auch Tribunal ist, findet zum Schluss zu einem klaren, von den nachfolgenden Deutungen befreiten Ausgangspunkt zurück: einer schlichten Evidenz Srebrenicas. Nachdem *Kukavičluk* sich im Verlauf der Aufführung gegen das Ausstreichen der gesamtjugoslawischen (Theater-)Tradition, gegen chauvinistische Haltungen, gegen die Kollektivverurteilung der Serben, aber auch gegen die Verantwortungsverweigerung in Serbien, gegen die postdramatische Leichtgläubigkeit in Bezug auf die Mittel der Darstellung, gegen das Selbstmitleid in Folge des serbischen NATO-Traumas und gegen sein Publikum wendete, endet *Kukavičluk* nach diesem regelrechten Anklage-Reigen damit, dass die acht beteiligten Darsteller nacheinander auswendig die Namen aller 505 identifizierten Opfer von Srebrenica rezitieren.

Die mündliche Wiedergabe der Namensliste lässt neue, ausgetretene Pfade verlassende, Saiten im Zusammenhang mit Srebrenica anklingen: sie ruft den pathetisch aufgeladenen Gedenkinszenierungskitsch auf, wie er von 9/11-Jahrestagen oder aus dem Spielberg-Film *Schindlers Liste* bekannt ist und spielt zugleich auf die sozialistisch-jugoslawische Rezitierpraxis der Pioniere anlässlich nationa-

---

am 26. Juni 2013). Frljić wird hier seine Inszenierung von Branislav Nušićs »Gospođa ministarka« in Zagreb angekreidet, die er nicht ins Kroatische übersetzen, sondern in serbischer ›Fremdsprache‹ aufführen ließ.

[41] Siehe dazu die Frljić-Interviews vom 16. Oktober 2011 und 16. Juni 2012 in www.novilist.hr: »Živimo u kulturi laži« und »Govorim o onom što svi znaju, a o čemu šute«.

ler Feiertage an (an die nicht nur das angestrengte Memorieren auf der Bühne erinnert, sondern auch die uniformierte Kleidung der Darsteller: weißes Hemd, dunkler Rock/Hose und die jugendlichen *Chucks*-Turnschuhe, die den *Borovo startašice* aus sozialistischer Zeit gleichen). Die Namensliste ruft aber auch mit ihrem »Aufzählen als Dokumentieren und umgekehrt«[42] die poetische Praxis des in Subotica geborenen Schriftstellers Danilo Kiš auf. Die Liste vergegenwärtigt die Toten und erschafft eine Wirklichkeit (wieder), die zwischenzeitlich von zahlreichen Debatten verstellt wurde. Gerade in der Vojvodina und dem Ort der von Kiš literarisch aktualisierten Verfolgung und Ermordung der serbischen Juden durch ungarische Faschisten hat die vergegenwärtigende »Poetik der Kataloge«[43] Wiedererkennungswert. Wie Kiš transformiert Frljić Authentisches und Augenzeugenmaterial und reduziert es in seiner dokumentarischen Theaterarbeit auf ›das Wesentliche‹.

Die Srebrenica-Szene beginnt mit dem expliziten Hinweis, dass das reine Aufsagen der Namen 12 bis 13 Minuten in Anspruch nehmen und dass sich darüber hinaus nichts Spektakuläres ereignen wird. »Alles, was sich ereignen wird, wenn sich überhaupt etwas ereignet, ereignet sich in Ihnen«, fügt der ankündigende Darsteller hinzu. Die bis dahin im Stück immer wieder gestörte Trennung von Szene und Zuschauerraum, die der Egalisierung von Szene und Publikum dient, wird an dieser Stelle durch die Ausleuchtung der Zuschauerplätze gänzlich aufgehoben. Die Schauspieler, noch mit den Namen der echten Personen/Figuren, die sie zwischenzeitlich spielten, versehen, sprechen vom Bühnenrand aus und stören darin ihre Fiktionalisierung als Figur mehrfach. Auf der Szene befindet sich auch noch das letzte Requisit: Kosovo als zertrampeltes »Herz Serbiens« aus Papierknäulen gelegt, darin Fähnchen mit den Namen kosovarischer Städte. Zu diesem Zeitpunkt haben die Bühnenagierenden, die vorher auf dem Kosovo Kolo tanzten, mit dieser verlassenen Szene »Kosovo« auch nicht mehr zu tun, als die anwesende Zuschauergemeinschaft.

Die hier stattfindende meta-theatrale Infragestellung der Grenze von Zugehörigkeit und Nichtzugehörigkeit, von Stimme und Stimmlosigkeit im Theater, setzt die Frage danach ins Bild, inwieweit auch der Zuschauer Teil des Theaters und zugleich alle am Theater Beteiligten Verantwortliche des dargestellten Ereignisses sind. Sprechen hier Schauspieler oder echte Personen? An wen richtet sich diese Namensauflistung eigentlich? Das Srebrenica-Thema treibt also noch eine weitaus prekärere Frage der Zugehörigkeit als die der Partizipation am Theatergeschehen hervor: Auf wessen Seite steht denn diese Aufführung? Wen geht Srebrenica eigentlich etwas an? Und: Wie denken die Leute, die mit mir hier im Theater sitzen, jenseits des Theaterraums?

---

[42] Lachmann: Zwischen Fakt und Artefakt, S. 95
[43] Lachmann: Zur Poetik der Kataloge bei Danilo Kiš.

Das Publikum durchläuft in der knappen Viertelstunde einen sichtbaren Polarisierungs- und Entwicklungsprozess. Während einzelne Zuschauer (teilweise unter empörtem Protest) das Theater verlassen oder ihre Mobiltelefone zur Hand nehmen, sich ablehnend zurücklehnen und die Arme verschränken, beginnen andere sich ratlos anzublicken, einige senken in Gedanken oder Trauer versunken den Kopf, nicht wenige beginnen im Laufe der Rezitation zu weinen.

Es dauert eine Weile, bis das monotone Aufzählen der Namen, denen keine konkreten Gesichter zugeordnet werden können, seine Wirkung im Publikum entfalten. Auch das Unvernehmen des Publikums wird erst allmählich vernehmbar und der Dissens unter den Zuschauern sichtbar. Die Frage Srebrenicas steht fühlbar im Raum, ohne dass sich die Einzigartigkeit der Aktion, das reine Aufzählen, ohne Weiteres in die »Logik und Begrifflichkeit des politischen Diskurses«[44] der außertheatralen Wirklichkeit übersetzen ließe. Srebrenica erlangt in *Kukavičluks* Schlussszene den Status der Ausnahme, die sich wie die Gnade im Verhältnis zum Gesetz oder das Wunder im Vergleich zum Naturverlauf[45] verhält. Wen oder was genau klagt der an bestehende Debatten schwer anschließbare mnemonische Akt der Namenswiedergabe an und wofür?

Srebrenica am Ende der Aufführung führt das postdramatische Theater weg von der vor allem per Zuschauerpartizipation ›engagierten‹ Inszenierung hin zum dokumentierenden Recherchetheater, das als reines Vor-Augen-Stellen besonderes Wahrheitspotential zugesprochen bekommt. Über die postdramatische Sichtbarmachung aller Teile des Theaters – sie verhindert das Illusionstheater – kommt das Theater zu einer ursprünglicheren Bestimmung, strittigen Fragen eine Bühne der Verhandlung zu verleihen, zurück. Dabei führt das Theatergericht und Gerichtstheater der Aufführung *Kukavičluk* nicht nur die Feigheit des Schweigens vor, sie bringt auch das Versagen der theatralen sowie gerichtlichen Sprache auf die Bühne. Das letztlich sprachlich organisierte Gericht, das Ereignisse im Verlauf einer Gerichtsverhandlung zunehmend in Sprache überführt und zuletzt im schriftlich festgehaltenen, sprachlich realisierten Urteil fixiert, wird in *Kukavičluk* rückwärts durchexerziert bis das bereits festgestellt und beschlossen Geglaubte in das vergegenwärtigte Ereignis rückgeführt wird, bis Sprache sich in die reine Evidenz auflöst.

Die Evidenz Srebrenicas darf dabei nicht umgangssprachlich verkürzt, sondern muss als aktualisierendes Vor-Augen-Stellen verstanden werden, das über die Aktualitätsfiguren des politischen und historischen Präsens wieder die beiden Ebenen des Theaters und seiner Bezugsrealität zusammenführt.[46] Rüdiger Campe beschreibt die Evidenz als Transposition des Redens zum Zeigen. Vergegenwär-

---

[44] Lehmann: Das Politische Schreiben, S. 17.
[45] Vgl. ebd.
[46] Vgl. Campe: Vor Augen Stellen, S. 209.

tigung kann in Aristotelischer Tradition das Zukünftig-Geplante durch gegenwärtig Geschehendes oder in Quintilianscher Deutung das geschehene Faktum durch ein augenblicklich Geschehendes ersetzen. *Kukavičluks* Vor-Augen-Stellen Srebrenicas aktualisiert im politischen Präsens (Aristoteles) die theatrale Gemeinschaft von Akteuren und Zuschauern als Verantwortliche und im historischen Präsens (Quintilian) das Gewesene als in der Gegenwart wieder zu Schauendes. Somit ist *Kukavičluk* als theatrales Tribunal mit der Wiederherstellung eines eingebüßten Äquilibriums und mit dem Austarieren von aus dem Gleichgewicht geratenen Waagschalen der Gerechtigkeit befasst, die die politische Gegenwart mit den stimmlosen Toten in Kommunikation bringt und Entscheidungen fordert. Die rhetorische Figur der Hypotypose spielt als affektisch aufgeladene wiederum eine zentrale Rolle für die Vergegenwärtigung des Gewesenen. Während Evidenz zunächst »affektlos und in belehrender Absicht«[47] im Erzählen beschreibt, ist die Hypotypose eine deskriptive Evidenz-Figur, in der sich das »narrative Moment aller (sprachlichen) Deskription enthüllt«[48]. Als Redefigur des »Zeigens-Statt-Redens«[49] realisiert Srebrenica als Hypotypose sich als reine Anschauung jenseits der Vergegenwärtigung über Metaphern, was erneut zugleich das Theater als solches mit kommentiert.

Literatur

Bandi, Nina / Kraft, Michael G. / Lasinger, Sebastian: Kunst, Politik und Polizei im Denken Jacques Rancières, in: dies. (Hg.): Kunst, Krise, Subversion. Zur Politik der Ästhetik, Bielefeld 2012, S. 167–181.

Campe, Rüdiger: Vor Augen Stellen. Über den Rahmen rhetorischer Bildgebung, in: Neumann, G. (Hg.): Poststrukturalismus. Herausforderung an die Literaturwissenschaft, Stuttgart / Weimar 1997, S. 208–225.

Fischer-Lichte, Erika: Die Entdeckung des Zuschauers, Tübingen 1997.

Fischer-Lichte, Erika: Ästhetik des Performativen, Frankfurt a. M. 2004.

Frljić, Oliver: Političko i postdramsko, in: teatron 154/155. Časopis za pozorišnu umetnost, Belgrad 2011, S. 53–56.

Gumbrecht, Hans Ulrich: Diesseits der Hermeneutik. Über die Produktion von Präsenz, Frankfurt a. M. 2004.

Handke, Peter: Rund um das Große Tribunal, Frankfurt a. M. 2003.

Handke, Peter: Die Tablas von Daimiel, Frankfurt a. M. 2006.

---

[47] Vgl. ebd., S. 219.
[48] Ebd.
[49] Ebd.

Jakiša, Miranda: Die Evidenz Srebrenicas: Oliver Frljić's Theatergericht in *Kukavičluk*, in: Susi Frank / Schamma Schahadat (Hg.): Evidenz und Zeugenschaft, Wien 2013 (im Druck).

Jakiša, Miranda: Ivana Sajko's Postdramatic Theatre of Disjunction or War on Stage, in: A. Jakir / M. Jakiša / T. Zimmermann (Hg.): Remembering War and Peace in Southeast Europa in the 20th Century. Split 2013 (im Druck)

Krämer, Sibylle: Zuschauer zu Zeugen machen. Überlegungen zum Zusammenhang zwischen Performanz, Medien und Performance-Künstlern, in: Europäisches Performance Institut. Die Kunst der Handlung 3, Berlin 2005, S. 16–19.

Lachmann, Renate: Zur Poetik der Kataloge bei Danilo Kiš, in: Rainer Grübel / Wolf Schmid (Hg.): Wortkunst – Erzählkunst – Bildkunst. Festschrift für Aage A. Hansen-Löve, München 2008, S. 296–309.

Lachmann, Renate: Zwischen Fakt und Artefakt, in: G. Butzer / H. Zapf (Hg.): Theorie der Literatur. Bd. 5 Helden als Heilige, Basel 2011, S. 93–116.

Lehmann, Hans-Thies: Postdramatisches Theater, Frankfurt a. M. 1999.

Lehmann, Hans-Thies: Das Politische Schreiben. Essays zu Theatertexten, Berlin 2002.

Lehmann, Hans-Thies: Just a word on a page and there is the drama. Anmerkungen zum Text im postdramatischen Theater, in: H. L. Arnold (Hg.): Theater fürs 21. Jahrhundert, München 2004, S. 26–33.

Lehmann, Hans-Thies: Prädramatische und postdramatische Theater-Stimmen. Zur Erfahrung der Stimme in der Live-Performance, in: D. Kolesch / J. Schrödl (Hg.): Kunst-Stimmen, Bonn 2004, S. 40–67.

Menke, Bettine: Prosopopoiia: Die Stimme des Textes – die Figur des ›sprechenden Gesichts‹, in: G. Neumann (Hg.): Poststrukturalismus. Herausforderung an die Literaturwissenschaft, Stuttgart / Weimar 1997, S. 226–251.

Mertens, Matthias: Vergegenwärtigung, in: Jahrbuch für Kulturwissenschaften und ästhetische Praxis, Tübingen 2010.

Rancière, Jacques: Die Aufteilung des Sinnlichen. Die Politik der Kunst und ihre Paradoxien, Berlin 2006.

Pewny, Katharina: Das Drama des Prekären. Über die Wiederkehr der Ethik in Theater und Performance, Bielefeld 2011.

Primavesi, Patrick: Theater / Politik – Kontexte und Beziehungen, in: J. Deck / A. Sieburg (Hg.): Politisch Theater machen. Neue Artikulationsformen des Politischen in den darstellenden Künsten, Bielefeld 2011, S. 41–71.

Primavesi, Patrick: Orte und Strategien postdramatischer Theaterformen, in: Heinz Ludwig Arnold (Hg.): Theater fürs 21. Jahrhundert, München 2004, S. 8–25.

Sasse, Sylvia: Wortsünden. Beichten und Gestehen in der russischen Literatur, München 2009.

Ueding, Gert: Grundriss der Rhetorik. Geschichte, Technik, Methode. Stuttgart 1994.
Vismann, Cornelia: Medien der Rechtsprechung, Frankfurt a. M. 2011.

Internetquellen

Frljić, Oliver: Should be art and politics at the same time, in: Zeitschrift maska www.maska.si
(http://nova.maska.si/en/publications/special_issues/bcc_balcan_can_con temporary/512/oliver_frljic.html, letzter Zugriff am 26. Juni 2013)
Frljić, Oliver: Govorim o onom što svi znaju, a o čemu šute, in: www.novilist.hr (http://www.novilist.hr/Kultura/Kazaliste/Oliver-Frljic-Govorim-o-onome-sto-svi-znaju-a-o-cemu-sute) (letzter Zugriff am 26. Juni 2013)
Frljić, Oliver: Živimo u kulturi laži, in: www.novilist.hr (http://www.novilist. hr/Kultura/Kazaliste/Oliver-Frljic-Zivimo-u-kulturi-lazi) (letzter Zugriff am 26. Juni 2013)
Ružić, Igor: Predstava predodređena za uspjeh, in: Kultura, 24. September 2012 (http://www.tportal.hr/kultura/kazaliste/216291/Predstava-predodredena-za-uspjeh.html#.UPZwfELEcbo) (letzter Zugriff am 26. Juni 2013)

Die Autorinnen und Autoren

Jürgen Brokoff, Prof. Dr., ist germanistischer Literatur- und Kulturwissenschaftler. Er ist Professor für Deutsche Philologie / Neuere deutsche Literatur an der Freien Universität Berlin. Zahlreiche Aufsätze zur deutschsprachigen Literatur vom 18.–21. Jahrhundert.

Christoph Flügge ist Jurist. Er arbeitet als Richter am »Internationalen Strafgerichtshof für das ehemalige Jugoslawien« (ICTY) in Den Haag (Niederlande).

Werner Gephart, Prof. Dr., ist Soziologe, Jurist und Künstler. Er ist Professor für Soziologie an der Rheinischen Friedrich-Wilhelms-Universität Bonn, Ancien Professeur de l'Institut d'Études politiques de Paris und Gründer und Direktor des Käte Hamburger Kollegs »Recht als Kultur«. Er ist Herausgeber des Bandes »Recht« der Max-Weber-Gesamtausgabe (MWG I/22-3).

Alexander Glodzinski ist Journalist. Er ist Redakteur beim ZDF und ehemaliges Redaktionsmitglied der Sendung »Kulturzeit« (3sat).

Miranda Jakiša, Prof. Dr. phil., ist slawistische Literatur- und Kulturwissenschaftlerin. Sie arbeitet als Juniorprofessorin für Süd- und Ostslawische Literaturen an der Humboldt Universität Berlin. Zahlreiche Publikationen zur süd- und ostslawischen Literatur und Kultur.

Dževad Karahasan ist bosnischer Schriftsteller. Er lebt und arbeitet als Schriftsteller, Dramaturg und Essayist in Sarajevo und Graz. Sein literarisches Werk wurde mit zahlreichen internationalen Preisen ausgezeichnet, u. a. mit dem »Leipziger Buchpreis zur Europäischen Verständigung« (2004) und mit der Goethe Medaille des Goethe Instituts (2012).

Rob Lemkin ist Regisseur. Er ist Gründer von »Old Street Films« und wurde für sein Werk mit zahlreichen internationalen Filmpreisen geehrt. Er ist Co-Regisseur und Co-Produzent des Films »Enemies of the People«.

Andreas Th. Müller, Ass.-Prof. Dr., ist Assistenz-Professor am Institut für Europarecht und Völkerrecht der Universität Innsbruck. Zu seinen Publikationen auf diesem Feld gehört die Studie »Der Internationale Strafgerichtshof als Faktor der Globalisierung« (Frankfurt a. M. / Wien 2005).

Ali Samadi Ahadi ist Regisseur. Für sein Werk wurde er mit zahlreichen internationalen Preisen, unter anderem dem Grimme-Preis 2011, ausgezeichnet. Er ist ehemaliger Artist in Residence des Käte Hamburger Kollegs »Recht als Kultur«.

Joachim Savelsberg, Prof. Dr., ist Professor für Soziologie an der University of Minnesota und derzeit Fellow am Käte Hamburger Kolleg »Recht als Kultur«. Er ist Autor vieler einschlägiger Studien auf dem Gebiet des Rechts, der Menschenrechte und der Erinnerungskultur.

Andrea Schütte, Dr. phil., ist germanistische Literatur- und Kulturwissenschaftlerin. Sie arbeitet als wissenschaftliche Mitarbeiterin am Institut für Germanistik, Vergleichende Literatur- und Kulturwissenschaft an der Rheinischen Friedrich-Wilhelms-Universität Bonn. Zahlreiche Aufsätze zur deutschsprachigen Literatur vom 18.–21. Jahrhundert.

Chandra Lekha Sriram, Prof. Dr., ist Juristin. Sie ist Professorin an der School of Oriental and African Studies der University of London. Ihre Publikationen beschäftigen sich mit Themen des Internationalen Strafrechts, der Konflikt-Prävention und der »transitional justice«.

Jan Christoph Suntrup, Dr. phil., ist Politikwissenschaftler. Er ist Wissenschaftlicher Mitarbeiter am Käte Hamburger Kolleg »Recht als Kultur« in Bonn. Seine Forschungsschwerpunkte liegen auf dem Gebiet der politischen Theorie und der Rechtskulturforschung.

Dubravka Ugrešić ist kroatische Schriftstellerin und Literaturwissenschaftlerin. Sie lebt und arbeitet als Schriftstellerin und Essayistin in Amsterdam und den USA. Ihr literarisches Werk wurde mit zahlreichen internationalen Preisen ausgezeichnet, u. a. mit dem Heinrich-Mann-Preis (2000) und dem Jean-Améry-Preis (2012).

Svjetlan Lacko Vidulić, Prof. Dr., ist germanistischer Literatur- und Kulturwissenschaftler. Er arbeitet als Professor für Germanistik an der Universität Zagreb. Zahlreiche Aufsätze zur deutschsprachigen Literatur und Kultur seit dem 18. Jahrhundert.

Annette Wieviorka, Prof. Dr., ist Historikerin. Sie ist Directrice de recherche am CNRS Paris und Autorin zahlreicher international anerkannter Studien zur Shoah, zur jüdischen Geschichte, zu den Nürnberger Prozessen und zum Eichmann-Tribunal.